OGILVIE
m. twice, unknown

ALEXANDER   HENRY   DAUG

DAVID R.N.
(?–1821)
. Mary Anne Lloyd
no issue

EDWARD R. M.
(1789–1821)
unm.

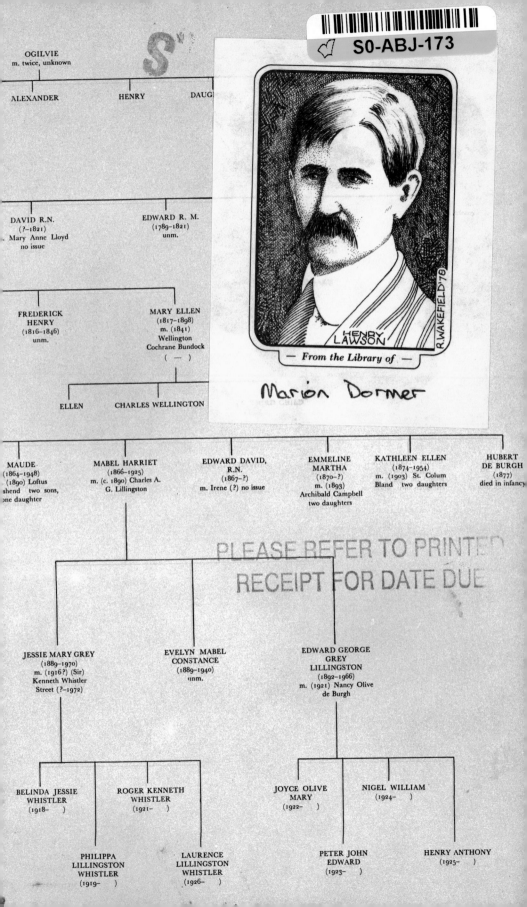

HENRY
LAWSON

R.WAKEFIELD '78

— From the Library of —

Marion Dormer

FREDERICK
HENRY
(1816–1846)
unm.

MARY ELLEN
(1817–1898)
m. (1841)
Wellington
Cochrane Bundock
(—)

ELLEN   CHARLES WELLINGTON

MAUDE·
(1864–1948)
(1890) Loftus
shend two sons,
one daughter

MABEL HARRIET
(1866–1925)
m. (c. 1890) Charles A.
G. Lillingston

EDWARD DAVID,
R.N.
(1867–?)
m. Irene (?) no issue

EMMELINE
MARTHA
(1870–?)
m. (1893)
Archibald Campbell
two daughters

KATHLEEN ELLEN
(1874–1954)
m. (1903) St. Colum
Bland two daughters

HUBERT
DE BURGH
(1877)
died in infancy

JESSIE MARY GREY
(1889–1970)
m. (1916?) (Sir)
Kenneth Whistler
Street (?–1972)

EVELYN MABEL
CONSTANCE
(1889–1940)
unm.

EDWARD GEORGE
GREY
LILLINGSTON
(1892–1966)
m. (1921) Nancy Olive
de Burgh

BELINDA JESSIE
WHISTLER
(1918–)

ROGER KENNETH
WHISTLER
(1921–)

JOYCE OLIVE
MARY
(1922–)

NIGEL WILLIAM
(1924–)

PHILIPPA
LILLINGSTON
WHISTLER
(1919–)

LAURENCE
LILLINGSTON
WHISTLER
(1926–)

PETER JOHN
EDWARD
(1923–)

HENRY ANTHONY
(1925–)

Squatter's Castle

Squatter's Castle

The Story of A Pastoral Dynasty

Life and Times of Edward David
Stewart Ogilvie 1814–96

George Farwell

Written with the assistance of
the Commonwealth Literary Fund

Lansdowne

By the same author

Mask of Asia
Last Days in Paradise
Land of Mirage
Down Argent Street
Vanishing Australians
Requiem for Woolloomooloo
Ned Kelly

Travel
Highway One
Sun Country
Australian Landscapes
Traveller's Tracks
The Outside Track
Cape York to Kimberley
Ghost Towns of Australia
Australian Setting

Drama
The House That Jack Built

Short Stories
Surf Music and other stories

For Children
Riders to an Unknown Sea
Seven Thousand Isles

First published 1973 by
Lansdowne Press Pty Ltd
37 Little Bourke Street, Melbourne, 3000, Australia
© George Farwell 1973
ISBN 0 7018 0255 3
Typeset by Dudley E. King Pty Ltd, Melbourne
Printed and bound in Hong Kong

Jacket: Montage design incorporating detail of
Tom Roberts' portrait of E.D.S. Ogilvie in 1894. Courtesy
Mitchell Library.

Frontispiece: Yulgilbar Castle with Mount Ogilvie in the
background. Photograph taken by Kathleen Ogilvie in 1894.

To those who made Australia
before the age of greed

Squatter:

'A soubriquet first applied to the
United States by means of derision;
to the respectable settler as ill-
applied as Shepherd Kings, a graceful and comely name . . .'

William Gardner, 1854

Castle:

'Defensive move in chess, designed
to protect the King.'

Everyman's Guide to Chess

Acknowledgments

I wish in particular to thank the late Sir Kenneth Street for the continu-
ing interest and support he gave this book, especially through the
loan of family letters and documents. My thanks are also due to Miss
S. Mourot, Librarian, and the staff of the Mitchell Library, the State
Government Archives and the Public Library of New South Wales; to
Basil J. Greenhill, c.m.g., director of the National Maritime Museum,
Greenwich, England, the Surrey Records Office, and Somerset House,
London; to Mr Allan Wilkes, Archivist, University of New England,
and Mr E. J. Adsett, Librarian of the Merton County Library, Surrey.

I have also had valuable assistance from many members of the
Ogilvie family, in particular, Mr and Mrs John Ogilvie, of Furracabad,
N.S.W., Miss Kathleen Bland, Winchester, England, Mrs K. Anderson,
of Sydney, Mrs F. J. Sabine, Yamba, N.S.W., Mrs Griselda Carson,
Wellingrove Station, N.S.W., and Mr Justice Street. I wish also to thank
Mr and Mrs Baillieu Myer for giving me permission to visit Yulgilbar
Station, and Mr and Mrs Alan Rogan for entertaining me there and
showing me around. Further thanks are due to Mr Robert Law, of
Grafton, for access to his father's personal records, Mrs L. T. Daley, of
Armidale, Mr Ian Robinson, m.h.r., and Mrs Robinson, and Mr
A. W. Wood, of Muswellbrook. I have also had much rewarding infor-
mation from Mr and Mrs F. W. Clark, of Lawrence, Mrs Hodgetts, of
Fine Flour Creek, and Messrs Herbert Rogan and Jack Hamilton, who
have associations with the Clarence going back for generations. I wish
also to acknowledge the help given by the Clarence River Historical
Society, Grafton, and Messrs Stephen, Jaques and Stephen, Sydney.

Finally, I have to express my gratitude to the Commonwealth
Literary Fund, whose fellowship made possible the research and writing
of this biography.

GEORGE FARWELL

Contents

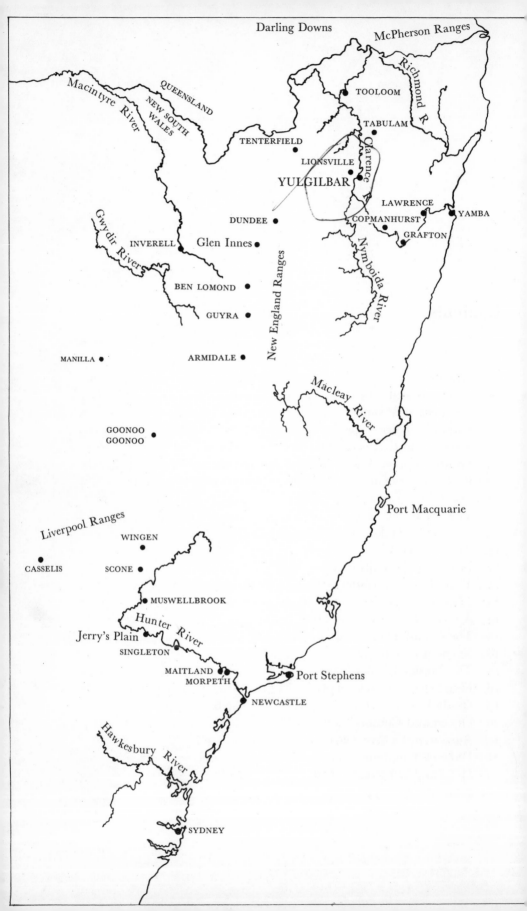

Prologue

We shall never again know anything quite like the pastoral age.

It was a grand age while it lasted; and it lasted a very long while; the best part of two centuries. It brought a special character to this harsh and lonely continent, created much of the ethos we still recognise as distinctively Australian. The squatter, however we feel about this particular type or that, was a special kind of man. He had to be. He had to contend with the savage as well as bountiful moods of a relentless, unfamiliar land. He was dedicated, inventive and hard-working, even if this dedication corresponded with self-interest and the hard work produced fortunes no others could amass. In time he became undisputed master of vast acreages he was determined to possess forever. He was often ruthless, arrogant, disdainful of lesser orders; but he could also be liberal in his attitudes, extravagantly generous and devoted to the land that bred him. Above all, he showed other men how to live with style and flair.

Style. That was the operative term.

This provincial society of ours, spiritually impoverished, has always lacked the civilising quality that goes by the name of style. The squatter fashioned a grand manner of living that our urban or suburban *milieu* can never hope to match. He created a unique life style; a zest for living; indigenous forms of architecture, either through the simple lines of his early colonial homesteads or expansive country houses in private parklands, and ornate Victorian mansions when he came to town. He transformed the once barren landscapes of the backblocks with his split rail fences, shady stock routes, drafting yards and clusters of outbuildings that assumed the proportions of independent villages. He fostered a national style of painting in the open air; a literature exploiting the rich bush vernacular; the folk songs improvised in shearing sheds, along the track, around campfires under the outback stars.

Yet frequently he himself was a dour, pragmatic, unimaginative man. He came from all classes and types: impoverished English gentry, grimly practical Scots, redundant officers from the Napoleonic wars, scholars and scoundrels, adventurers, gully-rakers and remittance men. In the beginning the squatter provided the one dynamic force for an ingrown, unproductive colony of petty officials, idling soldiery and transported felons. He alone had the courage to move out beyond the embryo cities and the coastal fringe. He followed in the tracks of explorers, filled in the empty spaces on rudimentary maps, found unknown river valleys, mountain passes and immense tracts of flat-ruled backlands whose only boundaries were bare horizons. He took his flocks and herds across the Blue Mountains, out to the Murrumbidgee, the Darling and the Condamine, spreading out like the nomad Arabs to the arid wastes of saltbush and spinifex in central Australia and even to the remote Kimberleys. There were many who perished out on the featureless frontiers; from thirst, or injury or starvation; or else from spear wounds in some confrontation with the tribesmen defending their own ancient rights to the land. Sometimes they responded with violence of their own. In rarer instances, as did Edward Ogilvie, some befriended the tribes and treated them in a humane and generous fashion.

These men transformed the once opprobrious term squatter—meaning those who squatted illegally on crown lands—to one of value and respect. I prefer it to more formal words such as pastoralist or grazier, because it has authentic Australian overtones. The squatter, through the old bush songs, the legends and the backblock's vernacular, has become recognised as an unique expression of his environment.

The Banjo's vision splendid nurtured a free-ranging adventurous existence that not even the recurring disasters of nature or the collapse of stock markets could long undermine. The squatter's world was sketched in bold and sweeping outlines against the massive canvas of the Inland, and he made it a source of legend.

A decade ago there were fifteen sheep to every man, woman and child on the continent. The squatter's wool cheque contributed more to the nation than the profits of industry and mining combined. Wool and wealth became synonymous; the squatter and social prestige. Now, almost without warning, the entire edifice has crumbled away.

Even now an Australia without sheep is inconceivable.

One might as well contemplate an ocean devoid of fish or the everlasting plains without their grasslands. How else are the vast regions of the back country now to be employed; the endless perspectives of grazing paddocks, improved pastures, river flats, blue-hazed mountain valleys, the forested uplands and level outback plains where the cloudless skyline comes down to a horseman's elastic-sided boots?

There is still something unreal in Haddon Rig selling stud rams for pet food at sixty cents a head, graziers from western Queensland seeking jobs as council employees, wharf labourers, salesmen in real estate; the owners of proud Western District stations waiting on paying guests or opening their manorial wrought-iron gates to Pioneer tours. For the big men of the pastoral world, the companies and syndicates, there is less need for sympathy. They have turned over their money many times, invested it in industry and city real estate; diversified as the modern saying is. The smaller, independent graziers have had the rougher passage; especially in sparser country, on soldier settler blocks or the arid and droughty holdings of the far outback. Yet even theirs has been a more rewarding existence than city clerks and counter hands could hope for; or those who, for generations, worked the big runs for small wages, long hours and no prospects of security in old age.

If sheep raising is no longer big money, most of us will recall the fantastic boom times of earlier decades. The annual excursions to Europe, the visit to Paris *couturiers*, the knighthoods and divine right of entry to Government House, the grey toppers and champagne at Flemington, the flunkeydom of social editors, the select invitation lists for picnic races or Bachelors and Spinsters Balls, the chartered aircraft taking guests and chorus girls out west for gay week-ends, the monied young larrikins causing mayhem in subservient country towns, the spendthrift entertaining in city hotel suites reserved by tradition for the squattocracy and now demolished for want of a carriage trade.

This country was surely unique in raising the owners of sheep into almost feudal aristocrats, exalting them to Shepherd Kings. Elsewhere in the world—on Europe's common lands or Asia's desert steppes—breeding sheep was a peasant's occupation. It may have been more to our benefit had we likewise fostered a peasantry, a race of men who lived closer to the soil, more frugally and wisely, bound to it by necessity and tradition, not by mere speculation in land and stock. Such men would have survived without a gambler's market, escalating labour costs and reckless money hunger. Under such conditions wool may well have retained its supremacy in world demand.

Perhaps it was in the nature of this hazardous continent to fashion a nation of gamblers. And, without this gambling spirit, the pastoral age would never have emerged at all.

These days we need to remind ourselves that the squatter was not always a feudal lord, not always the rich man mounted on his thoroughbred. Like William Ogilvie, he came often from humble beginnings, without prospects and with little capital. He made it by his own stubborn courage, selflessness and instinct for survival. No one has yet told the story of the pastoral age in all its scope and drama even though many books have been written and the archives are rich in private letters, diaries, notebooks, dusty records and official documents. In this narrative a selection of these has gone to reconstructing the rise of one determined family from the age of convict sailing ships to the creation of a baronial estate, built under immense difficulties in a river valley where, little more than a century ago, there were only jungle scrubs and primitive nomad tribes.

1

A New World

For a ten-year-old boy the sight was a traumatic one. Edward was to remember it all his life. A row of gibbets emerged from the drizzle as their launch passed down the Thames. Three shapeless figures hung there in chains on that raw late autumn morning, vanishing into the mist again. Thirteen weeks later, anchoring in Sydney Cove, the ship swung close to another gibbet; on Pinchgut Island a few cable lengths away.

In between were the enormous wastes of ocean.

The boy was to see masts and spars stripped under an Atlantic gale. Tropic squalls blacked out brilliant and unfamiliar stars, while decks blistered from days in airless calms. Huge following seas tumbled astern throughout the Roaring Forties. Scenes little less wild were enacted among the eighty-one female convicts aboard the robust little barque *Granada*.

It was a sobering induction into the new world his parents had chosen.

As symbols, those Thameside gallows may have been lost on so young a boy. His father would have better understood. William Ogilvie was always a reflective man. He knew the Britain they were leaving to be no gentle land. Unrest, violence, the protests of the poor and unemployed were spreading. Men wrecked machines, burnt hayricks, massed in strikes and riot, broke into houses, turned to highway robbery, filled gaols and convict hulks. The peaceful life, a secure future for his family seemed unlikely here; even if what was reported of the antipodes had not always been reassuring. As an old naval hand the hazards of a long ocean voyage would scarcely have troubled him. He would have been less sanguine on the prospects of that remote, little known continent ahead. One had heard of the presence of gallows there, too. Whatever transpired, it had to be a fresh beginning for a man, already middle-aged, with a wife in her early thirties and four children as well. There would have been misgivings enough to fill his habitual silences as they prepared to leave London for Gravesend. He sent Mary, with the six-year-old Ellen, direct by post-chaise to the dock, taking the three boys and all their possessions downriver by launch.

For the boys it was a day of rare excitement. Especially after the quiet of Merton.

Already that Surrey village must have seemed another life. It had been a good place for growing lads. One can almost hear the parents saying it. Open fields; a river; farm animals. And, if the need were there, only an hour to London by the modern turnpike road. Frederick had been christened there; Ellen born in the farmhouse; William Kitchenham and Edward had both paced around those meadows almost as soon as they could run. Then, if only briefly, they had been exposed to the crowds and varied happenings of London.

When, seventy years later, Edward dictated a short memoir on that voyage, he made only the sketchiest reference to their departure; none at all to the village they left or to their stay in London.[1]

The impact of the sights, sounds and smells of a riotous city can only be surmised. They must have overwhelmed the country-bred boy. The miles of cobbled or granite-paved streets; coaches rumbling past, carriages, some elegant chaise with postilions in scarlet and gold lace; the raucous costermongers, donkey carts, cockles and live eels under flaring lights; the stench of open sewers; darkies with turbans, pigtailed Chinese; monkeys dancing on barrel organs; truculent men in blue coats and tricorn hats, with crutches or a wooden leg from Napoleon's wars; the mysterious painted ladies in the Strand that boys were not supposed to look at.

They rode by hackney to the river. It was a grey chill morning. At Westminster Stairs they watched the Thames flow by, sucking at worn stone steps, eddying on again like curdled milk.

Father would have been much occupied at the landing, directing launch hands in brisk naval style, watching them load corded boxes, sea chests, furniture in packaged cocoons, Mary's household wares.

The launch, Edward recalled, was unlike anything the lieutenant had seen before, despite all his years at sea. His first steamboat. His fascination with that tall funnel, boiler and paddleshaft can only be imagined. Thumping downriver at two or three knots, it took them under London Bridge with its rows of shops, past the massive grey

[1] Bundock, Mrs E. W., *Early Recollections of E. D. S. Ogilvie of Yulgilbar*, 1894. Archives, University of New England.

Tower of London, past Wapping Stairs, the huddled cottages of East London's poor, then mud flats and those gibbets. Someone told Edward they were pirates, or what remained of them; as if it were their natural destiny to be strung up there as a caution to other Englishmen, or even boys. Then the first faint smell of salt reached them on the raw, damp air.

Father would have smelled it first. It came to him out of his past. The salt tang of it had been part of his life for more than twenty years. He had been only two years older than Edward when he first came down on these tides, shouldering his seabag aboard a man-o'-war at the age of twelve.

Now he was embarking on a more humble mode of travel. A convict transport. Women convicts at that. His fellow officers would have thought it damned undignified. After the trim, disciplined decks of Nelson's flagship, H.M.S. *St George*, or those graceful frigates patrolling South American waters and the Baltic Sea.

'We were coming out in a merchant vessel, commanded by Captain Coolin,' Edward stated in his memoir, 'but my father found him so unpleasant he was disinclined to do so. He got permission to come out in a convict ship instead.' Since the Government was paying their passages, the change was of no account.

It was a relief to find *Granada*'s master to be a friendly, powerful Scot. Captain Alex Anderson, also a naval man, must have had problems accommodating four children in the cramped quarters of a 400-ton barque. There were already nine other passengers. These comprised a government official, his infant daughter, a surveyor and his wife, and a Church of England clergyman travelling in style not only with a wife, but his sister and a young married couple as servants. At least Mary Ogilvie was not to be short of feminine company. The ship's doctor, who doubled as convict superintendent, was a thirty-five-year-old Royal Navy surgeon named Peter Cunningham. He, too, was a Scot. Since this was his fourth voyage to New South Wales, his local knowledge was to be of great value to immigrants like the Ogilvies.

There were also those eighty-one sad, defiant, shabby or bold-eyed women below decks. Sharing the same airless quarters were fifteen of their children; all females, too. Though obliged to remain in their own 'tween-deck purdah, these women were soon to have a powerful influence on the moods and routines of the voyage.

Granada sailed with the outgoing tide on 24 October 1824.

Edward was on deck 'to watch the anchor coming up, the sailors at the capstan keeping step to somewhat uncouth, if not inappropriate songs.' The phrasing belongs to an old man's recollections, not the excitement of youth. No boy could have been unmoved as his first ship cast off, spread its tall masts with sail, moving at last towards distant oceans whose adventures were as yet unknown, beyond the imagination.

When they reached the English Channel that rainy weather cleared. The passengers stayed on deck as the ship passed down the Margate Road. They looked at Dover Castle through Captain Alex Anderson's telescope, picked out the chalky cliffs of Folkestone and a steepled white church beyond. Within a few months the Ogilvies were to see an almost identical church in Parramatta, for the story goes that Governor Macquarie's wife chose its design as a reminder of that habitual last sight of English shores.

On board *Granada* it was too early yet for nostalgia. But one can imagine this family of six at the bulwarks, tightly wrapped against wind and cold, watching those green downs and cliffs recede in shafting sunlight, the only ones on board expecting never to see this land again.

In all likelihood they made a silent, closed-off group, all but William uneasy at the vaguely sickening lift and surge of unsheltered seas. Father would have been at the centre of them, a rock-like figure, shortish, thick of shoulder with ruddy weathered cheeks and feet planted wide in proper naval fashion; the knowledgeable one to whom the others looked for reassurance. Mary, too, would have appeared at least outwardly composed; a slender, yet large-boned, almost country-style woman of thirty-three. From the only portrait of her, painted later in life, she wore her dark hair brushed back firmly beneath tight bonnet, accentuating the full and rounded cheeks.[2] Everything about her, as always, would have been very firm; from the strong chin to the set of her mouth which, unless she smiled, downgraded her good looks. The children, scaling down from the eleven-year-old William Junior, with his lanky air of growing too fast, to Edward, a smaller, almost self-conscious replica of his father, and the two youngsters holding to mother's full, high-waisted skirts would have given this scene the air of a Millais engraving.

For William the real point of severance must have come with Cape Finisterre. This was where a fast-sailing French squadron had engaged them, twenty years ago. Finisterre had been a full-scale battle. His frigate dismasted; guns put out of action; nearly two hundred wounded or dead.

Soon *Granada* was plunging in the grey Atlantic. The wind rose alarmingly. That night a full sou'-westerly gale caught them, forcing them to lie to for three days and nights with tops'ls struck, lashed helm

---

[2] Portrait of Mrs Mary Ogilvie by Hay, Jersey 1857. Mitchell Library, Sydney.

and a double watch on deck. It was the kind of weather the North Atlantic alone can generate at the onset of winter; mountainous, surf-topped breakers, wind blasts of Arctic virulence, a fury of scudding, smoke-grey cloud. This rage of ocean was enough to turn anyone's thoughts towards God, firm earth and strong stomachs, none of which were accessible to these passengers amid the crash of tables and crockery in a lurching saloon.

As for the ninety-six women and children below decks, conditions were unendurable. In heavy seas hatches were always battened down, and every scuttle closed. No fresh air reached them at all. No ventilation of any kind. The stench was appalling. Nor was it possible for them to leave their close-set tiers of bunks. Each time a big sea crashed on the deck above several tons of water flooded down, drenching bedsheets, mattresses, clothes, sometimes even washing sleepers from their bunks, if any were able to sleep.

'The elders among our passengers became grave and anxious,' Edward recalled. 'But my brothers and myself, having got over our sea-sickness, thought it high fun to slide toboggan fashion upon a child's chair laid on its back across the deck from side to side as she rolled.'

Mrs Ogilvie's response to these games was not recorded. They were unlikely to have lasted long.

She was a tolerant woman in many ways, good-humoured and kindly as everyone who worked for her later agreed. She was also strong minded; a character of definite, if unconventional views, and a habit of expressing what her husband merely thought. You did not argue with mother. No woman of less vigour and resolve could have come through a voyage of this kind without stress or complaint. Confined to a narrow swaying cabin with four children, feeding them, keeping them amused, anxiously watching their health, forced to endure a life without privacy among strangers, she carried it all off with apparent calm. There was iron beneath that graceful, composed, essentially feminine manner. She was ably equipped to cope with even more critical demands the colony would make on her later.

By the time Tenerife was sighted, the ocean became quiet again. Land took shape in the form of a mountain soaring miraculously above horizontal dark cloud. The skies had never seemed so blue. The whole family went ashore in the jolly boat, marvelling at Edward's 'vine-clad slopes, laden dromedaries, swarthy and often hideous old women who excited our wonder and admiration.'

Again father would have talked of the wars. He had never landed here. No Britisher had in Napoleon's time. The boys must have heard him describe how Nelson—his hero figure—had unsuccessfully attacked the fortress, leading the assault in a flotilla of small boats under the Spanish guns. It was here that Nelson had lost his right arm.

Some days later they passed close to Gough's Island, a mere cluster of rocks in mid-ocean. It was the only land they would see for the next three months. Captain Anderson arranged for the men to have a day's fishing off the lee shore. The Reverend Frederick Wilkinson returned in triumph with the head of a huge sea lion, as if avenging those bygone Christian martyrs. He appears to have been a Dickensian character, the sporting parson. One imagines him as much at home with fowling piece or creel and rod as with the *Book of Common Prayer*. Whether or not he rode to hounds, he was to distinguish himself with some fast cantering when his material flock was in jeopardy some years later. On this particular fishing jaunt he also captured a live penguin which he gave to young Edward as a pet. The boy fed it with so much salt beef and enthusiasm that the bird died in a matter of days.

Equally distressing was the conduct of those other birds of passage. 'The ladies, as they called each other,' he said.

'One handsome young lady of decidedly warm temper, having been detected in a very unauthorised flirtation with one of the ship's mates, was so violent towards the poor doctor in both language and action, she was brought on deck and made a spread eagle, being lifted screaming and struggling on to the rail of the bulwark and main shrouds, to which her extended arms and wrists were bound until she cooled down. But her tongue was still free. The lady passengers scuttled away.'

A boy could learn much without formal schooling on a passage to the antipodes.

The wild, red-headed girl, Isabella Lloyd, was later assigned to George Wyndham, an early Hunter River settler. She worked there as a housemaid until the Wyndhams found her bashing their child's head against a tree stump. It could have done little to mitigate her seven-year sentence. The nature of her original crime was unknown. *Granada*'s convict manifest gave no information beyond length of sentence and where they were tried.[3]

Meantime Mr Cunningham did his best to control his uncontrollables with daily issues of lime juice. Since this was said to be an anti-aphrodisiac as well as insurance against scurvy, the ribald and randy shellbacks must surely have had their doses, too.

'Poor Jack is placed in a perfect garden of temptation,' Cunningham wrote in the book which he was to publish two years later. 'He sees twenty wicked fingers beckoning, and twenty wicked eyes winking; no

---

[3] *Register of Convict Ships, 1825*, Mitchell **Library, Sydney.**

wonder his virtue sometimes experienced a fall.'[4]

His *Two Years In New South Wales* reveals a more tolerant view of those 'fair seducers' than he showed aboard ship. Still his official options were minimal. Regulations had lately been introduced to prevent transports from becoming sail-driven brothels. At least that was the idea. He pointed out that in previous years prostitution had become notorious. Any man who attempted to curb it risked assault, knifing or an assisted dive overboard on some moonless night. Yet he believed that these voyages often produced lasting affairs, even marriage. If women 'lived promiscuously with the seamen', he wrote in his dry Scots fashion, the arrangement 'frequently brought more homogenity than now . . . By being suffered to live in concubinage with the sailors, they became inducted into the moral principles of *personal attachment.*' (The good doctor's emphasis.) The drawback was that, even if these amorous tars sometimes married, only too often 'Jack got tired of it and sailed off again.'

Nor was it much good, he added, if the guardians of morality succeeded. Women under such wowserlike control disported themselves 'like wanton colts' as soon as they went ashore. He wrote, too, of the seamen's cunning strategems. Even when doors were bolted and barred, they found ways of breaking into these 'tweendeck harems. 'They forced up a piece of board nailed over the coal hatch which, being under a bedplace, was completely hidden from view; then, entering the prison, puffed out the rushlight and continued their tête-à-tête until the inquisitive eye of the day began to blink in on them.'

Nice euphemisms the surgeon used. No wonder Isabella Lloyd had been brought on deck in such a fury.

For the saloon passengers it must often have been difficult to preserve decorum and small talk at the dining table. The doctor himself declared that anyone faced with so trying and saintly a job ought to be canonised on reaching Sydney. He was a master of the colourful phrase, classifying his types with botanical exactitude. He wrote of street perambulators, prima donnas, nymphs of the pavement, Newgate matrons, magnetic-fingered beldames, watch ticklers and connoisseurs of jewellery shops. There were other equally tricky souls who, 'having passed the grand climacteric', conned their bibles with such regularity it was always a surprise to find them 'overcome by the spirits, or using the religious tracts so eagerly accepted as curling papers for the hair'. Few of them were the simple convict maids of popular ballads. More often they were thieves, pickpockets, whores, blackmailers, with an occasional murderer

[4] Cunningham, P., *Two Years in New South Wales*, London, 1827.

or two among them. Of *Granada*'s eighty-one gaolbirds none had been given less than a seven-year sentence, the minimum qualifying them for transportation. Seven had earned fourteen years, while twenty-seven were lifers.

All the agony of Britain's industrial revolution and its outcome showed in their coarsened, leering, haggard and mock-deferential faces. These were women without hope, without menfolk, without anything to look forward to beyond the treadmill of a heedless convict regime ahead.

'If ever there was a hell afloat,' wrote another ship's doctor, 'it must have been in the fo'c'sle of a female convict ship—quarrelling, fighting, thieving, destroying each other's property from a mere spirit of devilishness, conversation with each other most abandoned, without feeling or shame.'[5]

Edward, though clearly fascinated, was too young to recognise their anguish. Nor was he aware of the punishments they were given. Though women were not flogged as male convicts were, it was accepted practice to whip their naked backs, arms or legs. Peter Cunningham may have been too humane to allow this to happen often. As he expressed it in his book, 'corporal chastisement, degraded in its very nature, ought certainly to be as much as possible avoided, and when necessary inflicted privately.' The greater indignity was to order a woman's hair cut off, or her skull shaved. For the more violent there was solitary confinement in the dark coal hatch, and a bread and water diet.

Standard dress for female convicts was shapeless calico, coarse woollen stockings and a black cap issued from slops. Mary Ellen wrote that the appearance of these women, especially in those dreadful caps, had terrified her. The astonishing fact was that they retained any tenderness or humanity at all.

Cunningham was a rare type of naval officer. Son of a land steward to the Laird of Dalswinton, he was born in the Dumfries village of the same name. He shared the literary gifts of three brothers, one of whom was a friend of Robbie Burns, and kept up his interest in farming throughout his active service years. The Ogilvies took to him immediately, while his youthful and candid outlook soon won the friendship of the older boys. During his four—later five—postings as a surgeon-superintendent, he claimed never to have lost a life at sea. It was a rare achievement, for the death rate on transports was often high. He attributed this largely to giving his convicts 'good and abundant rations'. He also had a shrewd understanding of prison psychology. He

[5] Clarke, T., Surgeon, quoted in C. Bateson's *Convict Ships*, Glasgow, 1959.

was well aware of the corrosive effect that hardened old lags had on younger elements among them, and believed in keeping his charges mentally occupied.

On *Granada* he devised a busy routine for these women. They rose at 4.30 a.m., parading on deck with their washtubs as soon as the barred gate was unlocked, then spent the morning holystoning decks and cleaning ship. In the afternoons they had organised deck games, if the seas allowed. After tea came concerts, masquerades, singsongs, dancing and other 'innocent amusements'. The cabin passengers were brought along as audience.

Sometimes the effects were spectacular.

Those 'tweendeck ladies enjoyed dressing up. Somehow they managed to rig themselves out in extravagant or bizarre costumes. One tough old moll in her fifties, Cunningham wrote, liked to set artificial flowers in her grey hair, teasing it out in youthful curls, then 'warbling sentimental songs about the false lover who stole her heart away'. One can only speculate as to what appalling crime had landed her in this company.

Personal visits were also encouraged. The more truculent may have ridiculed them as condescending, but they did break down barriers on what was, after all, a common voyage to the new land; and hopefully, to a free society of the future.

Mary Ogilvie took a special liking to one formidable lady known as Partridge The Elder. Her daughter, Ellen, had been transported on an earlier ship. Mrs Partridge was a gigantic woman, 'six feet in her stockings,' according to Edward, 'but did not appear so tall being well-proportioned.' Sentenced to life at the Lancaster Assizes, she behaved so impeccably aboard she was employed in the galley as cook. Some months later Mary offered her a similar job, and later employed Mrs Partridge's daughter as well.

For those with sensitivity, it seemed, this kind of voyage with Britain's outcasts or condemned became a two-way process in understanding. It may even have been a vital preparation for survival in a land unfamiliar to them all.

Most Australia-bound vessels put in at the Cape of Good Hope, taking on stores and fresh water for the last five thousand mile run through the Great Southern Ocean. *Granada* merely doubled the Cape and sailed south-east.

This must have disappointed William, who had twice patrolled this coast, while Cunningham had also been on active service here. Hence Edward and his brothers had to take this particular lesson in geography at second-hand, listening only to the two men's naval reminiscences.

That there were lessons can be taken for granted. Mary would have seen to that. She was always strong on education, and in subsequent years taught all four children herself. There were no other options in the solitudes of the bush. Though little is known of her own upbringing— her father, Edward White, was part-owner of Bishopsgate's Swan Inn —she was clearly an educated woman, well read, with a sharp intelligence. Her personal letters reveal an unusual command of language, a critical mind and firm, well-formed handwriting. William, too, was enlisted for his share of teaching, especially in those subjects with which he was better qualified; elementary science and mathematics. No naval man, even if he went to sea at twelve, could have reached lieutenant's rank without a trained intelligence. Examinations had to be passed; mathematics was needed for navigation; other disciplines for the command of men. It seems likely that the children were also helped by the Reverend Wilkinson, soon to be teaching classics in a school attached to his church at Newcastle, and by the surveyor Heneage Finch, whom the surveyor-general Major Mitchell was later to describe as a scholar and mathematician.

Above all, there was the teaching process of the voyage itself; the close contacts of shipboard life; the officers at work, talking with seamen on deck; and, of course, those earthy ladies of the lower decks. Again Edward's reminiscences are disappointing.

Perhaps it had all happened too long ago; or, having made that same sea journey several times in later life, he had forgotten just how it stimulated the boy.

It would be fascinating to know just how this unsophisticated lad reacted to what he saw: the storms; the immensities of ocean far from land; the eerie and oppressive atmosphere of the doldrums when even a full spread of sail could raise no wind; the sight of whales, or dolphins, or flying fish; the sea-birds skimming at wave level with not even an island within hundreds of miles; the talk of the shellbacks, how they worked, and how they treated him. Maybe a more mature mind was needed to describe the peculiar quiet and loneliness of nights, the stars swaying above tall masts, the bursts of sudden action as the watch rushed to stays, crosstrees or the fo'c'sle head to lengthen or furl sail, the thunder and rip of canvas after tense, overheated days of calm, the cut-water slicing and foaming past the hull.

On so small a vessel the passengers soon knew everything about each other. In that one all-purpose saloon there would have been unending talk of their plans, their hopes, their misgivings about the future. Quite early in the voyage it must have become apparent to the Ogilvies that they were not alone in rejecting their past. When William spoke of his order for a land grant in Van Diemen's Land, Cunningham would have surprised him with a Colonial Office order for a grant of his own. His was for New South Wales. Next, Captain Anderson would have produced a similar document, too. It began to look as if even seamen with settled jobs were deserting their British past.

At least one of them would have brought out W. C. Wentworth's best-selling book on the colonies. Published first in 1819, it had become the emigrant land-seeker's holy writ, running through four editions by the time they sailed.[6]

'There is no doubt,' the crusading young colonial had written, 'that in the course of the next few years the town of Sydney, for the excellence of its situation alone, must become a place of considerable importance.' He described a harbour large enough to hold all the world's ships; the incredibly cheap price of sheep and cattle; low labour costs; the quality of wool that matched the best German and Spanish fleeces; the millions of acres yet to be given out. 'The colonist had no expense in clearing his farm. No great preliminary outlay of capital is needed before he can expect a considerable return.' It offered the kind of paradisal conditions that North America could no longer offer.

As for Van Diemen's Land, Wentworth described it as more beautiful and potentially rich than the mainland. Yet Ogilvie would have been little reassured by what he had to say of the natives. He termed them 'the lowest predatory scale of the human species, ignorant of agriculture and often prone to killing. They expressed the most rancorous and inflexible hatred and hostility towards the colonials.' Was this, after all, the right place for a young family? And what of those alarmist tales they had heard in England; of escaping convicts, bushrangers, murders on lonely farms?

Yet it was a pity not to have sighted this beautiful, if notorious island. Since *Granada* was bound direct for Sydney, the Ogilvies would have to return on another ship. She was now on a fair weather course through Bass Strait, and all they saw of their first landfall since Tenerife was the distant and cloudy profile of Cape Otway. When Captain Anderson altered course for the last northward run, sombre mountains were all they sighted; none of the green and fertile land Wentworth had promised them.

Yet their last daybreak at sea brought a subtle change.

January is one of the better months to approach the Pacific coast. A molten sun rises out of a pale sea. The sky is lavender. Featherings of cirrus overlie an ocean quiet at last. Long, slow surges lift a steady ship

[6] Wentworth, W. C., *A Statistical, Historical and Political Description of New South Wales*, London, 1819.

that has plunged and wallowed for weeks. On the port bow, vaguely sketched still, there emerges the merest hint of a dun brown profile, hardly more solid than the sea; and beyond, tier upon tier of rounded green hills. This insubstantial outline, lean and arid, this weathering of sandstone headlands, russet cliffs and long arcs of breakers driving upon yellow empty shores, this low-lying bastion of land is only a fragment of the vast continent that, when *Granada* neared it before a light easterly, had yet to be explored.

In those windjammer days the scent of aromatic shrubs and trees gave off a musky perfume a mile or more out to sea.

The *Granada* came on course for a broadening gap between two abrupt, flat bastions of sandstone, with a glimpse of immense harbour beyond. On the southern headland was Francis Greenway's slender white lighthouse. A convict architect, Cunningham would have told them. Beside it a gaunt wooden semaphore began to signal their arrival to Sydney Cove six miles away.

Granada entered Port Jackson on 23 January 1825. She had been at sea just ninety days.

A pilot boat came out to meet them near the Sow and Pigs, the long oars stroked by Maoris with tattooed faces and chests. Flights of para- keets rose from the trees. Sea-gulls wheeled and dived. Cunningham would have pointed out the mansion built by Sir Henry Brown Hayes, transported kidnapper of Irish heiresses, and Captain Piper's elegant white home. Beyond was only bushland for miles. Small creeks rustled through dense bracken fern and tea-tree to sandy shores. First distant sign of settlement was a line of windmills on Woolloomooloo Hill; then the tapering copper spire of Greenway's St James; then Fort Macquarie's battlements and martello towers on the eastern arm of Sydney Cove. Under tops'ls only, they drifted past Pinchgut Island, a solitary gibbet upon barren rocks, and came to anchor in a shallowing bay.

Many ships were moored here; brigs and barquentines from Britain, India, the China Sea; schooners and South Sea traders; small sealing and whaling vessels back from the Bass Strait. At the head of Sydney Cove were bondstores ánd warehouses, rows of whitewashed cottages with trim small gardens, the long vista of George Street with its veran- dah posts, stores and inns, the army barracks whose parade ground was broad as a city square. From King's Wharf a dozen small boats approached them. Watermen, standing, stroked around the ship on long, upright oars, asking a shilling a head to row passengers ashore. Others simply called out for news from home. Others again hawked soft drinks, watermelons, lewdly gesturing women, oranges or beer. Behind the port officials came a most extraordinary character.

Cunningham, of course, recognised him. His name was Boongarre. He had a complexion like boot polish, shaggy, uncombed hair and a frayed blue cutaway coat, with gold facings and huge epaulettes. A short naval-type sword dangled from his belt. His broad black feet were bare.

He introduced himself, Edward said, as King Boongarre. He had one of his five wives with him; a lady with even wilder hair, a tattered dress too large for her bony frame and a short clay pipe between her broken teeth.

'His Majesty asked for the captain,' Edward recalled, 'then bowed with great formality, had all the passengers presented to him and let it be known that a glass of grog and a biscuit would be acceptable. And for the Queen likewise. Though a tumbler of rum and water was put in her hand, it was at once tossed off by the King.' Boongarre never failed to meet visiting ships. He was always good entertainment. Besides the seamen were generous with rum. If they had to pick him out of the scuppers afterwards, he was worth a few guffaws. Few of them knew, or cared to know, he had once been a leader of the Port Jackson tribe. Nor that he had sailed around the continent with Matthew Flinders, an intelligent guide and interpreter. The passengers aboard *Granada* may not have been among those who laughed. Perhaps the convicts did not either, for they would have known what dispossession meant.

Those watching his sad clowning on deck were exiles from another land. He was already an exile in his own.

2

The Nelson Manner

Clear sunlight and luminous skies gave Sydney an almost Mediterranean air.

Everywhere these newcomers walked they saw colour: flowering shrubs, trees in blossom, gaudy parrots in cages outside cottage or shop doors, street stalls piled with nectarines, plums, peaches, oranges, limes. The way people dressed was flamboyant after England. Even laundresses and servant girls wore gay bodices, scarves and saucily short skirts. Frock-coated gentry with bright cravats and vests strolled Macquarie or Pitt streets as though the universe were theirs. The vulgarly rich drove by in gigs, chaises, even carriages with footmen on the step. Soldiers in scarlet tunics idled around town, ridiculed as lobsters by sniggering colonial youth. There were foreign seamen in striped guernseys, mahogany-faced South Sea Islanders; sun-reddened farmers in from the Hawkesbury; waggon-drivers with wideawake hats and whips coiled over kangaroo-skin jackets; and hawkers gravelly voiced in praise of Botany Bay oysters and prawns, crayfish, cooked eels from the Harbour. Inexorably threading these restless street currents was the countertide of silent, sardonic, sweat-grimed 'government men' in canary-hued jackets or prison grey, tramping to unknown assignments. These anonymous men were what all this boisterous community was really about.

William's first response to the colony was revealing. He wrote a letter to *The Sydney Gazette*, having it signed by the other passengers as well. Complimenting Captain Anderson on his 'liberal and gentlemanly conduct on the voyage', he made it sound like a thanksgiving. It expressed a new buoyancy of spirit. As if he were glad, after all, to have come.

By good fortune he had also found somewhere for the family to live. An old friend of his service years, William Balcombe, had asked them to stay in his house while they remained in Sydney. Balcombe had been in great trouble the last time he saw him. He had been expelled by Lord Bathurst from St Helena, where he represented the East India Company, after he was suspected of aiding the exiled Bonaparte to raise funds through secret letters to Paris. Napoleon had rented a house on his estate; they had become friends. Now the same Bathurst, as Secretary for the Colonies, had been persuaded to appoint him to a post in New South.Wales. He was Colonial Treasurer, a man of influence.

The Ogilvies continued to see a great deal of Cunningham. He appears to have become almost an honorary uncle to the boys. They could have found no one better equipped to show them the town. In his book he wrote of it with intimacy and sometimes affection; from the verandahs of Government House down to those dubious backlanes, alleys, taverns and stews of the Rocks on Sydney Cove. As he saw it, the place was becoming two nations already. For the more fortunate there were the terraces of solid freestone houses, the homely whitewashed cottages with hedges of geraniums or picket fences, the open square fronting St James' Church and a broad carriageway from Hyde Park past the Horse Guards' Barracks and colonnaded Rum Hospital to splendid views of the Harbour. For the unprivileged masses there was the congested slum of the Rocks.

One can imagine him introducing William to the markets, probably with the older boys as well, assessing the impressive range of colonial agriculture, the weekly sales of oxen, draft horses, milch cows, poultry, sheep. Each Thursday drays and waggons filed through the red dust of Brickfields Hill, bringing in wheat and maize from outlying farms. Blunt-bowed, overloaded sloops and hoys drew into a ricketty jetty on Darling Harbour from the Parramatta and Hawkesbury Rivers. They would have spent many hours here at the back of George Street, watching sacks, baskets, barrels hauled ashore. The smell of animals, barley, manure; the uproar of bellowing cattle, human voices and idiot-bleating sheep; the press of carriers and porters, bare-footed market gardeners in straw beavers and ragged dungarees all gave a heady spicing to the scene. William's square-set figure would undoubtedly have spent many hours there noting stock prices, quality of breeding, the variety and abundance of what these burly, raw-voiced farmers grew beneath the strong antipodean sun.

The downtown scene was less appealing.

Newcomers like the Ogilvies must often have been shocked by the eternal labour lines. Down almost every street those cocky or soured faces confronted them; the hard stares, vile and scarifying language, the contempt for anyone who looked different, or better dressed, or even spoke with another accent. Alexander Harris, the emigrant mechanic, summed up the typical lag's reaction to those who had not been transported. 'He's one of those free objects, bad luck to 'em. What business h've they in this prisoner's country?'[1]

Long files of prisoners were forever slouching by in their broad arrow tunics or Parramatta smocks; iron gangs passed with a jingle of leg chains; leering, mud-flecked groups lounged beside half-dug drains or ditches, or leaned on picks and heavy hammers and desultorily broke up piled stones. Sometimes they laboured past drawing carts, as though they were bullocks; one of the humiliations that contributed new and scurrilous epithets to the Australian tongue. Bullocking was one of the mildest phrases to enter the language at this time. The Government stroke was another sardonic reflection of the all-pervading reluctance for real work. More chilling was the spectacle of some loutish and screaming character, carried half-conscious from the convict barrack's flogging yard to the hospital down Macquarie Street. Its iron-barred stone gateway was opposite the elegant Greenway church where Archdeacon Scott preached each Sunday.

The Ogilvie boys would have been much amused by Peter Cunningham's impromptu lectures on the new colonial English. Never use the term convict, he would have counselled them. It hurt men's feelings. Government man had a less offensive sound. Or Canary, by reason of his yellow-jacketed plumage. He was also well informed on the subtle grades of local society. These, he said, were as rigid as the castes of India. His 'Botany Bay Dictionary' began with the Pure Merinos, whose blood was worthy of a stud book; the Exclusives, those landed families who never spoke to their inferiors; the Emancipists, whose convict origins were unforgivable, however prosperous or law-abiding they became. There were mortal distinctions between Sterling and Currency; the former being English-born, the locally bred mere Currency Lads or Lassies. Again there were Legitimates, also known as Crossbreds, who had reasons of law for their emigration, the Illegitimates, paradoxically, having arrived of their own free choice. There were also Men of Title. These, if not acceptable to Burke's Peerage, were distinguished by such honorifics as P.B. and C.B. Such were the

Above: Sydney Cove at the time of the Ogilvie family's arrival. Engraving by J. Lycett, Mitchell Library, Sydney.

Below: A Government Jail Gang, Sydney, by Augustus Earle. Mitchell Library, Sydney.

[1] Harris, Alexander, *Convicts and Settlers*, London, 1837.

class distinctions between Prisoners' and Carters' Barracks.

The social functions of this self-styled aristocracy were to sweep the street, repair them, make bricks, break stones and create an easy-riding world for the despicable free.

At higher levels, he wrote, 'as in all small communities, private feuds, backbiting and scandal exist to a great extent. Etiquette is, if possible, more studied among our fashionable circle than in London itself. If a lady makes a call, she must not attempt a repetition until it has been returned. Cards are ceremoniously left, and the rules of precedence so punctiliously insisted upon by some of our *ultras* that the peace of the colony was placed in imminent jeopardy by the opening of a ball before the leading lady of *ton* made her appearance. The routine of balls, dinner parties and *petite soirée*, lately commenced by our worthy governor and his lady, tend still further to advance the hilarity of our social circles. The pride and dignified *hauteur* of some of our *ultra* aristocracy far eclipses those of the nobility of England.'

The Ogilvies were not much interested in dancing to this type of minuet. A week or two of card-dropping and debate on precedence were reasons enough to move on. William's only interest in Government House was to exchange his Colonial Office order for the promised grant of land.

The only likeness of William Ogilvie was painted very late in life. He was then seventy-five. It is a very good portrait. Hay, the Jersey painter, reveals him as a strikingly ageless man. He would probably not have been very different in his middle forties. Posed in a leather armchair, significantly holding a book, he has strong, blunt-fingered hands, accustomed to manual work. Alert, a little guarded, he seems not quite at ease, though the eyes are blue and steady. A good listener, one feels; a silent, but kindly man. The forehead is broad, high-domed; his clean-shaven cheeks, apart from grey muttonchops, have the ruddy, weathered look of a man who has lived always in the open air. He has a large, high-bridged nose that almost typecasts him as patrician Scottish.

Mary's portrait was painted, also by Hay, at the same time. She has aged a great deal more than William. But again the unchanging character is there. She is her husband's opposite in almost every way; complementing him perhaps. A downright, positive woman. The dominant one. Everything about her is firmly moulded, except the rather rheumy eyes. She had suffered considerably by this time with her eyes, and was then partially blind. If there are few hints of the handsome, unlined, entertaining young woman in her thirties described by those who knew her then, the painter has caught the direct, perceptive manner, the sense of knowing her own mind. It is just that her subsequent years of suffering have also been emphasised.

Edward appears to have inherited his mother's strength of character along with William's physical traits. The same dome of forehead, though with less filling out of the cerebral lobes; the same high-beaked patrician nose. Later in life this was to give him an air of arrogance, which his contemporaries claimed to find in more than appearance. He, too, had his father's Scottish look.

Yet, for all his efforts, he was unable to establish any such family connections.

This search for reputable ancestors, which so troubled him in affluent old age, was of small acount at the time of the Ogilvie's emigration. These obsessions belonged to a later stage in Australia's colonial ethos. William himself was among the most unsnobbish of men. He was also a Whig, a radical posture none too comfortable in the Tory-dominated Britain of his day. His only concern was to fit himself into the workaday fabric of a new, physically demanding country. 'Though much research was done,' wrote one of Edward's grand-daughters, 'no definite links have been found. There is, however, a strong family tradition that it belongs to the Findlater branch of the Ogilvie family. The Findlater lineage goes back to the first Earls of Findlater, created in 1638. The peerage has been extinct since 1811.'[2]

For Lieutenant Ogilvie, having rejected European feudal concepts, armorial bearings, primogeniture, the sagas of ancient chieftains were of little value.

All his second son was able to trace was a great-grandfather, devoid even of Christian names. According to the genealogy Edward had published shortly before his death, this Mr Ogilvie had two unnamed wives, four sons and two nameless daughters.[3] The eldest son, James, likewise married twice, had a son, also James, by his first wife and a daughter Ann by his second. James II, described by the College of Heralds as a 'civil merchant', inherited his father's house on Holborn Hill, London, married the sister of a Welsh merchant captain, William Lloyd, and entered the tomb of his father at St Andrew's, Holborn Hill, in 1796. How well he prospered is unknown, for his will—apart from leaving £30 to his half-sister—bequeathed 'the rest, residue and remainder of my estate and effects' to his widow, who lived on to the impressive age of ninety-two. Hence there is no record of any inheritance

[2] Miss K. Bland, letter to author, June 1971.

[3] *Burke's Colonial Gentry*, London, 1895.

passing to William and the other four surviving children. Since Elizabeth Ogilvie was left with a young family—an unnamed daughter (circa 1777), William (1782), David (no date), Edward (1789) and Ann (circa 1794)—one assumes that most of his capital went on their upbringing. All three boys were sent into the Royal Navy at the customary age of twelve. In William's case, the separation from mother and home took place only two years after his father's death. By the end of 1821 he was the only male child remaining, for both David and Edward were drowned in the same Channel shipwreck that year.

No doubt the three boys spent their shore leaves at home, for their mother had by that time moved to Alverstoke, not far from the Portsmouth naval base. But whether they had any source of income to enlarge their miserly naval pay is unknown. This leaves unsolved the question of what capital William could call on when he sailed for Australia to take up land. At all events, Elizabeth was still living in 1848.

The navy in George III's time was no great career. If this had not been the time of Britain's twenty-year war against Napoleonic France, perhaps none of the boys would have entered it. Even officer's rank carried little social cachet. Things were different from the army, where young men needed a private income to buy a commission, wore pretty and expensive uniforms, ran up stupendous mess bills and gained promotion largely through personal or family connections. To reach commissioned rank in the navy a boy had to join up when luckier lads were half-way through school. He became a first-class volunteer, endured barbarous conditions in the fo'c'sle, bullying quartermasters, almost inedible food and a wage of six pounds ten a year. At least he was better off than second or third class volunteers, who could seldom hope to become more than cabin boys, officers' servants or ordinary seamen.

Despite rising no further than lieutenant in more than twenty years of active service, William's record was not unimpressive. Few officers earned higher promotion, even though they had to accept more responsible duties. Lieutenants were frequently given command of smaller fighting ships; sometimes they were the real masters of larger men-o'-war, even when their listed chiefs were commanders or even captains. In terms of pay this meant great injustice. Many remained grey-haired, battle-worn lieutenants in a service for which Britain depended for its security against invasion, yet denied them official promotion for dismal reasons of government economy. Perhaps the prototype of William were the characters his friend Frederick Marryat, later the novelist Captain Marryat, drew of Peter Simple or Midshipman Easy. When Lieutenant Ogilvie retired from active sea-going at thirty-two, his career was given considerable space in official naval records:[4]

> William Ogilvie entered the Navy, in July, 1794, as Fst-cl. Vol., on board the TREMENDOUS 74, Capts. John Aylmer, Ceo. Hopewell Stephens, and Chas. Brisbane; in which ship he continued employed in the Channel and at the Cape of Good Hope, part of the time as Midshipman under the flag of Rear-Admiral Thos. Pringle, until his return with that officer to England in the CRESCENT frigate in 1798. After serving three years in the North Sea and Baltic on board the ST. GEORGE 98, Capts. John Holloway, Sampson Edwards, and Thos. Masterman Hardy, flag-ship latterly of Lord Nelson, and participating in the attack upon the Danish line of defence before Copenhagen, he was made Lieutenant, 27 June, 1801, into the RUSSELL 74, Capt. Wm. Cuming, with whom he proceeded off Cadiz. He left the RUSSELL in Nov. 1801, and was afterwards appointed—11 June, 1803, to the WINDSOR CASTLE 98, Capts. Albemarle Bertie, Thos. Wells, Davidge Gould, and Chas. Boyles, stationed in the Channel—about July, 1805, to the SAMPSON 64, employed at first in South America and then at the Cape of Good Hope, whence he returned in May, 1806—21 May, 1807, to the BANTERER 22, Capt. Alex Shiphard, under whom he was wrecked in the river St. Lawrence 29. Oct. 1808, suffering on the occasion many hardships—and, 29 April, 1809, to the VENERABLE 74, Capt. Sir Home Popham, in which ship he accompanied the expedition to the Walcheren, and served in the Channel until March, 1812. He became a Retired Commander on the Junior List, 11 Aug. 1832; and on the Senior, 9 March, 1846.

The last two rankings, as commander, somewhat anticipate events, for they were designed to increase his retirement pay long after he left Britain.

Nor does so brief a biography give much insight into what those long years of sea warfare actually meant. He was a twelve-year-old lad when first he climbed aboard the seventy-four gun H.M.S. *Tremendous*, which had just been refitted after severe damage and loss of men in the English Channel. Soon after his thirteenth birthday he was in action off the Cape of Good Hope. At sixteen, promoted to midshipman, he kept tense deck watches as Napoleon prepared an invasion force to cross the Channel. He was nineteen when Nelson's *St George* headed the British line of battle into Copenhagen Harbour against the Danish fleet. His was an especially dangerous assignment. The plan of attack called for a flotilla of small boats to enter the harbour the night before, charting and setting light buoys along a shallow channel, right under heavy shore guns. Among the midshipmen in charge of these boats was

---

[4] O'Byrne, W. R., *Naval Biographical Dictionary*, London, 1849.

Ogilvie. As soon as the battle was won, Lord Nelson had all midshipmen paraded on his quarter deck. He congratulated them personally, and promoted William to lieutenant.

This was the victory that won Nelson the admiration of even the most reluctant of his seamen in Britain's underpaid, ill-fed and forcibly recruited navy. William's later account of the Nelson legend created by this battle has, for quite other reasons, entered Australia's official records. This was when he chose to remind a colonial governor of his own wartime achievements, arguing a case for additional land:

> At one o'clock, after three hours of very hot fighting, two of the British ships were flying signals of distress, with no marked effect on the enemy. Admiral Parker flew the signal, "Leave Off Action." Nelson, who was second in command, said to his flag captain, "Damn me if I do, Foley. I have a right to be blind sometimes." He then put his telescope to his blind eye. The signal for "Close Action" was put to his own masthead, and he sent a man aloft to nail it there securely. By half-past two he had the battle won.[5]

The victory was celebrated, according to naval custom, with a distribution of prize money, which in this case comprised captured silver dollars. William had his coins melted down and made into forks and spoons for the officers' mess. Significantly, in view of the later search for ancestors, they were embossed with a lion rampant, plumbline in one paw. This was the Findlater crest. The cutlery is still in the family.

William's adulation of the admiral was clearly shown. It was by no means uncommon. He shared this feeling with almost every member of the fleet; from senior deck officers down to the most potentially mutinous rating. 'Nelson was a pattern of kindness,' C. G. Trevelyan has written. Yet few of his men had much cause for loyalty to a service that forcibly recruited them by press gang, flogged them, condemned them to seaborne squalor and kept them eternally on short rations and poor pay. Having fought on Nelson's own flagship, shaken him by the hand, won promotion from him, he felt a personal sense of identification with his hero that was to sustain him for the rest of his life.

Though he was posted to another squadron before the death of Nelson at Trafalgar, another Ogilvie was on board H.M.S. *Victory*, being twice mentioned for his part in the battle. This was Midshipman David.

Four months earlier William was on *Windsor Castle* when she was badly hit by French gunfire near Cape Finisterre. Thirty-nine of her

[5] *Historical Records of Australia*, Series i, Vol. XIV.

crew were killed, four times as many wounded. Then followed two more
years of Atlantic patrolling, the boarding and capturing of foreign
ships trying to run the blockade. Next, while based on Nova Scotia,
he survived a shipwreck in near freezing seas off the American coast,
returning again from home leave in Britain to join a poorly led
invasion force that was battered by Napoleon's shore guns on Walcheren
Island. Also involved in this Netherlands battle was Lieutenant
Marryat. The subsequently famous author may well have drawn on
this disaster for his critical analysis of conditions in the navy. These
naval men, it seemed, could often be of independent mind.

After another three years of Channel blockades, according to
O'Byrne's dictionary, he was discharged from active service. This did
not mean retirement, for Mary Ogilvie wrote many years later that
he remained at sea for another two years.

This meant that, for the first two years of their marriage, Mary rarely
saw him. The wedding took place two months after he signed off
H.M.S. *Venerable*.

Presumably he had known Mary White for some time, for he was
staying at her father's Swan Inn in Bishopsgate when the unexpected
event occurred. The family story goes that Edward White disapproved
of William's attentions, not wanting a junior officer without sound
prospects for a son-in-law. It has also been suggested, though without
evidence, that he and Mary were cousins, which might also have
accounted for her father's objections.

The Ogilvies had a curious propensity for marrying within their own
clan structure. David married his first cousin, Mary Anne Lloyd, his
mother's brother's child. Anne Ogilvie also married the son of her older
sister's husband, Major Benjamin Baynton, by his first marriage. Since
there was seventeen years between the two girls, the elder was a middle-
aged woman by the time she attended the wedding of her stepson and
twenty-seven-year-old sister.

Edward White's feelings probably had a more material basis. He appears
to have had larger ambitions for Mary than the thirty-year-old William.

But Mary even then was a determined girl. She had also just come of
age.

Early one morning the pair went off as usual to communion at
St George the Martyr in Southwark. They returned to shock the breakfast table with news that they were married.

Their first child was born the following year.

They appear not to have stayed long at the Swan Inn. William, of
course, would have returned to naval duty. But Mary was living at
Mitcham, Surrey, when she registered the birth of William Kitchenham

in February 1813. She had moved to Tottenham, Middlesex, by the time Edward David Stewart was born on 25 July 1814. When their third child, Frederick Henry, arrived in April 1816 they were living for some unexplained reason in Nice, then the capital of Italian Piedmont. The boy was named after his godfather, Lieutenant Marryat. How they came to be living on the Mediterranean has not been accounted for. It could hardly have been a naval posting; no such station existed. Possibly William had been given some other government mission, for there was then much tension between Italy and France, which had just lost the province of Savoie under the Treaty of Paris. Nice was certainly no pleasure resort at that period.

It was two years before they returned to England, when they settled in Merton. This was the beginning of William's life as a farmer. There is no record of him there before 1820. His arrival can be dated by the birth of Mary Ellen on 10 September 1818. The church register has a simultaneous entry of Frederick's prior birth in Nice, as if the Ogilvies wanted to ensure his British nationality.

This Italian sojourn was to have an unconscious influence on Edward's life. Having spent his second and third years here, he returned half-a-lifetime afterwards for prolonged periods. Despite his solidly Australian career, he confessed that this was the country in which he felt most at home.

Meantime there was Merton.

William had been lucky to make any kind of living at all.

As a career, the navy had evaporated for most officers by 1815. In the long, costly struggle against France the service had been built up to seven hundred warships and nearly 150,000 men. Now Napoleon was defeated and in exile. Four thousand lieutenants alone were pensioned off or unemployed. Victory at Waterloo had made them redundant as haystacks in a land smoking with iron and cotton mills. The industrial revolution was ruthless to earlier affinities with the land. Nor was it anyone's responsibility that the proclaimed heroes of wooden ships had saved the newly rich class of ironmasters, mill owners and war profiteers from the dangers—and dangerous ideas—of revolutionary France.

There was no place for them in the new money-focussed society. They were simply retired on half-pay. This meant trying to live on five shillings a day. Moreover it was a period of widespread unemployment. Nor had they any skills or training to make a living in peacetime.

No wonder naval officers were by tradition Whigs. Recruited largely from the sons of country gentry, mostly with little capital, they saw the

Tory party as representing the middle classes and rising masters of capital. Britain was now the strongest power in Europe. Yet it could not find its own people work. The choice was to take low-paid jobs in factories and sweatshops, or stay unemployed.

It required some courage for people like the Ogilvies to take up farming. The industrial revolution, in its one-eyed drive for factories and profit, was rapidly destroying the agricultural scene. Yet there was not much option for them, apart from turning to the land.

That they chose the village of Merton was not accidental. William's attitude to Nelson had much to do with it.

Merton, wrote Mary Ellen of her birthplace in retrospect, was the place 'hallowed by Nelson, whose favourite village it was'.[6] It became deeply etched in their affections. It was to condition their outlook for many years to come. The atmosphere it evoked, truthfully or not, was of an eternal, unchanging England.

Saxons had fought the Viking invader across these fields. Cynewulph, their king, was said to have been buried here. It was mentioned in the Domesday Book. Thomas Becket studied in its long-vanished priory. Gilbert Norman, Sheriff of Surrey, built the monastery in which Henry III's chief justice, Hubert de Burgh, took sanctuary and, back to the altar, defied twenty thousand armed pursuers accusing him of high treason. Later this became part of Merton Abbey. After the Reformation, it was converted to a private mansion and occupied by several notable figures. The dramatist Sheridan lived here. William Morris set up his tapestry looms here and made it a pre-Raphaelite centre. Isaac Walton wrote of the pleasures of angling on the Wandle. Rear-Admiral Isaac Smith, Captain Cook's cousin and cabin boy on his voyage to Australia, was still living in the ruined abbey's gatehouse when the Ogilvies arrived. Cook's widow came to stay here frequently. Above all, there was the mansion where Nelson had planned the life of a grand seigneur. Trafalgar put an end to that.

Merton would have been widely discussed in the wardrooms when the admiral bought his eighty-acre property. After shocking his lawyers by paying £9,000 for the neglected, rundown house and grounds, he proceeded to scandalise Britain by installing his mistress here. Renovations ran him into serious debt. The Hero of the Nile hired workmen by the dozen to enlarge dining room and kitchen quarters, modernise the guest wing, equip all eight bedrooms with newly invented water closets and create a lavish *décor* for dinners, house parties and receptions. There were rambler roses on the upper balcony, lover's walks, a coach house,

[6] Bundock, Mrs E. W., *Early Recollections of E. D. S. Ogilvie of Yulgilbar*, 1894. Archives, University of New England.

wine cellars, sunken gardens, ponds stocked with carp and a man-made moat diverted from the Wandle which Emma Hamilton at once christened The Little Nile.

What probably impressed William more were the practical improvements. Nelson had briefly fashioned a manner of living that had style. There were special quarters for domestic and farming staff, a kitchen garden, dairy, stables, and pastures for livestock. He was also negotiating to buy another ninety-two-acre farm between Merton Place and the Abbey, but died too soon. This would have provided more ground for his sheep, with an elegant park-like atmosphere. His ideas were to have a potent influence on Ogilvie in future years.

Nelson was a man strongly drawn to land instead of warfare and the sea.

Yet, even in Merton, the Wordsworthian tranquillities were passing. It was too close to London. A mere eight miles. City men had already bought up the better houses; men like Abraham Goldsmid, a cultivated London banker, his financier brother Benjamin, and the owner of a city newspaper. It had become fashionable to live the life of a bucolic country squire, discussing the points of horses or pig-breeding over the nightly port. Those who worked the land were mostly tenant farmers. Owners had given up the struggle, harassed by high rents and taxes originally imposed to win the war, and, as usual, never repealed.

Epitomising this rural decay was Merton Place itself.

It was already becoming a ruin. Emma's lavish gardens were overgrown with weeds and thistles, windows smashed and doors broken. Vandals had carved their trivial names on woodwork and outbuildings. It must have been a great place for the boys to explore in secret, perhaps tickling the forgotten carp in Nelson's moat, or playing in the ghostly coachhouse and cobwebbed cellars. The place had been empty since Lady Hamilton left in debt and disarray, some three years after her lover's death in battle. Its extravagant furnishings were auctioned off in 1808, though the property remained unsold until Abraham Goldsmid decided to buy it two years later. Even so he never lived there. His own speculations collapsed soon afterwards, and he shot himself one sunless afternoon. No one occupied the place again. Locals said the house had a curse on it.

No record exists of where the Ogilvies first lived, nor why they chose

Above: St Mary's Church, Merton, England. An engraving by W. Ellis published 1 July 1793. Courtesy Mr E. J. Adsett, Merton County Library.

Below: Lord Nelson's villa at Merton, England, published by J. Strutford, Holborn Hill, March 1830. Courtesy Mr E. J. Adsett, Merton County Library.

to come to Merton. There were several reasons why they might have
been drawn to it. Mary appears to have spent some time here as a girl,
perhaps at the house of Charles White, who may have been a relative;
perhaps an uncle. One of her favourite stories later in life was of being
kissed by Nelson at a ball in Merton Place. This was probably the
children's ball he gave early in 1803 for his nephews and nieces. He
announced that he would kiss all the pretty girls in the room; and he
did so. She would then have been thirteen. Again, while William was
still at sea, she must have stayed with the Marryat family at nearby
Wimbledon, for the lieutenant's wife was her closest friend. Admiration
for the romantic admiral was something both she and William shared.

According to the Surrey land tax returns, William became a tenant
farmer in 1820. He was shown as paying an annual rental of £100 to
Susan Harper, owner of the farm. Yet he may have been in occupation
earlier, for the previous tenant Richard Dallett ran several other farms
as well. A possible explanation has come from Merton's borough
librarian, Mr K. Adsett.[7]

He wrote that Dallett, having married Mrs Harper's daughter,
'succeeded his uncle, one of the wealthiest farmers, in 1813, and went to
live at Merton Hall farm, his uncle's former home. Ogilvie could therefore have lived on the Harper's farm while working for Richard Dallett.
It could have been on this farm that he first learnt the art of sheep
farming from the Dalletts, among the most successful sheep farmers of
the day. All the land in Merton was low-lying meadow, mostly with a
clay soil, not the usual sheep country. But animals could until 1819 be
pastured on Merton Common nearby, and the Harpers did have rights
to it. When it was enclosed the Harpers received an extra field in
return.'

And higher rent. When a newcomer bought this farm, William
found his rent increased three times in as many years.

The enclosure of that ninety-acre common was also significant. A
private Act of Parliament divided it up among local farmers, each of
whom gained an extra field, so that open grazing was no longer possible.
The whole pattern of the region was changing. London's industrial
growth was pushing drab streets and sub-standard homes further and
further out. The urban tide had now reached as far as Wimbledon. To
cater for the increasing mass of city dwellers, farms were being converted to market gardens, orchards and small-scale dairying.

No one had to read Malthus to understand his dismal warnings.
Over-population allied to falling productivity was corroding English

[7] Letter to author, March 1971.

life, forming giant slums; and brutalising the inhabitants, too. When Merton Place was finally sold, the speculators arrived, cutting up its grounds for building. 'The ancient nobility and gentry of the kingdom,' as Cobbett had foreseen nearly two decades before, 'have been thrust out of general employments . . . A race of merchants and manufacturers and loan jobbers and contractors have usurped their place.'[8]

It was no climate to encourage people with other values, like the Ogilvies, to think in terms of a constructive future for their children.

Yet what may have finally decided them to leave could have been something else entirely. Many years later, when they were firmly settled in Australia, the son of an old naval friend, Captain Charles Tindal, came to stay with them. In one of C. G. Tindal's letters home he told his father that 'Mrs. Ogilvie showed me the original "firebrand" letters from Honiton to Merton, Surrey, and seemed to regret very much that you deserted the scheme having drawn them into it.'

What was this scheme? The Tindal family letters contain no other reference. It appears to have been a joint proposal for the two men to take up a farming venture in Australia. Captain Tindal is then said to have withdrawn from it, promising to send out one of his sons later in life. The term firebrand is itself intriguing. William may have appeared outwardly to be an easy-going man. He was capable, if the occasion came, of considerable anger, and even radical expression.

A possible escape route had been found by William's younger brother early in 1821.

This was the year when David Ogilvie made a brief visit to the antipodes. After leaving the navy, he joined the East India Company's merchant fleet, eventually gaining command of the transport *Juliana*. Among his junior officers was the third brother, Edward. In 1820 *Juliana* was chartered to take convicts to Van Diemen's Land, reaching Launceston in January the next year. David's wife was also on board. When the ship sailed for Sydney two weeks later, it carried among other despatches a letter from the Lieutenant Governor, Colonel William Sorell, to Governor Macquarie in Sydney. The despatch was dated 17 January:

> I have the honour to transmit copies of letters that have been addressed to me by Captain Ogilvie, commander of the Juliana, and Mr. Graham, superintendent of that ship, expressive of their desire to become settlers in Van Diemen's Land . . . I accordingly stated to them my readiness

[8] Cobbett, William, *Political Register*, London, 1802.

to reserve land in such situations as they might point out, but until their application could receive Your Excellency's decision.

In the event of their request being sanctioned by Your Excellency, I understand it to be their intention to fix upon the lower parts of the Macquarie River, not far from where that stream joins the Lake River; which last joins the South Esk on Norfolk Plains about fifteen miles from Launceston.[9]

This would place the land somewhere between what are now the towns of Longford and Cressey, noted from the beginning as a centre for Tasmania's best superfine wools. It is also country of great beauty, green as England beneath the rain shadow of the Western Tiers.

The seafaring Ogilvies had a shrewd eye for good pasture lands.

David must have called on Macquarie after berthing in Sydney Cove, for his grant was approved. Six weeks later *Juliana* sailed for Madras and London by way of Batavia, where she loaded cotton and coffee. She entered the English Channel in the third week of December. The weather, as usual, was wild. The barometer dropped so rapidly that Captain Ogilvie made for the nearest port, put his wife ashore and beat on stubbornly up channel. That was the last anyone saw of *Juliana*. Except for the wreckage.

The crew of forty were drowned on Christmas Day.

Whether or not William had considered a partnership, he must have thought hard about David's tragically aborted plans. He would have had at least one letter describing the country during that leisurely voyage home. David's widow must also have talked of it in England. Besides Australia was coming more and more into the news. First there had been Wentworth's crusading book; then reports of the new boom in locally grown wools. The first large exports reached London in the year of his brother's death. The textile trade was enthusiastic, stating that the Australian fleeces were comparable, if not better, with those of Germany or Spain. Reports from New South Wales spoke of wool rising from 2/6 to 5/6 a pound within three years. Many men able to raise some capital were already planning to leave England, especially army and naval officers for whom the land offered no scope at home.

The decision was made at the end of 1823. On 2 January he wrote to the Under-Secretary for the Colonies, Wilmot Horton, asking for an appointment to discuss his brother's grant. Three weeks later a despatch went out to the Lieutenant-Governor of Van Diemen's Land, Colonel Arthur, in these terms:

I am directed by Lord Bathurst to transmit to you the memorial of Lieutenant Ogilvie, praying that a grant of land, which was formerly

[9] *Historical Records of Australia*, Series 1, Vol. XIII.

made to his brother and which is now in the occupation of Mr. Wilson, may be assigned to him. Mr. Ogilvie having stated that Mr. Wilson has expressed to him his readiness to resign his claim to the land upon Mr. Ogilvie's taking his stock off his hands at a fair valuation. Lord Bathurst has no objection to the arrangement proposed, and should Mr. Ogilvie satisfy Mr. Wilson for his stock and receive his permission to take the grant, you will have an order made out to Mr. Ogilvie to occupy the same.

Wilmot Horton ended by saying that, should someone else have since occupied the grant, Ogilvie was to be given another. It was just as well he did.

It appeared that T. B. Wilson, yet another ex-naval surgeon employed in ferrying convicts, had been given David Ogilvie's grant on the Macquarie River six months after the wreck of the *Juliana*. Men were following hard upon one another in the search for land.

Late in January, William applied for a free passage out and arranged to terminate the lease of his farm. The new owner, Payne, found another tenant farmer to take over. His name was William White. Once again the records are confusing. Mary's younger brother was named William, and it would be pleasant to think that he moved on to the farm, acquiring two years' experience before he, too, joined them in Australia. Yet the Surrey land tax returns list a William White as tenant for at least another twelve years. White, after all, was a fairly common name.

Whatever the facts, when Mary's brother followed them out, he found the Ogilvies established on land of their own.

3

Land of Silences

Government House, at the top of Hunter Street, commanded a dress circle view of the blue harbour. From its French windows offcialdom could watch each newly arrived ship reduce its spread of sail between Bradley's Head and Benelong Point, bringing these days more free settlers, less convicts. It was here that William came to present his credentials to Sir Thomas Brisbane.

The downright, efficient governor saw no difficulty in arranging Ogilvie's grant. Instead of passing him through routine channels to Van Diemen's Land, he suggested other action. No one, after all, knew what T. B. Wilson planned to do, since he was still in England. According to Ellen's memoir, her father 'at the personal request of Sir Thomas Brisbane, went to inspect some lands in this colony.' It could hardly have been as simple as that.

There was to be much confused correspondence with London over the next few years. Meantime Brisbane cut the legal knots, ignored the southern colony and gave William the option of staying in New South Wales.

It may even have been that William himself suggested it. He could have been prompted by Peter Cunningham. Since they were both in search of land, why not go out together. Why not pool their resources, take up neighbouring blocks if possible, minimise their common inexperience of local conditions. The problem was that most good land within a reasonable distance of Sydney had already been taken up. The frontiers were now over the Blue Mountains, south along the Murrumbidgee and northward on the Hunter River. The Government Surveyor, Henry Dangar, had just completed his survey of the Hunter. A new land rush to this fertile river valley had now begun.

Dangar's map was then on display in the Surveyor-General's Office, where prospective settlers could apply for detailed information. The two men assessed their prospects and decided to travel north together. But first, because of the primitive nature of the back country, William had to make arrangements for his family.

Again the freemasonry of the navy proved its value.

They were offered a rentable cottage out at Parramatta. This was on a 750-acre farm owned by the widow of a former governor, Captain Phillip Parker King, R.N. The lady was then in England, trying to extract a pension from the reluctant Government, and the cottage was vacant.

The Ogilvies travelled up the Parramatta River by the *Rose Hill Packet*, following the course taken by *Granada*'s convicts some weeks before to the Female Orphanage, which locals called less elegantly The Factory.

With ex-convicts alternately raising sail or pulling at the oars, this clumsy ferry was hardly designed for family comfort in a February heat wave; nor in winter westerlies or rain. 'I can still remember how tedious it was,' Ellen recalled, 'and how cold and hungry we were when we returned in the same manner about three months afterwards.'

Those surly oarsmen took them past the moored cutters and trading schooners of Darling Harbour, past the walled compound on Cockatoo Island where their more luckless brethren were kept in irons, past bush-lands and the bark huts of lonely grass cutters, the waterside salt pans where convicts laboured with heavy shovels under a blistering sun, past Squire's Tavern, then a few scattered orchards until they came to Hannibal Macarthur's rustic Vineyard Cottage amid orange and almond groves. Beyond was Parramatta.

If Parramatta was no Merton, it did have the settled air of a village. Lord of the manor here was the governor, whose country mansion dominated the green slopes and open parklands beyond. In the foreground were rows of whitewashed or sandstone cottages between gentle hills, the twin steeples of St John's Church, several coaching inns and a village green which, in harsher times, had been occupied by the flogger's triangle and stocks for petty criminals. The heritage of convictdom remained in the frowning grey walls of the prisoners' barracks and the Female Factory. In one of his rare poetic moods Cunningham saw this as 'a village of purest white, shining in a clear cloudless sky, like transparent alabaster, gemming over the fresh green undulating carpet beneath that cannot fail to occasion a thrill of admiration. But during the summer heats what a woeful reverse . . .'

A family fresh from Britain would certainly have found it so. Ellen was driven to complain that 'the heat and the myriad of mosquitoes, which are always worse to newcomers, made a lasting impression on my mind, but what was worse, they stung my brother Edward and the irritation was so great that mother had to call in a doctor.'

The doctor was yet another naval surgeon. John Dobie, then staying in Parramatta between convict transports, was to figure largely in their lives a decade or so ahead.

One might have thought that all Australia was in process of being taken over by naval or military officers. This was very nearly true. No longer was this to be the utopia Macquarie had envisaged for reformed criminals from the British Isles; nor his pastoral dream of independent yeoman farmers after the mildly socialist pattern of Robert Owen. Colonel Macquarie's liberal ideals were discarded when the caustic report by Commissioner J. T. Bigge reached parliament. Convicts were no longer to be coddled; ideas of rehabilitation then were too costly and unreal. Now the colony must pay its own way, attract a new class of free settlers, turn towards capitalist enterprise, and produce revenue for itself through the export of home-grown commodities. As John Macarthur had shown there was only one product with an overseas demand: wool.

Even in Parramatta the Ogilvies would have noted the standstill in public building, abandoned public works, the absence of convicts around the streets. The new policy of the mid-1820s was differently geared. Instead of working for the Government, convicts were now being sent out bush, assigned to private settlers, supported by them, and, in many cases, treated with greater harshness, as though they were feudal serfs.

Soon this was to become a test for Lieutenant Ogilvie's capacity to handle men. And for his conscience.

Back in Sydney, he rejoined Cunningham and shared a cabin with him aboard the *Lord Liverpool* on its weekly voyage up to Newcastle.

King's Town, as it was still known officially, had become a somnolent little township since the commandant, Captain Francis Allman, had opened up a new penal settlement for felons at Port Macquarie, a hundred and fifty miles further north. It consisted of two houses for government officers, a couple of passable inns, the almost empty hospital, quarters for the mounted police and, reminder of other days, the gaol and convict barracks. Only activity was on the harbour jetty where coal was loaded for Sydney.

Captain Allman, now returned from Port Macquarie, did what he could to make the visitors comfortable. There was little he could offer them for their expedition, except passing hospitality.

Peter Cunningham's advice to new chums going upcountry was simple enough. All a man needed, he wrote in his book, was a horse, a saddlebag for spare clothes, one blanket to sleep in and a packhorse to carry tucker and gear. With these, he informed them, travellers could exist for weeks along the track. The only trouble was a shortage of horses.

Not a single animal was available in King's Town. Even the police horses, aged and slow as they were, could not be spared. The troopers needed all they had for urgent patrols in search of escaped convicts, bushrangers or troublesome Aborigines. Any of these, the newcomers were warned, they were likely to run into from time to time.

They had obviously two choices only. They could return to Sydney; or walk.

Without hesitation, they chose to walk.

At least they would be reduced to walking once they reached Wallis Plains. This was the last settlement, thirty river miles inland. Even this was only a single hut for passing police patrols, with a few small farms along the river banks.

Wearing the customary cabbage-tree hats, rough bush shirts and moleskin trousers with pouches for tobacco and flint matches clamped to their hide belts, the pair set off on the small packet boat making the twice-weekly passage upriver. Since it was so slow, the Hunter River so winding and its shallows tricky, men mostly went overland by a bridle track through Hexham Swamp, putting only their baggage on board.

Along that narrowing waterway, with its steep clay banks, they would have seen no habitation before Morpeth, where the only settler, a retired army officer named Lieutenant Close, was building a homestead. At Wallis Plains they landed on a makeshift jetty and slept in that government hut.

Articulate as he was, Cunningham left no account of that strenuous inland journey. There is no way of knowing how these novices to the bush made a round journey of some two hundred miles on foot, with only faint wheel tracks to follow and barely a habitation. Nor how they managed for food, what they carried with them, nor where they slept. Cunningham wrote of the advantages of taking 'a steady white man who is a good bush-ranger [dangerous misuse of the term in those hazardous times] and a black native. Also a tinder-box to make fire on camp.' He suggested the use of 'a few slips of bark peeled from a tree as shelter against damp and cold, a good fire at the feet, a tin of hot tea before sleep, you will rest well. Also a musket for birds, and a brace of greyhounds for emus and kangaroos, for your bush fare is a true sportsman's feast.'

Probably they had not much more than that tinder box and a gun. It was possible, though unlikely, that Captain Allman went with them, for he was to register an upriver land grant a month later. Possibly he sent a guide, either convict or black. There were blacks, after all, around Wallis Plains. But they were nomadic groups, little interested in the few white men they saw. The swamps and plains beyond Wallis Creek made life too easy for tribesmen to trouble about with the dubious handouts of passing whites.

Here the travellers would have had their first close look at tribalised Aborigines, men whose hunting skills and independent outlook made them very different from the sad, ingratiating derelicts they had known around Sydney. These lithe, sleek-skinned hunters had been in the habit of gathering here for centuries. They speared fish that bred in great quantities here, snared waterfowl in nets of woven reeds, tracked game across the grassy plains, returned to their mia-mias of boughs and bark to feast on wallaby roasted on the coals, fish cooked in balls of clay and wild duck, water hen, heron, plover and geese.

The two white men were faced with a more restricted, hard-won diet on their journey into solitude. From the small hill above that swamp they saw nothing but flat horizons and dry plains ahead.

The silent land closed in around them, ebbing away to eternity. It was like a sea without tides. Zone after zone of silence. It was uncanny. At first there was dense scrub, a green world tangled with trailing vines, heavy undergrowth and tall, stout-boled cedar trees. Then came empty plains, stark hills, stony creek crossings, gullies heavy with boulders, more hills, more eerily still plains. The lonely country they walked through had the quality of a vast, blue-domed cathedral in the open air. Early morning and late sunlight shafting through the frieze of green foliage had the suggestion of stained glass. Yet the atmosphere was of Greece rather than Anglican. This was a timeless Arcadia filtered through the blue eucalyptus haze. Instead of goatherds they came upon a rare idiot shepherd shuffling behind his small browsing flock of sheep. The silence engulfed their wraith-like passing; and they were alone again. Sometimes a rough slab hut emerged in a clearing; or someone's deserted sheepyard of adzed posts and saplings. Often they would have an awareness of being watched. Yet saw no one. These remained presences they were dimly aware of; observing them from behind some outcrop or tree. Perhaps here and there they came on the embers of an Aboriginal fire; charred emu bones; a heap of mussel shells on the river bank. They were not often near the river. The track mostly kept far from it, so they heard only the rare hushing of water over rapids at a distance. Rank after rank the splendid trees spread away on either side; myrtle trees, great figs, the noble cedar others would soon come to shatter indiscriminately from these park-like forest lands. The air shrilled with cicadas on the hot still afternoons. Scores of kangaroos propped motionless as they approached, bursting away in scattered fright through the underbrush. Ungainly emus pounded from their tracks. In the scrubs there were mysterious rustlings, stirrings, outlandish sounds they could never quite identify. Especially at night.

Almost everything, it seemed, remained invisible. They never quite saw anything before it disappeared. At other times they would have been startled by a parrot's harsh cry, the warning of a sulphur-crested cockatoo. They heard the lyrical song of magpies; and bellbirds chiming, sure indication of nearby water.

In the dark there were bullfrogs, the whine of mosquitoes, mopokes like banshees, bats shuttering overhead, and the soul's agony of remote dingoes penetrating sleep. As they trudged on they would have seen native bears, possums, spiny goannas like miniature dragons; coiled snakes with evil bright patternings. Let's hope they had stout boots for this long pilgrimage towards what still seemed to be nowhere. There were rock-strewn gullies to cross, sharp-bladed grasses, bindy-eyes, thorny trees and mile after mile of sun-hardened, dusty earth.

The track eventually brought them to the river again. Beyond a shallow ford was a shanty named Singleton's Inn. James Singleton, whose 600-acre selection was all that existed of what surveyors called Patrick's Plains, would have given them beds and fresh directions in the morning. From this wayside tavern it was two, perhaps three more days to a great northward bend in the river. This was the location they were making for; the present limit of settlement.

Beyond Singleton's they had to cross a large expanse of ploughed land where an ex-marine, Lieutenant James Mudie, now styled Major, was experimenting with wheat as well as stock-raising. Allman would no doubt have warned them to avoid the notorious owner of Castle Forbes, the grandiose name he had given it in sycophantic tribute to the chief justice. It was protected by a pack of Newfoundland dogs. He was reputed to treat his fifty convict servants with unremitting harshness, liberal only in his use of the lash. These men, too—as they demonstrated later—could be as savage as the homestead dogs.

Next it would have taken them a full day to cross the sheep pastures recently taken up by George Forbes, brother of the chief justice, who had exchanged a land grant in Jamaica for six thousand acres here. He had named his still sparsely stocked property Edinglassie, after the family's centuries-old home in Scotland.

At last they sighted a strange, double-domed scrubby, long hill. It crouched on the landscape like a stone lion in Trafalgar Square, head facing the western sun, its heavily timbered back parallel with the river. They climbed its southern flank, saw a serrated, violet-hued range of low mountains ahead, and then the great river bend below.

Henry Dangar's map had called it Twickenham Meadows.

Cunningham wrote of these later:

> On disentangling yourself from among the undulating hills and ridges which bound these beautiful meadows, one of the richest natural prospects presented itself. The flat alluvial lands spread out before you, being matted with luxuriant herbage; branching evergreens scattered singly or in irregular clumps; the river winding through the midst; while dark-foliaged swamp oaks, bordering with a deep green fringe its steep and grassy banks; and the gently rising hills beyond, thinly clothed with wide-spreading forest trees, extend in diversified magnificence as far as the eye can reach.

It must have surprised them to find rich and open pastures of this quality as yet unclaimed by any man. Nothing had ever grazed upon these splendid grasslands. Was there anywhere else on earth where men could still say to one another: these are your lands, those are mine?

They walked along the river for several miles. They climbed the basalt ridges, through open forest, noted the tall trees ideal for timbers, the outcrops of stone to be dug away for building. Below them dense grasses rippled away like ripening wheat in the summer wind. There was one segment of the plain of at least fifty acres where no trees grew at all. Those rich soils seemed even then to be waiting for the plough.

At the very time that these two men were measuring, plotting and examining these lands, pegging them out, calculating distances, responding to a new and unfamiliar sensation of belonging, a party of horsemen rode across Twickenham Meadows unaware that anyone else was there. The explorer Allan Cunningham—no relation to Peter—spent a night camping by the river, then rode west along the Goulburn River to cross the Liverpool Ranges for the first time. He discovered a low gap he named Pandora Pass, becoming the first European to sight the fertile treasure box of Liverpool Plains beyond.

Back in Sydney they lodged their applications. Cunningham had his 1,200 acre grant approved on 11 March. Ogilvie had to wait another month for his 2,000 acres, due no doubt to the complications of Van Diemen's Land. They had also pegged another claim on the far side of the river for Captain Anderson, who had been unable to leave *Granada*.

Peter Cunningham at once named his land Dalswinton, after his Highland birthplace. William called his Merton.

Could he have given it any other name?

4

Settlers and Convicts

The family was united again on board *Lord Liverpool*. She cleared Sydney Heads on a late April morning. They were unlikely to have regretted leaving, despite warnings of bad weather ahead. 'Edward and I were fearfully sick,' wrote Ellen, 'and the voyage occupied two days, a violent storm obliging us to put into Broken Bay.'

Town life had never been of much appeal to the Ogilvies. Probably it was less so than ever at this time. Too often, they found, it resolved itself in the perennial drunkenness, street brawls, the stink of raw Bengali rum, the jostling groups of larrikins baiting authority, truculent lags and ex-lags shouldering their betters off footpaths and the equally offensive patronising of Macarthur's Camden Park set. At times the whole town seemed to coalesce into a multiple provocation. The warring sects and classes simmered constantly within a few degrees of explosion point. Every week newspapers like the *Gazette* reported fresh robberies, violence, back street assaults. The most recent issue had warned that 'even brick walls were a sorry defence against expert and ingenious burglars.'

There had also been a report of the public hanging of a housebreaker at the top of Grosvenor Street. On the scaffold, so Father Therry assured the massed spectators, the condemned man had said his sentence was just. He was expecting more merciful treatment from his Redeemer in the hereafter.[1]

Urban living, as Cunningham saw it, had nothing more virtuous to offer. He wrote:

> It was no very extraordinary spectacle to see an arraigned murderer carousing among his friends in a pothouse adjoining the court, in the

[1] *Sydney Gazette*, 31 March 1825.

very presence of the constables, on the day of his trial; to see 'thieves
of rank' walking up to trial arm in arm with their equally dignified
associates, receiving the blessings of all the sympathising community
as they tripped along, accompanied by the fervent prayer that they
might get safely out of "this trouble"; the respectful constable walking,
like a common lackey, behind; to see the receivers of stolen goods
driving up to court to receive sentence in their carriages with liveried
servants. While all this existed, one could not wonder that the larcenous
portion of the population of England should feel a strong disposition to
take a pleasurable trip to our shores.[2]

Not that the back country was much better. There were frequent
reports of tribal raids on settlements, of clashes with stockmen or police.
A special force had just been formed to deal with incidents of this kind,
while the Governor proclaimed a £20 reward for the capture of bushrangers.

For the quality, of course, there were other pleasures. The *Gazette*
had just announced the formation of the Sydney Turf Club, with such
notables as W. C. Wentworth, William Balcombe, Captain John Piper
and Sir John Jamison 'the genial knight of Regentville' among its
foundation members. There were now to be two race meetings annually
and a grand ball.

Present plans were for William to leave his family in Newcastle, pick
up the six convict labourers assigned him and return to the Upper
Hunter with Cunningham. Francis Allman had offered to share his
house with Mary and her four children until they had somewhere to
live at Merton. This was a happy arrangement, since the Allmans had
a large family of their own.

The change in the Ogilvie children must have been considerable.
Nearly three months on that Parramatta farm would have matured
them. One can imagine how they had filled out in the clear air, the
sunlight and the freedom of the bush. They would have learnt a great
deal, too. This may well have been where the oldest boy, Will, first
developed his interest in cattle, which was to become his main occupation within a few years. Perhaps Edward's single-minded concern for
sheep also had its origins at this period.

Other learning processes continued in the Newcastle house which,
Ellen noted, had been built by the commandant's notorious predecessor, Colonel Morriset. Unlike Francis Allman, he had been 'a very
cruel ruler over the convicts.' The chief difficulty, she added, was a
local shortage of food.

'The government allowed us to buy salt pork from the commissariat

[2] Cunningham, P., *Two Years in New South Wales*, London, 1827.

store,' she wrote. 'As for meal, all we could get for some time was from the convicts, who sold the coarser part of their maize meal to father.' A friendly gesture from the new aristocrats. A convict baker also supplied them with bread, the Allman's cows gave them plenty of milk, and some garrison officer occasionally returned from a day's shooting with a present of game. There were other problems with the more valuable possessions brought out from England.

'To guard them we were allowed a constable, who was a convict, to live in the house, but he was soon detected stealing them. Mother in her walks was much struck with some smoothing irons a woman was using very skilfully, and, on investigation, found they were some of her own which the constable had stolen.'

William hoped for a higher tone from his own assigned convicts. They were Irishmen, a type that, according to Cunningham, 'possess an anxiety to oblige, and have a light-hearted civility about them, of which the English are notoriously destitute. The latter consider everything in the shape of work a degradation.' Cunningham had applied for one man only. He had no plans yet to build.

Travelling upriver they may have reflected on the changed atmosphere since Morriset's brutal time. The commandant had been in the habit of travelling with a triangle rigged at the bows, and a fully employed scourger.

At Merton they shared a tent beside the Hunter. While Cunningham laid out his farm, William put his men to work on a cottage for his family, quarrying freestone from a nearby hillside. The site he chose was on rising ground, well above flood level, with a superb view of river flats and violet-hued ranges beyond. The sun set behind them in flaring ochres and the delicate afterglow of a galah's wing. Through a steep cleft in those serrated ranges, where the Goulburn River flowed down to the Hunter, he could see the dark and massive dromedary's hump of Mount Dangar. Henry Dangar, without inquiring of the locals, had modestly named it after himself. For the Kamilaroi, who knew it as Biame, it had mystical influences reaching back many thousands of years.

This was the abode of an ancestral spirit who spoke through the thunder, whose inspiration came from the heavens in shafts of lightning. If the practical William was unconcerned with savage myths, his older sons were soon to become familiar with them. Tribal memory is still preserved by a township and creek named Baerami.

It was a modest little cottage these Irishmen built. Yet solid and enduring. A century and a half later it is still here, derelict, without windows or doors, its shady verandah gone, the remnants of a shingle

roof replacing the earlier thatch. The first home built on the Upper
Hunter, it has acquired a patina of age its original designer had never
contemplated.

Little more than a rectangle of freestone blocks two feet thick, with
hand-adzed beams and horizontal timber slabs, it comprised only two
rooms and a kitchen in its earliest form. An ingenious feature of those
heavy wall blocks are holes bored in either side, enabling men to hoist
them easily with iron hooks and tackle, a naval technique used in loading ships. The Irish builders used local pipeclay to whitewash walls,
mixing it with powdered earth for floors. The chimneypiece of hand-
made bricks was set outside the kitchen wall, within which was an open
fireplace with hanging iron pots, camp oven and heavy kettle on
smoke-blackened chains.

He brought Mary and the children to Merton towards the end of the
year.

Summer had begun. The plains were heating up. The country
revealed a different, harsher mood.

The boat reached Wallis Plains in heavy rain. The river was brownish
and running fast. They spent the night at the government cottage on
Stockade Hill. 'It rained so heavily that night,' Ellen wrote, 'that in the
morning the whole plain was flooded and, in a lagoon where the plain
had been, we saw blacks paddling in canoes made of bark, the ends tied
with kurrajong bark, and sealed with grass-tree gum. We were detained
at this house for some weeks.'

The newly-formed mounted police, with black trackers, arrived
expecting to move into the cottage, 'but the officer, a gentlemanlike
man and very kind, would not have us disturbed, and set his men to
weave sticks of wattle between the verandah posts to accommodate
them.'

Their sense of isolation would have been mitigated by the small
farms along Wallis Creek. An inn and general store had just been
opened up, while the celebrated Molly Morgan had taken up a 159-
acre grant near the embryo town. Now married to her third husband,
Joe the Marine, this twice-transported lady queened it over everybody,
though her language and manners were something less than regal. Her
original crime, the theft of three shillingsworth of yarn from a Shrop-
shire store, had put her behind Parramatta's bars for five years. Then
returning to England a free woman, she aggravated a bigamous
marriage by burning down her new brassfounder husband's house, a
performance that sent her back again, this time to Newcastle. Now,
backed by some mysterious protector, said to have been an army
officer, she was prospering, due largely to trading in illicit rum. Wallis

The ruined cottage at Merton in the Hunter Valley, 150 years after it was originally built. Photograph by the author.

Creek, as one old settler later put it, was 'a great place for widows.' When these ladies wanted a spree, he said, 'they would dispose of five acres of land for five gallons of rum, and then, my boys, look out for squalls.'

Three weeks later the flood went down. The family 'started for Merton in a very primitive conveyance,' Ellen wrote, 'a covered cart drawn by a horse and bullock—the latter being a very quiet one lent by a neighbour. But most of the party, including mother, preferred walking.'

Their single cart jolted over boulders and rocky creek crossings, sometimes bogging down in mud, behind the ill-matched pair of draught animals; Mary and her children walked with a file of convicts following. Among this company was the massive Ellen Partridge, now employed as cook. There was also a bull-terrier named Turpin. This was a gift from the police officer at Wallis Plains.

'We found him very useful when the dray, laden with luggage, bogged where the Maitland bridge stands today,' Ellen wrote. 'The animals could not move it until Turpin flew at their noses, when they wildly struggled out. Another time he was not so useful at Merton, when a valuable calf was being dosed for an ailment. Turpin flew at his nose, too, and had his hind leg bitten by a man before he would release the calf. This dog was dreaded by the blacks, though very gentle with all of us. His end was mysterious. We missed him, and, making inquiries from the blacks, heard that he had been seen walking towards a large waterhole. He was tracked to the edge, but there were no return tracks.'

The blacks, obviously, had no intention of talking.

What men overlooked in the first exuberant spread of settlement was that the land was occupied already. There were few overt signs of it.

Now and then a party of lean, naked hunters would file across Twickenham Meadows, each with slender spears and a woomera with which to hurl them, or with a wallaby carcass over the shoulder. Other parties emerged from the back country, camped by the river with their women and piccaninnies, improvising temporary shelters, then vanishing again. No one knew—or cared to know—that these camp sites and hunting grounds were regarded as inalienably theirs, that they were accustomed to fight men of other tribes trespassing on them, that these waterholes, springs, creeks, hills and open plains were essential to their survival.

Nor was it only the game, fish, water, edible roots that bound them to these lands. There was an invisible mesh of myth, sacred ritual and personal identification with many natural features that, if shattered, would destroy the meaning of existence altogether. The alien dispossessors cared as little for these matters as their illiterate, rum-soaked employees, the shepherds lusting only for lubras, or the scared hut-keepers who fired muskets at the first shadowy figure they sighted with hunting boomerang or spear in hand.

Had these landtakers troubled to find out, they could easily have done so. As William Gardner pointed out, the boundaries belonging to each tribe or horde were clearly defined, and had been so since antiquity.[3] Carved rocks and prominent outcrops bore markings that other groups were careful not to pass, unless invited to some conference or inter-tribal ceremony. To cross these borders meant death at any other time. It was an honour to be invited to enter another's territory. One can imagine the shocked reactions of each tribe when Europeans ignored

[3] Gardner, William, *North & Western Parts of N.S.W.*, Sydney, 1854.

these traditional limits. Their sanctity had been impressed on every young man, who at the time of his initiation was led around them by the tribal elders. Others asked for permission before they entered, held up a green bough as a peace symbol, or else invited attack. No wonder the crude and ignorant whitefellow met with relentless hostility.

Again, when white settlement began to make native animals scarce, the hungry nomads turned to spearing cattle or sheep for the protein they needed. They also resented these imported animals fouling their waterholes. When the inevitable armed clashes began, the murderous reprisals, the greater savages were often those of white complexion.

The Ogilvies appreciated these realities from the beginning. They treated the native people they encountered as fellow human beings. They brought up their children to do likewise. Merton became, in the Nelson fashion, a pattern of kindness.

To win their confidence was not easy. Sometimes they made them gifts of food or tobacco, though they had little enough to give away. They appear to have reached an early understanding with the chief tribal elder, whom they called Jerry.

According to contemporary sketches, they were a pretty wild lot, as difficult to approach as wild horses. Their long hair was shaggy and tousled; they wore little but pubic tassles, often not even that. Their womenfolk, by European standards, were hardly attractive, with their great splayed feet, broad and flattened noses, pendulous dugs of breasts. They knew nothing of hygiene.

Yet the Kamilaroi were said to be an elite. They were of higher intelligence and craftsmanship than others, who both respected and feared them. Their magico-religious ideas had some parallels with Christian concepts. They believed, for instance, in a good spirit named Potoyan, which was opposed by the satanic Koyan. Kamilaroi itself was a generic name, representing a large group of tribes. According to Gardner, they covered an enormous inland territory; from the Warrego, Maranoa and Balonne Rivers right down to the Murrumbidgee. A similar language was spoken by all these tribes.

Among those who achieved some understanding of them, though he published only a glossary of words, was Archdeacon Greenway, son of Macquarie's architect. He wrote of their 'many acts of bravery, kindness, their tender care of the afflicted, especially their aged blind, their faithfulness as servants, and at times true friends of the whites.'[4] It would be difficult to find a more civilised race, he added. Their menfolk were well-formed and tall, many over six feet. When he first knew them

[4] *Mankind*, Sydney, 1895.

in 1845, they numbered between six and seven thousand. Half a century later they had been reduced to less than two hundred.

At Merton the most rewarding contacts were probably made through the children. Both Edward and Will quickly learnt to speak the language. They learnt it probably by associating with uninitiated boys of their own age. At all events, it was to prove immensely valuable when they came to take up further back country lands.

In Edward's case, the knowledge was later to save his life on two occasions.

Nonetheless, William's efforts to employ them on Merton had no success. According to Cunningham's book, many lived on the station quite early. Work was another matter. Yet he mentions one working group he saw on the way home from Wallis Plains. While stopping the night with an unnamed settler he watched a group of fifty picking and carting maize, for which they were rewarded with cauldrons of boiled pumpkin into which they dived spoons, flat sticks and fists, demolishing the meal in minutes. There was no mention of any pay.

The surgeon's own recipe for friendship was cutting their hair. They enjoyed his barbering, because it was so much quicker than using fragments of mussel shell.

That they were quick to pick up English is clear from this story of 'a young friend of mine', Will, who shot by accident a long-legged redbill wader. The bird, a favourite of his father's, was always to be seen alongside a particular waterhole. One day, when the thirteen-year-old boy accused one of the Aborigines of stealing corn, the man's lubra interrupted him.

'Ah, Massa Milliam, who shoot de redbill? I tell your fader!'

The interrogation was dropped.

Cunningham wrote also of one friendly character named Ben, whom he considered far more clever than any Botany Bay thief, and equally adept at accusing others when confronted. He was said to be a great influence among neighbouring tribes, and also to be the instigator of frequent robberies and murder. Others were described as good marksmen, whenever they managed to steal firearms. They were 'subtle and dangerous enemies,' especially sharp sighted at long distances, brilliant at tracking animals or men in the bush. 'It is quite impossible to surprise them,' he added, 'except early in the morning, through the assistance of a native guide; while they can always steal in on the whites by gliding from tree to tree; for even when you do see them, it is no easy matter to distinguish them from a burnt stick.'

Cattle were always nervous of them, disliking their smell, and would either gallop away, kicking up their heels, or charge them, forcing them up trees 'with the nimbleness of monkeys.'

The realistic Cunningham concluded that, in general, there was no way to handle them when hostile except with a show of force. He believed that every tribe contacted had initially attempted a trial of force and that 'when once fairly satisfied of their inferior power, live ever afterwards in perfect harmony.'

There was clearly much unrecorded tension around Merton, for he wrote of them being 'fearful to attack the whites, though ever so few in number, if armed with muskets. The best way of retreating safely is by only pointing the muskets at them, to keep them at bay, as at the moment it is fired they rush in and spear their victim.'

In view of later happenings, it was unfortunate that more settlers failed to listen to his advice. He warned that blacks with a sense of wrong did not trouble to discriminate between whites, and would attack and kill the first they came across. They neither forgave nor forgot. Having murdered, they would expect violent retaliation, whatever the show of friendship. 'Hence, until some of the tribe are killed by the whites, they never conceive themselves safe, and usually continue their murderings until, in retaliation, blood is expiated by blood.'

Whether this were true or not, his belief was soon to be put to a tragic testing.

The new year brought a quickening of life along that lonely track to Merton. It was to be a long while before the most optimistic could call it a road. Yet increasing numbers were travelling that way, wearing deep wheel tracks through the springy grasses, and over the long steep haul of Ironbark Hill half-way to Patrick's Plains.

Crop farmers were ploughing rich alluvial soils out from Wallis Creek. At Singleton's Inn a ferry now took waggons across the Hunter, while bullocks and horses swam behind with a rope secured to their heads. At Castle Forbes flocks of wild turkeys moved among the heavy crops of maize and wheat. Beyond Mudie's open paddocks James Glennie was struggling to establish wheat and sheep. Beyond again was ex-naval surgeon James Bowman's Ravensworth. Having married John Macarthur's daughter, he had capital enough to spend on large buildings for packaging and sorting wool from the best crossbred flocks in New South Wales. Retired officers like Dickson, Carter and Mills were grazing along Twickenham Meadows to the boundaries of Edinglassie, while Captain Pike had imported merino and Saxon sheep to Pickering across the river from Merton. There were even a couple of settlers further out along Martindale Creek. At the back of Mount Ogilvie was the well stocked property just taken up by George Blaxland, whose grandfather, 'Old Gregory' had made that first crossing of the Blue Mountains a decade before.

It seemed as if only Cunningham and Ogilvie were unable to afford sheep.

Their problem was to find some immediate source of income. Cash crops, for instance. Both now ran a few cattle, and had dairies for making butter and cheese. They planted tobacco, originally described as the valley's greatest promise. They set convicts to breaking the soil for maize and wheat.

Cunningham, in his book, advised hopeful settlers against emigrating without at least £1,200 in ready cash. It was doubtful if either of them had arrived with as much, although Cunningham wrote to the Colonial Office in August, 1826, stating that 'I have already expended £1,100 in stock and farming expenses.' This was probably not all laid out in actual cash. The mystery is how they raised any capital at all. In William's case, his half-pay would have been totally inadequate, even if his grant were free. He had inherited nothing from his father, though Mary may have had some financial help from hers.

According to Henry Dangar, whose published guide to the Hunter River carried much practical advice,[5] a combined pastoral and agricultural venture needed an initial outlay of between £500 and £750, providing it was close to a settled district. For more distant regions, such as Merton, without ready markets, he set the minimum at £1,000. These sums, he said, would meet the cost of, say, two hundred ewes in lamb at £2 each, twenty cows in calf, a bull for breeding, one brood mare, a saddle horse, essential farm implements and seed, and rations for convict workers.

Like Cunningham, William cut his outlay by not buying sheep. Yet it remained a gamble to survive.

Obviously they had been able to produce assets enough when first applying for their grants. In London they had to show they possessed capital equivalent to £1 for each acre granted, promising to pay two shillings per acre in quit rent after six years. They were also required to put one acre in every three under cultivation, or to feed and clothe three assigned convicts, or to make £50 worth of improvements within five years. Then, in March 1825, the very month they selected their land, they were confronted with new regulations that increased their commitments further. 'No grant will be made to any person,' Brisbane announced, 'unless the governor is satisfied that the grantee has both the power and the intention of expending in the cultivation of the land

---

[5] Dangar, H., *Index and Directory, The Hunter River*, Sydney, 1828.

a capital equal to half the estimated value of it.' That intention had to become fact within seven years, when three shillings an acre quit rent would be payable.[6]

Both men, however, passed the governor's scrutiny.

In theory, convicts appeared a cheap source of labour. It was an almost feudal form of serfdom; no wages, only food, clothing and quarters. All the same, as Cunningham put it, 'I doubt whether many English labourers live better than our convict servants, whose weekly ration consists of a sufficiency of flour to make four quartern loaves at least, of seven pounds of beef, two ounces of tea, one pound of sugar and two ounces of tobacco.' Thus began the modern shearer's traditional rations; ten, ten, two and a quarter—the award rate in pounds for meat, flour, sugar and tea.

Regular issues of this order meant a considerable outlay. Especially as, by the census of 1828, Ogilvie had fifty-eight convicts assigned to him.

Nor was this forced labour noted for its efficiency. It was impossible to drive them hard. To depend on the lash as men like Mudie did was no solution, for flogging also rendered a man unfit to work for at least a week. William began to acquire quite a different reputation. Some of his less squeamish neighbours said he was too soft and called him an 'old woman'. Peter Cunningham disagreed with them.

'The convicts are very easily managed,' he wrote, 'the punishments awarded only required to be *certain* rather than *severe* . . . A flogging may serve effectually to check the poor cowardly pitiful thief; but it only hardens the bold and courageous, while it essentially debases the feelings of both.'

One had only to read this book to appreciate how exacting was the process of adaptation to the new land, how much they had to learn and improvise. They had to discover its very different moods, the vagaries of climate, irregular rains, the effects of strong sunlight on plant life, the limitations of native pastures, how to plough and cultivate stiff clay soils, to sow and reap in new ways, to put in fallow crops, to cope with the destructiveness of white ants, dry rot, caterpillar and grasshopper plagues, to use natural materials like the bark of kurrajongs or stringy-bark for making rope, to burn off rank grasses in winter to encourage sweet new growth. There was no end to what they did not know.

In this isolated backblocks setting the entire family was involved in learning. The boys roaming these meadows, birdnesting, fishing, bringing in cattle, taking over routine jobs, would also have responded

[6] *Historical Records of Australia*, Series 1, Vol. XIV.

quickly to the new environment. Instead of blackbirds, thrushes, larks, they learnt to identify strange new birds like reed warblers along the river, mournful curlews, the flocks of redbills, the laughing jackass known as the settler's clock.

Yet, from Cunningham's writing, their life was not all work. He wrote of fishing for perch and river cod, collecting mussels, catching eels in the river, shooting wild turkey and wonga pigeons for food. He wrote of hunting the kangaroo, which fed in large numbers when an early dew was on the grass. Horsemen had to keep at a full gallop behind their dogs to catch them. He was amazed too, by the speed of the emu. 'I was mounted on a swift blood mare, and kept her at a hard gallop, but they left me always with the most perfect ease.'

These folk hunted like English gentlemen. But in so doing they became essentially Australian, too. As his book progresses one senses this growing feeling of identification. He begins to write of 'our colony', 'our commerce' and 'our bush'.

And yet, by the start of 1826, he was beginning to feel the financial strain. At one stage William made an unsuccessful voyage down to Sydney to arrange a loan for Cunningham, who decided at last he would have to return to sea. He sailed for England on another transport, intending to raise money at home and come back, which he was unable to do for another two years.

In his absence Ogilvie agreed to manage Dalswinton, as he was already doing for Captain Anderson, whose Martindale across the river was still in a rudimentary stage. As if he were not busy enough already, he accepted an appointment as honorary magistrate in May, 1827.

Yet this was an essential post.

Merton, with its increasing number of employed convicts, was the only sizeable settlement west of Wallis Plains. The police saw it as a strategic outpost for controlling the back country. Now and again troopers rode in with an escaped convict in chains, or a bushranger, or some troublesome Aborigine. Their captives were passed on to another police post at Jerry's Plain, thence to Wallis Creek for escort down to the coast at Newcastle.

William's new responsibilities were summarised by Cunningham. 'Every district magistrate has a district constable and two ordinary [i.e. ex-convict] ones under his command, and also a scourger to inflict corporal punishment. The district constable is always a free man, but the others are often convicts . . . A magistrate can inflict punishment to the amount of fifty lashes, and sentence to a certain extent of labour in a penal gang employed upon the roads or in clearing land, or else in the gaol gang or treadmill.'

Whether or not Ogilvie wanted these powers, he was so committed by his official post. Knowing the man, one imagines he saw it as a matter of public duty.

Merton had already put down permanent roots in the pastoral world. If only Ellen had written her memoir before her memory began to fail. She left little on record as to how they lived during those formative years at Merton. All she had to say on this particular subject was this:

'Our energetic and clever mother was always busy, and she educated us all, father assisting in some branches. Her great recreation was her garden. We soon had a beautiful garden, orchard and vineyard—and a great deal of which she planted with her own hand.'

We are left to imagine just how she coped with the teaching of four children at different age levels, with few books, writing materials scarce and only nature to draw upon outside the cottage. The clearest insight into how she managed came through her own daughter, for Ellen was subsequently obliged to educate her own children, too. She was then living on her husband's property, Wyangerie, on the equally remote Richmond River, far from what then passed for civilisation. The parallels are clear.

Looking back to his childhood, Ellen's son, C. W. Bundock, described how among other things she made all the family's clothes.

'In addition,' he added, 'she educated us all. The school hours were regular, even though we might have had to say our lessons while my mother was cooking and ironing. Generally, she did her sewing while lessons were being done. My father taught us Latin. Many a time did I say my lessons to him while he was mending saddlery or pruning grape-vines, or doing other jobs about the place.' He added that, so well had they been taught by their parents, they found themselves placed in classes above their age when they went later to a formal school.

In the Ogilvies' case there was no higher school to follow. Everything they knew was learnt at Merton. Yet Ellen grew up to become a capable teacher of her own children. Nor was Edward any less intellectually equipped than the worldlier men among whom he was to pass his adult life. If neither Will nor Fred often left their stockbreeding environment, they occupied themselves with more than normal station routines; the elder brother in legal work, the younger in handling the family's complex financial affairs. Besides, both died long before their promising careers could be fulfilled.

5

Frontier Under Arms

Edward's twelfth birthday came at a time of great tension along the Upper Hunter. The Aborigines, who had been peaceful enough since settlement began, had suddenly become truculent and difficult to manage.

Early in July 1826 a number of settlers appealed to the new governor, Sir Ralph Darling, for protection. However, on the 18th, Captain Allman wrote from Newcastle to Lieutenant de la Condamine, Military Secretary, assuring him that 'no acts of violence have been committed by the Aborigines in this district for some weeks past. There is every reason to hope for permanent tranquillity. Having made an offer of assistance from troops stationed in this town to Wm. Ogilvie Esq., the resident magistrate in the district beyond Patrick's Plains, I am happy to say this gentleman did not think that at present any part of the infantry is required.'[1]

Perhaps Ogilvie misjudged the situation. Eleven weeks later he was one of eleven Hunter landowners, all of them in Sydney, to remind Darling of 'the very disturbed state of the country by the incursions of numerous tribes of black natives, armed and threatening death to our servants, and destruction of our property.' While commending him for having sent horse patrols to the area, they deplored the later action of withdrawing many soldiers for an investigation in Newcastle. They appealed for immediate replacements to protect them against 'the infuriated and savage people.'[2]

Darling was angry. Though it took him seven days to express his wrath, he accused the signatories of all being 'persons who constantly reside in Sydney'. He said he had been informed that 'not one of the

[1] *Historical Records of Australia*, Series 1, Vol. XIV.
[2] *ibid.*

whole number was on the spot when the outrages took place ... Everybody knows that, from the natives as a body, at the utmost few in numbers, nothing is to be feared ... vigorous measures among yourselves would more effectively establish your ascendency than the utmost power of the military.'

The Governor's strictures were hardly fair to Ogilvie, among others, for there had been good business reasons for his coming to town. Besides the Hunter situation was then serious enough to warrant decisive, if careful, handling.

Trouble had first begun late in July, when an Aboriginal party stole maize from two farms bordering Bowman's Ravensworth. Horsemen chased the marauders into the hills, only to be stopped when the blacks began rolling great boulders down on them from a ridge. Next came several robberies and ambushes of travellers and drays along the lonely track between Ravensworth and Patrick's Plains. Several men, stripped of their clothes and belongings, were left naked in the bush. Some days later the blacks appeared on Martindale Creek, where the Scottish selector, John Greig, having gone to Sydney, had left a clergyman cousin in charge with an Irish shepherd. As the parson sat in the doorway reading Burns, Cunningham reported in his book, 'a tall, lame villanous-looking ruffian named Nullan-Nullan glided behind him, and with his club plastered the floor with his brains'. The Irishman was later found dead fifty yards away. Having plundered the hut, the blacks went off to Wollombi Brook, where another selector was 'waddied while a gin tried to beguile him, actually singing in English'. (Cunningham, who was then in London, was not often given to poetic licence of this order.)

There was said to have been no motive for this raid. Perhaps not, if one excepts the fact that Grieg was said to have hated Aborigines, whom he had always hunted off his land. A month later, according to the *Sydney Gazette*, he, too, was 'found a corpse with his head beaten to a mummy'.

It was at this stage that Darling ordered troops up from Newcastle, led by Captain Foley of the Buffs. They arrived to find the tribe dispersed, so the soldiers were posted in small groups around nearby stations, including Merton. Now and again some suspect was arrested and sent to Newcastle gaol, while soldiers fired on those who eluded them.

A second phase began late in September with the spearing of a stockman on Edinglassie. Mounted police were at once sent up from Newcastle. Immediately there was another raid on Bowman's head station, apparently in retaliation for the police locking up an Aborigine they had arrested on some unspecified charge. Two days later one of Bowman's watchkeepers was killed in his hut, while his fellow shepherds were out on the run. Outside another lonely hut a shepherd named Chilcott was surrounded, having to struggle with the leader, a man named Cato, for his musket, saved only by the arrival of several stockmen who commendably fired only at the attackers' legs as they went bush. After two of Bowman's fencers had been badly wounded elsewhere, events moved to Merton.

'Among the recollections of my childhood,' wrote Ellen, 'was playing with Fred outside the house, when we suddenly saw the whole hillside covered with blacks, all armed except for our chief, Jerry.'

She described how this 'fine, dignified man' had walked up to the children, shaking them repeatedly by the hand as if to convince the others he was a friend of the family. He was dressed in a possum skin rug, with strips of fur around his loins, and had the customary waddy in his belt. William was again in Sydney, so that Mary was left virtually alone to look after her children, apart from what Ellen termed euphemistically 'our protective force. This was composed of the constable, the scourger whose business it was to chastise the convicts and five soldiers.'

A strange reflection on the times. This nine-year-old girl took for granted the presence of a resident flogger.

The good-natured Jerry 'kept going among the natives to quieten them, and at last they melted away over the hill to our inexpressible relief, having taken only a little corn from a shed, after shaking all the constable's rations to the ground. The cause of all this trouble and anger was an act of treachery committed by the constable and soldiers.'

This had actually occurred the previous evening.

Before sundown Mary had been on her way down to a temporary garden she had by the river, probably for seedlings, when she saw the six uniformed men struggling with two Aborigines. One broke away and escaped. The second was dragged into a hut. Mary recognised him as Jerry and ordered the soldiers to free him. Which, of course, being Mary, they did. Immediately.

Some sharp questioning revealed that the soldiers, having been told to search for a suspected killer named Jerry, had arrested the wrong man.

The soldiers, Ellen continued, 'fearing the indignation of the blacks, deserted us, clearing away in the night, and leaving us to reap the consequences of their bad conduct, which might have resulted in the loss of all our lives. The blacks said to the last that, if they had found the constable and soldiers, they would have murdered them for their treachery.' She added that the field commander, Captain Lowe, then wanted to court-martial these deserters, 'but at mother's intercession they were spared'.

No question as to who was the real commander at Merton.

The following night the very blacks Mary had been able to control so easily surrounded the overseers hut on Lethbridge's cattle run, drove his wife and child under a bed while they fought stockmen with waddies and spears, leaving four dead and two wounded. They were pursued into the ranges two days later by an armed detachment of settlers and soldiers, fought a brief battle in a forest clearing, left several casualties behind them on both sides and disappeared in the direction of Mount Dangar. That, for the time being, was the end of it.

Ellen's remembered account of what happened at Merton was somewhat incomplete. Cunningham's version, if slightly different, made a more vivid story. He said that Mary Ogilvie had been inside the house when she heard men shouting outside. There she found two soldiers surrounded by a crowd of furious Aborigines, who were shaking them by their collars, threatening them with raised waddies and spears and whatever scraps of English they knew. Ignoring their weapons, Mary ran in among them and 'with a firm persuasive manner awed and soothed them. In half an hour they left on the most cordial terms, the leaders even shaking hands all around, rattling their spears and shouting warnings to "tell sojda not come meddle Massa Ogilvie blacks".'

It must have been a magnificent scene. This slender, firm-mouthed woman of thirty-five, with two children at her skirts, confronting that angry and naked mob with their rattling spears. And all the brave soldiers gone bush.

According to Darling's subsequent report to London, the Aborigines had been more than two hundred strong, which seems unlikely in view of the party of twenty or so reported elsewhere. 'Mrs. Ogilvie, who appears to have acted with much judgment and spirit, then gave them some maize and tobacco, and they left the premises without being guilty of any irregularity. They then proceeded to Mr. Lethbridge's place where, I presume, not being managed with the same spirit, they fell on the overseer and stockmen, killed and speared four men.'[3]

What no one except Ellen reported was the panic inside Merton homestead. As soon as the uproar began outside, that giantess of a cook Mrs Partridge ran about in terror, demanding that another convict servant named William help her hide in a small wooden cask. It was, in every sense, a tight situation.

When William returned he found Captain Foley at Wallis Creek,

[3] *Historical Records of Australia*, Series I, Vol. XIV.

where they discussed opening some kind of dialogue with the tribes as the only hope for restoring peace. This would entail using a friendly Aborigine as go-between. Foley sent down to Newcastle, asking for the release of one of the men being held in gaol. Captain Allman came upriver himself with a black named Dennis. He was a Merton man. William, who knew him well, assured them he was trustworthy. However, when they reached Helenus Scott's Glendon station, Dennis became uneasy about being seen in the company of whitefellows, so William suggested they send him ahead alone. It was arranged that he should contact the tribal elders, arrange a parley and meet them again at James Glennie's.

The others were unconvinced. They were right. They never saw Dennis again.

It was some time before the broader issues were brought into focus. Darling appointed two local magistrates as a committee of inquiry into the whole affair, one of the members being Helenus Scott. Reliable information suggested that the initial hostility had been provoked by a more distant tribe. This was said to be located somewhere beyond the headwaters of the Goulburn River. The same tribe was suspected of having caused similar troubles along Wolombi Brook earlier in the year, raiding and pillaging farms, as well as having been the directing force behind armed clashes with settlers around Bathurst back in 1824, when nine stockmen were killed.

These repeated forays may well have come from the heart of the Kamilaroi country; a planned campaign. No doubt its inner council of elders was troubled by the spread of white settlement, the takeover of their ancient lands, and the corrosion of tribal unity. Similar campaigns are known to have taken place well into the present century; notably among the Pitjandjara in central Australia as late as the 1950s. This was virtually an underground resistance movement, organised by a secret society known as the Red Ochre, dedicated to intimidating the detribalised and forcing them back to traditional ways.

In the case of the Kamilaroi too, there was no other solution. Unless they fought back, the loss of their lands was certain.

But Darling's policy was no solution either.

To encourage settlers to take the law into their own hands, to subdue the blacks by force, had the makings of disaster. This was one of the issues over which he quarrelled with his attorney-general, Saxe Bannister, a man of Whiggish views, sympathetic to the Aborigines.

When the Hunter outbreak was reported, Bannister recommended declaring martial law. He wanted, in fact, to freeze hostilities and examine the whole Aboriginal question. 'Experience proves,' he informed the governor, 'that, if the Crown does not take the lead in a decisive manner and on a large scale, both in the coercion and improvement of the Aborigines, they will fall into a miserable way in contact with white people.' The Bathurst troubles, he added, proved what could happen when settlers, having been refused military aid, began shooting it out themselves, with casualties on both sides.

As usual in this fractious colony, there was uproar. The autocratic Darling, though an efficient administrator, was fatally prone to allow personalities to get in his way. Bannister's letter, he wrote to Under-Secretary Hay in London, was 'very offensive and insolent. I shall cease to correspond with him . . . Who is this Attorney-General who prescribes the persons to be admitted to my table, would dictate the measures of government, the proclaiming of martial law, the assignment of the troops, and, last of all, like another Quixote would proceed himself in search of adventures!! His eccentricities would amuse, were it not for the impertinent style of his observations.'

The ex-Horse Guards general gave no more thought to the Aboriginal question. When Bannister resigned, the regime blundered through one feud after another. There were arguments with W. C. Wentworth, with Waddell of the outspoken *Australian* and *Monitor*, with his own colonial secretary, Alexander Macleay, and chief justice Francis Forbes. Finally, when Darling was recalled in 1831, Wentworth celebrated his departure with bonfires on the lawns of Vaucluse House.

A somewhat melodramatic footnote to that guerilla war of 1826 came from a German missionary, the Reverend Thredkeld, stationed at the London Missionary Society's ineffectual mission on Lake Macquarie. Writing to his superiors in Sydney of Mary Ogilvie's courageous stand, he added that:

> No one can tell how I am perplexed respecting the Aborigines. Many will be shot and if the English will be murdered in retaliation their land is taken from them, their food destroyed and they are left to perish or driven upon hostile tribes where death awaits them . . . The Attorney General told me last week that there are many who would banish us from this Colony, and prevent every attempt of a missionary nature among the blacks if they could . . . Some wish that they should be shot and no further notice taken of it. God alone knows what will be the end of those things. Forget us not at the Throne of Grace, we have need of every support in this vile, hypocritical country . . .[4]

What had worsened matters, as a police inquiry showed, was the casual shooting of several Aborigines captured, but never charged, by

[4] Bonwick Transcripts, Missionary volume, Mitchell Library, Sydney.

the mounted police. Evidence was also given that one man, who had agreed to lead a detachment to the site of a supposed murder up a steep range, was forced to travel on foot, while tied by a picket cord to the trooper's saddle. When he broke away, he was—in the still-current police jargon—'shot while escaping'. James Glennie also told the inquiry of a scene he had watched on his own property. This was after a man named Cato, suspected of leading the first raid on Ravensworth, 'refused to cross the brook. The soldiers were obliged to use the flat of their swords to urge him on. The soldiers were nearly half-an-hour endeavouring to secure him. It took four men to hold him.' Under questioning, Glennie said he had not seen Cato killed. He had only heard the pistol shot.

No wonder Dennis never kept his rendezvous.

The year 1827 was a memorable year at Merton. It was the year that the Ogilvies acquired their first sheep.

'Father,' Ellen recalled, 'with difficulty obtained a flock of sheep at £3 a head from a gentleman, who, having built a new house, required to replenish his purse.' The gentleman was Captain Pike across the river at Pickering. Though the number he bought was only eighty, it would have been a strain on his finances. He may well have followed the usual practice of paying one-third down and the remainder after end-of-year wool clip. At the same time he found an additional way to build up a profitable flock. This was probably sponsored by the Reverend Frederick Wilkinson, just appointed to the curacy of Newcastle.

Arrangements were made for the Church Lands Corporation to agist its sheep and cattle at Merton. The Corporation had been formed in 1817, had sole responsibility for the colony's schools, and was entitled to one-seventh of all land open for selection. Despite a board that included the colony's chief administrators, pastoralists, Archdeacon Scott and other church men, it was run in an erratic, pinch-penny fashion, and did nothing to find its own land. Yet it badly needed those flocks and herds as a meat supply for its orphanage at Liverpool as well as various schools.

William's opportunity came when two selectors out from Parramatta told its youthful secretary, Charles Cowper, they could no longer handle the stock. The first complained of 'the hostile tribes of blacks that frequently appear', the second—and Ogilvie should have been warned —of clerical accusations that he had allowed his sheep to contract scab.

Over the next few years William's reports and letters of complaint were to fill a bulky file.[5]

In November William rode across country to Wilkinson's property and took delivery of 351 clerical ewes, sixty-eight wethers, four rams, 205 horned cattle and one working bullock named Traveller. With these animals came six Irish convicts. Presumably he bought more stock of his own soon after, for the 1828 census listed Merton as running 1,610 sheep, 600 cattle and nine horses.

In less than three years his achievements had been remarkable. Just how hard he had worked was shown in a memorial he addressed to the Colonial Office in July that year. This appeal for an increase in his free grant was sent through Darling, whose own enclosure described him as 'a most respectable man and highly deserving of the attention of government'.

After reminding Lord Bathurst of his thirty-four years as an officer in His Majesty's navy, his association with Nelson and his commendation after Copenhagen, he went on to describe the 'unprecedented bad seasons' since his arrival. 'The total failure of his wheat and maize crops,' he wrote, 'have put your memorialist to the necessity of purchasing these articles for a large establishment at the high prices consequent upon their scarcity, together with the great expenses incurred in the important and extensive improvements made on the land.' Now that 'his means had been so completely exhausted, it was quite impossible to pay for the additional four thousand acres he had been allowed under conditional purchase, though he had already put improvements upon them.' He asked, therefore, for these to be made an addition to his original grant.[6]

He could hardly have improved his case by an oblique, but incautious reference to the Australian Agricultural Company, which had been granted 464,000 acres of free land near Port Stephens in 1823. His memorial 'humbly submits that large tracts of land have been granted to companies and individuals on the sole condition of their investing capital to the amount of one pound sterling an acre, which your memorialist has already done.'

The list of improvements attached to his appeal made impressive reading. Estimating them to be worth £2,000, William listed them in this meticulous fashion:

5½ miles of 4 and 3 rail fence
150 acres of land cleared and enclosed for cultivation—80 under crop

[5] Stock Returns & Correspondence, Church Lands Corporation, 1818–31.
[6] *Historical Records of Australia*, Series 1, Vol. XIV.

2 acres garden fenced in, planted and cultivated
4 acres orchard enclosed and planted
9 acres of tobacco ground, fenced and cultivated
Stone house, 60 front. Walls up and roofed
Barn 60 feet by 20. General store 50 feet
Butter dairy, cheese do. Do store. All complete permanent substantial
    buildings
Cottage for present residence and various offices and temporary
    buildings, 17 in number, besides tan pits, lime kilns, etc.

Though Bathurst's reply was a brief refusal, William revealed himself
as a persistent man. In November that year, he applied to Colonial
Secretary Macleay in Sydney for a 5,000-acre reserve adjoining Merton.
He asked to be allowed to occupy this during His Majesty's pleasure
and according to the terms of government notice of 16 October.
Having added 'my humble need of praise of the notice', he said it was
'calculated not only to confer much positive benefit on the steady and
respectable settler, but also to check many of the evil practices carried
on by means of the wandering herds of cattle with which this country
is inflicted'.[7]

This was the first reference anyone had made to the prevalence of
cleanskins in the district. These ownerless cattle not only consumed
valuable pastures in time of drought, but encouraged a new class of
duffers and gully-rakers who were soon to become as great a menace as
bushrangers in the back country.

The notice to which he referred was a new regulation allowing larger
land grants to all army and naval officers emigrating in or after 1828.
It was swiftly pointed out that he, Ogilvie, did not qualify.

He was also having problems with the Church Lands office, which
had expressed its disapproval of his use of milk from their cows. The
milk of Christian kindness, it seemed, did not include its conversion to
cheese or butter-making for his own profit. Ogilvie replied, with his
usual dignified manner that, for the sake of their health, cows had to be
regularly milked. He told them also that he had divided them into dry
and milking herds, kept them on good pastures with two separate herdsmen and was sending beef cattle as well as wethers for school meat.

What else could a man do for so small a return?

Merton, which now had fifty-eight convicts on the roll, also had two
additions to the family. These were Mary's younger brother, William,
and her sister, Susan. Both had decided to emigrate late the previous
year, probably after Edward White's death. There are no further

[7] Governor's Despatches, Public Record Office, Mitchell Library, Sydney.

references to him at the Swan Inn. The remaining two girls both married and went to live in Jersey.

William White remained at Merton at least a year, where his brother-in-law would have welcomed another hand, even if it meant teaching him a great deal. He was clearly a good learner, for Ogilvie secured for him a 2,000-acre grant nearby in 1829.

Peter Cunningham had also returned to Dalswinton. He reached Sydney in March 1828 by the convict transport *Morley* with sheep of his own on board. Evidence of these flocks was to be found in a letter to the Colonial Office soon after his return from Australia to London late in 1826. 'I have already expended £1,100 in stock and farming expenses,' he wrote. 'I am also taking out a supply of agricultural implements and of Saxon merinos to the value of several hundred pounds more.'

Now a successful author—though his book, in a second edition, had been strongly criticised by exclusives for its liberal ideas—Cunningham was able to relieve William of at least one of his many commitments. This time he began by building a comfortable house of his own half-a-mile away, as if he intended to settle permanently.

But nature had begun to make things difficult for all these Hunter settlers. In the summer of 1827 hardly any rain had fallen. 1828 remained equally dry.

The year following William wrote to Cowper in Sydney, 'The drought, I am sorry to say, continues, and the country is in an alarming state. Unless a decided change takes place very soon the wheat crop will again fail.'

In November that year he offered to buy the clergymen's wool clip at seven pence a pound, 'the highest price yet reached'. They accepted his generous offer. This helped to make his shearing economic, for the river had fallen so low that no boats could reach Wallis Creek, or Maitland as it was now called. He was obliged to pay a bullock driver for the cost of carting wool bales right through to Newcastle.

The following month Cowper underscored the obvious by demanding an explanation for the drastic fall in Merton's lambing. Still writing in his tolerant fashion, 'I have the honour to receive your letter of . . .', William reminded him that drought had inevitably affected the condition of lambing ewes, that paddocks were almost bare and, as a post-script, 'that the black natives have been very mischievous, and have destroyed a number of cattle belonging to myself and others. We found the remains of a steer and heifer calf belonging to the corporation's stock that had recently been killed and eaten by them.'

Yet, by adroit husbandry, he had managed to build up the church property to 704 sheep and 354 cattle. This did not include his own third share of the increase.

In November he also made yet another application for extra land, asking for permission to rent 'all land on a small creek falling into the Goulburn opposite Mount Dangar, containing about seven thousand acres and commonly called James Creek. The said creek is now and has for some time been occupied by me as a cattle station.'

A note scrawled by some anonymous clerk on the back of his application read bluntly: 'Inform him as usual that, as it does not adjoin his own property, he cannot obtain it.'

William quietly took other action. He did exactly what many other enterprising men had been doing. He simply took his surplus sheep and cattle further along the Goulburn, running them in the outside country no man yet owned.

'If the breeder does not possess as much land as would feed the number of sheep he might want to keep,' Wentworth had written long before, 'he would only have to send his flocks beyond the limits of colonisation, and retire with them as the tide of colonisation approached. He might exclaim in the language of Abraham to Lot: "Let there be no strife, I pray thee, between my hersdmen and thy herdsmen; for we be brethren. Is not the whole land before us?" '[8]

Ogilvie had become—in the contemptuous term of the day—a squatter.

The isolation of Merton made possible few of the outlets that a normal child enjoyed. There was little variety to their lives, no friends beyond the home, no school companions, not much opportunity for pleasure or play. They grew up as a close-knit family group, very much dependent on one another, generating strong emotional ties and loyalties that, later in life, moulded them into a forceful, perhaps even formidable, clan. From an early age their home life would also have been disciplined and somewhat austere. The emphasis would have been strongly on work. Their one relaxation appears to have been music.

There is no indication as to just when the boys first took a serious hand in station work. Undoubtedly it would have been in their early teens.

First hint of this was in a letter Cunningham sent to the *Sydney Herald* in April 1829. He described how 'my young friend, Edward Ogilvie', had come upon a fossilised bone, which the surgeon immediately sent to England for analysis. The thirteen-year-old Edward had found it on a

[8] Wentworth, W. C., *A Statistical, Historical and Political Description of New South Wales*, London, 1819.

sheep run along the Goulburn River, some ten miles west of Merton. This would have been one of their many out-stations. The assumption is that he had been out with a convict shepherd, whose semi-nomadic and irresponsible attitudes needed constant supervision. Edward, even in boyhood, was clearly the sheep man.

Will appears to have gravitated towards cattle from the start. Maybe he enjoyed the rough riding, the back country, or simply the greater freedom that comes with mustering cattle.

As the Ogilvie sheep increased, they moved their cattle further and further out, where they had room to forage on timbered hillsides or the heads of valleys. Their flocks required much closer watching. Rather more, in most cases, than those sunstruck, simple-minded shepherds gave. This would have kept Edward out in the bush for long periods, sometimes days at a time. Each flock was grazed at a considerable distance from the next.

Sheepmen normally divided their animals into flocks of three hundred or so breeding ewes, or four hundred wethers, each with their own shepherd. These assigned convicts had to take their flocks out before sunrise, returning by sundown to portable yards made of hurdles or brush fences. A watchman had to count them in, while the shepherd counted them out again next morning. And woe to the man whose tally was short. The watchman slept in a flimsy wooden structure like a tall sentry box, keeping a good fire and a dog to scare the dingoes away. The hurdles, usually cut from swamp box, ironbark or gumtrees, had to be shifted daily to fresh ground, a precaution against footrot, catarrh or the dreaded scabby mouth, which could rapidly infect a whole flock.

Edward would soon have learnt how to treat this often fatal disease. It was unpleasant work. You cut away wool from the infection, bled the skin and bathed it in a strong mixture of turps and tobacco water. There was also a prevalence of blowflies. Cutting out the maggots was not romantic either. Nor was the castration of lambs, nor the cleaning out of yards in a stench of sheep's urine and trodden ordure.

Equally difficult at times was handling the shepherds themselves. Theirs was perhaps the most monotonous occupation known to man. They lived in utter solitude on greasy mutton chops and doughy damper they baked themselves. Only the most witless of them remained at this dreary work. Crawling after sheep, the less docile, sharper types called it, absconding whenever the chance occurred. The rest degenerated into lonely hatters, mumbling all day around vacant, sun-baked landscapes, drawn on compulsively by the tinny bells on leading wethers, or drowsing under a kurrajong till an angry master stirred them, often threatening a taste of the cat-o'-nine-tails, especially if a sheep or two was lost. Mostly they were simple, unlettered, sour-mouthed derelicts stupefied by raw grog and the soporific sun. Keep the flock moving, were their instructions, but unhurriedly, let them feed as they go, check the front runners, weed out the sick and maimed and aged, watch for the wild dogs that attack even by day, rest them under the shade trees in the midday heat, never crowd or hustle them, for a broken-winded sheep is as good as dead.

'The shepherd who walks quietly among them,' wrote Cunningham, 'is a gentle and careful man.'

From Merton's records there were not many such men.

The Ogilvies took extreme care over the shearing, which happened in November; and over the sheepwashing that preceded it. Each flock was made to swim a creek, preferably with a clear sandy bottom, for three days in succession. Only then did the washing begin. Two men entered the water, the downstream man lathering each sheep with a softening grease, passing it to the second who scoured the fleece, after which the animal was forced to swim upstream as a rinse. If the landing place was sandy or bare, the sheep was bedded down on newly mown grass. After feeding, the flock was penned closely together in straw-bedded folds, or on well-grassed earth, until each fleece was fully dry. Once the yolk stood up clean and yellowy-white, William pronounced it ready for shearing.

Without cheap labour, painstaking work of this order would not have been possible. Yet it was just this intensive care that enabled Australian wools so rapidly to dominate the English market. Back of it all were those homeless wandering shepherds, tailing after the tin-tinkling sheep bells in their white smocks or moleskins and cabbage tree hats.

Edward too, would have had interminable days in solitude, comfortless camps in the hot nights or when cold westerlies seethed down the funnel of the Goulburn Valley.

'The silence of the Goulburn with its majestic spurs rising up on every hand,' wrote H. H. MacKenzie, 'engenders a feeling of melancholy. As night closes in, and the dark green foliage of the rugged heights grows like ink against a golden sky, with all bird life hushed and no sound but the breeze sighing through the lofty pine tops, like the sound of surf on some rock-bound coast, the gloom increases. Happy are they who heard in every murmuring brook a tongue and a voice in every whispering wind.'

What did Edward think of on those occasions? Back to that other, more gentle Merton he came from; or forward to some vision of grander pastures on which he might one day be master of his own?

6

Road to Survival

Perhaps these Hunter men should have known their first successes were too good to last. They had overlooked a semi-arid climate—or had not been here long enough to understand it. This beautiful valley was not to be all sunshine and hock-deep pastures. The sun continued to shine; but more ferociously. It shone without respite through the hot dry summer months; with bland indifference for three dry winters when scarcely any rain or even cloud came. The grasses withered and dried.

Those drought years of 1827 to 1829 were like the visitations of Job. Just what had such enterprising men done to deserve them?

There could have been no worse period for new men to enter the country. Yet several did. Among them were the Reverend Wilkinson, dividing his time between his curacy in Newcastle and Wollombi Brook; William White now struggling to keep his few stock alive; and another English newcomer. This was George Wyndham, a man who was to bring new zest for living to the upper Hunter. The Ogilvies and Wyndhams were soon close friends. Reaching Sydney on Christmas Eve 1827, Wyndham at once set about the energetic clearing of land at Dalwood, upriver from Maitland, and was soon to have wine grapes as well as sheep. Each time William rode down to the river port he stayed at Dalwood. There was always good talk, books, a sense of common purpose. They were of like mind, these two men. In so distressing a time the sense of companionship was essential to morale. Wyndham was not only a good agriculturalist, but a man of firm ideas and principles. Though here he was to keep his opinions to himself, he had acquired a reputation in England for free-thinking and campaigning for political reform. He had, in fact, turned down the lucrative offer of a government post because he disliked Tory policies.

Meantime several men found themselves unable to withstand the drought. Several were ruined. These included William Carter, Captain

Wright, shortly to be found drowned in the river, and Alex Anderson, who had finally decided in 1828, the worst time he could have chosen, to resign his captaincy of *Granada*. Having just settled his wife and daughter on Martindale, he had to apply within a year for another position at sea. His daughter remained. To help support her mother, she found work as a servant on another property.

Peter Cunningham was also forced to retreat.

Once more, in May 1830, he left Dalswinton. He turned over its running to William White, either as manager or lessee, and sailed for England to another active service post. It was a decision he made reluctantly. He had worked hard for the past two years. He had put in many improvements. Yet he was still operating at a loss. In a submission he made to the Colonial Office a year earlier, he spoke for most of his neighbours, claiming that he had insufficient land. He sent home an accounting of just what he had done. He had built himself a shingled freestone cottage, outbuildings for his men, a stone barn, several miles of fencing, dairies for butter and cheese making and put ninety acres under crops. But, he added, his land was fundamentally suited only to grazing and he could not live by grazing alone. Since conditions made it possible to run only one sheep to three acres, one head of cattle to every ten, he was simply unable to support his six hundred fine-woolled sheep and more than one hundred cattle on a mere twelve hundred acres. He applied for a larger grant.[1]

When Downing Street rejected this, he resolved to leave.

Next time the Ogilvies heard from him he was on his way to Rio. He wrote frequently from the naval station there, sent out South American cuttings and seedlings, many of which found their way into Mary's garden, and on occasions published papers on botanical subjects in England. He spoke always of returning to Dalswinton. He never did.

All that today remains of those hard-working years—Dalswinton was sub-divided long ago—are ten massive stone blocks for weighting his bygone cheese presses. Some are now gateposts on a modern farm. Others can be seen in the Hunter River Historical Museum beside Glenbawm Dam, displayed as examples of pioneering ingenuity. The foundations of his roomy cottage can still be traced on rising ground a mile from the Ogilvie home.

Merton was one of the places that weathered the crisis best.

William had not over-capitalised, as others had. Nor had he over-stocked it. Somehow he endured by supplying produce to Sydney,

[1] *Historical Records of Australia*, Series 1, Vol. XV.

making cheese in summer, butter when the winter months made it easier to preserve, and a few crops to support his convict workers.

What really aggravated the colony's difficulties was an economic slump as well. Its origins went back to 1825. In England a Tory government had tried to combat depression by reducing import duties. This enabled wool producers in Spain and Germany to undercut their competitors in distant Australia. The colonists decided to stockpile their wool instead of exporting. It was a drastic decision, since the sheep population had reached half a million. Even so wool prices failed to rise in the next three years. In fact, by 1828 these had fallen from fifteen pence a pound to one shilling. When they began selling their sheep on the local market for meat, mutton prices also dropped, from sevenpence to threepence per pound. It became hardly worth while shipping wethers down to Sydney. Despite a slight revival in 1829, *The Sydney Gazette* reported 'a crisis of Public Distress, and of almost general insolvency . . . the auctioneer's hammer forever a-going . . .'

Lieutenant Carter's bankruptcy was to involve the Ogilvies in a bizarre scandal.

It all began with that sporting parson, Frederick Wilkinson.

Despite his parish duties—he had also become a teacher of classics in Newcastle—he had managed to acquire four flocks and a hundred head of cattle. This had run him into debt, for sheep were commonly bought 'one-third down, the balance on the clip'. When Archdeacon Scott hinted that he was neglecting his spiritual for a material flock, he arranged for them to be depastured by William Carter on shares. In 1828 he offered to sell both stock and land to Carter, naming a modest Christian price of £3,500. But Carter likewise had no cash. He arranged to give the curate adequate security, paying off the purchase price at seven and a half per cent. Regrettably, before the papers were signed, he borrowed £1,000 from the well-to-do James Brindley Bettington. This meant that the unlucky clergyman had to accept only a second mortgage. The following year Carter advised Wilkinson he could not meet his annual repayment of £400. The obliging parson then arranged to buy back two flocks, twelve merino rams and fifty breeding cows for £2,000. When Carter found himself still embarrassed for funds, he agreed to take back the rest of the stock and return the man's security.

Carter's overseer was instructed to deliver the cattle to Captain Allman's place for agistment, and the sheep to Ogilvie as Wilkinson's agent. But, under drought conditions, Merton could carry no more, so William had them sent back to Carter's where the overseer consented to look after them on thirds.

These complicated manoeuvres were only a beginning.

In May 1829 Wilkinson had an urgent letter from Merton. This warned him he was in danger of losing all his sheep. One Joseph Josephson, a Maitland storekeeper, was sueing Carter for a £3,000 debt and intended to have all sheep on his run sold at auction.

Panic.

Wilkinson applied to Archdeacon Scott for leave. He was refused. He sailed for Sydney, tried to arrange a *locum tenens*, failed and hurried home on the *Lord Liverpool*. Back in Newcastle he saddled up a horse and went bush.

The result was uproar. For months afterwards acidulous letters passed between Sydney and Newcastle. There were charges of disloyalty, being absent without permission, insulting his superiors. The affair permeated the governor's despatches to London. All manner of dignitaries were drawn into the embittered action; Sir Ralph Darling, Scott's successor Archdeacon Broughton, the Bishop of Calcutta, His Grace the Archbishop of Canterbury and heads of the Colonial Office. All the clamour over some peaceably feeding sheep.

'The spectacle of a clergyman riding at full speed through the country,' rumbled Broughton, 'is little calculated to impress the public mind with the reverence which ought to be entertained from the Established Church.'[2]

Whether in clerical collar or not, the galloping parson made fast time on his hundred mile dash for the Upper Hunter. He reined in first at Dalwood, picked up George Wyndham, J.P., rode on to James Glennie, J.P. near what is now Singleton, gathered up William Ogilvie and George Blaxland, both justices as well, and led the cavalcade to the rescue of his flocks.

'In the morning after I arrived at Mr. Ogilvie's,' he wrote later in explanation, 'his son accompanied me to the place where the sheep were penned, and my sheep were separated from Mr. Carter's. The head shepherd requested Mr. Ogilvie's son to allow them to remain with mine till they could be provided for, as it would save a man. Mr. Ogilvie's son agreed with them.'

Whether this was Will or Edward was not clear. But the move was a mistake. When the flocks were eventually removed to the safety of Blaxland's run, they found several of Carter's sheep among them as well. The parson hurriedly returned them to their rightful owner.

He was at once accused of theft. And all his accomplices were justices of the peace.

The Archdeacon's response was choleric. The issue was to grow worse

[2] *Historical Records of Australia*, Series 1, Vol. XV.

yet. After Carter and Wilkinson emerged from the sheriff's office in Newcastle, where they had persuaded him to delay the court proceedings, they were confronted by the angry Josephson. The confrontation took place right on Church Hill. Bystanders declared it had almost come to fisticuffs. They were members of Wilkinson's congregation, too.

The Archdeacon accused his sheep-stealing curate of bringing the cloth into contempt. Among other charges were the neglect of his school and parish duties.

'A base and wicked assertion,' Wilkinson wrote back. 'I tell you, Reverend Sir, you are deceived. I detest a lie in any shape. It is insolence towards God, and cowardice towards man. You were appointed my judge, and like the celebrated character in Scripture, you have sacrificed me to the outcry of my enemies.'

This was too much. Governor Darling ordered his suspension.

As he prepared to leave the parsonage, Wilkinson received a letter from eighteen Hunter settlers regretting his dismissal and expressing admiration for his 'character as a clergyman and gentleman'. Among those who signed were William Ogilvie, George Wyndham, George Forbes, James Glennie and William White.

Church officials merely saw them as disaffected radicals, freethinkers and Whigs. Few of them actually were.

Merton's survival in those drought years was due entirely to William's capacity for work. He could never have had a moment to himself; from daylight until well after dark. When he was not in the paddocks he was writing reports and letters by the light of a slush lamp. Yet in 1832 he even found time to make a survey of Newcastle Harbour, a hundred miles from home.

He did this without charge to anyone. Working with the harbour master, Captain Livingston, he charted the dangerous entrance, worked out ways to strengthen the breakwater and sent a report to the governor urging immediate action to make it safe for shipping. He had reasons to do so, of course. It was an essential port for the Hunter, the only throughway for their produce and wool. It was when he applied for the site of the old prisoners' barracks as a depot for stores he brought officialdom down on him. On the back of his application someone wrote in spider-fine writing: 'I think Mr. Ogilvie is very much indebted to the Govt. and cannot therefore be in a position to build. R.D. Jan 8/31.'[3]

[3] Colonial Secretary's correspondence, Land Grants, New South Wales Government Archives.

The pen spluttered. It was angry.

This reasonable request touched off a departmental enquiry. 'To be reported whether indebted,' wrote another hand on 31 January. 'Documents to Deputy Commissary General: Collector of Internal Revenue; Auditor General.' The Internal Revenue clerk, as always, was the most devastating. He reported in this fashion:

(1) Under Sir Thomas Brisbane's Regulations his debt is as follows:

Deposit due 16/19 May 1825	£100
Balance of price 16/19 May 1828	£900
	£1,000
Interest up to 31 Dec 1830	212.11.8
Quit rent at 2/- 100 acres	10. 9.7
	£1,223. 1.3

(2) Under the Regulations of 23rd Oct, 1828 his debt for the same land is as follows:

Deposit due 16/19 May 1825	100. 0.0
Balance price due 16/19 May 1828	233. 6.8
	333. 6. 8
Interest up to 31/12/30	93.16.11
Quit rent at 2 pence p acre p.a. to 31/12/30	87.13. 5
	514.17. 0

The land remaining liable to annual quit rent of 2d.—or yearly £33.6.8

The clerks were spinning a long-delayed web around him. Attached to this perilous document was a further memorandum from the Internal Revenue department. The crucial phrases of this document were: 'If he pays for this land under Sir Thomas Brisbane's regs—£1,223.1.3, or under Refs of 23/10.28 £514.17.0. I refer to my letter No. 31/136 for Mr. Ogilvie's reply to my application for payment of that debt. Wm. Macpherson, Coll. Int. Revenue.'

Clearly it had not paid him to ask for something outside official ordinances. 'I have the honour to receive your letter,' he replied in his usual polite fashion from Merton. Then continued:

On taking possession of the said land I had not the smallest doubt of being able to comply with the conditions on which it was reserved and commenced immediately to make extensive improvements upon it; and the subsequent years of unprecedented drought having absorbed the whole of my very considerable capital in effecting the said improvements and the necessary purchase of stock, I find myself from the circumstances and the extraordinary revolution that has taken place in the value of every species of property and more particularly livestock, wholly unable to make the payments required or any part of them; nor can I relinquish the land without ruin, having expended the whole of my capital, upwards of £3,000 upon it.

I beg further to inform you that I am in correspondence with His Majesty's Government on the subject and feel confident that when the circumstances above alluded to are duly considered it will be found necessary to deliver me and others similarly situated from the claims.

I have the honour to be,

Sir,

Your most obedient servant

William Ogilvie.

The game old boy. They had pushed him to the limit. They had demanded money he did not possess. He was fighting back. He was the young deck officer of Channel blockades all over again. Still patiently enduring. Still resisting. Petty officialdom could pleasure itself in the burrows and stews of Sydney Town, evade the intolerable pressures of frontier life, the malice and stubborn resistance of a convict labour force, the wary hostility of an alien nomad race, the corrosive bush silences, impassive and engulfing nothingness of forest land and stony hills and sun-withered plains waiting, patiently waiting to obliterate everything they had laboriously gained in year after year of unrewarding struggle, and all these high-collared gentry in their city pigeon houses could think of were regulations, references, payment on due dates.

The final comment was inked into the bottom left-hand corner of his letter of appeal: 'Inform Mr. Ogilvie that until his debt to Govt. be satisfied, his applcn cannot be entertained.'

The dispute was to continue intermittently for years.

Yet it was no longer a lone protest. Two months after his last letter fifty-four of the colony's leading pastoralists sent a petition to Darling, urging the suspension of quit rents until conditions improved. It was the first time that hitherto opposing factions had come together: Exclusives and Emancipists; Tories, Whigs and the uncommitted. First to sign were men as influential as John Blaxland and Richard Jones, land-owner and founding director of the New South Wales Bank. William Ogilvie's signature was third.

The petition emphasised that, even after the three-year drought, wheat was down to four shillings a bushel, maize one and sixpence and tobacco cured on the leaf sixpence a pound. If there were a good harvest that year, as expected, prices would fall even lower, below the cost of production. The true fact was that 'land beyond the [Blue] Mountains and in the distant parts of the Colony cannot be employed in tillage . . .

It becomes a simple question can the grazier, in the interests of the Colony, afford to pay rent for the land he occupies and to what amount?' Furthermore sheep that four years earlier had brought £4 were now sold for as many shillings. There was no sale for cattle at any price. With butcher's meat at one penny a pound and wool averaging a shilling, grazing, they insisted, was a losing concern.

On a second front William was still being harassed by the Church Lands Corporation.

Back in 1830 the clerics had told him of a decision to withdraw all ewes over four years old from Merton, fattening them at Liverpool instead. He wrote back, in his tolerant way, that he would meet their wishes. However, 'I must remind you that this new arrangement will greatly prejudice my interests. It will require a greater subdivision of the sheep, and consequently an increase in shepherds. As the ewes at four years old are in their prime and making the best return in lambs, it will also diminish the force from which alone my payment is derived.' Pointing out that he had already maintained them for a full year since the previous lambing, and at no cost to the Corporation, he added:

> The committee is aware that I am bound by my agreement to furnish rams for the flock, to drive our sheep and cattle twice a year to Liverpool at my cost, and to pay all expenses, and that even the freight of the wool to Sydney has been charged to me. The profit, therefore, of one-third of the increase, if indeed there can be any, is certainly not such as will bear diminution. Indeed when the diseased state in which the sheep came to me is considered, the great expense of forming out-stations, and the increase of all other expenses from the disastrous seasons ever since, profit hitherto could hardly be expected.[4]

He suggested they might care to make some other compensation. None was forthcoming. He seems to have delivered only 149 ewes to Liverpool before another clerical complaint arrived. They accused him of failing to control scab. It was impossible to do so, he replied, so long as other men were allowed to walk diseased sheep through the Valley. What was urgently needed was legislation to stop this practice.

Among the suspects was his own neighbour, George Blaxland. Presumably he took up the matter with Wollum Hills, for his monthly stock return in March 1831 carried a covering letter from Blaxland himself. It had been William's habit always to have a witness at Merton when he drafted his own share of new lambs. Blaxland in the past had signed willingly enough. Now his letter suggested a break in their friendship. Addressed to Cowper, this read:

[4] Stock Returns and Correspondence, Church Land Corporation.

'I request that you will inform the committee that Mr. Ogilvie, after keeping the accompanying communication two months in his possession declined forwarding it.'

After confirming the stock tally, he spoke of the need to have 'an alteration made in the sheep yards, to have those sheep in hurdle folds would be most desirable, but should they remain in hedge yards, the sweepings of them should not be allowed to remain so near the yard, but carried some distance off.'

One can imagine William's indignation. Was this an attempt to strike back at him for that complaint about scab infection? Following a reprimand from Cowper, he wrote again, protesting that 'where there is a difference of opinion between Mr. Blaxland and myself, it may at least be a question whether I am not as likely to be right. I have every reason to believe that my flocks were infected by Mr. George Blaxland, as he was moving about diseased sheep in the direction of the station that became infected.'

As for the implication of dirty folds, he had found this to be a single case in which a shepherd had neglected his instructions. William insisted that he had always been meticulous about clean yards, which he preferred to moveable hurdles anyway. Each time hurdles were moved, they created dust that filled the sheeps' eyes and nostrils, affected both their health and the fleeces. He demanded that someone be sent up to inspect his methods.

No one, of course, came. The corporation was almost moribund. It had been declared insolvent back in 1829, though it continued to exist in muddled fashion for another three years. While Edward rode the paddocks month after month, supervising the reluctant shepherds and their flocks, his father was forced to continue the wrangle with those spiritual shepherds in their increasingly musty Macquarie Street files. He lost patience after the Blaxland controversy, though not until February 1833 did he allow his exasperation to show.

'I have received a written notice from you,' he wrote, 'that our agreement was to close at Christmas 1831, and the stock to be delivered to your agent, but it did not suit your convenience, and I kept it till July. When I came to Sydney I was again informed by you that the committee had decided to remove the stock. I then made out the account for six months to the end of June, charging at the very low value of six shillings p. annum pr. head for the cattle, and for the sheep, only the expense of the shepherds, at the modest rate of twenty pounds pr. annum each. But the sheep were left with me near 8 months more, and the cattle upwards of 10 months.'

He ended by asking did the 'gentlemen of the committee', mostly stock breeders themselves, have some superior knowledge of how to run sheep and cattle for so miserly a return. He was finished with them all; if they took offence, he no longer cared.

It had been a hard, frustrating way to build up Merton's flocks. Nor had they been particularly good sheep.

Yet, after 1831, his situation began to improve. The Hunter was again entering a run of good seasons. Wheat was growing well again, improving in price. The region was on the way to becoming the granary of New South Wales. With the proceeds of good crops, William bought a flock of much superior sheep from Colonel William Dumaresq, who had established a pure-bred Saxon stud at St Helier's some thirty miles upriver. Dumaresq, who had named it after the Jersey town of his Huguenot ancestors, would have had an immediate affinity with the Ogilvies since Mary's two remaining sisters had recently married and gone to live in Jersey. The quality of that stud much impressed young Edward John Eyre, who studied sheep-breeding there in 1832 before beginning his marathon journey on foot around the arid shores of the Great Australian Bight. In his diary he wrote of the 'intelligent, enterprising and liberal settlers' he met when those fine-woolled Saxon rams were offered for sale.[5]

Enterprising or not, it seems likely that Ogilvie had to raise a loan at steep interest in Sydney, as most others had to do. They were all speculators. The nature of the country forced them to be. They were all subject to the whims of dry times, flooding rivers and the unseen manipulation of their markets.

1832 was something of a vintage year.

William, who had been unsuccessfully nominated for Darling's small legislative council back in 1827, was again among the names put forward by the new governor, Sir Richard Bourke. The vacancy, Bourke wrote to Viscount Goderich, 'was occasioned by the incapacity of Mr. John Macarthur, who has been pronounced a lunatic. The physical temperament of this gentleman is such as to afford little hope of his restoration.' Conceding that his first choice was the ubiquitous Sir John Jamison, he added that 'some are certainly not of sufficient influence, and perhaps Mr. William Ogilvie is the only person on that list I could venture to recommend.' Sir John, however, was given the seat.

Before this was decided, William was informed by the Admiralty that he had been promoted to commander. Now on the Royal Navy's

[5] Eyre, J., Unpublished Journal, Mitchell Library, Sydney.

retired list as junior commander, he was entitled to an increased half-pay of two shillings daily.

Also in September a large party left Merton for Newcastle to celebrate the first Upper Hunter marriage. The bride was Susan White. The groom, James Glennie. Commander Ogilvie was the natural choice to give her away. There must surely have been, for the first time in many years, champagne. Most of them travelled right through by horse. Others took the new steamship *Sophia Jane* from Morpeth. This curious melange of square sails and paddlewheels was now making a weekly voyage to and from Sydney.

The wedding in Newcastle was actually a double one. As soon as Mr and Mrs Glennie left the vestry, the Reverend Wilton—Frederick Wilkinson's successor—went on to marry another Merton couple. These were the Commander's ex-convict overseer, John Dawkins, and a ticket-of-leave girl, Penelope Kelly. Miss Kelly, not long released from Bathurst gaol, had been transported for the improbable crime of 'assisting in a rape'. She had only been eighteen at the time.

Mary had been so satisfied with her earlier that she recommended her for the annual Lady Darling award for good conduct. The lady, incidentally Colonel Dumaresq's sister, was back in England by the time her prize was given.

The Ogilvies were soon to have second thoughts about Penelope. Within a month the Commander took her before two fellow magistrates for refusing to work. She claimed that, married, she was now free. Captain Pike and George Forbes remanded her, waiting for the attorney-general's opinion. Some weeks later, after a second refusal, they gave her six months in Newcastle's house of correction. Though ordered to return to her master, she was next heard of at Wollombi Brook, where her husband was charged with selling sly grog to convicts. The Commander fined him £30.

With the drought gone, labour was now the major problem. Convicts, being virtually serfs, had never been satisfactory. Reluctant and inefficient workers, they had no interest in the job, and when ruthless employers drove them, tended to vanish into the bush. During the 1830s the situation worsened. The earlier convicts had rarely been vicious types. Mostly they were petty thieves, rickburners, the maladjusted victims of an inhumane society back home, or pauperised Irish driven by famine or anti-British sentiment to minor crime. Now Britain had changed the rules of transportation. It was sending out only its hardened criminals. The new mood was harsher.

The change can be read in the Merton bench books, which the Commander wrote up in his meticulous hand until Will was officially appointed Clerk of the Court in 1834 at a salary of £70 a year. As senior magistrate he presided over monthly court days, with one other, sometimes two local magistrates to assist him.[6]

The charges followed a monotonous pattern. Mainly these were insolence, malingering, theft, drunkenness, absconding, neglect of flocks, killing sheep, assault or harbouring deserters. Punishment, too, had little variation. Hence the resident scourger.

Typical cases and sentences for January 1832 were that of a lifer reported by the eighteen-year-old Edward for shirking his duties. Fifty lashes. Another neglecting to milk Captain Pike's cows. Seventy-five lashes; two instalments. A stockman not only refusing work, but illegally harbouring a lubra in his hut. One hundred lashes; fifty at a time. A woman charged by the Commander with enticing a man into her quarters, the pretext being she wanted to marry him. She was already married. One month in the Female Factory. A drunken stockman who absconded. Twenty-five lashes.

From a modern standpoint these punishments were barbaric. Men were stripped to the waist, bound by their wrists to an iron triangle, flayed by a professional flogger who, being a convict himself, had to flog well or risk being flogged himself. It was the accepted practice of the times; and that was it. Cunningham, a humane man, even said that flogging in New South Wales was lenient compared with the services. For similar offences the army or navy would have ordered five hundred lashes instead of fifty. A consoling thought; perhaps.

The convicts may not have been so philosophic.

Nor, for that matter, was Alexander Harris. He saw physical punishment as a form of class tyranny. One landowner, he wrote, would order a flogging for his neighbour's stubborn servant. His neighbour would then return the compliment by having his flogged. What troubled him was the brutalising effect on the population at large. 'I have seen young children practising on a tree, as children in England play horse,' he reported one man as saying. 'I saw one man walk across the yard with the blood that had run from his lacerated flesh squashing out of his shoes. A dog was licking the blood off the triangles, and the ants were carrying away great pieces of human flesh that the lash had scattered about the ground.'[7]

By the 1830s matters were slightly improved. Regulations were introduced preventing magistrates from giving more than fifty lashes

[6] Merton Bench Books, State Archives, Mitchell Library.

[7] Harris, Alexander, *Convicts and Settlers*, London, 1837.

at any one time. At Merton this appears to have been the norm, with less awarded for minor offences.

The Commander, according to A. W. Wood,[8] 'used his influence among other magistrates and settlers to stem the excessive use of the lash. This made him unpopular, and he was derided by the more extreme settlers. He and his friends were called "convict pleasers".' Wood also mentioned that, when new boundaries were being marked on the Gwydir River in 1848, one surveyor was told that a prominent tree had long been known as 'Mother Ogilvie's'. John Robertson, who grew up at Plaskett, near Jerry's Plains, before entering politics, described Ogilvie as 'humane and a true liberal, believing in the dignity of man'.

Those worn, cloth-bound bench books from Merton reveal a factor never discussed in the histories. The wool industry was founded on the cat-o'-nine-tails. Australia was not riding on the backs of sheep. It was riding on the scarred backs of convict labourers.

This was feudalism with violence. Yet how else could these men have formed their runs. Free labour did not exist. Nor, had it existed, could they have paid for it. Despite their free grants, they had to borrow at high interest, live often at subsistence levels, force their reluctant, inefficient slave labourers to work if there were to be any shepherding, sheep washing or shearing done at all. They left scars also on the human psyche, on the land itself.

The early men, like Cunningham, wrote of how the land responded to careful husbandry. Morning dews refreshed the native grasses, ensured fertility. Then, to increase carrying capacity, they cleared scrub, cut down shady trees. The dews came less frequently. The earth became parched and powdery under the hooves of sheep. Rains and wind eroded bare flats and gullies. The topsoil was washed away. This region has never recovered the fertility those first settlers found.

The Ogilvies were among the few who refused to cut down trees. Others ridiculed them at the time.

A frontier environment offered few outlets for a normal childhood. The Ogilvie boys were virtually adults by their early teens. As mere lads they had to learn the handling of grown, tough-fibred convicts— truculent, embittered men. They had to supervise them, give them orders, search their huts for stolen goods, send them to the lock-up whenever they showed defiance. 'A man, to enforce his authority,' wrote Cunningham, 'must go among them and beard them without timidity.' It had equal application for these boys.

[8] Wood, A. W., *Dawn In The Valley*, Sydney, 1972.

Will was frequently alone with them; many miles from other support at home. Edward, too, had to deal with surly, rum-soaked shepherds out on the Gumman Plains, as the Goulburn River country was called. They had to prove themselves stronger in will than devious and dissolute men.

Edward was seventeen when he brought one sullen shepherd to court. He charged him with having failed to yard his sheep one night, neglecting to report several killed by dingoes. He said that he himself had been obliged to spend all night riding in search of that flock.

Again in April 1832, he told George Forbes, J.P., that 'the prisoner came over to the farm before the river rose and told me he would not stay any longer with the watchman, as he would not grind the mess. I told him to stay where he was told. He refused. I immediately ordered him to the lock up. I went over to the sheep station and made the watchman swim across the river to me.'

One can imagine the scene; two lonely hatters, miles from anywhere arguing over trivial idiocies; a teenage boy ordering one to swim a fast-flowing river in flood. Later the same year he had the court order another flogging, again to a potty shepherd who let a wild dog break into his sheepyard.

Court hearings often became recitals of violence. On one occassion, Captain Pike brought in a stockman who refused work till he was given new boots. Pike, when threatened with a chisel, 'gave him a thrashing with a stick. I then told him to clean out his sheepyard. He took up his shovel and said you bloody bugger if you come in here I'll stroke you. I took the shovel away and gave him a few strokes with the whip. I then called on the shepherd to take him to the lock-up.'

This was the fashion in which wool was won.

The ultimate in violence occurred at Castle Forbes in 1833. Happily this was beyond Merton's jurisdiction. Provoked by James Mudie's relentless brutality, his seventy convicts mutinied. Six of their leaders robbed the store in his absence, attempted to kill his overseer, John Larnack, who was also his son-in-law, then turned to bushranging before once more raiding the station for firearms, horses and food. Led by Larnack, mounted police eventually captured them and had them sent to Sydney for trial. They were young men, skilled artisans and might well have worked as peaceably as on other runs, but for the atmosphere of Castle Forbes. In the Sydney courthouse these men took off their shirts one by one. They shocked spectators with the empurpled fretwork of scars on their backs. They were found guilty nonetheless. Five were publicly hanged. The sixth was sent to Norfolk Island.

In 1836 Governor Bourke failed to renew Mudie's commission as a magistrate. The angry Mudie at once sold up his property, returned to England and published an embittered attack on colonial attitudes, *The Felonry of New South Wales*. Its theme was his famous dictum on convictism, 'Nothing could wash away their guilt and obliterate the brand.' But these sentiments were fast going out of fashion.

Nothing illustrates this more clearly than George Wyndham's experience at the peak of the bushranging era.

When building his freestone homestead at Dalwood, he equipped it with bolted window shutters that also had loopholes for firearms. One afternoon he rode home to find a rough note nailed to the front door. The anonymous visitor assured him he had nothing to fear. He had always been a good master to his convicts. Nonetheless, Mrs Wyndham retained the habit of carrying a revolver, even when indoors.

In 1834 Fred Ogilvie, then fifteen, described in court how he and Edward had faced the revolt of twelve convicts. They had complained of bad and insufficient food, and of wheat crawling with weevils. On other information, Fred had ordered constables to search their hut. They found good and plentiful wheat hidden beneath mattresses. The men were marched to the lock-up.

Later that year Fred was in court again. He told of riding after cattle, out near the Liverpool Range, when a stranger had entered his hut. He recognised him as a bushranger and had him brought home, presumably alongside his horse, to the cells at Merton.

At this stage bushrangers were not free-riding men like Thunderbolt or the Kellys. These were simply absconding convicts, on foot, hunted men ready to kill. Typical was the fugitive from an iron gang, John Davis, who was arrested in 1834 for horse stealing and sent by Ogilvie to Sydney for trial. Under his brother's leadership, he became a member of the six-man Jew Boy gang that later raided Puen Buen station, flogged the manager at his own whipping tree and eventually went to the scaffold in Sydney.

The increasingly tough situation obliged Merton's magistrates, during the same year, to write to Sydney asking urgently for a new scourger. At present, they explained, they had to send convicts forty miles to Patrick's Plains for punishment, 'a very serious inconvenience as it wholly employs the constables and prevents them attending to their other duties.'

The same three justices—Ogilvie, Pike and Blaxland—recommended that the colonial secretary find some other punishment for escapees than the chain gang. Men had been found to make repeated breaks for freedom, convinced the iron gangs treated them better than some local station owners. They advised also against a proposal to send young delinquents to the Hunter, because there was no way of keeping them from the general depravity. The Commander proved his point next year by demanding the withdrawal of a new constable, who had shown himself a master only of drink and misconduct.

Occasionally a magistrate would find in favour of an accused man, dismiss a case or find some landowner guilty of breaching the law. This was rare.

One such case involved Ogilvie himself. This was when Cunningham's new manager, John Harley Pagan—his recently arrived nephew —complained that Merton had commandeered five of Dalswinton's workers. The Commander's stubborn defence failed to convince his fellow magistrates.

Ogilvie, who was later commended for his achievements in suppressing bushrangers, also had one long-sought character's ticket-of-leave cancelled for cattle stealing in the Goulburn Valley. The man later worked on explorer Charles Sturt's property on the Murrumbidgee, before taking up a violent career in Tasmania. His name was Martin Cash.

In October 1836 a murderer named Hobson was committed for trial in Sydney. Known throughout the back country as Opossum Jack, he had a long list of charges against him, including a violent attack on Edward after breaking out of Merton's cells. Nothing more is known of the incident. A letter to the Crown Solicitor urged him to subpoena the local surgeon at Jerry's Plains, since Dr Graham had been called in to treat Edward's wounds.

Neither lock-up nor courtroom did much to add dignity to the law. Since only slab walls divided cells from court, prisoners could listen in to every case, while magistrates were only too conscious of the night tubs. To make his escape all a man had to do was to push open one of the slabs.

Another justices' letter to the Colonial Secretary in 1836 read like a manifesto. Deploring the lack of interest shown by George Forbes in the court, magistrates Ogilvie and Pike revealed that he had only attended eleven times in two years, and then only when he had a personal interest in the cases. On the other hand, Forbes complained to Sydney that neither of them would award 'proper punishments' to his convict servants, often giving none at all. He also sued them for libel, only to find the attorney-general opposing the case on two occasions, which forced him to withdraw his charges. 'He takes every opportunity of evincing hostility,' the two men had written, 'especially when it has been our duty to decide against him on many cases wherein he has appeared discreditably on complaints of his honesty.

'It is unnecessary for us to point out the evil consequences that must arise,' they concluded. 'If a magistrate who takes no part in the public duties of the magistracy is permitted, for his own private ends, to put aside government regulations, and to encourage and abet prisoners to do the same, and to set at defiance those magistrates who devote a great deal of their time to the honest and conscientious discharge of their public duty, all our endeavours to preserve the peace and good order of the district must be in vain.'

It was a distressing admission. They had revealed a facet of Hunter settlement too often ignored. That the region had been conceived in convict misery, breast-fed on violence towards its original owners and matured only by the kindness of a few more sensitive settlers. Its lyrical beauty had gone too often unobserved.

7

Beyond the Limits

Merton was no longer a mere family outpost on the edge of nowhere.

The cottage was now one of a whole cluster of buildings. There were barns, a stone store, dairy, quarters for constables, overseer, head shepherd, blacksmith, as well as the bark huts of convict labourers. The addition of a courthouse and the first licensed inn, the Green Gate, began to give it the air of a self-contained village. It was, in fact, officially proclaimed a township, though it remained a private one, not subject to outside control. The town of Merton was very much the Commander's domain; as landowner, magistrate and benevolent squire. It was almost a reversion to the manorial life of mediaeval Britain.

Commander Ogilvie was the feudal lord; the convicts his serfs.

The old cart track around Mount Ogilvie to the river, crossed by a ford, had now become a well-used road. Police patrols, stockmen, carriers passed this way frequently to the country further out. Now and again a teamster put his bullocks out to grass across the river. There was also a semi-permanent encampment of Aborigines on the nearby flat, their humpies of bough and bark ranged about cooking fires.

Others of the tribe had come to live on Merton itself. Some even worked for the boss now. When Charles Grant Tindal, son of William's old naval comrade, came to Merton for 'colonial experience' some years later, he wrote, 'Captain Ogilvie is very particular about the natives, and the tribe call themselves his blacks. One day I was introduced to them by Mary Ogilvie as another son of hers from England, and therefore brother to all blackfellows. They are finer and more intelligent than I expected, the best are employed at the outstations to track cattle.'[1]

[1] Tindal Family Letters, Mitchell Library, Sydney.

The manor, it seemed, extended even to the Aborigines. And some had begun to call him Captain.

Tindal's letters home made frequent mention of the Ogilvies, and described how the homestead had been enlarged. Additional rooms were now set at the back; the roof was thatched; a front verandah with stout posts and palings gave shade in the hot months; the whitewashed floors that Ellen had called 'very troublesome to keep clean', had been overlaid with pitsawn timber. 'The principal room of the original hut is now papered and made very comfortable. The rest of the house consists of two detached rooms, one called the barracks, where the young men sleep, and the other is a room for strangers. The kitchen and servants' quarters are also detached, so that the whole looks more like a small township than a house.'

In modern parlance Mary would have been termed a pioneer. But she had no mind to rough it more than necessary. When Partridge the Elder left to work for Hannibal Macarthur nearer Sydney, she engaged this massive woman's daughter Ellen as cook instead. Then, in 1836, she made quite a stir among Sydneysiders by advertising in *The Gazette* for a lady's maid.

Though Tindal casually mentioned having killed two five-foot snakes in her sitting-room, he had nothing to say about Mary's furnishing. Some were distinctly unusual for these rude times. Among the sea chests, improvised tables and chairs was a beautifully polished cedar sideboard made by some convict craftsman; an elegant silver tea service; and, William's special pride, the portable oak washstand from Nelson's cabin aboard *Victory*. Family tradition has it that this was a personal gift from the admiral, though it seems more probable that his brother David acquired it after Trafalgar, since it must still have been in use until Nelson's death at sea.

'At a short distance from the house,' Tindal added, 'is the garden which Mrs. Ogilvie delights in, and close to it a large vineyard. The garden is full of oranges and all kinds of foreign fruit trees.'

Presumably these fruit trees were gifts from Peter Cunningham in South America. The young Englishman failed to mention two other prominent features. Outside the house was a stone sundial which must have been carved by a convict mason, and a large bronze bell beside it. It was from these that the convicts' hours of rising, feeding and ceasing work were regulated.

All that remains of that splendid garden now are a few rosebushes gone wild, several of Cunningham's exotic trees and a crumbling stone archway through which Mary took guests to admire her shrubberies and beds of flowers.

The vineyard has gone without trace. Yet this was one of the earliest along the Hunter, now celebrated for its wines. The Commander, too, made wines that men thought well of. Ellen wrote of the white he produced from an undated vintage that 'is still remembered for its excellence'. It was a blend of Gouais and Sweetwaters, she said. 'A German named Luther, a highly educated man, and a descendant of Martin Luther, on tasting the wine, could not believe it was not hock. As he appeared skilled in the arts of wine-making father kept him to assist.'

His chief assistant at the vineyard and maturation vats was Edward, 'who was excellent in the cultivation of wines and wine-making.' Later in life he was to produce many good wines of his own.

Meanwhile Merton's vintages became so successful that, in 1841, William applied for a permit to import two vine-dressers and a cooper from Europe. Clearly the old reliance on unsophisticated convict labour was coming to an end.

A succession of good seasons was giving the whole region a rare taste of prosperity. As James Macarthur wrote to W. E. Riley, the Liverpool pastoralist, from Camden Park in an undated letter—probably 1836— 'the wool market has risen considerably. Mr. Ogilvie's wool is said to have averaged 3/9 per lb. Montefiore's London are reported to have received the catalogues of sales, but are keeping the matter quiet.'

To keep the Commander quiet was less easy. He continued to ask for more land. His offer to buy 640 acres, described as adjoining the village, was refused on the grounds of being already listed for sale. In the same year the Admiralty notified him of a new promotion. He was now a senior commander on the retired list. He offered at once to trade his complete pension for a further grant of land. Downing Street replied that no such precedent existed. Whereupon he produced—or borrowed at interest—enough cash to buy two blocks, totalling two thousand acres, across the river. A year later the colonial treasury, his old adversary, expressed its pleasure that the last instalment had been paid on 1,200 acres bought from the land originally offered to him on optional purchase back in 1825. The Lands Office listed his total payment as £321.13.9. This amounted to five shillings an acre, with interest.

By this time he was possessed of very much more land than was officially recognised.

This was revealed when Governor Bourke gazetted new regulations late in 1836. These brought to an end the extra-legal practice of squatting. No longer would squatter be a term of contempt. A new sub-class of 'gentlemen squatters' was to become acceptable. They would no longer be classed with lawless elements, cattle duffers and runaway convicts who squatted on any segment of Crown Land they happened

Merton. the residence of W. Ogilvie Esqre
on the river Hunter — visited by me in March. 1853.

Conrad Martens

Above: A sketch of Merton Cottage by Conrad Martens in 1853. Mitchell Library, Sydney.

Below: All that remains of Merton township today—the graveyard overlooking the Hunter River. Photograph by the author.

to fancy. The administration would henceforth issue 'licences to depasture Crown Lands beyond the limits of the colony'. They would be registered and pay an annual fee of £10.

The new deal began to reveal just how active the Ogilvies had been in the outside country of which officialdom knew so little.

The movement of men and stock beyond the prescribed Nineteen Counties had been gathering momentum since the depression lifted in 1831.

These so-called limits of location were quite unreal. They had been fenced in only by the bureaucratic mind. Throughout the colony men had simply to ride their boundaries and look out at the unoccupied plains, or valleys, or hills beyond. Allan Cunningham, the explorer, had ridden beyond the Liverpool Ranges across the Namoi and glimpsed, north of the McPhersons, the widespread promise of the Darling Downs. Hume and Hovell had opened the overlander's track down to Port Phillip Bay. Major Mitchell had found his Australian Felix below the River Murray. Sturt's epic small-boat voyage down that grand river had touched off plans to establish the new free province of South Australia.

Men everywhere were on the move.

Besides a legal precedent had been set when the influential A.A. Company was allowed to cross the Liverpool Range in 1833, taking up a vast 249,000-acre grant at Warrah. Its announced capital of £1 million to develop a million acres was all-persuasive. Soon they were to add the 313,000 acres of Goonoo Goonoo on the Peel River to their original 464,000-acre grant inland from Port Stephens. Yet the company, with Henry Dangar as chief land-seeker, had not by any means been first over the range. Several squatters had to be ejected in their favour.

Other men had taken the route past Merton, up the Goulburn and over Cunningham's Pandora Pass to fan out across the Liverpool Plains. It was easy at first to find land. A man took what he pleased. He chose a great stretch of open plain, or river flats, or a valley walled in by stony, or scrub-covered hills. The cattle roamed free. Some men, like the Ogilvie clan—which now included James Glennie and William White as well—formed a network of interlocking holdings. It became important to keep johnny-come-lately out. Especially as these were so often men of dubious character. There were no surveys. No legal boundaries. Nothing to mark the start or the end of a man's run except blazed trees, blackened stumps, prominent rocks, a creek bed or even the impermanent lines cut by somebody's plough.

Beyond the mythical black stump the country was open to all.

The issues were soon to be summed up in that much quoted dictum of a subsequent governor. As Sir George Gipps expressed it:

> As well might it be attempted to confine the Arabs of the desert within a circle, traced upon their sands, as to confine the graziers or wool-growers of New South Wales within any boundaries that can possibly be assigned to them; and as certainly as the Arabs would be starved, so also would the flocks and herds if they were so confined.[2]

Glennie, first man on the Gwydir, had only a small mileage com-

---

[2] *Historical Records of Australia*, Series 1, Vol. **XVIII**.

pared with the Ogilvies. The records remained haphazard for a long time after Bourke's Act of 1836, so there is no way of identifying all their runs, nor when they were first formed. For varying periods they had at least nine cattle stations, mostly on the Peel, Gwydir and Maranoa Rivers. All of these had distinctive Aboriginal names; which probably explained the manner of finding them. They included the 51,000-acre Culpa, Whyomoy, Tali Tali, Pal Lal, Gala, Oak Oak and two additional sheep runs, in Will's name; notably the 23,000-acre Tarella. None of these had ever carried a single hoof before.

One imagines that the family had to borrow money, at heavy interest, to finance these ventures. Everyone else was doing so. Credit was easy, and the land cost nothing before 1836. They were gambling in futures. If things failed, that was too bad. Meanwhile the all-important fact was to breed more stock. Saddle up and shift out to the everlasting plains.

Merton, at this time, became little more than a depot for cattle movements up country and back, apart from the breeding of sheep. The way they ran this country was well described by Tindal. He wrote, in his new chum fashion, of one journey out to Manilla with a party of stockmen, led by Will.[3] This was no doubt Terniax, the first outside run taken up by the Commander in the early 1830s. There were four white men, two blacks and eight horses. Their first camp was made four miles beyond Muscleton (Muswellbrook), after which they put up at a station near Wingen, then 'crossed the boundary of the colony', and camped outside Cuerindi. 'It was pleasant camping out in summer, when there was plenty of grass and water. First you look after the horses, then select a great log against which a fire is made for tea and damper, then arrange your blankets and lie down to drink tea, yarn and sleep. Before sunrise you get the horses in, take more tea and damper and saddle up, riding until the heat of the day obliges you to rest your horses.' They came at last to a place called Perimbungay, and next day reached the Ogilvie station at the head of the Manilla.

'The station', he explained, 'is a row of four huts built of slabs, covered with large strips of bark stripped by blacks, and an earth floor. The owner's hut has a long narrow verandah to keep the sun off. The furniture consists of a small table and stretchers around the sides for beds.' There were other huts for stockkeepers, stables and a small yard for holding cattle.

Tindal described how these rivers 'unlike England are dry most of the year, except for deep waterholes. Watercourses are only run-offs

[3] Tindal Family Letters, Mitchell Library, Sydney.

from the hills. They may be hundreds of yards wide when full. At the other side of the river is a large camp of blacks working for them, especially for bark.' He wrote of going out with these Aborigines, picking up a few words from them and making himself understood. 'It is astonishing how readily the blacks can pick up food where the white man would starve.'

At this period curious rumours began to circulate about the Ogilvies, and their friends. It seems doubtful if they had much basis in fact. It was as if the less fortunate or curious resented their success.

It was repeatedly said, for instance, that William and Captain Pike were hard masters to work for, over-keen on flogging. Yet it had long been known the opposite was the case. There were also whispers of strange doings at Dalwood; suggestions of witchcraft. What, one wonders, would the Wyndhams and Ogilvies have been up to behind those heavy shutters? Freethinking orgies; black masses? Was Pan, perhaps even Satan, disporting himself among Dalwood's cloven-footed rams?

Again there was talk of Will being 'wild'. Even Tindal mentioned it years later, writing that 'he was rather dissipated when he was a young man'. He gave no further explanation. Possibly it was connected with vague bush talk at the time of a young man's interest in lubras. He became known as Billy the Bull. Edward, too, had his share of that talk. So, for that matter, did most single men who ranged the backblocks alone for long periods—especially those known to be sympathetic to the Aborigines, or those who spoke the language. 'Boong-lovers' was becoming Australia's special racist phrase.

It appears far more likely that they were making excellent use of tribal friendships to find more land for grazing.

More fascinating is an unexplained entry in the magistrate's letter book for 24 October 1837. This is a copy of a letter written to the Colonial Secretary by the Commander, asking for investigations of a charge made against Mr E. Ogilvie 'for having aided and assisted some black natives in some of their fights being stopped for want of proof of the death of a black belonging to the Gumman tribe'. This man was 'stated to have fallen from the effects of a shot fired by Jerry. We request you to forward every evidence that can be found.'

It seemed that no further evidence was forthcoming. More desperate events overtook them all. Individual inquiries became meaningless in the general disaster crystallised by the massacre at Myall Creek.

Since 1836 an undeclared war had begun to smoulder across hundreds of miles in the back country. A government committee later disclosed that it extended from the Ovens River, south of the Murray, where W. M. Faithful had eight shepherds murdered at the one time, to the Liverpool Plains. James Glennie reported fifteen similar killings on the Gwydir within thirty months, and entire flocks and herds slaughtered just to obtain kidney fat. Five hundred sheep were killed on the Darling, though wild game there was abundant. The Reverend David Mackenzie, who employed fifty Aborigines, felt he could no longer trust them and warned his European employees to be perpetually alert. There were other reports of tribes massing in particular areas. It began to look as if the whole country were turning against the invader. There were, of course, two sides to this confrontation. As C. D. Rowley explained it in pithy fashion: 'When shepherds came together it was not unusual to potshot natives in exactly the same way that pigeons are shot at shooting-meets.'[4]

For the Kamilaroi the new aggressions were a final gesture of despair.

The *Monitor* reported that a violent backlash appeared among stockmen who, 'that their cattle might never more be rushed, resolved to exterminate the whole race of blacks in that quarter.'

The first shots were fired at Myall Creek station. Not to be confused with a smaller holding of Ogilvie's also known as Myall Creek, this large cattle run had been formed on the Gwydir by Henry Dangar, who had now left the A.A. Company. Dangar himself was then away on another of his runs. According to L. L. Payne[5] the flashpoint occurred at Terrie-Hie-Hie, a western out-station where 'a white youth was murdered, and his body cut up and concealed in a case of salted meat. The meat was packed on top of his body. When the remains were found, the men in the area were gathered and the argument advanced that "the blacks must have done it".'

In retrospect, it seems more likely to have been a European murder, the result of some all too common perversion. The blacks never troubled to conceal their victims.

Payne continued:

> Everybody was in favour of getting rid of the blacks altogether these days; now was the time to make a start. A party of horsemen were gathered. They systematically drove every Aboriginal they could muster into the bed of a watercourse beneath a sheer mountainside. A number of warriors made good their escape, and fled east to what has henceforth been called Slaughterhouse Creek. A band of seven horsemen pursued them. The chase and running battle went on for

[4] Rowley, C. D., *The Destruction of Aboriginal Society*, Canberra, 1969.

[5] Harrison, B. W., *The Myall Creek Massacre*, B.A. (Hons.) thesis, University of New England, 1966.

eight days with mixed success . . . Savage and frustrated, the riders
then commenced calling around on every holding within reach, urging
an immediate "kill the blacks" campaign. Stockmen they met informed
them that the well known peaceful Myall tribe had returned three
weeks before from the direction of the MacIntyre run and were again
settled on Dangar's property.

On 7 June the station's superintendent rode off with a mob of cattle,
leaving two convicts in charge. The same evening a neighbouring
cattleman arrived in search of Aboriginal workers, took ten away and,
along the track, heard that the posse was making for Myall Creek. The
men he sent back to warn the others arrived half-an-hour too late.
The vigilantes had tied them up with long, rawhide ropes—men,
women, children all together—and shot or axed them to death in a
lonely gully. Two small boys alone escaped. A couple of younger lubras
were spared; for the usual reasons.

Next morning, after a good breakfast, one of the convicts, suitably
named Kilmeister, helped them pile the bodies on a log fire. When
reports reached E. D. Day in Muswellbrook, he spent seven energetic
weeks hunting down the killers. Eleven of the twelve were finally
arrested and sent to Sydney for trial. At once there was an outcry.
Local squatters organised a defence committee, engaged expensive
lawyers and campaigned against Gipps. They declared he was imperil-
ling law and order, pandering to the blacks, making life impossible for
white men in the backblocks. The men were acquitted on a technicality.
The attorney-general ordered a second trial, at which seven were found
guilty and hanged. The rest were freed for 'insufficient evidence', or
because Aboriginal witnesses were 'insufficiently instructed in religion',
and thus unable to swear an oath on the Christian bible.

Christian ethics indeed.

Sydneysiders were soon given news of yet another massacre. The
authors this time were the newly formed Border Police. Forty to fifty
Aborigines were said to have been slaughtered on the Namoi; even the
exact number was unknown.

It had actually occurred five months earlier than Myall Creek. But
Bourke had left for England, Gipps not yet arrived and the Acting-
Governor, Colonel Snodgrass, saw no cause for investigation. Several
months went by before the new governor set up an inquiry. Even then
it was much delayed. This was because the three-man committee's
presiding magistrate, E. D. Day, was out in the backblocks hunting the
Myall Creek killers.

The other two magistrates appointed were Commander Ogilvie and
Captain Pike. The evidence was to be taken in Merton's courthouse.

Since no other witnesses could be found than mounted police, the inquiry was able only to take depositions. One can imagine how sympathetic men like Ogilvie, Pike and Day chafed at the lack of Aboriginal testimony. But the tracks had long ago grown cold. The police commander, Major I. W. Nunn, inadvertently explained the initial cause of that panic action. He had been briefed by Snodgrass, a Pickwickian ex-cavalry officer of the most witless kind.

'There are a thousand blacks out there,' Snodgrass told him. 'If they are not stopped, we may find them presently within our boundaries.'

Nunn dutifully swung into the saddle. He assembled some thirty troopers at Jerry's Plains, riding out through Merton to the Namoi cavalry-style. In the courthouse he admitted that their three-hundred-mile ride, with sabres clattering, could have made him too eager for action. The police cantered into every station en route, made indiscriminate arrests for alleged cattle killing, then at the headwaters of the McIntyre shot one captive 'while escaping'. He had been ordered to 'clear the Namoi'. Now he was charging about nearly a hundred miles further north. Tribal reaction was instantaneous. But waddies and spears were useless against Nunn's cavalry charge across the paddocks of Invermein. An unknown number were killed. Two hours after resistance ended, the troopers opened fire again.

No decorations were won at the Battle of Invermein. But no action followed the inquiry either. The Executive Council filed away the transcript, giving cautious support to police handling of unspecified 'aggression by the blacks'. It concluded that, owing to the delay in collecting evidence, 'no object either in Justice or Humanity could be attained by making the transaction in question the subject of further judicial inquiry.'

Gipps, unnerved by public hostility to the Myall Creek hangings, made no effort to have Nunn tried. His report to London drew only a mild reply from yet another new Secretary for the Colonies, Lord John Russell. Asking was it necessary for police always to carry firearms, the philosophic earl wote, 'the object of capturing offenders was entirely lost sight of, and shots were fired at men who were apparently guilty only of jumping into the water to escape from armed pursuit . . . It is impossible to contemplate the condition and prospects of that unfortunate race without the deepest commiseration.'[6]

Yet contemplate it he did.

He urged Gipps to try making 'that unfortunate race' more aware of 'the blessings of Christianity, knowledge of the Arts and the advantages of the civilised life.'

[6] *Historical Records of Australia*, Series 1, Vol. XVIII.

The Aborigines had seen enough of those blessings in action. They began by avoiding contact with Europeans even when these made friendly overtures. When Gipps signed the Border Police Act in March 1839, partially designed to protect the native people, the news travelled by bush telegraph at great speed through the tribes. The big white father in the city, they believed, was now on their side. They became more and more aggressive, or 'cheeky' as the whitefellows termed it. They renewed their attacks on unprotected outposts, slaughtering so many stock that squatters had to withdraw from the region altogether. Between 1840 and 1846 no stock whatever grazed on the Liverpool Plains.

It was the world's first expression of black power. If a man's complexion was white, he had little hope of staying alive, friendly or not. The frontier had become a whirlpool of racial hatred.

William's reactions were understandable. His careful investigation had been so much waste of time. Fifteen years of humane treatment was in the discard. He had lost at least a hundred square miles of grazing lands. No wonder he responded with such black humour to a questionnaire from the Legislative Council. Prompted by a proposal from Gipps that something be done to solve the Aboriginal problem, possibly through regular employment, the four-page printed document was circulated to all pastoralists.[7] The response from Merton was sardonic.

1. Have you been in the habit of employing any of the Native Blacks on your establishment?
   —Yes, occasionally.
2. What numbers, do they work constantly, what class of work, are you satisfied with their assiduity?
   —I have one Native Black, or shepherd, and a very good one, and constant. He was wounded on the foot by a spear, and is lame in consequence, and can therefore earn his livelihood more easily than as a hunter. No other of his race ever satisfied me with his assiduity.
3. Have they been accustomed to receive wages, or other remuneration?
   —Roger my shepherd, is well fed and clothed.
4. Can you suggest any means by which they may become readily induced to engage in the above?
   —Much could be made of them in every way, provided only they were caught young.
5. Can you suggest any means by which they may be more induced to engage in the above?
   —By cutting off their great toes. They could not then climb the trees for opossums. Two hours so spent or in fishing will supply them

[7] Committee on Land Bill, Notes and Proceedings, Legislative Council, 1839.

with all they want for the day; why then should they vex themselves with the drudgery of labour? They are not fools.

6. Please state the amount of labour you have known any of them to accomplish, by the day, week or month; what do you consider their average service compared with Europeans; and in what manner may they be most readily induced to exert themselves?

—They are not labourers at all, and for the same reason that any other gentleman is not, viz. that he can live without labour. So also can they, and as comfortably as they wish to live.

7. What do you consider their prevailing character?

—They realise the philosophy that Diogenes only dreamt of, yet are no Cynics, rather Gymnosophists. But surely the Council will not encourage a "degraded class" among our pure population.

The last two questions were answered in a different hand, alongside the signature of George Wyndham. It suggests that the two men worked out their answers together, perhaps over a bottle of Dalwood claret or Merton hock. The effrontery of those replies. Their mockery of the Victorian gospel of work. One just did not speak of primaeval savages as gentlemen. No wonder the now faded documents William signed carried a testy front page note: 'Memo for Clerk of Council. As it conveys rather more insult to the Committee than information, I shall be authorized to exclude from those selected for publication.'

It may also explain why Wyndham, in 1839, had refused to accept nomination for the Council. The principles which made him quit England hardly encouraged hobnobbing with Torydom here.

Before those boom years ended in frontier strife, the Ogilvies had taken to visiting Sydney less infrequently. The regular steamer service made travelling easier. They had a little money to spend. William had his agent to see on matters of wool shipments, banking and loans. Mary, too, would have found it a welcome diversion from bush monotonies.

No doubt, like that unknown young naturalist aboard H.M.S. *Beagle*, Charles Darwin, they found the town still 'rancorously divided on almost every subject; the whole population, rich and poor, bent on acquiring wealth.' They might have agreed with him in 1836 that 'much jealousy exists between the children of rich emancipists and free settlers.' Yet a mere two years brought a remarkable change. Evidence of this was the formation of a new club to promote 'the social and literary interests of individuals resident in the Colony, and for country gentlemen.'

For the first time exclusives and emancipists, Whigs and Tories, were prepared to make common cause. There were sound reasons for it, chiefly centered on their growing differences with Gipps, though he was named the Australian Club's patron. They saw him as a threat to their landowning ambitions and a champion of London's plans to end cheap convict labour. The eighty-six foundation members included such prestigious names as Richard Jones, Hannibal Macarthur, Alexander Macleay, and three Blaxlands.

The Commander was also invited; so were his two sons, Will and Edward, now both in their twenties. The Ogilvies had arrived.

Other members included Dr John Dobie, retired from the navy to become port health officer; James and John Mylne, pastoralists recently arrived from Scotland; shipowner J. H. Grose, and Francis (Frenchman) Girard, a one-time baker now prospering in timber. A curious omission was the gruff, once radical crusader, W. C. Wentworth who had, a decade earlier, called exclusives 'the yellow snakes of the colony', and was now the largest landowner of them all. He was admitted soon after.

If there was little reading or writing, members at once set about living well. Comfortable quarters were rented in the Pulteney Hotel. They sent a draft of £1,500 to London for dinner and breakfast services, sterling silver, wine glasses. Accounts approved for the first year included twelve guineas for champagne to celebrate St Andrew's Day, with another fiver for the 58th Regiment's band, which played again on St George's Day, this time without champagne. Generous payments were also made for French burgundies, brandies, truffles, cheeses and a billiard room.

It was around this period that the Ogilvies began their friendship with Wentworth. They were soon to become his active supporters in campaigns for pastoral security. He formed a special attachment for Mary, giving her a gold chain and locket she was rarely seen without. It contained a lock of his own curling, elder-statesman's hair. The gesture was worthy of Gladstone.

The Australian Club was also a handy place for picking up information. Here, early in 1839, the Frenchman passed on to Dobie, the Ogilvies and the Mylnes some valuable news.

He told them of a large, unknown river valley up north, where he and Grose both had men cutting magnificent stands of cedar. It had no other name but the Big River. Protected from the outer world by steep and rugged mountains, it possessed fertile grazing lands without a hoof on them, a warm climate, unlimited water and untouched forests. Grose thought so much of it he had already sent up a trial batch of sheep.

The response was immediate.

The club asked Gipps to make an investigation. He was reminded of the severe drought, now in its second year, the fears of a depression to rival 1828 and the almost total loss of the Liverpool Plains. The governor agreed at once. He released his deputy-surveyor-general, Captain S. A. Perry, ordering him to mount an expedition to the north coast. The proposed survey was made public by *The Sydney Gazette* on 14 May 1839.

> The steamer *King William* will leave Sydney to explore the Big River on Wednesday the 15th May, calling at Newcastle and Port Macquarie on the way out and home. Those gentlemen who wish to secure berths for the trip are requested to apply for tickets (£10 each) at the office of J. H. Grose, George Street, or at his Steam Packet Wharf.

A number of gentlemen did. Among them were Gregory Blaxland Junior, William Forster, James Mylne, and Dr Dobie, who was about to resign his health post to take up a land grant near Cassilis. Grose, who owned *Sophia Jane* as well as *King William*, did not make the trip himself, but took the precaution of applying formally for his land at Smith's Creek (later Copmanhurst) before she sailed. This was at the head of navigation, where he had cedar cutters at work already and his first sheep.

It was surprising how the Big River had remained virtually unknown. There were, after all, numerous mentions of it in official files.

Back in 1825 Port Macquarie had reported the arrival of four escaped convicts from Moreton Bay, Captain Logan's paradise for floggers on the Brisbane River. They spoke of travelling southward along coastal beaches, crossing some sixty rivers and streams, two of them very big ones indeed. One year later another runaway had described the region as being 'beautiful beyond description', while several others lived for varying periods among the Aborigines.

Most notable of these runaway convicts was Richard Craig. Some time in 1830 he reached the Big River, as it was then known among convicts, lived with a local tribe, learnt its language, slept in their bark shelters and shared their cooking fires. He survived in this fashion for more than a year.

The problem of survival was not new to him. Son of an immigrant mason, he had been sentenced to death at sixteen. It was a harsh sentence for stealing a few head of cattle. Some said his father inducted him into the art of duffing, others that he had been framed. In 1829 his sentence was commuted to seven years at Moreton Bay, a term he was skilful enough to reduce to one by escaping. Why the Aborigines later handed him over to the Port Macquarie authorities was not explained. Perhaps they tired of supporting him, or found him too much of an intruder during their food gathering cycles, hunting and ceremonial life. At all events he was spared a return to Captain Logan's barbarous settlement by volunteering to search for some lost working bullocks. Through tribal contacts and his gift of language, he found them and was assigned to a job in Port Macquarie. His tales of the Big River prompted the commandant to send a cutter north, but bad weather prevented her crossing the rocky bar at its entrance. But his information earned him a £100 reward. In 1836 he was sent down to Sydney on a ticket-of-leave, worked at Thomas Small's Kissing Point shipyard on the Parramatta River and talked so much of the Big River's cedar that both Girard and Grose sent vessels to explore it. First vessel to travel upriver was Small's 22-ton schooner *Susan*, with Craig on board as guide. She sailed fifty miles up to a large island, later named Susan Island, loaded cedar and left a party of sawyers there to establish a timber camp. This was at the end of 1837.

The cedar traders, fearing competition, kept these voyages quiet. It seemed the colony had forgotten the publicity given a decade earlier to Captain Rous, R.N., who had even taken Governor Darling on his warship's voyage of exploration up the north coast. He had been much impressed by another big river he named after the Duke of Clarence, unaware that the explorer Oxley had already called it the Tweed. Yet public interest in the northern coastline he charted had entirely lapsed until Grose announced his new venture with *King William*.

The men who cut cedar were, in their own crude fashion, the true pioneers of all these northern rivers. Wherever they took their crosscut saws and splitting irons, others followed. They were a brawling, drunken, dissipated class of men who, according to *The Sydney Gazette*, practised 'vice of the most abominable kinds'. These were centered about the rum keg and lubras. The *Monitor* claimed that these 'drunken sawyers' travelled the rivers well armed, provoked the Aborigines to reprisals and shot them when the situation became out of hand.

One week before *King William* left, Gipps gazetted new regulations. Perhaps this was a coincidence; perhaps not. These were designed to give more security to men grazing on crown lands beyond the limits of location. There were other vital clauses; notably in the powers given to nine crown lands commissioners, backed by border police, in remote areas. But, in general, it was a signal for the adventurous to go ahead.

One wonders why the Ogilvies held back. Perhaps they were too heavily committed already; or believed they could still return to Liverpool Plains. Whatever the case, Captain Perry's report was soon to impel them into action.

This time the dominant figure would be Edward. No longer would he be merely the Commander's son.

8

The Big River

The first man came from the land where the sun rises, and was called
Uli-tarra . . . In the beginning was no sea or water, except a deep well
on a mountain which Uli-tarra made. This was where the eagles
drank . . . Uli-tarra led his tribe across the mountains to fight the
tribe occupying that land. They painted themselves with red ochre
and white ochre . . .

Having conquered their enemies, they returned rejoicing, but found
the ocean had covered up what was dry land before. They crossed
safely with a long rope made of the entrails of the wild bear . . .[1]

Those who related the Big River's mythology to A. C. McDougall
endowed it with an Old Testament air. According to the Kumbainggiri
people, 'the earth was once covered with water, except at Bellira Mira,
a very high mountain which was formed by many mountains or hills
being piled one upon another. To this those of them who could, fled,
and were saved from drowning . . . This tribe believed that the earth
was once consumed by fire before it was peopled. They point to the
black or fire-burnt rocks and burnt black soil. Then the water was
divided into seas, rivers, lakes and creeks as they are at present.'

The Big River, which they called Booryimba, had been truthfully
conceived with volcanic fire, laid down in lava and ashes, flooded by
great storms and downpourings from high mountain ridges that carved
abrupt canyons, gorges, valleys and narrow, rock-choked creek beds.
Its genesis was in the eruption of a vanished volcano whose diminished
remains is the leaning triangle of Mount Warning, dominating the
Tweed River valley further north. There was also the universal legend
of a great flood. This was no fiction, even in recent times. The coming

[1] McDougall, A. C., 'Manners, Customs and Legends of the Coombagoree Tribe',
Science of Man, Vol. 3, No. 7.

of man here was of fairly recent occurrence. Perhaps twenty or thirty thousand years ago. This made the presence of Europeans at its southern approaches a matter of quite ludicrous brevity. Tribal occupation of these mountain valleys, whose semi-tropical vegetation was of astonishing lushness and density, gave them no minor claim to ownership.

Not surprisingly they were willing to defend them.

When the first runaway convicts entered this great bowl of ravines, rain forests, fast mountain streams, flood plains and winding, 250-mile river it had an estimated sixty thousand people. There were three major tribal groups here, with similar languages and material culture, each having its own sharply defined hunting and ceremonial grounds.

Had he been a more intelligent man, Richard Craig might have brought back information of immense value, for he had been reliving the prehistory of mankind. Instead he spoke only of commercial matters, prompting cedar traders to begin the destruction of both forests and native culture.

Most important were the Badjelang, north of the river, and the Kumbainggiri, to the south and west. They were complete masters of their environment.

Building low gunyahs of bark and boughs, mostly in dense scrub, they moved on every month or so as food supplies dwindled, clothed themselves in rugs, aprons and waist girdles of possum skin, teased and spun the fur into yarn, used kangaroo tail sinews as thread, made carrying bags of grass and string twisted from hibiscus bark, and dried and hardened wooden implements by passing them through fire.

'The man's duty,' Ellen Ogilvie wrote later, 'was simply to hunt and fight. Each man carried his weapons; a club (or nulla nulla), a couple of spears and three or four boomerangs, while the stone tomahawk was thrust through the twist of cane around his waist. Preparing and cooking the food, carrying all the implements, such as possum rugs, wooden bowls, water vessels, string and grass bags, with generally a baby on the top, fell to the woman's lot.'[2]

Family groups shifting camp filed silently through the tall, close-set trees and jungle scrubs. The males went first, their long hair tied on top of the head, a great protection in fighting, and necklaces of dog's teeth, cane or shells ground to an oval design, their hunting weapons thrust into cane belts; the women following with their possessions suspended from headbands of plaited dingo tails and, unlike the menfolk, devoid of ornaments, their hair cut short and naked but for an apron of

[2] Bundock, Mrs E. W., *Early Recollections of E. D. S. Ogilvie of Yulgilbar*, 1894. Archives, University of New England.

possum skin. The piccaninnies came last, usually without clothes of any kind.

The men hunted in the mornings, though seldom stirring before the sun was well up, tracked wallabies, pademelon, kangaroos with their special eyesight, sometimes following them at a run for hours, wearing them down, cornering them at last in some thicket to hurl waddies with incredible force, and rarely missing even at a distance of fifty yards. 'At certain seasons,' Ellen wrote, 'they drove the kangaroos to some place where they had fastened nets to trees and added wings of brushwood in some narrow valley. The whole tribe took part in these drives, young men being posted along the drive to take up the running. They get flying foxes by going to their camps when raining heavily, for then they will not fly. They hang by the hundreds on a tree, and by hundreds of thousands in a big camp. In very wet weather the blacks cut down a tree and return with as many as they can carry.'[3]

Thomas Bawden described how they also caught these bat-like creatures by posting men at the base of a tree with boomerangs and waddies, then sent another climbing to scare them off while the men below, waiting for the lowest point of flight, hurled their weapons unerringly.[4] They climbed trees also to rob bees' nests, to dislodge possums from hiding places inside hollows and boughs, and to seize by hand the sluggish, succulent koalas, whose needle sharp claws were no mean defence. The way these men climbed trees, whose first branches may have been sixty or so feet above the forest floor, was miraculous. First man to describe these feats was Charles Tindal. 'At Merton,' he wrote, 'the blacks cut notches in the bark for their toes; but here Charlie merely throws a vine, the thickness of a small rope, round the opposite side of the tree, and holding the ends, one in each hand, he places his feet against the trunk and runs up it faster than a man can walk on level ground. I have seen him run up a tree sixty feet high, quite perpendicular, the bark perfectly smooth with the greatest apparent ease. If he wants to use his hands on the way up, he twists one end of the vine round his leg and holds it between his toes.'[5]

Other luxuries were carpet snake, whose white meat, when roasted, tasted like fish; flying squirrels, the spiny lumbering goannas, echidnas which were rolled in clay before roasting. The brimming channels of the Big River, the swamps and lagoons all carried wildfowl in immense

---

[3] *ibid.*

[4] Bawden, Thomas, *Three Lectures on the Early History of the Clarence*, 1886–1888, republished by *The Argus*, Grafton.

[5] Tindal Family Letters, Mitchell Library, Sydney.

quantities: magpie geese, wild duck, teal, shags, cranes, ibis, brolgas, all of which were cunningly panicked into flight towards some pre-arranged ambush among reeds and shrubs. Ground birds like quail and curlew were easily knocked out with waddies as they rose in flight; the superb scrub turkey was an even easier prey on the mound incubating its eggs. Huge piles of mussel, clam and oyster shells along river banks left their records of great feasts, while swamp eels were grilled on sticks over a slow fire, and crayfish, crabs and fish of many kinds were caught either by hand or pronged spears.

They also made a kind of bread of beans stripped from the Moreton Bay Chestnut and roots of the arum species known as *congevoi*. Both beans and roots when raw were poisonous, but they roasted them, then broke them into grass bags, leaving them in running water until the slime came out, finally pounding them into paste to make flat cakes cooked over a fire.

These people could have set the Europeans an example in matters of conservation. As D. Macfarlane put it, 'Seldom would the blacks kill any living creature they did not eat . . . It was one of their customs not entirely to destroy tree life, and this principle was observed in respect to animal vitality. The Aborigine refrained from killing except what was needed for his subsistence, even venomous reptiles were immune from his weapons.'[6]

Their genius in tracking ground life was almost instinctive. More than a matter of keen eyesight, it was an ability to infer movement and direction from a displaced stone, a bent blade of grass, a broken twig or fragments of feather, fur or even saliva left on some object in passing. They cut no paths through heavy forest, or the jungles fashioned by multiple loops of lawyer vine, strangler fig and liana, yet their sense of direction never failed in this tangled, exhausting terrain through which it was often impossible to see more than a few yards. Even in times of flood they crossed rivers and creeks in fragile canoes made from a single sheet of treebark, moving at speed by paddling with tree limbs or blunt segments of wood. Every weapon and utensil they used had to be fashioned, often with considerable labour, from whatever natural materials they could find.

'If this primitive people has any special quality or virtue,' wrote R. L. Dawson, 'I should put it down as patience. With such insufficient implements as stone tomahawks, flint knives, shell scrapers and pointed sticks, imagine the infinite patience required to cut most of their living out of hardwood trees and logs, to strip bark for their shelters, and to

[6] Macfarlane, D., 'Aboriginal Races', *The Examiner*, Grafton.

Hay's portrait of Commander Ogilvie painted in 1855. Mitchell Library, Sydney.

Mary Ogilvie, painted by the artist Hay in 1855. Mitchell Library, Sydney.

shape and fashion their weapons of war and the chase. Indeed the manufacture of a stone tomahawk itself, from grinding to a sharp edge to the fixing of an adequate handle, must have been a task needing no end of patience and perseverance.'[7]

What they revealed also was that stone age man did not live by material values alone. Uti-tarra, like the Christian god, was a dweller among the stars. Their Son of Man was a great doctor named Uloorie, 'who protected their hunting grounds, cured the sick, healed the wounded in battle and decided all questions affecting the welfare of the tribe'. So wrote J. F. Small, nephew of the Kissing Point shipbuilder, who described this ancestral figure as 'a great medicine man, high priest and judge combined. This office was always held by the oldest man of the tribe. When he dies his eligible successor leaves the tribe and goes away alone to the mountains, where the spirit of his predecessor endows him with supernatural powers, and enables him to cause death without a wound or mark of any kind, this death being inflicted on anyone offending him or refusing to obey his commands.

'Next to him,' he added 'and under his control was a chief whose duty was to train the young men in war and hunting, and act as general on the day of battle. The chiefs are polygamous, being allowed a number of wives, but all the other men of the tribe must be content with one.'

Among these nomadic people all were equal, except the doctors, or as A. P. Elkin has expressed it, 'the men of high degree'. Each tribe and sub-tribe, or horde, had its own time-sanctioned areas of land which none other could enter without permission; each family had its totems which, in the form of animals or plants, defined its marrying and genetic code.

It was an essentially moral society, disciplined as Europeans have seldom known the term, with strong taboos against incest, and harsh punishments for theft, adultery or promiscuous behaviour by youths before their final initiation, which usually occurred about twenty. There was a traditional emphasis on the sharing of food: half to the man who caught it, the other portion divided among the clan.

Initiation ceremonies were designed, above all, to perpetuate ethical standards among the tribes, to enable them to live in harmony with nature and their fellows. These were barbaric, rich in drama and ceremonial power. Aliens like Richard Craig would never have been allowed to watch them; just as the women and children were not.

[7] Dawson, R. L., 'Some Recollections and Records of the Clarence', *Clarence River Historical Society Journal.*

They were as sacred as any mass; the secrets as well kept as any high order of masons.

The great tribal event was the Murrawin ceremony, the initiation of young men at puberty. After ritual preparations on the sacred bora ground, much chanting and thrumming of bullroarers, each initiate was taken from the women's camp by ochre-painted head men, and led within a circle of older men amid the flourish of firesticks and clapping boomerangs. Men rushed at him with firesticks, pointing them close to his face as if to poke his eyes out. He had to endure various physical ordeals through the night; shocks, enacted threats of violence, fearful noises, magical apparitions like a man apparently dancing in mid-air and the display of mystically carved stones and wood, said to be the work of Dharroogan, a malevolent spirit. [8]

In this atmosphere of religious awe and violence to the senses the novices were given insight into the eternal cycle of birth, maturing life, death and the hereafter. These people were not primitives in the modern, debased sense of the term. In the years to come it was the invading whitefellows that appeared savage and callow.

So long as a belief in Uli-tarra persisted, so did the morale of these inner-disciplined and hardy tribes.

Their first glimpse of modern technology must have alarmed them. Hitherto they had seen only small cutters, visibly driven by wind. Now came this astonishing *King William*, with a thin stem amidships smoking like a burnt tree, paddlewheels threshing on either side so that the thing appeared to crawl against the tide.

For the gentlemen of Sydney on board, they might have been cruising up another Amazon. Dense screens of vegetation walled in the broad, sluggish river, Tall trees were matted with creepers and strangler figs. Tangled lawyer vines reduced visibility to yards. Strident bird calls brought the jungle alive. The still air was unbearably humid. Sweat dampened their faces and clothes from the early hours.

The vessel remained at anchor for several days in the two-mile-wide estuary where, according to Captain Perry's report, the passengers had an 'interchange of civilities with the blacks, who were in a sort of temporary village.' He was much impressed with the craftsmanship of their canoes. He found them greatly superior to 'those in the neighbourhood of Port Macquarie and other places visited, their fishing nets, baskets, water vessels and utensils being constructed with peculiar care.

[8] Ryan, J. S., *Land of Ulitarra*, University of New England, 1964.

These people were delighted with being presented with some fish hooks.'

So far so good.

But the surveyor added, 'They were terrified at the first appearance of firearms. Like most savages, they were addicted to thieving. The propensity has unfortunately led to outrages on the part of the whites, the affects of which will be difficult to avert.'

They steamed sixty miles or so upriver, ran aground once, honoured Queen Victoria's birthday with a twenty-one gun salute that must have panicked both wildfowl and watchful tribesmen, they drank Our Gracious Sovereign's health in brandy, went ashore several times, examined the native pastures, had an ochre-painted group aboard to perform a corroboree, noted several sawyer's camps, including one—where Phillips and Cole had set themselves up on a grand three-quarter-mile bend—that had an improvised slipway building a brig from local timbers. Returning downriver they lost two seamen ashore, gave up the search after eight days and, just as the engineer was getting up steam to depart, sighted them on the headland of Yamba. They were surrounded by Aborigines. The watchers on deck feared trouble.

A whaleboat was sent towards the beach. Suddenly, with much yakkai-ing and laughter, two blacks began to carry the seamen out to the boat on their shoulders.

The men said that the blacks had been very friendly from the start. As Thomas Bawden, son of the steamer's engineer, later reported it, 'They gave them kangaroo and fish, and made a gunyah for them to sleep in, while all they seemed to covet was their pocket knives.'[9]

King William's passengers coveted rather more. Back in Sydney they applied immediately for a large part of the Badjelang's tribal lands. Legally, of course, they were entitled to do so. Had not a British naval captain named Phillip long ago claimed the entire continent, sight unseen for King George, having then walked on only a few square yards of it?

Within weeks the best of these potential grazing lands were gone.

Thomas Small and a brother already had Woodford Island, where their sawyers were at work. Girard's overseer, Williams, claimed a bank of the South Arm that Perry had not even sighted. Girard himself made plans to backload cattle to his cedar concession at Waterview, opposite Susan Island, where Phillips and Cole had their depot and slip. Next came the well-grassed flat country granted to the Mylnes on the

[9] Bawden, Thomas, *Three Lectures on the Early History of the Clarence*, University of New England.

north side of the river. Then Dr Dobie's Ramornie on the southern side, from Mistake Creek to the Orara River junction. Finally, James Hickey Grose's land at Smith's Flat, the head of navigation.

Grose at once made a shrewd move. He had bought eight thousand sheep at Lake George, much reduced in price because of drought, and sent them overland to the Macleay River. To take them on to the Big River he engaged the one man who knew the country. This was Craig. The ex-convict contracted to take them through the ranges for £50 and expenses, promising delivery in no more than two weeks. Dobie was quick to follow this up. His sheep were in a bad way at Cassilis. He arranged with Craig to pick them up in New England for the final hazardous journey. The Mylnes, too, bid for Craig's services, arranging for him to take delivery of their cattle.

A major expedition was beginning to take shape.

In October Gipps responded to Captain Perry's recommendations that a town site be selected for future use, preferably on that great bend opposite Waterview. A private surveyor, W. C. B. Wilson, was at once commissioned to travel north. A month later, since no one had bothered to mention Boorymiba, the governor rediscovered Captain Rous' report, naming the river after a man who had never seen it, the Duke of Clarence.

The Ogilvies must have been aware of Dobie's plans. After all, Merton was on the only road to Cassilis. The portly doctor, after his return, would have passed through at least once, probably staying the night. Besides the entire back country was discussing the newly found Clarence River, and the planned movement of stock north.

Many Hunter men had already moved into the New England Ranges in recent years.

In essence this was an extension of a migration that had been going on for some years. H. C. Semphill began it back in 1832, taking sheep from Belltrees to Nundle. E. C. Cory cut a shorter route over the steep Moonbi Ranges to form Gostwyck. William Dumaresq followed, and bought it off him. Peter McIntyre drove his sheep four thousand feet up to Guyra. Then Alexander Campbell and the Macdougalls, retreating from the Liverpool Plains, tracked the Namoi to its high source with cattle herds. By 1839 at least fifty Scots alone had stations as far north as Stonehenge, near the present Glen Innes, Thomas George Hewitt having founded the station for Archibald Boyd. They wrote into the rough survey maps names such as Dundee, Ben Lomond, the Vale of Glencoe. There was even talk of changing the region's name to New Caledonia.

All these squatters had been baulked by New England's eastern escarpment. Many had reined in their horses on some exposed bluff or basalt outcrop, staring down into sheer ravines and gorges, at precipitous drops of a thousand feet and more, at glimpses of rain forest and ripe green valleys that must have been the headwaters of coastal rivers. The grasslands up here were fertile enough; there were rushing mountain streams and good rainfall; but it was cold as Scotland in winter, much given to frosts, sometimes even to snow; and they longed for the lush, sub-tropical savannah lands below.

The problem was how to get there. It seemed as if there was no way down. This steep and fractured escarpment was country for goats; not sheep and bullock drays. One of the few that had attempted it was Archibald Boyd; probably with the aid of that shrewd bushman Hewitt. They had succeeded, with horses only, in making a laboured descent as far as the upper reaches of the Mann, later recognised to be a tributary of the Clarence. The surveyor Heneage Finch, according to his unpublished maps, had also in 1838 cut his way up to the Dorrigo Plateau, then down again through even wilder ranges to the Big River.

Richard Craig assured his sponsors that, from his experience of the region ten years earlier, he could find a safe route for their stock.

But first he had to take Grose's sheep from the Macleay. He had spoken of two weeks. It was to take him thirteen. Finding two thousand of those sheep to be scabby, he travelled up the headwaters of the Macleay with the other six thousand, struggled over the Dorrigo Range and promptly lost direction. It seems likely that he had travelled close to Finch's track, perhaps even using the surveyor's blazed trees as a guide. Running short of food, he left drovers and sheep among friendly Aborigines, then continued alone, on foot, in search of the Clarence. There he located the Phillips and Cole depot, bought rations and a pack bullock to carry them, returning for the sheep. This time he would have had his own marked trees—or possibly Finch's—to keep him on course through trackless scrubs and ravines.

On New Year's Day, 1840, he was back at the great river bend, where he borrowed a raft used by cedar-cutters to ferry his sheep across. The rest of the journey to Smith's Flat was reasonably easy.

Meantime Dobie had set out on 5 January for what was to be a five-month journey.

Arranging for his head stockman, Ben Sellars, to drive his sheep from Cassilis through Pandora Pass to the Peel River, he returned to Maitland where he had assembled a large mob of cattle. With this second party, he rode across the Liverpool Range, using the steeply winding Cedar

Brush Track to a now well-known overlander's camp named Doughboy Hollow. The two parties made their rendezvous at Goonoo Goonoo.

Only eventful occurrence en route was the bailing up of those sheep drovers in the ranges by the Jew Boy Gang. It was almost their last exploit before Edward Denny Day captured them.

Reaching Falconer's Plains, they had a long wait for Craig. They had plenty of company. Overlanders and men looking for northern lands were constantly arriving. Among these were Patrick Leslie, Gregory Blaxland Junior and his uncle, William Forster. Of these three men, Leslie alone had stock. He was travelling in a grand manner, with twenty-two convicts, five thousand sheep and three drays, which he left on McIntyre's run while he rode north with his brother to investigate the Darling Downs, hitherto explored only by Allan Cunningham. Six weeks and four hundred miles later he returned with an exuberant report of saddle-high grasses, big lagoons and rich chocolate soils. He had named his huge selection Canning Downs. 'Tried hard to induce Dobie to follow me,' he noted in his diary on 4 April. 'He remained wedded to the Clarence.'[10]

When Craig at last arrived, he rode into Falconer's with the Mylne brothers and their two cattle herds, as well as Grose's last two thousand sheep. It had been an exhausting journey already. It was nothing to the succession of ranges they had yet to cross, even though he had cut some kind of track through the more overgrown sections and set frequent axe marks on trees.

The heroic journey was later described by Thomas Bawden, whose ship's engineer father was now in charge of Dobie's two-wheeled bullock drays. Young Bawden—he was then a boy of nine—had ridden with his mother on a horse-drawn cart right through from Maitland.

'After leaving Falconer,' he recalled, 'our cattle led, the stockman in charge being Ben Sellars. Then followed the Mylne brothers' cattle, next came our sheep, then the various teams, our cart bringing up the rear. Immediately behind came Grose's sheep. These had to be kept back to avoid our sheep being infected. Many became too weak to travel, and they were at once tomahawked.'[11]

Later he described how the men's boots began to wear out. '"Shampoos" made of raw hide drawn over the feet were used as substitutes for boots. In order to clear the way for the drays the grass had frequently to be burnt. This made it very unpleasant for walking when

---

[10] Russell, H. S., *The Genesis of Queensland*, 1933.

[11] Bawden, Thomas, *Three Lectures on the Early History of the Clarence*, University of New England.

almost barefooted, and I suffered intensely when, my riding horse having been taken for some special and urgent duty, I was compelled to tramp it.'

Frank Stevens has estimated that the party consisted of at least thirty shepherds and stockmen, probably very many more.[12]

Fifty miles out they made camp on the Guy Fawkes River, beneath the 5,250-foot mass of Mount Ebor. It was a magnificent setting. On one side was open forest; on the other a fast-flowing river, which swirled abruptly over a broad apron of rocks to plunge into a smoke-blue ravine below.

Here they rested their horses and stock for a day or two. The most hazardous part of the journey was yet to come. For generations this as yet uncleared track was to be known as Craig's Line. It is fitting that it should still carry his name, even if he could by no means have been called its discoverer.

What Craig actually did was to capitalise on his earlier experience among the coastal Aborigines. Each year, as winter ended, they were in the habit of migrating to the mountain plateau. The route that Craig selected was precisely that taken by generation after generation of Badjelang tribesmen for thousands of years.

Once again, without the original owners of the land, these inexperienced Europeans could never have found their way.

[12] Stevens, F. and Sabine, J. F. *The Pathfinders*, manuscript, Mitchell Library, Sydney.

9
The Great Trek

When the Ogilvies acted, they acted fast.

A party of four horsemen left Merton towards the end of March. They rode north across Twickenham Meadows for Muswellbrook and the long stock route into the high country of New England. When Thomas Bawden saw them, they were all wearing bright red flannel shirts above their moleskins and long blucher boots. They would have provided the only colour crossing those bleached and desiccated plains. Though the long drought had broken—Bawden said the first heavy rainfall bogged their drays the very morning Dobie left Maitland—no grasses had begun to cover the bare, cracked soils. They travelled light, with a single packhorse between them. Since they had also a number of fast-running kangaroo dogs, they clearly planned to live off the country, running down or shooting whatever wild game they could.

Leader of the party was Edward, now a lean, hard-muscled young man of twenty-five. There was an adventurous set to him now, with his fiercely twisted black moustache, shaggy Dundreary whiskers and resolute, outthrust chin. 'He was a born bushman,' his nephew later wrote of him, 'one of those who can go straight to anywhere they wish.' He described him as 'a small wiry man, of great strength of character and body, a first-rate rider and very athletic. He could best even the blacks at sprint running and long distance diving.'[1]

The rest of the party consisted of his brother, Fred, an unnamed Aboriginal stockman and a third European whose identity was never made clear. Ellen and Bawden both referred to him merely as a 'new chum'. A. W. Wood believed this to have been John Harley Pagan. Yet Pagan was hardly a newcomer, having been the manager of Dalswinton for the past five years. It is more likely to have been his brother, Peter Cunningham Pagan, who had recently arrived from

---

[1] Bundock, C. W., *The Sydney Morning Herald*, 1911.

Scotland, or their brother-in-law, W. T. Evans, then managing Old Skellatar. The young red-shirted Aborigine was certainly Jimmy Cobbera, a Merton-trained stockman who was soon to figure largely in events on the Clarence.

It is hard to account for the Ogilvie's long delay in following Dobie. Or why, having made no move to join him, they now set out so belatedly on their own.

There had been reasons enough to make this long ride for several months. After all, the whole colony had been in crisis. No stock feed, no loan money available, no market worth speaking of for sheep and cattle. With the entire back country closed by the Aboriginal revolt, it was impossible for Merton, or any others, to carry the vastly increased stock numbers they had been obliged to bring back.

The final decision was probably forced on the Ogilvies by another event of tragic proportions. The death of Mary's brother William.

The cause remains a mystery. None of the family ever spoke of it. There was no known grave. Perhaps even no body. The sole record of death is an entry in the Muswellbrook register for 7 March 1840. Perhaps even the date was arbitrarily chosen. Some legal proof of death had to be given before White's estate could be wound up. Within three months his executors—the Commander, Edward and Will—swore its value to be less than £2,500. White's stock, then being held on Merton, was kept in trust until prices improved, after which the proceeds were to be sent to White's sole legatee, his mother in England.

Wood has suggested that he died somewhere out on the Liverpool Plains. There appears to be no other explanation. Such tragedies were not uncommon at this troubled period. Sometimes they were accidental; caused by a fall from a horse, becoming lost in the bush, or perishing far from a waterhole. Sydney newspapers often carried notices asking for information of 'missing friends'. Missing was usually a euphemism. All too frequently the end came from a spear thrown into some lonely hut; an ambush; a dispute over slaughtered stock.

Writing of that mass retreat from the back country in 1840, William Gardner said that 'most of the abandoned stations had two or three men killed before they left. The number of whites killed was twenty-five, and upwards of a hundred horses.'[2]

The loss of her brother affected Mary profoundly. It struck hard at the Commander, too. It was as if the land itself had risen up against him. The long drought was only a part of it. The new mood of tribal aggression reflected the unrelenting hostility of a continent that wanted

[2] Gardner, William, *North & Western Ports of N.S.W.*, 1854.

nothing of them. His personal attempts to win the friendship of the tribes, to shield them against the more ruthless of his own people had now proved futile. He and his sons had become as much a target for their hatred as the others.

In this bitter reappraisal, he would have recognised another factor. He was an ageing man. At fifty-six, he had reached an age when most of his kind might expect to live with some degree of comfort. Yet he was still an outsider; still in debt. He had been unable to give his sons security or prospects of a settled future. There is evidence that Edward in particular resented this. He wanted to be more than his father's employee, a glorified station hand. Strong-willed at any time, he determined to break away from all this parental domination. He persuaded his younger brother to cut loose with him, resolved to leave the stagnation of life at Merton forever.

They saddled up and rode after those other Hunter squatters. This was within a week or two of White being declared officially dead.

In his recollections, Bawden spoke of Craig having made camp on the Guy Fawkes River, 'near the present crossing, a short distance from the magnificent falls, where a party of men clothed in red shirts made their appearance. They did not stop at our camp, but pressing onward encountered considerable privation on their way to the Clarence.'

Presumably he meant they did not stay overnight. They could hardly have ridden past friends like the Dobies and Mylnes. Besides it was the bush tradition to dismount for at least a yarn or a meal.

What in fact happened was that Edward asked if they could join the expedition, riding down to the Clarence together. Craig refused.

'Very well,' Edward is said to have answered, 'I will go my own way and be there before you.'

The same writer, C. W. Bundock, also described Craig as 'a very surly man', who took a set on Edward from the moment he arrived.

Nonetheless, he had good reasons for refusing. His contract was to act as guide exclusively for Dobie and the Mylnes. They had an extremely difficult journey ahead. He had scabby sheep to worry about, and little enough food to take so large a party through to safety. Why should he jeopardise it for a fresh lot of men who had come in uninvited? And now two other men, Blaxland and Forster, wanted him to carry them through as well. They, too, were refused, but shrewdly waited a few days before tracking Craig right down to the Orara River by following wheel tracks and the droppings of cattle and sheep.

I suspect also that Craig's bushmanship has been overrated, and that he knew his limits. He had already been bushed on the Dorrigo, taken more than three months to reach the Big River instead of his promised two weeks. Hitherto he had been able to rely on Aborigines to guide him. Now, with all this slow-moving stock, he had to face this fantastic maze of ridges, ranges, broken gorges and swift-running rivers on his own initiative.

Nor was there even any record of Edward offering to pay.

It was a dramatic confrontation. The dour ex-convict and Edward beside his thoroughbred horse. And all around them the mournful cattle and bleat of sheep; the men in their cabbage tree hats watching; the heavily loaded drays. Above it all was the great organ music of the Ebor Falls. Minute by minute the flood of water swirled by, remorselessly, foaming and tumbling into the vast maw of the gorge. Down there was a void of silence that had brooded among tall trees, rock faces and rapids since antiquity. Beyond were the sombre profiles of scrub-dark mountain peaks and ridges and spurs that had yet to be climbed or circumvented in the unpredictable weeks ahead.

Edward swung a leg over his saddle, called to the others, rode with them past the spume and spray of the waterfall and they were seen no more.

What route they took was never stated. Perhaps they were able to pick up at least some of Craig's blazed trees. They would have tried, wherever possible, to follow the watercourses. In the denser scrubs they must have lost themselves repeatedly, turned back, tried some other slope or shoulder of the ranges. An experienced bushman like Edward would have known to keep to the ridges, but these frequently led only to some precipitous cliff and rockface, with only wind-flurried treetops below. The rain forest gullies were out of the question, so dense was their vegetation. Ride a yard or two into them, and a horse entangled itself in lawyer vine thick as a man's biceps. No man could penetrate that undergrowth, the moraines of sodden, decaying tree trunks and fallen logs. There were poisonous stinging trees, leeches in every boggy creek, mud for a horse to sink into, all the rotting, slushy, treacherous debris that had covered the forest floor for centuries.

'Food ran out,' wrote Bundock. 'They lived on what they could shoot with a muzzle-loading gun and black powder. The kangaroo dogs at first caught game, but after a time got so poor and weak they were compelled to kill them one by one, and feed the roasted flesh to the others to keep them alive. There was only one left when they finally reached the Clarence. Every bird shot was cut up and lots drawn for the different portions. If a bird fell far downhill it had to be left, as they were too weak to climb back uphill. Parrots were the principal food, with a crow and a magpie now and then. My uncle always declared that a crow was excellent eating, tasting like mutton.'

Ellen also described her brother's insistence on dividing a meal of crow as fairly as possible; drawing lots for each portion. 'The black boy, having his eyes bandaged, was made to touch which part was for which as each name was said, he who got the part with the head being envied by the others.'

According to Bawden they were also, at one stage, reduced to eating part of the dogs they killed.

If they kept at all close to Craig's Line, they would have followed the main range north, high above the Guy Fawkes and Nymboida Rivers, crossing deep cold streams like the Bo-bo and Wild Cattle Creek, which meant swimming their horses against strong currents, then down a great spur later known as Harness Cask after one of Craig's jettisoned water casks, then over the Blick's River, now known as Craig's Line Swamp, over Aitken's Crossing, the Nymboida again, then Kangaroo and Sheep Station Creeks. Somewhere, too, they must have negotiated a mountain spur so rocky and uplifted that when Dobie's bullock teams reached it, they were unable to haul up the drays, even yoked in pairs. Men had to unload those drays, hauling loads and vehicles separately from tree to tree with blocks and tackle.

Ogilvie's party would have been too saddle-weary and weakened by hunger to take much note of the wild splendour all around them. Yet, now and then, they must have dismounted on some ridgetop or exposed sheet of rock to look out at the landscapes below. The great dark sweep of mountains surrounded them still. Then, gradually, they would have become aware of a huge and vaguely defined amphitheatre taking shape ahead. The creeks, the distant threads of waterfalls, the contours of ridge and spur all pointed down towards it. And—at last—someone saw, and checked his horse, and pointed.

There it was. Remote; silvery; a glint in the sun. The Big River.

It had the curve of a boomerang laid flat on the land. Everything around it was silent and still; the abruptly rounded, intensely green foot-hills, the emerald flood flats, the dark stains of forest land, the soaring and vertical knife-thrust of a shadowy gorge from which the gunmetal river emerged. It was all hazy out there, opaquely blue as distant gum smoke. The silence was overwhelming. It was a silence without begin-ning; eternal. They looked across those distances and saw the shapes of islands in mid-stream, sandspits, small crescents of sandy beach. The long valley had the air of a natural park. Away to the north and west ridge upon ridge rose up, gloomy, sullen almost, as if impervious to man. To European man, at all events.

They rode on, certain of their direction now, guiding their horses with surer touch, approaching the lower, gentle slopes of the valley.

They were out of the thin mountain air now. They felt the air thicken around them, grow dense and humid, palpable upon the moist flesh. It was like entering a greenhouse; a rank, warm smell of jungle vegetation, the cloying atmosphere, the brilliance of orchids and flowering creepers festooning immense trees. No more silence here. From impenetrable rain forest came swelling waves of sound; cicadas in thousands, crickets, a barrage of insect life. The men rode on in a haze of exhaustion, rocking in the saddle. Their horses were coated with lather. Only when they came to the wide and brimming river did it begin to seem possible that their ordeal was over.

Here, too, they were lucky.

A schooner was anchored near the shore.

It was loading the last of a consignment of cedar for Sydney. 'Had that schooner not been there,' Bundock declared, 'they must have perished. They were too weak to get food for themselves.' All they had, Ellen wrote, was a few uneaten birds shot that morning; enough to last one more day.

It was easy then to find their way on to Phillips and Cole, where the Wilson brothers and a third surveyor were also camped. They were able to confirm landmarks and boundaries, directing the Merton men on to the last settlement at Smith's Flat. They would also have been reassured by the town site already surveyed across that three-quarter-mile channel inshore from Susan Island. With the prospect of a settlement and river port, the Clarence no longer seemed so inaccessible.

A week or so after they reached the Clarence, Craig brought his long, straggling caravan of footsore sheep and cattle into the depot. Edward had made good that boast of his at Ebor Falls. He had done without Craig's help and beaten him to the river. It was an impressive feat of bushmanship, a triumph over that implaccable barrier of mountains no one had explored. Yet Craig's achievement was even greater. With several thousand head of stock, clumsy drays and thirty or more men inexperienced in this mode of travel, he had covered the distance almost as rapidly as those free-riding, unencumbered horsemen.

It was said that he never forgave Edward for coming through first. What did it matter? Craig's Line had become a matter of legend. Craig's was the name future generations would remember.

The first great trek to the Clarence ended when Dobie's cattle were delivered to Ramornie on 16 June. The doctor's sheep and cattle had been on the track for exactly five months and eleven days. The Ogilvies were in the saddle for just over two months.

At Smith's Flat, where they passed a night at Grose's cedar camp, the party saw its first consignment of sheep grazing on the river flats, then rode into unoccupied scrub again. This was no-man's-land.

They were the first Europeans to enter it. No tracks. No survey marks. Nothing but that splendid river flowing gently between high grassy banks, or cliff faces of sun-hardened red soils, or massive black boulders piled one upon another. Sometimes the river was broad and sluggish, sometimes it narrowed between loose banks of shingle and stones, or between rock walls whose tumbled and eroding boulders must have been washed from mountain gorges in ancient times. In mid-stream, there were often long, narrow islands with strips of white sand and rock pools, but mostly overgrown with tangled tea-tree scrub whose downswept branches had been shaped by floods of great violence and velocity.

All along this moody river were formidable silences. It was all so isolated, so devoid of human occupation that a man might feel himself back among the reverberating stillness that followed Creation Day. It was not, in these aspects, a friendly river.

They refrained from following its perpetually curving course. To do so would have taken them many days. It carved its way down through sombre gorges, black cliffs, and the downswept ridges of the New England Ranges. Besides they knew that Dobie and the Mylnes had already claimed these lower reaches. They rode instead for the centre of the valley. Old hands say they went northward from the densely forested Coal Range, riding through the centre of the long valley. They soon found this to be not a single valley, but a complex of undulating hills, deep gullies, flat plains intersected by creeks so screened by tea-tree, wattle, pines and casuarinas that they could only hear the unseen rush of water over stones and shallows. Here and there they came to reedy swamps or lagoons crowded with waterbirds.

All this sunlit land around them was theirs for the taking. Mile upon mile of it. Everything they could see from the crest of each hillock as they rested momentarily in the saddle. And beyond, almost encircling this untouched little kingdom of deep grasses and permanent, interlacing streams, was the hazy blue profile of the mountains.

A long day's ride would have brought them to the main river again. It curved and looped grandly around the northern extremity of the well-grassed open country, entering another gorge. Behind it rose a steep hill, dark with scrub and blackened rocky outcrops.

They made camp here. It was a perfect site.

A perfect site for some future homestead, too. Upriver from that gorge, whose dominant hill they named Mount Ogilvie, was a broad, gently flowing reach, glittering in sun. Black swans cruised here in

North-east view from the summit of the ruggard Gibraltar Ranges over which Edward Ogilvie and his brother Fred raced in 1840. Photograph by R. Paine.

leisurely fashion. Ibis, spoonbills, herons fished along the banks. Above, flights of magpie geese arrowed towards the river's upper reaches.

They slept that night beneath an ironbark tree.

At daylight that gunmetal reach would have acquired fresh beauty. The sun rose directly behind it. The clear still water reflected the dawn sky. The far bank had emerald pastures among the shade trees. On the near side a reddish cliff swept upwards to a grassy knoll, fringed with grass trees, whose tall black stamens were like spears rising from bunched green skirts. Their camping place was sufficiently high above the river to be beyond flood level, and they could hear the swirl of water over rapids directly below. There were indications of an Aboriginal camp down there. It was clearly a traditional fishing place.

Whether or not people were then camping there was not on record. But, somehow or other, they learnt the native name for that reach. Perhaps Jimmy Cobbera made contact with them. Perhaps Edward or Fred attempted an exchange of words.

They learnt it was called Yulgilbar. *Bar* was a common term in the region for place; but the other two syllables have been variously interpreted. Ellen said they meant 'little fishes', her husband, W. C. Bundock, 'platypus'. J. S. Ryan has more recently translated it as 'a log of wood; something caught in a tree'.[3] All three were valid enough in this context. Generations of blacks caught fish in quantity here. Platypus still surface and dive under the red clay cliffs. In times of flood—and there were to be some devastating ones—logs, great branches, flotsam of all kinds were swept high into downstream trees.

All that really mattered was that Yulgilbar became Edward's instant choice for a head station.

When, some days later, they prepared to leave, the two brothers had made a fair assessment of these immense pasturelands. They decided to claim the entire floor of this long valley; on both sides of the river. The limits of occupancy would be the ranges on all sides. They esti-

[3] Ryan, J. S., *Land of Ulitarra*, University of New England, 1964.

mated their river frontage to be approximately fifty-six miles. It was clearly more than a modest sheep station they had in mind. It was a minor kingdom of several hundred square miles.

Instead of returning home along the same formidable route over which they had barely struggled through alive, Edward decided to cross the mountain range to the north-west. What he hoped to find was a less arduous track, a way to bring their sheep down to the valley.

They rode upriver, cut westward through the jumbled foothills, worked their way up the head of one valley, crossed to another. They were forced to change direction repeatedly, doubling back on themselves, climbing gradually higher. Tracing Edward's course many years later, Norman Crawford of Tenterfield wrote that 'seeing a likely gap in the distance [Hamilton's Gap] he crossed the Cataract River and made for it, and got over towards Wallangarra and went round the north side of Tenterfield [as it was soon to be]. The intervening hills prevented him from seeing the Tenterfield Plains.' Had he done so, Edward told another early settler later in life, he would have taken them up instead of Yulgilbar.

At last the party reached the blazed track Patrick Leslie had taken through the Darling Downs. They turned south. There were more wearying climbs. Huge granite outcrops loomed above them; hundreds of giant boulders poised in perilous fashion on the hillsides. They rode among silent forests, seeing nothing for days but the endless ranks of trees: blackbutt and ironbark, bloodwoods, mahogany, red cedar, blue gums, manna gums and massive hoop pines that soared like Roman columns to an interwoven canopy of dense foliage that barely allowed the sunlight to filter through.

Then they were back in the cool thin air of the tableland.

It was winter now. The air was misty. Beads of frost stayed on the ground for hours after sunrise. They rode in silence. Everything was silent. Even the horses' hooves were muffled in the dense carpet of leaves. They were still a very long way from home; a long way from their prior objective. This was the Crown Lands Commissioner's headquarters on the Beardy River. Edward wanted to reach it before any of Craig's party, or those who followed it, returned from the river.

Within a few years the hamlet of Armidale would begin to take shape around Commissioner George J. 'Humpy' McDonald's lonely hut. Meantime he and his border police camped here in solitude. He was a power in the land, nonetheless. He had to ride constantly around his vast district, interpreting and policing Gipps' 1839 Act. Without his approval no squatter could occupy a single square mile of country. The

Above: Ellen Bundock's watercolour of the original cottage at Yulgilbar on the writing case used by Theodosia Ogilvie, c. 1850.

Below: Watercolour of Castle Waters, Yulgilbar, by an unknown artist, c. 1890. Reproduced by permission of Mrs Griselda Carson.

Edward Ogilvie wrestles with Toolbillibam painted by Donald Friend. Reproduced by permission of Mrs W. O. Anderson and the artist.

area he supervised extended from the coast to the western limits of New England; from Port Macquarie right through to the Darling Downs.

The act decreed that no man could own or even lease the land he selected. He was issued with a licence to depasture stock; and that was all. This could be withdrawn at any time, whenever the commissioner felt that he had reasons for doing so. Nor was there any right of appeal. The licence holder was told he must not cut down a single tree, except for his own use; he must not harbour convicts or felons, nor store liquor for sale or profit, keep no native women in his dwellings, allow his servants to misbehave, nor commit any injury or offence against the Aborigines. This last clause was a crucial one. It was to be tested again and again, compromising McDonald's successors.

The commissioner was also entitled to withdraw any licence if its holder failed to give a half-yearly account of his stewardship. This included regular reports on the quality of his stock, and the amount of land left idle or insufficiently developed. To pay for the commissioner and his mounted police a half-yearly levy was made on each squatter's land. This was calculated on the basis of a halfpenny a head for sheep, three halfpence for cattle, and threepence per horse. The licence itself cost £10 a year.

Not surprisingly, the squatters were soon campaigning against these costive restrictions. Their principle complaint was that the act gave them no security of tenure. With the risk of losing grazing licences at any time, perhaps at the whim of some dogmatic official, they could hardly be expected to develop their runs properly, put up permanent buildings or plan for the future at all.

Meanwhile Edward filed his claim with McDonald. He had it registered in his father's name, putting himself down merely as superintendent. Why he gave so unimaginative title to it as Swanlea went unexplained. It could only have been derived from those black swans nobly cruising the Yulgilbar Reach.

It was a triumphant homecoming to the Hunter. They had been absent a long while. Nothing had been heard of them for more than four months. At Merton no one even knew if they had won through to the Clarence at all. Now they were back with news of great tracts of unoccupied lands. Subject, of course, to the commissioner's pleasure.

Relief, excitement, fresh hopes. One can imagine the reactions at Merton. The suspense was over; the long dead weeks of anxiety; the uncertainties as to what to do next. They could even forget now about the Liverpool Plains; at least for a while.

Probably the brothers remained at home for a month or so. It had

been an exhausting journey. Edward especially had felt it. 'The responsibilities as well as the anxiety and rough life told on his health for some
time,' Ellen wrote. Yet they had not all that much time to spare. As
soon as possible they had to be on the road again. A condition of these
licences was that runs had to be stocked within six months; or some
newcomer could simply jump the claim. And the Clarence was well
over four hundred miles away.

Towards the end of 1840 they began their preparations. They had to
select sheep in good enough condition to travel the great distances,
muster and cull them, and shear them, before they left. Eventually
they drafted twelve thousand sheep for the journey. They also took
three heavily loaded bullock drays.

Two other men arranged to travel with them, also taking sheep. They
were Peter Cunningham Pagan and C. R. Haly, representing William
Tucker Evans, who intended to travel north with his wife, by sea, later.
Though Pagan and Evans yet had no licence, they had decided to take
a chance in forming a new Clarence run in partnership. Edward doubtless assured them there was plenty of land available.

Talk of the Clarence had become widespread up and down the
Hunter Valley. Others were preparing to leave for the north as well.
There were flocks moving up that New England stock route every few
weeks. A. W. Wood has estimated that more than a hundred men left
the Hunter between 1838 and 1840.

Another who considered going, but could not, was Wellington
Cochrane Bundock. Here was another naval officer's son who had come
to Merton, arriving to learn sheep-breeding in 1836. He came with
letters from Mary's old friend, Mrs Marryat, as well as gifts for Fred
from his godfather, the now well-established author Captain Marryat.
Soon afterwards he took up a nearby block of his own; but at the very
worst time. In the existing economic climate, he found it impossible to
dispose of either land or stock. Edward would no doubt have noticed
that Bundock was also giving his sister a great deal of attention.

The final assembly point was Terniax. All told, fifty-two men travelled
with the long columns of sheep from Merton and Dalswinton. In charge
of three heavily loaded bullock drays was one Robert Smith, who had
arrived a year earlier with his family and letters of introduction to the
Ogilvies. Smith's affairs were complicated. Some years earlier he had
made a runaway marriage with the daughter of a Kentish baronet. On
reaching Sydney with a daughter and two sons, the lady had been so
alarmed by the sight of a sailor falling overboard, she had thrown up
her hands and promptly lost her handbag, money and papers in the
harbour. Since she was also about to give birth to twins, her husband

left her in Sydney, taking the two boys on to Merton. Now he was obliged to take them on this long overland trek as well.

One marvels at the way Robert Smith set off on so demanding a journey with one son aged ten, the other only seven. They must have been unusual lads, for they were said to have made themselves very useful with the horses and bullocks. There was also a married couple from Ireland.

Edward guided the horsemen, sheep and drays up the headwaters of the Namoi from Terniax, up the western escarpment of the Moonbi Range, moving them from one previously noted creek to the next until, beyond Ben Lomond, they could follow the snow-fed Beardy Waters to the northern limit of the high country. Winter had started early.

'It was so cold,' wrote Ellen, 'that the sheep ran most of the way through New England trying to keep warm, and they were disinclined even to stop and eat sufficiently.' All kinds of disasters occurred, she added. In the steep ranges dray shafts broke under the strain on several occasions. Once Edward had to fell a tree and cut a fesh pole for one of the drays. Beyond Tenterfield, according to an early settler, W. S. Cowan, they 'had to come down a very steep mountain where, I believe, the dray had to be lowered by ropes.'

Ellen also recorded some strange behaviour by that Irish couple. Among their possessions was a weighty box. 'After many accidents, breaking of shafts, etc., the brothers found it necessary to overhaul the loading to see what could be left behind. In the first place dropping many of their own things. Then they proceeded to open the Irish couple's box, to which they most reluctantly consented. It was found to contain many large stones put in to give themselves importance as possessing much luggage.'

From its beginnings, the trek must have taken at least two months, most of it in wintry conditions. They reached the Clarence through an upland valley known to the Aborigines as Tabulam. The river was narrow here; but it was good country, open and flat. On Edward's advice, Pagan and Haly decided to stop here, dispersing their sheep on each side of the stream. The Ogilvies went on. They came within sight of that long reach at Yulgilbar towards the end of April. The exact date is unknown. First evidence of their occupation is the sheep journal they kept, beginning on 1 May 1841.

But before that, accompanied by Robert Smith, they made another quick journey back to Merton. They rode north again with Mrs Smith, her daughter and the one surviving twin.

In the matter-of-fact climate of the times no one ever mentioned how two women and five children, one an infant, managed to adapt to the crude and perilous conditions of this isolated valley.

10

Abode of Demons

The Ogilvies had been well advised to make a quick return to the Clarence. In the brief interval between those two expeditions all the remaining land had been occupied.

Captain Crozier had formed a new run on their southern boundary, naming it Gordon Brook. This one-eyed naval veteran—his sound eye, Bawden noted, was a 'piercer'—had already gone home to Sydney, leaving a cousin in charge, Gordon Sandeman; hence the station's name. West of the river Robert and Charles Walker had taken up Newbold; a grand sweep of hilly country on the eastern flank of the Clarence. Those who had followed Craig down from New England had established runs at the foot of the now celebrated Line; Gregory Blaxland on Nymboida, Forster on Geergarrow, and Thomas Coutts on the subsequently notorious Kangaroo Creek.

The Mylnes, who had now named their station First Falls, after the rapids where *King William* went aground, had rewarded Richard Craig by employing him as head stockman.

At Tabulam, Pagan and Evans shortly found themselves in trouble. Having just spread their flocks along both sides of the river, they were confronted by two newcomers with travelling cattle. The land, they insisted, was theirs. They had a licence from Commissioner McDonald to prove it. Messrs Clay and Stevenson, it appeared, had first reached Tabulam soon after the Ogilvies left for Merton. They registered their claim, returned south for stock and sent up supplies by schooner to the Clarence. It was their bad luck to have arrived just two weeks after their six-month term of grace expired. Fortunately they proved to be reasonable men.

'As, at that time,' Bawden wrote, 'the whole of the country to the eastward was unknown, Pagan and Evans guaranteed to find them an equally good run, providing that they gave up all claim to Tabulam.

To save litigation this was accepted. On the following morning the party mounted their horses and proceeded eastward. From the top of a high range they traced the course of the Richmond River [then unnamed], and saw some of the plains along its banks. They then drove their cattle on to the Richmond River, and took up the first station there at Tonki.'[1]

They named their cattle run Cassino.

The next problem was to find their supplies. They had come to rest a mighty long way from the Clarence. To reach what was now called the Settlement, behind Susan Island, they had to cut a new track through cedar scrubs and mountains, and eventually located the schooner up at Copmanhurst. The charges they had to pay—for sea freight, storage and carting by bullock dray back to Cassino—were astronomic. Their flour alone, said Bawden, cost them £102 a ton. Pioneering these distant regions could be a costly enterprise.

Costly in terms of human lives as well.

From the moment of arrival these new settlers had been treated as invaders. The Aborigines, when not openly hostile, watched them with suspicion, appearing frequently on the runs as men set about building huts, yards and tracks through the bush.

William Forster was the first to feel their enmity. He had not even unloaded his bullock dray on Nymboida when his party was attacked. One man was fatally speared; another had a spear pass between his shirt and flesh, losing his hat brim to a boomerang. A third, having no time to pull the ramrod out of his musket, fired it right through the attacker's body. The dray was plundered, while sugar and flour, not then known to be edible, were scattered over the countryside. Some days later, when Major Oakes brought a police party up from the Macleay, he was attacked by his own native guides, whom he pursued into the ranges, shooting several of them.

Blaxland, with rueful humour, renamed his run Pandemonium, which in the original Greek meant 'the abode of all demons'. Forster, after those harrowing experiences, called his Purgatory.

Yet it was no moment for men to amuse themselves with classical allusions. An explosive mood was developing. The flashpoint came at Tabulam. 'At this time,' Bawden remarked, 'every man carried a musket wherever he went.' While Pagan's workers were struggling to haul equipment across the river, someone reported the theft of blankets outside an unfinished hut. Impulsively Pagan ordered them to ride after the thieves.

[1] Bawden, Thomas, *Three Lectures on the Early History of the Clarence*, University of New England.

'They immediately started on the tracks, but without ammunition, except what was in the guns,' Bawden continued. 'Coming over a hill, they found themselves within two or three hundred yards of the blacks' camp. Mr. Pagan, being in advance, immediately fired the only shot he had, and then seized the gun of one of the men who accompanied him and fired it also. The party then turned away when a blackfellow, who was concealed behind a tree, threw a boomerang which killed Pagan. Upon reaching the hut, the whole party, consisting of eight men, got all the sheep into one flock, and barricaded themselves in the hut, although their number was ample to drive off 500 blacks.'

Pagan's body was left in the bush.

Next day one of the men rode for the police post just set up at Red Rock, five miles downriver from Smith's Flat. It was an eighty-mile journey, and took two days and a night. Major Oakes saddled up immediately and led a party of eight horsemen north. Among them were one of the Mylnes, Robert Walker of Newbold, Grose's manager Alfred Lardner, and some ex-convict police. They reached the Ogilvies the first night, camping on Yulgilbar Reach.

Here they heard that a hutkeeper had been murdered out in the hills. This was a young Englishman, who had been asking to leave for a long while, only to be put off by Edward.

Oakes swore in everyone present as special constables, led them on a fruitless chase through the back country, flushing out nothing but emus and kangaroos, then made for Tabulam.

They arrived to find Pagan's men still barricaded in that hut. Their attackers had long ago vanished. For three days they followed tracks through the bush until both men and horses were exhausted. Edward then rode back to Swanlea for reinforcements. Finally Oakes was given a report of a tribal party seen building gunyahs some miles out from Yulgilbar. Assuming these to be the killers, Bawden wrote, Oakes called a conference beside that tranquil reach. He continued:

> It was decided as no one knew the ground well, that they should start at 3 a.m., one section proceeding down the river bank, the other inland within hail of each other; another to the head of the valley where the blacks had been seen; the intention being for the river party to drive the blacks up the valley, and the valley party to intercept them. At daybreak they were taken by surprise, but took to the river. On the valley party reaching the scene, several of the blacks were seen to have been shot, while a New Zealander, the police flogger, tomahawked all he could get at—young or old. Nothing was found in the camp belonging to the murdered man.
>
> One of the policemen and two of Pagan's men then went to follow up the tracks of another party of blacks. On the second morning

suddenly rounding a cliff on Rocky Creek, they found themselves between two camps. The policeman dashed through, firing right and left with a double-barrelled gun, while his companions bolted and reported the policeman killed. Much to their surprise he returned to the station next day, having single-handed driven off the blacks and recovered Pagan's hat out of the camp. Such is the difference between a brave man and a coward. At this time, such was the dread of firearms among the blacks, there is little doubt that three determined men, who did not fire except in self-defence, would have been able to disperse 100 blacks.[2]

Instead of dispersing them, these men had given way to desperate panic. According to Major Oakes' rather confused report, eight Aborigines were killed. When their comrades fled to Ramornie, Dobie's homestead was attacked three nights in succession and a hundred and fifty sheep slaughtered. Oakes then wrote of a great number of Aborigines discovered on the Orara River nearby. 'A cordon was formed during the night, hemming the camp in, with the river behind it. At a given signal at daybreak, the camp was rushed and men, women and children were shot down indiscriminately. Some took to the river, and were shot as they swam. Their dead bodies subsequently floated down past the Settlement.'

An appalling fact was soon to be revealed. Had McDonald troubled to ask the right questions, he might have discovered that the Swanlea hutkeeper had not been murdered by Aborigines at all. 'It turned out afterwards,' Bawden said, 'that the man was probably killed by a fellow servant. But, as any proceedings would have entailed a journey to Sydney, the matter was not investigated, and the suspected person leaving the district soon afterwards, no more was heard of it, and no inquiry held.'

It was the tragedy of Myall Creek all over again.

The sins of the whitefellow had been visited once more on black brother. Yet no one thought either regret or compensation necessary. They might have been so many animals they had disposed of. Crime was to be compounded with crime; the tension increased; hatred added to hatred. Edward said later that the Aborigines had been so terrified by those manifestations of white violence that it was nearly two years before the least contact could be made with them. The first parley was one that he brought about; under great difficulty.

Even Pagan's death could have been avoided, had men kept their heads. As Bawden described it later, drawing on statements made by Lardner, 'a well-known blackfellow for many years about Yulgilbar,

[2] Bawden, Thomas, *Three Lectures on the Early History of the Clarence*, University of New England.

known as King Billy, who was present at Pagan's murder, said that Pagan was very stupid to come too near the blacks, and that the blacks kept making signs to him to go away.'

They buried Peter Cunningham Pagan near the river where he died. He had been only thirty-two.

At this stage the Ogilvies must surely have begun to wonder was this whole brave venture worth their while. They had lost more than a close friend. They had lost a comrade in their joint endeavour to make something of this land; a man who believed, as they did, that humane principles and racial understanding were possible. And in one uprush of uncontrolled impulse, they had discarded reason and set every man's life in jeopardy. Perhaps they remembered also, with black irony, that it had been Pagan's uncle and namesake who had first taught them tolerance towards the Aboriginal race. Now men of that very race had killed the nephew.

Almost as a postscript to his official report, Oakes mentioned a very different response by these men. Regrettably he did not elaborate. He ended his account of the affray at Ramornie with the simple statement that 'six children were brought back to be civilised'. Exactly what was intended no one made clear; with one exception. A young boy named Pundoon (the Wallaby) was discovered by Edward, hiding in a hollow log. He put him on his saddle and rode home.

The lad's mother had presumably died in the shooting. There was no further reference to her. Edward took him back to the two bark huts he and Fred had built for themselves by the reach, treated him with kindness and took him everywhere he went. Towards the end of the year, Pundoon even travelled down to Merton with him. He was still there more than a year later, when Charles Tindal arrived. In a letter home, he wrote, 'there is a wild black down from the Clarence River. He was taken prisoner by the Ogilvies some time back. He cannot yet speak a word of English; but he is very fond of Edward, who speaks their language well.'[3]

On Edward's own admission, this was his chief reason for adopting the boy. He recognised that the key to mastering these wild tribes was to learn their language. Ellen said he spoke it fluently in a remarkably short time, and even produced a grammar. No trace of this has since been found.

Edward was a very determined man.

Meantime the situation remained so tense that neither man nor stock could be dispersed over the run. 'Huts were robbed,' said McFarlane,

[3] Tindal Family Letters, Mitchell Library, Sydney.

A boy like Pundoon. Photograph by J. W. Lindt, Grafton. Mitchell Library.

'sheep stolen and men killed, and it was unsafe to go out in the open run alone.' The Ogilvies kept their flocks near the reach, grazing them on one side of the river only. They were also short of shepherds. A number of them had cleared out altogether, escaping down to the Settlement, where they stowed away on schooners returning south with cedar. The first census, taken towards the end of 1841, revealed only twenty-nine men at Swanlea; another twenty-two on Tabulam.

Nor was it only tribal enmity the Ogilvies now had to endure. Dingoes bred in great numbers throughout the hills, coming down at nights, sometimes even by day. One has only to read the faded entries in their first sheep journal, with its damp-stained cloth cover and pages eaten by insects. Day after day this was written up, laboriously, in a spidery, rather unformed hand, probably Fred's. Though its notes were restricted to sheep numbers, dispositions, and the names of shepherds, it reveals something also of the hazards and frustrations of that period. It was a catalogue of woes. The first date was 1 May 1841. Page one carried the ominous heading 'Deaths'.[4]

The first entry lists the loss by one Jas. Murphy of five unmarked and eight marked lambs. All told, fifty-five sheep died in that one month, many of them from attacks by dingoes.

Because of the emergency, flock sizes were then unduly large. On two successive days, for instance, the journal records, 'Counted to Robby 2,356 sheep; to Moyle 2,470.' In June the complete tally was 10,555 divided into eight separate flocks, each with its own shepherd. This figure was nearly two thousand less than they had arrived with six months earlier. By the end of July another 180 sheep were dead, including thirty-two lambs in Murphy's flock on the one day. Frequently wild dogs were mentioned. At other times no cause of death was given. So high a mortality rate must have worried them greatly. It could have been due to cold snaps, the negligence of shepherds or perhaps poor pastures. Unless another entry for July was any pointer: 'served 12 balls and powder for every man to last them six months'. Whether these items were for self-defence or use against dingoes was not explained. Edward had a firm policy, making it clear to the Aborigines that any shepherd molesting them would be punished; and vice versa.

It was at this time that Major Oakes decided to add to their troubles.

When McDonald found his large area too difficult to administer, Oakes was appointed Crown Lands Commissioner for the Clarence and Richmond only. His headquarters remained at Red Rock, so named for the red cliffs on the river's southern bank, opposite his police huts. Some time in mid-1841 he began his first tour of inspection, officiously aware of his absolute powers. In cases of boundary disputes, grazing rights, the treatment of workers or Aborigines, his instant decisions allowed for no right of appeal.

One can picture the former police major, from E. M. Curr's description of a similar official, as he rode at the head of his 'cortege' across Swanlea's pastures. Curr wrote of sighting the Commissioner on a magnificent chestnut, followed by a mounted orderly, sergeant and three border police troopers, variously armed with pistols, carbines and a cavalry sabre. 'The Commissioner's horse was likewise accoutred in

[4] Yulgilbar Sheep Journal, Mitchell Library, Sydney.

the manner of a cavalry charger, and his dark green costume, fixed spurs, Hessian boots, blue cap and braided band were decidedly military.'[5] Any conflict between settlers, he added, 'which in later times would have taken a judge, with his jurors, barristers, witnesses and attaches of the court a week to dispose of—Bah! the Commissioner settled them in half-an-hour, probably hearing only one of the claim- ants, and sometimes neither. I should say that our particular Commis- sioner kept few records of his official acts, if any; and never caused any marks to be made on the trees or the land in connection with boundaries. Indeed I fancy he considered things of this sort mere red tape nuisances; his custom in the case of disputes being to hear but short statements, giving his decision in a few words, change the conversation, light his pipe and ride away.'

Something of the kind must have happened beside Yulgilbar Reach. In this case Oakes' opinions were challenged. He was obliged to defend his attitudes in a letter sent to the Colonial Secretary, E. Deas Thompson, in Sydney during August.[6] A complaint had been made by William Ogilvie, as the legal licencee of Swanlea. Oakes was accused of having favoured James Mylne in a disagreement over their common boundary.

Oakes replied that Edward claimed more land than he was entitled to, even had he possessed five times as many sheep. 'His claimed run extends 56 miles on both sides of the river, at 196,000 acres. The land in dispute is on the opposite side of the Clarence from Ogilvie's head station, 22 to 25 miles away. Ogilvie once had sheep there, but removed them when they began eating poisonous herbs.'

Furthermore, the commissioner wrote that shepherds had complained of being given very poor quarters. They were only bark gunyahs, not proper huts, giving inadequate protection against the weather and marauding blacks. He had even considered withdrawing Ogilvie's licence altogether.

Oakes had chosen to ignore two facts. The licence to that huge area, rightly or wrongly, had been legally granted by Commissioner McDonald. As for the shepherds' housing, this was only a temporary arrangement. Once the Aboriginal emergency passed, flocks would again be sent into the back country, where Edward planned to build more durable timber huts. At all events, the licence was not withdrawn.

But official records give no indication as to who kept that disputed tract of land.

[5] *Reminiscences of a Squatter in Victoria*, Melbourne, 1883.

[6] Oakes, report to Colonial Secretary, 17 May 1841.

Though Oakes had also reported that the whole region was in a state of near disaster, the Ogilvies not only kept their main flocks alive, but even sent wethers in good condition down to Merton. In June the journal noted that they 'started Murphy with 508 wethers from Malmut's flock and 639 from Barry's to the Hunter'. Whether they were sent on that rugged five-hundred-mile journey for fattening or for Sydney's mutton trade was not recorded. A year later, other flocks were travelling in the reverse direction: 'added all the yearlings which came from Merton to Barry's flock, making his number 1,862. Total from Merton 576.'

Despite the isolation, those two runs were being shrewdly worked in a joint operation.

Isolation. This was the critical factor. Apart from a few distant neighbours like the Walkers, Mylnes, Gregory Blaxland—Dobie was temporarily overseas again—the two brothers rarely saw any but their own reluctant labourers. Nor was there much pleasure in rare visits to the Settlement. The embryo town now had three stores, an inn and a shipping wharf; very little else. On the south bank, three-quarters of a mile across the strongly flowing Clarence, a second settlement was growing around Phillips and Cole's depot. One or two teamsters were now in business, but they did not travel far upriver. If Swanlea needed supplies of any kind, someone had to ride down to Smith's Flat, then take Tom the Boatman's two-masted ketch into town, which came to life only when the cedar-gangs were in for a spree. On the north bank Bentley's store was already becoming notorious.

'The scenes to be witnessed when cedar cutters brought down their rafts were beyond description,' Bawden remembered. 'It was no uncommon sight to see a cask of rum rolled out, and spirit ladled by the pannikin full. Men became raving or hopelessly drunk. The person who refused to drink at an orgy such as this was abused in the most ruthless manner, even to the extent of personal violence.'

It was an extension of the convict's traditional self-immolation and despair; a death wish almost. These transported townsmen hated this alien land, hated the bush, its indifference and hostility. Many free men were likewise to become demoralised with cheap Bengali rum. They drank themselves insensible, totally unable to adapt to the harsh conditions as peasantry, had there been one, would have done. The alcoholic stupors were the other face of the pioneering coin. Alexander Harris summed it up perfectly by writing that 'after earning their money like horses, they spent it like asses'.

It was hardly the atmosphere to impress Aborigines with the virtues of a white civilisation.

Yet officialdom remained supremely optimistic. Late in 1840 Gipps had forwarded Captain Perry's report to London, adding enthusiastic touches of his own. It was, he wrote, 'a promising field for the employment of capital in agricultural and commercial pursuits. In the lower part of the district alone there is room for a large body of industrious immigrants, and, such is the nature of the soil, that little apprehension is entertained for the labour that may be bestowed on the cultivation of wheat, the maize, the vine, tobacco, sugar, indigo and many other articles of consumption, and even of export.'[7]

This emphasis on immigrants was new to the colony. Transportation had now ended. The age of the convict was over; or nearly so. Its remnants would still provide labour for years to come, But, when the last convict ship reached Sydney in 1840, both administrators and pastoralists had to begin thinking in terms of free settlers; which meant paying labour for the first time.

This remained scarce for some years in the more remote districts.

Even Hunter squatters were hard put to it finding the class of men they needed. The Commander had made this clear when giving evidence before the Legislative Council's immigration committee in 1838. 'I have to pay a carpenter two pounds a week,' he said. 'Mechanics are impossible to find. If ten thousand labourers were imported for the next two years, they could find work. This farm has subscribed to 22 Chinese labourers. Another to 22 Indian coolies.'

Subscribed they might have done. Those Asians did not arrive. William Ogilvie was one of 772 pastoralists who had signed a petition to the Colonial Office, calling for the import of cheap, reliable workers to replace the outmoded convicts. The new Pastoralists' Association, formed to campaign for this scheme, met strong opposition from free immigrants, who had the governor's support as well. Coolie labour, said Gipps, 'would tend to deteriorate the community'. He had no regrets when the Association's remittance—treasury bills worth £1,500 —somehow went missing in Singapore.

Nor were those recruits needed. The large increase in free migrants from Britain in 1838-40 unexpectedly met the demand. But it did so for one reason only. There was just no demand for labour. The colony had entered another depression. This was the second economic collapse in little more than a decade.

Once again there were dismal prospects to be discussed at Merton. Edward and his brother made another long journey from the north

[7] Governor's Despatches, 1840. Mitchell Library.

towards the end of 1841. It was their first visit for twelve months. The occasion was Ellen's marriage.

The wedding took place in the homestead on 3 December. The groom was the former jackeroo Charles Bundock. The Commander and his sister-in-law, Susan Glennie, acted as witnesses.

It must have been a grand reunion. The clan had become scattered. All of them must have noted the changes that year had brought. It had been a rugged, toughening period on the Clarence. Both Edward and Fred would have matured, grown leaner perhaps, more tense. They, too, would have found their parents beginning to age. In another year Charles Tindal was to describe William as being 'still very active and busy, riding up and down all kinds of places', but 'he stoops a little, even if he looks as though he has always stooped'. He found him also 'a very quiet little man when his wife is present, only correcting, prompting and acting as general reference. She is very clever and entertaining.'

For those who did not know her well, Mary tended also to be somewhat intimidating. There is a family story of her at that wedding. Late that evening, no doubt under the influence of champagne, the atmosphere became gay. One of the younger men was said to have told Bundock, 'You know, old man, you're marrying the wrong one. The great old girl here is her mother. Worth much more than her daughter.'

Mary appeared behind them. She had her special look on. It froze the two young men.

'The old girl is perfectly happy with the way things are, thank you,' she said, 'And it's time you young gentlemen were in bed.'

By 1842 the economic trough had deepened. The causes were again embedded deeply in reckless capitalistic practices none seemed to understand; either in Britain or the fast-spending antipodes. The land and stock boom of the late 1830s had attracted more overseas finance than anyone could readily invest. At the same time the once booming wool prices in London had collapsed, due partly to the recent drought. Again the vast increase in sheep and cattle had glutted the market, for there was just not enough population to consume all that mutton and beef. Horses, which had fetched up to a hundred guineas, could hardly be sold for as many shillings. Sheep crashed from sixty shillings a head to one shilling, even with the wool on its back worth another eighteen-pence. One landowner sold his nine thousand sheep at a shilling a dozen. In New England another disposed of his station, with five thousand head on it, for £505, and the wool clip thrown in.

The most reckless speculation had been in the expanding Port Phillip district, where land had continually changed hands at fantastic profits and squatters lived like Persian kings.

While the land boom lasted, thousands had sent overseas for luxury goods, built grand houses, imported costly furniture and drank only champagne. French champagne, wrote Judge Therry, was even the common drink of bullock drivers, who called it 'the gentleman's grog', and quaffed it in pannikins outside wayside shanties and inns. The reaction, as Therry described it, was disastrous. He wrote, for instance, of the glut in imported pianos, 'soon tuneless and silent; splendidly appointed carriages, soon sacrificed for a mere trifle at auction, and converted into rows of hackney coaches in Sydney' and such shiploads of fine wines that the Governor in Council said 'the whole country, almost a hundred miles around Melbourne, was strewn with champagne and porter bottles.'[8]

Though Gipps blamed the banks and moneylenders for the crisis, especially through their improvident, high-interest loans and mortgages without security, Therry held him to be equally blameworthy. The major question, to his mind, was the Land Fund.

The fund, based on the proceeds of Crown Land sales, was the principal means of financing the shipment of immigrants to swell the labour force. By 1840 this had risen to £300,000 a year. Next year it was only £85,000; in 1842 a mere £17,000. There was just no money in the government treasury. The damage had been done by the governor's sharp increase in the upset price of land. Back in Bourke's day the minimum selling value had been fixed at five shilling an acre. In 1838 Gipps raised it to twelve shillings; three years later to a pound.

His action, though he did not say so, may also have been a subtle device for checking the desperate inflation. How else was anyone to combat this appalling spectacle of greed? When challenged by the squatters, Gipps asked publicly whether anyone had the right to assume that Australia was destined to become no more than a gigantic sheep-walk. He saw no reason why pastoralists alone should be coddled. Who knew, sometime in the future other uses might be found for the immense lands they had monopolised.

All that his unpopular views achieved, of course, was to unite every landowner, whatever his status or political beliefs, into determined opposition. The Ogilvies, hitherto regarded on the Hunter as 'revolutionaries', were now allied on this issue at least with the most rigid Tories. The economic slump, after all, threatened them as well, despite their canny management.

[8] Therry, J., *Reminiscences of Thirty Years in New South Wales and Victoria*, London, 1863.

11

Leave Us the Hills

Back on the Clarence these two young men must often have longed
for the companionable warmth of Merton. For people of their own
kind, and the company of women. It was a lonely and totally masculine
scene.

The silence along that smooth-flowing river was profound. Only the
soporific sound of those rapids downstream, the sad calling of crows;
the leisurely movement of herons and cranes fishing; the bleating of
sheep, which were still being closely watched near the reach. At night-
fall Edward and Fred returned to the two cramped huts they had built
side by side. Their walls were of pisé, and roofs thatched with dried
grass. They stood on high land near the rapids, where currents swirled
fiercely through divided channels, surest measure of high rivers or low.

Of the native inhabitants there was never a sign. They seemed to
have abandoned the region.

The same mood was apparent right down the river. An uneasy,
brooding tension overhung the country; even the Settlement itself.
In mid-1842 two surveyors, reprimanded for having spent six useless
months in town, revealed the widespread fear of roaming the bush.
It was still unsafe for any but the most wary travellers. Now and again
fresh reports came in of raids, thieving and reprisals. Frontier life had
resolved itself into a contest of muskets versus spears. It was not enough
to dismiss these unrepentant tribes as deadly savages. They had no
conception of the whitefellow's attitudes to property, especially when
these disputed their right to ownership. Besides they had 'tasted the
flesh of the monkey', as the newcomers referred to their vulnerable
sheep; they had learnt that the sugar and flour they pilfered were
edible loot.

Edward was determined to end this impasse. The brothers must have
discussed it often over their monotonous suppers of mutton and

damper, or when riding tensely around their flocks. Unless some kind of dialogue could soon be opened, it was clear they had little hope of developing their lands. The problem was how to make contact.

The chance came at the end of May.

It was a dramatic confrontation. Edward himself wrote a moving account of it. He wrote it in the form of a long letter to *The Sydney Morning Herald*, which considered it important enough to publish in full. Dated 4 June, the letter described a meeting some days earlier with a party of Aborigines somewhere in the back country. Edward sent it, he wrote, 'in the hope that it may tend to remove the belief that these people are an utterly irreclaimable and ferocious set of people.' They were, he insisted, 'of very unrevengeful spirit', not at all the 'wild beasts those who knew nothing of them had come to believe'. He went on:

> Since the hostile encounters about a year ago, they have rarely shown themselves, but have kept among the mountains, always making off as fast as possible if accidentally seen. Though they have occasionally crept unobserved upon the huts, and carried off the shepherds' blankets and axes. I had several times tried to bring them to a parley, to establish a better understanding, but always without success. Until having seen a smoke rising amongst the hills, some miles distant, my brother and myself mounted our horses, and set out to make another attempt. After clambering about the hills some time, we entered a narrow valley. We suddenly came in sight of a camp situated upon a small flat, surrounded on three sides by a creek, and backed by a mountain.
>
> Setting spurs to our horses, we galloped across the creek into the camp. We found it untenanted, however, except for a woman with an infant at the breast, and a child apparently about four or five years old. On our approach they fled up the mountain, the woman carrying her child astride her neck.
>
> As we neared them they cried out in great fear. The woman took the infant from her shoulders, and clasping it to her bosom, threw herself upon her knees and bowed her face to the ground, thus concealing and protecting her little one with her body. The other child crouched at her side, and hid its face in the grass. I dismounted, and taking the child by the shoulders, raised her face from the ground, but she set up such a terrible squalling, that I let go again, when she dropped quite stiff and stark into her former position, and was again silent. I sat down near them, and having some knowledge of their language, which I had gained from a young boy Pundoon who was taken in one of the forementioned encounters, and who has since remained with me, I addressed the woman, telling her not to fear, as we had no hostile intentions, and would not harm her. After a time she raised her head and looked steadfastly at me. She seemed to have been reassured, for she began to speak.
>
> She first said that she was afraid of the horses, and asked if they

would not bite her. We told her that they are harmless and lived upon grass; upon which she seemed to lose all fear, answering all our questions, and saying a great deal more that we could not understand. We learned from her that the men were hunting upon the surrounding mountains. After a great deal of shouting and calling in which the lady joined— though not until she had made me repeat several times that I was not an enemy—we heard an answering shout from a hill top. All was then silent again for some time. As we felt assured that the blacks were reconnoitering, we concealed our only gun in the grass, and assuming as unwarlike appearance as possible, sat down beside our horses.

We had not long remained thus when we were roused by a sudden shout upon the mountainside, and as we got upon our feet, two men, armed, but perfectly naked, came in view over the shoulder of the hill, about one hundred and fifty yards above us. One of them, a large finely proportioned man, immediately stood forward, and waving one arm in the direction of the river, in a most undaunted and uncompromising manner, told us to begone. I called out to him that our intentions were friendly, that we were unarmed, and that I wanted to speak with him, but he talked so loudly himself, that he could not hear me. He also spoke so rapidly that I could but partially understand what he said, which was, however, something to this effect:

"Begone, begone, and take away your horses—why do you come hither among the mountains to disturb us? Return to your houses in the valley, you have the river and the open country, and you ought to be content, and leave the mountains to the black people. Go back— keep the plains, and leave us the hills. Go, go, begone."

Having at length induced him to attend, I advanced some distance towards him. After again assuring him that my intentions were not hostile, calling upon him to observe that I was not armed, I said "Lay down your weapons and approach me."

He regarded me for a moment, and then, with great deliberation, threw from him his spears and his boomerang, and came forward a few paces, retaining his parrial (or wallaby stick) in his hand. I told him to put that down also, and he did so with some reluctance, but would not consent to come any lower down the hill. I therefore slowly ascended towards him, keeping a steady watch upon his movements.

As I approached, he seemed uneasy, and went behind a tree but, as if ashamed of this, he soon stood out again. By this time, feeling satisfied from his bold and open expression that he might be trusted, I walked straight up to him and took him by the hand.

He asked "Are we friends?" I again assured him that we had none but friendly intentions towards him.

He appeared to be much delighted at finding me speaking his own language, and soon became quite at his ease. His companion, who had till this time remained some distance in the rear, now threw down his weapons, and joined us. They, however, still showed great fear of the horses, and would, on no account, consent to their being brought near.

An Aboriginal hunter and his wife on the Clarence River. Photograph by J. W. Lindt, Grafton. Mitchell Library.

My brother, therefore, fastened them to a tree, and came up the hill, carrying in his hand a tomahawk that we had brought with us, and which we presented to our tall friend, whose name we found to be Toolbillibam. He was overjoyed at the gift, and leaped and shouted with delight. We were now upon the best terms possible.

Toolbillibam began to shout loudly for the rest of his tribe on the surrounding mountains to come in and see us. I then asked him if he knew anything of Pundoon; at hearing the name, his countenance brightened. With great earnestness of manner, he told me he was the boy's second father, or uncle, and that the father was among his companions. To bring him to me he now redoubled his shouting. In a short time five of them made their appearance, running along the mountainside towards us.

Toolbillibam called out to them, telling them how matters stood, and they instantly threw their weapons out of their hands.

He pointed out one of them as Pundoon's father, calling him by his name of Pundoonbam. Upon Toolbillibam calling out to him that he had news of his son, the old fellow came running down, with out-stretched arms. Coming first to my brother, he gave him the full benefit of a most literally sweet embrace, as the old gentleman had evidently dined on honey. For want of a spoon, he had used his fingers, besides having smeared his face and beard a good deal more than was pleasant. He asked me many questions about his son, much more quickly than they could be answered. Upon learning that he lived in a house and ate bread, and wore clothes like ourselves, and that we would soon bring him back to the river, and that he should see him, the old fellow's joy was unbounded. Having, by this time, eight or nine of the blacks about us, we told them to sit down in a row, and made them a regular harangue.

We said that we had made war upon them because they had killed white people, but that now our anger was gone, and we wished to live at peace with them; that we wanted nothing in their country but the grass, and would leave them their kangaroos, their opossums, and their fish. Toolbillibam here interposed to know if we would not leave them the honey also. We assured him that it was quite at their service, and that he might make himself perfectly easy about rats, bandicoots, grubs and all other small game.

All this appeared to be extremely satisfactory to our audience.

We told them that if they would not rob or injure our people, nor kill our sheep, that no person would harm them; but on the contrary, would give them bread when they came to the stations. We promised that, if they conducted themselves peaceably for a time, we would give each of them a tomahawk. We pointed out to them the direction of all our stations, and told them that when they visited them, not to sneak from tree to tree, but to walk up openly and call to give notice of their approach, and put their weapons out of their hands—all this they promised to attend to. The sun was now sinking. After distributing amongst them our pocket knives, our handkerchiefs, and such articles of our dress as we could spare, we told them that we must go.

On the Clarence River by C. Hodgkinson 1845. Mitchell Library.

They all rose and accompanied us to the camp, which lay in our route. Toolbillibam walked before, and with much care parted the long grass with his hands, and cleared away all obstacles from our path.

Before parting with our wild-looking friends, we remained a few moments to examine their household goods and utensils which were in the camp. Hanging near each fire was a large bag, about the size of a two bushel sack, very ingeniously fabricated of grasses or rushes woven together, which appeared to contain all their property. Some spears were piled against the trees, and clubs, boomerangs and shields were scattered about.

Of opossum cloaks they appear to have a very scanty supply, as I saw none but very old and well worn ones, but as a kind of substitute they had large bunches of the skins of flying squirrels' tails tied together, which they use as a covering at night. The blacks appeared uneasy at our taking so much notice of their valuables. Therefore, having attempted in vain to persuade some of them to accompany us home, we took our leave.

Toolbillibam, who was evidently the head of his tribe, again preceded us, clearing our path as before, until he had conducted us as far from his camp as was consistent with his notions of politeness. None of these people could speak or understand a single word of English, and some had possibly never seen a white man before. I have not since seen them, but they have visited some of the out-stations, always approaching as they were desired, calling out to give notice of their approach, and laying down their weapons.

I shall not fail to follow up this first step by all means in my power, and hope it may prove the commencement of a friendly intercourse with the natives of the River.

Though it was never recognised officially, this remarkable exchange in the hills changed the whole course of tribal relations. The two races had come to understand each other, learning something of each other's strength and motivation. This did not in the least obscure the fact that, ultimately, there could be only one victor.

It seems likely that Fred personally took his brother's letter south, and that he went by sea. Schooners and ketches were now making frequent voyages, obviating the need for that long overland journey by horse. He was certainly in town when the letter appeared. Late in July he gave evidence before a Legislative Council committee, discussing the future prospects of free immigrants from Britain. The information he gave revealed a good deal about Swanlea's progress.

Despite tribal harassment, he and Edward had been able to establish eleven sheep stations along fourteen miles of river frontage, grazing to a depth of two or two-and-a-half miles on each side. Their sheep numbers had risen to nearly thirteen thousand. To help feed their thirty employees, they had twelve acres under crops, though he admitted this was not enough. 'I intend to cultivate more, and anticipate in good years to be able to do so. In poor ones we shall be obliged to purchase.'

His use of 'I' was significant. He appears to have gravitated to the management side, leaving Edward to handle the sheep.

He said also that this was the second year they had sent their wool clip down to Sydney by sea, that the returns from it were sufficient to make so remote a station pay—if managed with 'their whole attention, and with frugality'—and that finding labour was now no problem. 'I have not for the past 18 months found any difficulty in hiring men in Sydney, and defraying the expense of their conveyance to the Clarence River.'

Fred's was an optimistic outlook, since they were in the midst of a depression.

From a labour viewpoint, of course, it was a hirer's market. Wages had been much reduced. In the past year thirty-nine immigrant ships had brought nearly six thousand adults to the port of Sydney alone. Most of these were agricultural labourers from depressed areas in Britain. Fortunately they were inured to unemployment. There were also more carpenters, builders, gardeners, dairymaids, housemaids and farm servants than the impecunious colony could now afford. Hence Fred was able to say that current wages of £20 a year, plus rations, were not too great a burden on Clarence squatters. Despite the economic squeeze, Swanlea was still able to engage the four or five temporary hands they needed at lambing time, and another ten to twelve for the two-month shearing period. It looked as if they might ride out the economic disaster better than the over-capitalised south. The new country had many advantages. So did a navigable waterway like the Clarence.

Others were coming to recognise this. Especially in New England.

Soon after that crucial parley with Toolbillibam, Edward must have been astonished to see three bullock drays arrive down the track from Tabulam. They were loaded with baled wool. This difficult journey had been made possible by Thomas Hewitt, one of the tableland's greatest bushmen. Having left the A. A. Company four years earlier to form Stonehenge for Archibald Boyd, Hewitt had long wanted to find a dray route down to the coast, enabling him to ship wool direct to Sydney. Early in 1842, he had followed the Ogilvie track down from Tenterfield, cut a less hazardous route of his own here and there, cleared scrub in the tougher places to allow vehicles to swing and turn and, reaching the Settlement, bought up Bentley's notorious store. Having converted it into a wool depot, he sent word back to Stonehenge that he was open for business.

The teamsters, Noakes and Skinner, took to the track with New England wool, passing through Tabulam, Yulgilbar Reach, Gordon Brook, Smith's Flat and Ramornie to Hewitt's depot, where a schooner was waiting to take delivery. The teamsters returned again immediately, this time taking the Irby family and all their possessions up to Richard Windeyer's new station at Deepwater. New England and the Clarence were no longer separate worlds.

At the year's end Edward felt secure enough to ride over the ranges to the next valley north. Men were now talking of a new utopia on the Richmond River.

It seems incredible that, at so early a stage, his own run still undeveloped, he should be thinking already in terms of yet more land. But he was always a man to think ahead. Besides, unless he acted at once, the opportunity would be gone. A new land rush had now begun. Despite the depression, indeed because of it, the valley was drawing further land-seekers from the south. It was, in fact, more reasonable for men to take up new country than buy at the inflated rates in settled regions. Since the Clarence had no more land available, they were now making for the Richmond. 'In times like these,' wrote L. T. Daley, 'it was not surprising that five of the squatters who settled on the Richmond had already been through the insolvency courts. For those who had failed, almost the only course open was to assemble their station hands, collect their worthless sheep, and start again in some distant part of the colony until conditions improved.'[1]

First of these so-called new poor was Ward Stephens, formerly a founding partner of *The Sydney Herald* and owner of several stations. Having sold these for a depressing two shillings and threepence an acre, he formed Runnymede, Virginia and Stratheden on the rich soils of the Richmond River plains. By the time Edward rode up at least half-a-dozen men had already taken up sheep and cattle lands.

To reach the valley Edward retraced that familiar track to Tabulam, then followed Clay and Stapleton's route down to Cassino, stayed with them, and rode northward again along the Richmond. The first thirty miles he travelled were already occupied. He came eventually to a well-grassed plain narrowing between the Tooloom and Razorback Ranges. It was beautiful country. The intensely green pastures and gentle hills, the clear river flowing over pebbly shallows were a little reminiscent of England.

He adopted the native name for the place: Wyangerie.

His brother-in-law, Wellington Bundock, was later to describe it as the most beautiful sight he had ever seen. Sighting it first from a low gap in the range, he looked down at 'a sea of kangaroo grass in full seed, waving in the breeze that blew over the plain. The lagoon on the far side of the river was known as the Pink Lily Lagoon.'

Edward, riding through that gap, must have been well aware that no other European had ever seen these lyrical landscapes. He was quite alone. He came as an alien into a densely populated region. 'It was a risky thing to do', wrote Ellen, 'coming so unprotected. He was to encounter a number of very warlike blacks on the bald hill opposite. However, he addressed them in their own language. One of the blacks said to another, "He speaks, he speaks," recognising him thereby as the white man they had heard of who spoke their language. They soon became friendly. He had a duck he had just shot hanging on his saddle bow, which they tried rather roughly to seize. But, after a little talk,

---

[1] Daley, L. T., *Men And A River*, Melbourne, 1967.

he shared it with them, so as to gain their confidence. He wished to convince them that so long as they were quiet they had nothing to fear.'

She added that, in the time he stayed there, he used to roll himself up in his blanket, sleeping on the ground near their camp. 'One night he heard one of them say to another, "Take his tomahawk,"—upon which he made no remark, but quietly put his hand on it—so they understood he knew what they said and did not fear them. They made no further attempt to molest him.'

Edward returned to Yulgilbar without further incident.

(It is not clear when the original Swanlea was dropped, though it became officially known as Yulgilbar about this time.)

When he wrote of his find to Merton, the clan moved into action. Edward's unusually lyrical description decided Bundock to follow him north. Since Ellen wrote that they then had a son aged six months, he must have disposed of his rented property around February or March 1843. Leaving Mary to take care of Ellen and the baby, Bundock rode through New England with one Aborigine and a packhorse, following the Ogilvie track down through Tabulam and the Richmond River. The block he selected was in more settled country on Myrtle Creek, well south of Wyangerie. Next came another thousand miles in the saddle; back to the Hunter, north again with his sheep. He had a brother with him now, Frederick, having just arrived from England. His drovers were the convicts assigned to him seven years earlier; almost the last of their breed.

As others were soon to find, this was deceptive country and not really suitable for sheep. Heavy rains made the ground too damp. Footrot and a disease known as bottle soon became a serious worry. They bought a block nearer the Richmond from the Pagan brothers; the price merely thirty-three cows. Subsequent transactions became somewhat involved. When Commissioner Oakes refused to grant Edward both sides of the river at Wyangerie, he was so exasperated he sold it to Edward Hamilton in exchange for portions of what were to become Dyraaba and Wooroowoolgen stations, then sold these to the Bundocks, who in turn traded them with Hamilton for Wyangerie. Within a couple of years Wellington was in occupation at Wyangerie; Fred at Dyraaba.

Meanwhile, having helped to establish his brother-in-law, Edward was free to concentrate on Yulgilbar once more. His larger plans for it had yet to be shaped.

Fred's attitudes before that committee on immigration had been surprisingly mild. This would never have done for his so-called firebrand father. Nor for the forthright Edward. He had shown himself to be a pragmatic young man, giving quiet, pragmatic answers. He evaded controversy. On matters such as leasehold rights, security of tenure, land prices, he remained non-commital.

The Commander had no such inhibitions. When asked to stand for the broadened Legislative Council in March 1843, he spoke with his usual bulldog idealism.

His political opinions were well known, he told a public meeting in Muswellbrook, nor had he been backward in declaring them.[2] In bluff naval fashion he said he stood by free and liberal institutions, liberty of conscience and opposition to all forms of class legislation. His only reason for standing was because he had no confidence in the other candidates. Richard Windeyer, he said, might be a successful city barrister, but he was unknown out here. Robert Scott was a nonentity opposed to free speech and the emancipists. *The Maitland Mercury* published a leader regretting that he had been 'so late a starter', and praised his candour and vigour in local affairs.

Throughout the colony the general election made a strong impact. It was the first gesture towards representative government, even though voting was limited to property owners. Hitherto Council membership had been restricted to government officials and safe nominees. Now twenty-four of the thirty-six seats were open to public vote. Fought out against a background of economic depression, the elections stirred up acid debate. Figures like W. C. Wentworth attacked the governor's policies. Wealthy pastoralists demanded a new deal on their lands.

At Hunter River gatherings the Commander was given some rough treatment by his rivals. Richard Windeyer questioned his right to speak for farmers, because he had failed to grow wheat. Actually Merton then had ninety acres awaiting harvest. Scott asked sharp questions about his support for importing cheap coolie labour, which the Commander said was a matter for individual conscience not the Government. Henry Dangar dubbed him 'a cocktail aristocrat'. The end was in sight when Scott rode into Maitland at the head of a long cavalcade of 'gentlemen on horse or in gigs', welcomed by flags, bunting and a brass band. But the man first past the post proved to be Richard Windeyer.

The Sydney Morning Herald reported a corrupt poll in Durham country. It made no difference to Ogilvie's position, for he had finished last.

In Sydney, polling day was celebrated by a riot outside the Council's

[2] *The Maitland Mercury*, 21 March 1843.

colonnaded building in Macquarie Street. It was a protest against the depression none knew how to cope with. Two of the seven banks had now failed, one of them being the Bank of Australia, the squatters' bank so proudly founded by exclusives less than two decades earlier.

'Bankruptcy is almost universal and confidence in mercantile matters lost entirely,' wrote the Murrumbidgee squatter Hobler in his diary for 12 June. 'So valueless has property of all kinds become that no monied engagement can be met at the most dreadful sacrifices. Sheep are sold at 6d. and 7d. each, stations given with them, horses at £7 and fat cattle 50 shillings. The whole country seems horror-struck and nothing that can now be forseen can avert general bankruptcy.'[3]

Hobler noted also that 'I consider Dickson, Dee and R. P. Cummins the only three solvent men left in Maitland, and it would be difficult to name three in the neighbourhood of the town of whom so much may be said.' Miraculously William Ogilvie appeared to be one of them. Three years later Hobler added a marginal note to that diary entry, reading: '1846 Cummins took to drinking and died insolvent. The other two weathered the storm.'

Among the indignant W. C. Wentworth's first utterances in the new Legislative Council was a speech he made on the crisis.

'It is notorious,' he declared, 'that nine-tenths of the houses, lands and mansions of the proprietors are mortgaged up to their full value. As to the squatters' interest, it was known that gentlemen with 10,000 sheep could not get credit for a bag of sugar or a chest of tea. The insolvency list, in fifteen months, has swelled to nearly two million, while in six months previous to August 1843, 6,000 writs had been issued out of the Supreme Court. There were merchants without custom, traders without business, and mechanics and artisans were pining for want on the streets.'[4]

Judge Therry added that, so great was the glut of sheep, 'small carts, laden with legs of mutton, were driven into town in the morning, and on giving the driver 6d. any passer-by might take one.'

Why only legs, a stranger might have asked. The answer was simple. Sheepbreeders had found at least a temporary solution to their troubles. Its originator was Henry O'Brien, a Murrumbidgee pioneer, who began boiling-down his sheep for tallow rather than sell them at a few pence each. If street hawkers continued to sell legs of mutton, this was only because these yielded less tallow than the rest of the beast.

Boiling-down spread rapidly throughout the country, until almost

[3] Hobler manuscript, Mitchell Library, Sydney.

[4] Therry, J., *Reminiscences of Thirty Years in New South Wales and Victoria*, London, 1863.

every inland town had its great iron pot bubbling away, reducing whole flocks to a mess of stinking grease that soon became worth £350 a ton on the London market.

John Macarthur's grand vision of the golden fleece had vanished in the stench and fumes of sixty boiling-down works polluting the outback air. 'The effluvia was almost overpowering half-a-mile away,' wrote a Victorian squatter of the period.[5] 'It was all right if you did not have to endure the smell and sight.'

Entire flocks of carefully bred Saxons and Spanish merinos were driven to these macabre factories, slaughtered in thousands, stripped of their hides and thrown into large vats whose manholes were secured tightly to prevent the escape of steam. The meat was disintegrated under high pressure, dissolving into fat, which was then drawn through taps as a steaming liquid. Next the remaining solids were boiled again for further reduction, then the bones extracted and the entrails sold as 'a fine wallowing mess for a herd of pigs that has no Board of Health to look after them.'

'The destruction is immense,' wrote Hobler ruefully, recording that the great Wentworth himself had opened a large works at his Windemere station on New Year's Day, 1844. With a capacity of two hundred sheep daily, he catered for most of the Hunter region's needs. Soon these huge iron or wooden vats were boiling away profitably as far north as the Clarence, where Joseph Sharp opened his works at Alumni Creek, near the Settlement.

By this time nearly two hundred thousand sheep had vanished in steam. Three-quarters of a million were to go into the vats by 1845. Squatters began to sing rorty songs about transforming their flocks into candles, but each animal killed brought them from five to seven shillings. Desperate reversal though it was of pastoral ambitions, it paid them better than keeping sheep alive for shearing. Wool prices had now dropped from three shillings a pound to elevenpence-halfpenny.

There could have been no worse time for a young man looking for colonial experience to arrive. The twenty-year-old Charles Grant Tindal, who disembarked at Sydney in mid-December from England, was dismayed by the depressed atmosphere he found. He had even brought 120 sheep with him on the sailing ship *Hamlet*, hoping to buy or lease land at a reasonable price.

Discouraged by Sydney's high living costs, he arranged to stay on board until the vessel sailed. By good luck the Commander, to whom

[5] James, G. F., ed., *A Homestead History*, Melbourne, 1942.

his father Captain Tindal R.N. had given him a letter of introduction, happened to come to town. A second letter, addressed to the governor, he decided not to use, because 'I heard that Sir George was accustomed to treat people who present them rather rudely.'

The Ogilvies were certainly more help.

Soon after leaving the ship, Tindal was on his way up country to Merton. 'There is no chance of obtaining a situation as superintendent anywhere,' he wrote home to his father. 'Most owners who are not insolvent are so far reduced as to be obliged to go beyond the boundaries to look after their affairs themselves. Now, however, things are beginning to take a slight turn, the colonists having found two new articles to export; tallow and horses for India and China. So I think I had better take my £60 from Captain Ogilvie in sheep at 5s. each, he taking the whole for their keep.'

This letter, written the following March, was sent from Terula, the Ogilvie station at Manilla. It was the first of a long series giving close insights into bush life. Tindal, in fact, was soon to become chief chronicler of the Ogilvie fortunes.

The Terula letter also reflected the current pastoral mood. 'The governor intends to limit each station to twenty square miles. This has caused a great commotion and the Council intends to stop supplies if he insists.' This was clearly an echo of the 'Captain's' own views. Ogilvie was about to take an active role in this commotion himself, siding with the big landowners against Gipps.

Since the governor had recently stayed at Merton, presumably on an inland tour, one wonders how those two uncompromising men rubbed along together. Yet both were staunch idealists in their differing ways. William stood by Wentworth, already leader of the Council, in his anti-Gipps campaign. Mary even wrote to her sons at Yulgilbar, urging them to sign a mass protest Wentworth organised.

The struggle became a complex one, not all fought out on the surface. Some of the argument was contained in confidential despatches sent by Gipps to the Colonial Office, while the squatters consciously over-simplified their case for political advantage, or self-interest. The general public, as always, remained utterly confused.

On 3 April Gipps issued a new set of Occupation Regulations. These proposed that separate licences be issued for each run, instead of allowing one to cover several tracts of country; that each should be limited to twenty square miles; or, in poorer country, sufficient to support 4,000 sheep, or 500 head of cattle.

The reaction was savage and instantaneous.

Alarmed by the squatters' anger, he then drafted a new set of proposals, sent them to London, and leaked a copy to one of the Council's nominees. Further uproar. What he now proposed was to allow each squatter, after five years occupation, the right to buy a 320-acre homestead block, and to occupy the rest of his run for a further eight years undisturbed. His opponents made it clear they would have nothing to do with licences at all. They wanted ownership. Protest meetings were arranged for every town and district of any size.

The largest and most clamorous—great violence of language, Gipps reported—assembled in Sydney's Royal Hotel on 11 May. William, no doubt, was present at the Muswellbrook gathering; Edward and Fred at the Settlement.

In Sydney 350 squatters formed a Pastoral Association to defend their rights. They voted for resolution after resolution condemning the governor's proposals as unnecessary, unjust, unreasonable, oppressive, ruinous and, finally, unconstitutional. They resolved to send a mass petition to Queen Victoria.[6] In the Port Phillip district, lines of mounted squatters called for separation from New South Wales. The sharp-tongued lawyer turned landowner, Robert Lowe, wrote of raising a republican flag and training 20,000 armed insurgents. In some outback parts they flourished their saddle carbines and talked rebellion.

It was great melodrama.

Nonetheless, it was only talk. To keep the issue simmering, Wentworth, himself the owner of fifteen stations, persuaded the Council to set up a new inquiry. This became known as the Land Grievance Committee. Grievance was a word well chosen. Long repressed resentments were loosed upon the committee, old feuds with crown lands commissioners, denunciations of the governor, Colonial Office and the economy. During June twenty-eight graziers gave evidence, while another 122 distant ones answered a lengthy questionnaire.

Ironically, the most devastating case was presented by that liberal humanist, William Ogilvie. His reply from Merton was so articulate and impassioned it could well have been adopted as the pastoralists' manifesto.[7]

Doubling the upset price of land, he asserted, 'had been one of the chief causes of the present depressed state of the colony'. It was a mischievous act, had annihilated the land fund, entirely stopped the immigration of capitalists and all demand for land. He continued:

[6] Gipps to Stanley, *Historical Records of Australia*, Series 1, Vol. XXIII.

[7] Land Grievances Committee, Votes and Proceedings, Legislative Council, 1844.

The free use, for grazing purposes, of the waste lands of the colony, or what is now called squatting, is the only advantage this colony had, or ever had to offer; it is that alone which has attracted settlers to these shores, who by their enterprise produced a degree of prosperity through-out the whole community, almost unparalleled in colonial history, in which the government equally partook, having the largest revenue ever raised from a community of equal numbers.

The true policy, therefore, of this government is to afford every facility to those who are desirous of turning to profit those pastures, which the hand of nature has so bountifully spread over the wastes of this country, and to content itself with the indirect advantages which the general prosperity, thereby occasioned, will produce, which, as all experience has shown, will fill its coffers much more plenteously than any direct imposts on stock or stockholders, the latter being the policy of the silly boy who killed the goose for the sake of the golden eggs.

It was not by chance that the 1844 census listed Ogilvie as the largest occupier of crown lands and stockholders in the Clarence district.

This credited him with three separate runs, which totalled 159 square miles. His livestock comprised 15,610 sheep, 380 cattle, ten horses; the carrying capacity was 118 sheep to the square mile, or five and a half per acre. Through his two sons, he had now entered the big league.

The cause of his embittered diatribe was to be found in the later passages of his Grievance Committee submissions. Here he wrote scarifyingly of 'arbitrary and despotic government, property held at the will or caprice of the executive, or the good or ill-feeling of the commissioner [which] tends to destroy every manly and independent feeling, and to degrade the character. The uncertainty of tenure must also prevent the formation of those improvements which the comforts and decencies of life require, and which would take place as a matter of course under a different scene.'

He then went on to condemn the old system of quit rents, the sudden demands for payment of arrears long ignored and the consequent loss of lands which he termed confiscation.

Obviously he was still brooding on his long fight with the Lands Office during the 1830s, when he had battled through drought, depression and financial shortages to establish himself.

He continued:

The unfairness alluded to, applies chiefly to those parties who came to the colony under the impression (which was general in England) that a free grant of land would be made to them on arrival here, in pro-portion to their capital; but who found themselves afterwards saddled with a heavy quit rent. When about to emigrate, I communicated with the Colonial Office to ascertain the terms on which grants of land were made, and came to it under the regulations promulgated by that office in November, 1824. By the 13th article of those regulations, all lands granted without purchase were made liable to a quit rent of five per cent of their estimated value; the 15th article runs thus: 'In the redemption of his quit-rent the grantee will have credit for the one-fifth part of the sums which he may have saved the government by employment and maintenance of convicts.'

With this means of redemption there was no great hardship, but without it no such amount would have been put on, as it would be quite preposterous. The rack rents in England do not amount to more than two or three per cent upon the value of land, although provided with dwellings and all other necessary improvements. Under these regulations I redeemed my quit-rent before any was demanded of me, and when it was demanded, of course claimed that redemption. My claim was refused, on what ground I am still ignorant; and I was under the necessity of giving bills to the Colonial Treasurer for the whole amount of arrears claimed, to prevent the levy of distress upon my goods. I had subsequently a personal interview with His Excellency the Governor, and the matter has since been in abeyance, but it is still hanging over me. There are very many individuals whom the enforcement of these claims, at the present time, would drive into the Insolvency Court.

And thus Gipps, constantly harassed, in poor health, beginning to break under the pressures, found himself confronted with decades of injustice by officialdom, long before his own regime began.

Ultimately it would be the Colonial Office who pondered and decided upon policy change. Meanwhile, restless and uneasy in Government House, he had to bear with the unremitting hostility of men he had come to recognise as more powerful, in terms of argument as well as possessions, than himself.

The colony had reached a crisis in its affairs. One side or the other must eventually give way. The shepherd kings were increasingly confident.

12

Toolbillibam Wrestles

Yulgilbar had lost its air of impermanence.

Everywhere was movement; the imprints of man's activity. Here and there trees had been cleared. Grasses along the river banks, eaten down by three years of grazing, grew less uncontrollably now. Sheep pads meandered through them to habitual watering points. Dray wheels had worn tracks to various flock stations and away through the hills to Ramornie and Smith's Flat. Across on the north side of the river a woolshed had gone up; stout posts, slab walls and roof of bark. On the homestead side a cluster of buildings had taken solid root: stockmen's huts, blacksmith's shop, a large store for the station men stocked with tea chests, bagged flour and sugar, casks, saddlery, boots and working clothes.

The brothers Ogilvie appeared to have taken Gipps' pledges for fact. The half-promise of longer tenure had encouraged them to build a permanent homestead. Moreover, the newly arrived Commissioner Fry at Red Rocks was much more amiabily disposed than Oakes, taking no hard line when inspecting the run.

They were just completing it when Charles Tindal arrived overland from Merton. He had ridden that five hundred mile journey with Bundock and a plant of horses, taking five weeks instead of fifteen days because of heavy rains and flooded creeks. Arriving late in October 1844, he saw men putting the last touches to a comfortable home.

It had been built around the core of those two original huts, which now became living rooms. Three more bedrooms had been added, all opening on to a shady verandah. The place had slab walls, was white-washed inside and out like Merton, and had roofing of six-foot sheets of stringybark. There was a detached kitchen, and a small garden in front. Young fruit trees were already growing here, as well as some beautiful native creepers. The soil had also been prepared for vines.

By this time Tindal had travelled across the ranges to Wyangerie, returning with a herd of cattle Edward had temporarily depastured there. These carried the same W.O. brand on their rumps as Merton cattle. He wrote also of reduced costs on the Clarence. 'The large immigration pouring in has lowered wages, and shepherds can be had at £15 to £16 per annum and rations. I am comfortably settled with the Ogilvies, and think I can make myself useful.'

It was an understatement, for the brothers had plans to work him pretty hard. He was soon to be put in charge of their cattle.

Yet they were a long way off security still. Tindal told his father that 'the Ogilvies have been in difficulties, but as they have managed to get through to the present time, I have no doubt this year's wool clip will set them right again.' He added that an unnamed Clarence station had been sold a few months earlier, 'when the sheep did not average five shillings each, stations and all improvements given in'. This was probably Pandemonium, for Forster had given up the struggle, selling to his neighbour John Dobie. Before long Blaxland's adjoining run was also to be added to Ramornie. It soon became a commonplace for a head stockman to tell his masters, 'I'll ride across to Pandemonium this morning, boil the billy and meet you in Purgatory after dinner camp.'

Maybe fires burned more strongly in the abode of devils.

There were no further signs of devilry among the tribes. The Ogilvies were on excellent terms with them. Young Pundoon was back with his relatives. Men, women and their piccaninnies had set up semi-permanent gunyahs beside the long reach. Their leader and spokesman was the tall, muscular Toolbillibam. The masters of Yulgilbar had developed an easy friendship, based partly on respect for tribal attitudes, partly on physical competitiveness.

Both Edward and Fred challenged the sturdiest tribesmen to bouts of wrestling. Even the redoubtable Toolbillibam. They ran foot races against them. They challenged them to swimming and diving contests along Yulgilbar Reach. It was great sport. The blacks hugely enjoyed it. But all this had begun as something more than sport. There had been elements of real hostility in those vigorous and exhausting bouts. For the powerfully built chief and his supporters this was a testing of the white men. They had to win; or at least to prove themselves. They had to prove their strength if they wanted to be masters of this country.

There is a family story, told by later generations, that Edward, after the first wrestling bout, was shut in a gunyah for the night, during which the tribal elders debated whether or not he should be allowed to live. Had he not fought so gamely, so the story goes, he would have been killed. Next morning he was relieved to see Toolbillibam's wife approaching the gunyah, leading one of her piccaninnies. It was well known that, when violence was planned, women and children were withdrawn from a camp.[1]

Only later did these fierce and resolute combats descend to the level of more even-tempered play. Even Tindal was drawn into them. As a new chum he, too, was expected to display his manliness.

In November he wrote to his father, 'This afternoon we had some wrestling matches with the blacks. I began with Toolbillibam. He is the biggest man about here. The first round was undecided. In the second he managed to throw me. After this Edward Ogilvie threw his brother Charlie twice out of thrice. Some time back we wrestled with a black named Jemmy. Edward Ogilvie and I threw him, but he had the best of Fred Ogilvie.'

The entire scene was almost unimaginable anywhere else in the country. These hardy, outgoing young Ogilvies had created a sense of harmony no other outback squatters enjoyed. It had achieved more than muskets could ever do. The outcome was made clear by a further entry in Tindal's letter: 'I have just been making a bargain with a black for a belt, which he had round his loins, and which constitutes his only clothing. He gave it to me for a fish hook. It is made from the hair of his own head. Another is to get me some of their baskets, and I hope to have some of their weapons by and by.'

No wonder the new Crown Lands Commissioner, Oliver Fry, was able to write in his annual report of the remarkable improvement in racial relations. 'Their feeling seems to have quite changed,' he wrote of the tribes, 'for scarcely a day elapsed, throughout the entire year, in which they were not at some of the stations, frequently encamping within sight of the huts, and manifesting the utmost confidence and good feeling. Nor have I to report a single outrage on the Clarence.[2]

A pity he lacked the good grace to describe exactly who had brought about this state of affairs.

Yet matters were not so good further north. Late in 1844 a shepherd and hutkeeper were killed at Tabulam, and their entire flock driven away. On the Richmond another stockman was murdered, though he had only himself to blame. Fry reported that he had been foolish enough to 'go armed into a blacks' camp with a view to having improper intercourse with women.'

[1] Sabine, F., The *Daily Examiner*, Grafton, 1960.

[2] Report to Colonial Secretary, 13 January 1845.

Fry, being a young man, was more energetic than the elderly, overworked Oakes. After the major's death in 1842, the twenty-three-year-old commissioner spent much of his time patrolling the huge region. Stylish in dress, flamboyantly good-looking, with a cavalry-twist moustache and curling black hair shiny with Macassar oil, he had arrived with a great reputation from the Liverpool Plains. He had actually won his spurs near Goulburn, almost single-handedly breaking up Scotchie's gang of bushrangers, who had threatened to kill him. 'On their approaching his hut,' Bawden wrote, 'Fry barricaded the doors and windows, directing his men to keep their guns loaded, firing at the besiegers through loopholes in the slabs. Fry succeeded in potting Scotchie, who had shown his body slightly round a tree, immediately started in pursuit of the others and arrested them.'[3]

If anything, Oliver Fry was too headstrong. Richard Craig was to make serious allegations against him, following his action in March 1845 against a party of Kumbainggiri who killed two shepherds on or near Archibald Boyd's station in the hills at Buccarumbi. Craig, who could not write, had Ward Stephens compose a letter of protest to the Colonial Secretary, accusing Fry and his border police of firing without provocation on a native camp near the Boyd River. 'Afterwards I met some of the tribe, who counted on their fingers seven men, four women and five children killed. I applied to the court for a subpoena to bring forward Ross and McAvoy, who were eye witnesses to the murder, but was refused!'[4]

Trouble of this kind was now rare at Yulgilbar. The only incident was one mentioned by Tindal in March, after returning from a trip downriver to buy cattle. He was told that the brothers had both ridden after a party found to have stolen flour and blankets. They brought back one captive, who promptly made a hole in the hut's roof and escaped. 'The blacks all agreed that it was right they should be punished for stealing,' Tindal wrote to his sister Ana. 'But the chief said he had beaten the man already, and that was enough.

'Another tribe, who had heard nothing of the matter, came to the house, but the chief being a notorious thief, I secured him, and Edward Ogilvie, when he came home, threatened him. Two hours afterwards he managed to get off, having wrenched open the padlock with the thigh bone of a sheep. After a long chase with men and dogs he got clear off.'

[3] Bawden, Thomas, *Three Lectures on the Early History of the Clarence*, University of New England.

[4] Colonial Secretary's correspondence, 1 July 1845.

Fred's sheep journal also recorded an occasional ram or wether stolen and eaten. Mostly the losses were due to dingoes or some flash flood. But sheep numbers were now rapidly increasing. Back in 1844 they had been able to send a draft of more than 800 wethers back to Merton. After the next lambing, their tally had risen to nearly twenty thousand.

They were now grazing a great deal more territory. Many of their flocks were on beautifully grassed, undulating country known as the Front Run, south of the homestead. Another large flock, in charge of a shepherd named Nett, was further east at Waterfall. They had a separate run named the Plains Station along the track to Tabulam, while the cattle were away down on the Mann or Nymboida, known as the South River. Tindal said it took a hard day's riding to cover the distance between north and south boundaries in a day.

'Shearing is just over,' Tindal wrote in the New Year. 'It is hoped the clip of wool will relieve the Ogilvies of some temporary financial difficulties.' A month later new optimism was apparent. 'The yearly cost of sheep is one shilling per head and they yield 2½ lbs of wool, worth a shilling a pound. This shows a net profit of 1/6 per head. For 1200 sheep the cost would be: wages for two men, £32. Rations, £12. Licence for station, £10. Shearing and packing wool, £10. My own personal expenses, £20. Total, £84.'

These figures, presumably, were hypothetical. But he calculated the Ogilvie profits, too, estimating their expenses on 15,600 sheep at £1,092, and their yield of wool at £1,950. This gave a net profit of £852. Yulgilbar was beginning to pay.

On the Richmond, sheep were not doing so well. Men were beginning to find the climate wrong for sheep-raising; too humid, the grasses too rank; diseases like fluke, catarrh, footrot and bottle eroding their flocks. Dobie reported one grazier having lost a thousand sheep, which obliged him to abandon his run altogether. He added that his own losses had been so large it would take him four to five years to recover. Yet the genial doctor—now 'a stout old gentleman', as Tindal described him—was shrewd enough to take over an additional run, Stratheden, after Commissioner Fry had cancelled Ward Stephens' licence to it for claiming too much country. The pioneering Clay and Stapleton went broke completely, and were bought out by Stephens, thereby restoring his vast acreage.

The Bundocks were also having trouble; this time from the local tribe. Fry reported that Wyangerie was twice attacked without casualties in June, and a third time soon afterwards, leaving a watchman with three spear wounds. Cattle were also killed on five other runs.

Nonetheless, Wellington Bundock had also built a permanent home, planning to bring his wife and children up from Merton as early as possible.

Riding south in mid-1845 to sell off the rest of his stock, he returned with them on board *William The Fourth*. Proudly described by its owner Girard as Australia's first locally built steamer, she was dubbed by Ellen 'an old tub of a ship', and took five days on a voyage to the Clarence. Even more discouraging was the news given them on arrival.

Fred, they learnt, had been in town but had ridden back to Yulgilbar, leaving them without transport. On the wharf someone then told Bundock he had heard his new homestead at Wyangerie had been burnt down, all their stores destroyed, the overseer killed by the blacks and their sheep stolen.

Ellen, being Mary's daughter, insisted on her husband riding across country to the Richmond. She would find her own way up the Clarence. Fry offered to put her up, with the children, at Red Rock, so she took them up river with Tom the Boatman, stopping later with the Mylnes at First Falls. Meantime a message went through to Yulgilbar, and both brothers came down for her with a buggy and saddle horses. The final stage of that journey took a further two days. For Ellen, having so long heard of Yulgilbar, it must have seemed like coming home.

The suspense over Wyangerie remained until, a week or so later, Bundock rode in with news. Rumour, as usual, had slightly overplayed matters. There had been no tribal attack. But the homestead had been destroyed, due to the cook's folly of burning off timber and rubbish outside. In the panic the overseer's horse had bolted, run him into a tree and killed him. The sheep had gone bush, after which a few hundred eager tribesmen had captured some of them, roasting them in a sequence of feasts. The rest of the flock was safe.

Worst news was that a completely new homestead had to be built. All Bundock's months of labour had gone for nothing. Ellen and the children had to remain at Yulgilbar for months. Being the first woman to live in this homestead, she would doubtless have taken control. As strong-willed as her mother, domesticated, practical, she must have made a big impact on this rough-hewn establishment of bachelors. She helped to create a more relaxed atmosphere as well.

'We had a picnic the other day,' Charles Tindal wrote, 'and with a blanket for sail, went up the river for six or seven miles, landed, had dinner and got home after dark. The Bundocks, Edward, myself and a gentleman staying here, guitar and singing. The Ogilvies are all musical.'

It was to be a long while yet before further musical evenings occurred.

Most popular song of the day along the Hunter was *The Ballad of Billy Barlow*. It told of the sad fate of an English-born squatter, down on his luck. The blacks speared his cattle, his sheep had scab, his pastures were withered in drought, the moneylenders had foreclosed and bushrangers taken his money and horse. Then came the bailiffs.

> What I'd left of my sheep and my traps he did seize,
> And he said, "They won't pay all the cost and my fees",
> Then he sold off the lot, and I'm sure 'twas a sin,
> At sixpence a head and the station giv'n in.
>   Oh dear, lackaday, oh,
>   "I'll go back to England," said Billy Barlow.

There was no stigma in being insolvent any more. It was happening to the most eminent, respectable folk. Even the late chief justice's affairs had ended in the bankruptcy court. The Ogilvies were particularly affected, for Sir Francis Forbes and his wife had been close friends. In 1845 Mary Ogilvie was among those who attended the auction of Lady Forbes' furniture and effects at Old Skellatar. It was saddening to watch strangers bidding for the possessions she had seen so often in her friend's homestead; a valuable mahogany piano, chinaware, silver, engravings.

Yet this was the very year that William was described at a public meeting as having 'an ample fortune'. If he had, it was on paper only.

Having decided to have another attempt at politics, he stood for a Legislative Council by-election caused by the retirement of Richard Windeyer. This meant campaigning in the three boroughs of East Maitland, West Maitland and Newcastle. His sole opponent was a former police magistrate, Patrick Grant, whom *The Mercury* described as having no aim but 'to serve himself; to make a stepping stone of the suffrage; to secure for himself a snug berth.'[5] Ogilvie, recently appointed warden of the new district council of Merton, was strongly recommended by the newspaper, which praised his character, record of public service and outspoken criticism of the governor's policies.

At the final meeting at East Maitland's court house in September, with E. D. Day in the chair, the Commander was given even livelier praise. His chief sponsor, a Mr Lipscomb, ridiculed Grant's slanderous campaign. What was all this talk of Ogilvie being an arrogant, wealthy squatter?

'So far as being wealthy,' he declared, 'the squatters have produced

[5] *The Maitland Mercury*, 12 July 1845.

more Billy Barlows than any other class. In fact, they're so poor I never knew of an instance of one having the gout. I've only known three men who have—two auctioneers and an undertaker.'[6] As for the renewed gossip about the Commander being a severe magistrate, he was now supposed to have been not only a rabid flogger of convicts, but to have actually branded his employees with hot irons. 'I didn't quite know what to make of that one,' Mr Lipscomb said amid laughter, 'Perhaps it was some mysterious rite of freemasonry. Later I found that what Mr. Ogilvie was branding were the men's trousers.'

Richard Jones, the banker-pastoralist, was also angry about those manufactured rumours. 'Many of the parties most active in circulating those rumours are present at this meeting. I call on them, if they have any manliness or honesty, to come forward and accuse Mr. Ogilvie face to face.'

No one came forward.

The finest testimonial came from the newspaper's correspondent at Jerry's Plain. The Commander, he wrote, was 'a gentleman of ultra-liberal opinions, who speaks of the natural right that all should be treated on a footing of perfect equality'. He asserted that the electorate had been deceived with false rumour, the truth being that Ogilvie did not 'punish too severely, but that his sentences were too lenient'. Ten years earlier, he recalled, a certain gentleman from the West Indies on the local bench, of which the Commander was senior magistrate, had uttered extreme opinions about 'keeping the slaves of the estate under proper discipline'. This was, of course George Forbes, a man of more reactionary views than his brother, the chief justice. 'These ideas,' he continued, 'soon found supporters among the great majority of superintendents, and among many settlers, including some of the magistrates, and a vast increase of police-office cases resulted against assigned servants. At that time, when Mr. Ogilvie could have had no electioneering purpose, he stepped forward to put down the cruel tyranny that was becoming every day more shocking. For his efforts, Mr. Ogilvie soon fell in bad odour with the "proper discipline" party, who did all they could to throw ridicule upon his lenient decisions. Finally none was more pleased than him at the total discontinuance of capital punishment.'[7]

The anonymous correspondent was believed to have been either the young poet Charles Harpur or John Robertson. It seems more likely to have been the second for 'Ironbark Jack' Robertson was an outspoken character, noted in everyday speech for his 'gift of profanity'.

[6] *The Maitland Mercury*, 3 September 1845.
[7] *ibid.*

Perhaps it was this very liberalism that caused Ogilvie to lose the election. The autocratic Grant was returned by a small margin. *The Mercury* hoped that those who voted for him 'might have no cause to regret their choice.'

At least it allowed the loser more time to restore his alleged fortune.

The economy was slowly beginning to right itself. Station folk were finding that, even if wool and sheep prices remained low, they could survive through the new tallow industry. 'Captain Ogilvie tells me,' wrote Charles Tindal, 'that tallow produced from the surplus wethers by boiling-down will, under good management, pay all expenses leaving wool a clear profit.' Moreover, peace had returned to the Liverpool Plains. The Hunter men were driving their stock out once again. 'Instances of the outrages of the more distant tribes are becoming less frequent,' read the 1845 report from the regional commissioner for crown lands, F. Allman Junior.

Will Ogilvie was among those who had returned to grazing on the Gwydir and Macintyre Rivers.

In one of her few surviving letters, Mary described the quiet routine into which their life had settled at Merton. Written to her daughter at Wyangerie, it was a gossipy letter about local folk that also revealed, for the first time, just how much those twenty years of tension and struggle had affected her.[8]

> I need not tell you how glad we were to see Mr. Bundock both for his own sake and for the information he could give us viva voce about you and the dear little piccaninnies, and also to see him looking so strong and well. I fear he finds Merton but a dull sejour, for your father and I naturally grow more prosy. However, the Muswellbrook races take place this week and doubtless he will be repaid for all the dullness he has had to endure. Mind, I do not say he has betrayed any symptoms of being particularly ennuied. But he is getting into a fidget about the return of the steamer, for the wind is blowing from the south and rain has been falling. I cannot wish the rain to cease, though I should grieve if he were detained, because I cannot bear the idea of your being left without a gentleman . . .
>
> I am not so good a correspondent as you deserve, for I have suffered very much lately from headaches, after an attack of which I am very much afraid to use my pen at all. I believe they arise from the very inactive life I have, for the weather has been such as to prevent my taking any outdoor exercise except driving out of an evening, and that has been discontinued of late from the absence on more than ordinary business of the groom in consequence of collecting and sending horses to Bungarabbee. But as I am extraordinarily embonpoint I cannot be very harsh, and your father too is recovering his lost flesh.

[8] Ogilvie Family Papers, Archives, University of New England.

She went on to discuss her staff problems: 'those honest folk,' Mr and Mrs Hollis, thankfully, had decided to stay and run the house for them; 'poor Catherine,' presumably one of the maids, 'is moving with her, I fear, idle husband from place to place. She has not bettered her condition.'

She was concerned also at lack of news from Edward, who was then making an expedition to inspect new country in the Moreton Bay district. 'I shall be glad to know he is safe.' She had an additional reason for this anxiety, as she had long been expecting him back at Merton so that they could travel north together, making her first visit to the Clarence and Wyangerie. 'I shall be pleased to find that Willy remembers Grandma, and indeed I look forward with very great pleasure to seeing you and Willy and Mary.'

Mary was to make that voyage north much sooner than she expected. And in very different circumstances. The tragic news reached Merton before her daughter even received that letter.

Edward, returning to the Clarence without taking up fresh land, remained long enough to arrange for Charles Tindal to graze four thousand Yulgilbar sheep on a half-share in the increase, then sailed for Sydney.

Subsequent events were related by Charles Tindal in a letter to his sister. 'Poor Fred Ogilvie died very suddenly on Monday morning. Edward had left for Merton. It appears he was taken unwell on Saturday night, and during the Sunday broke two blood vessels at different times. I sent a messenger to catch Edward. But he arrived two hours after the steamer had left.'

Fred had been alone when he had this seizure, for Tindal was then fifteen miles out mustering cattle.

Arrangements for the burial were made by Tindal. They carried the coffin to the crest of a steep, stony hill overlooking the homestead. The rocky soil was hard to dig. It was a beautiful, if lonely setting. West of the hilltop they could look down at the homestead, and the sombre mass of Mount Ogilvie behind. Northward was the sunlit expanse of Yulgilbar Reach. To the east, lagoons and swampy plains reached away to the distant Richmond Range; and south were the rolling and fertile pastures of the eight-mile Front Run. The splendour of this valley was spread out all around them. It was a sunlit little kingdom that Fred and his brother had struggled to make their own.

Fred had only had his thirtieth birthday eight days before he died.

Ellen was first of the family to hear the news.

Someone, presumably Tindal, rode the hundred-mile track to Wyangerie. Since her husband was still at Merton and Tindal unable to leave Yulgilbar, now being in sole charge, they decided to send her brother-in-law, Fred Bundock, to inform Edward and the parents. Yet this meant leaving Ellen and her two small children virtually unprotected, for tribal attitudes along the Richmond were still unsettled. Ellen poignantly described the situation in her memoir.

'The day my brother-in-law went to Merton, joining Edward on the road, to break the terrible news of our brother's death, I was left all alone. On looking across the plain I saw a number of blacks coming towards the house. I went into the kitchen and asked the man cook if he could fire a gun. He answered yes, but turned very white. Luckily it was not necessary for him to do so. Although they were very bold and came about the place, they did not molest us and seemed content by being allowed to come in as none had been permitted to since the shepherd had been speared by one of the tribe.'

As it turned out, this was the final breakthrough. Ellen's restrained handling of these wondering visitors within her homestead brought the tension to an end. Though Wyangerie cattle were now and then speared, they never experienced further trouble. Only casualties reported by Oliver Fry for the whole Clarence–Richmond region that year were three men speared on Heifer Station, the motive being an attempt to steal flour or bread.

Edward returned north with his parents by the first possible steamer.

It was a tragic time for the ageing couple to see Yulgilbar. For five years they had lived with their sons' description of the great valley on their minds. Now they saw it through the veil of mourning. Mary, growing stout, no horsewoman any more, would have remained at the homestead. The Commander, though now sixty-one, must have ridden up that stony hill and looked down for the first time at the magnificent scene spreading away below.

Two months later, when Tindal wrote home again, the Ogilvies were still there. Mary, he said, appeared 'a little more reconciled'. She kept herself busy around the garden and vineyard her sons had planted.

Life was not quiet at Yulgilbar for long. What troubled Edward now was not the Aborigines, but bushrangers. The Wilson gang, notorious as far south as Port Phillip, had first appeared on the run during Christmas week. When several station horses went missing, Commissioner Fry sent up two of his border police to search for the gang. They found Wilson on the Bellingen River, more than a hundred miles away. 'But instead of securing him,' wrote Tindal, 'he secured them, taking their horses and arms, and sending them back on foot.'

Oliver Fry, himself an old hand in bushranging incidents, just missed a personal confrontation with Wilson at Woolport. Both men had actually slept the night at Sharp's Hotel. Wilson overheard the Commissioner telling some friends how he intended to deal with the bushranger and, riding out of town, sent back a challenge to meet him in the open, 'not sheltered behind a slab wall as he had met Scotchie.'[9] Fry rode out at once. Two of his troopers were stuck up as they forded a creek and were forced to surrender their horses and carbines. The gang was next heard of in New England, where Gardiner's station was raided. In July they reappeared on Yulgilbar.

There were rumours that Wilson had threatened to shoot Edward. It was a grudge that went back many years to the Hunter. Perhaps he also knew that William Ogilvie was there, for his father had been one of Merton's convicts, and no favourite of the Ogilvies.

'We have had seven soldiers here, and three prisoners, for more than a fortnight,' Tindal told his father. 'The soldiers have been despatched from the Hunter River after Wilson. Having at last received intelligence of his robbing a station 50 miles from here, they went to the station with a black boy and after a day's search, got on his track. They followed it over the mountains for three days.'

The horse tracks led them directly towards Yulgilbar homestead. Ten miles out, from a forested ridge, they sighted smoke from a camp-fire in a narrow valley.

> On dismounting and crawling down to the fire, they were seen by one of the bushrangers, who was on watch. He gave the alarm and then bolted, with one of his companions. The other two retreated to some trees, where they fought until Wilson was shot dead, and his companion through the shoulder. One of the police was hit in the back.
>
> In the evening the corporal came for a dray to fetch the wounded man in, and on his return captured one of the runaways. The gang is now broken up. They had intended to take this station in the evening, hearing there were plenty of good horses to be had. Thirty stands of arms were found in their camp, including double-barrelled guns, rifles and blunderbusses.

Wilson himself was buried near the ford, just across the river from Yulgilbar homestead.

The parents remained at the station until October. Before returning to Merton, they offered Tindal a fifth share in the property for £2,000. The young man considered it, but decided it was beyond his means.

[9] Bawden, Thomas, *Three Lectures on the Early History of the Clarence*, University of New England.

His present capital, he said, amounted to no more than eight horses, twenty head of cattle, 420 sheep and £170 cash in the bank. Yet, he added wryly, it was 'more than many people have in this colony'.

The following year, after his first trip to Sydney in three years, Tindal accepted another offer from Edward. He was appointed station manager in Fred's place, with the additional inducement of acquiring 160 Yulgilbar sheep for his own account. 'I am to have all the increase,' read an exuberant letter, 'and the wool over the expenses of keeping them, which is taken at 17 or 18 pence per annum.'

A subsequent letter he wrote, clearly in answer to some forthright comment on the Ogilvies from his father, made a mysterious reference for which there now seems no reasonable explanation. 'In reply to the objectionable part of the Ogilvie character,' he wrote, 'I can understand the reasons which induced you to be silent, and I hope and believe that these conditions are now changed. I have already noticed that at least outward forms are now kept up, which I am sorry to say is not generally the case beyond the boundaries. With regard to myself, I hope I shall never give you cause to regret the confidence you reposed in me.'

Possibly this was only a reference to religious matters, for the Commander was well known as a free-thinker. Perhaps those 'outward forms' related to a passage in his previous letter noting that 'the service was read last Sunday to a congregation of twenty, which filled our sitting room.' It could, however, have had sexual connotations. Edward was widely supposed to favour local women.

More significant was this earnest young man's account, during 1847, of economic improvements along the Clarence.

On Yulgilbar, he reported, 'the gigantic lucerne and clover are growing well. I sowed in three different places, and it has come up strong everywhere. Kangaroos are beginning to disappear and give way to sheep and cattle. Plenty are still found in the mountains, but difficult to get at. I daresay I shall find some use for the kangaroo knife.'

Most important asset for local squatters was the newly opened boiling-down works at Woolport. 'Thousands of cattle are boiled down every year,' he wrote. 'A good bullock is worth 50/- to 60/- this way and, as cattle cost very little expense in management, it pays well enough.' Several station owners, notably the Mylnes, were soon to begin boiling-down as well, using great iron pots heated over open fires. Edward saw no point in following them, finding it more profitable to travel his stock on the hoof to Joseph Sharp's works outside Woolport, which had now been renamed after the new governor's grandfather, the royal Duke of Grafton. It was characteristic of the period to prefer the names of obscure Englishmen of title than those of local significance.

Stability now seems to have settled on the Clarence. The tribes, though reconciled to the new order, showed not the least intention of working for the newcomers. They had at least given up attacking them. They returned to their more ancient habit of fighting each other. These were almost ritualised conflicts in which the first blood shed was usually sufficient to end the battle. They had the spectator appeal of a bloody football match. Tindal was taken to see one of these encounters by Edward and Toolbillibam.

> It began in the afternoon, 26 men on one side and 30 on the other. Presently I heard a great shout, and the army came in column two abreast. They deployed into a circle and marched round the ground twice, stamping and shouting. One party then advanced throwing spears and boomerangs till dark. Next day they began again and fought for three hours. Two men on the opposite side were speared, and others hit with boomerangs.[10]

The replacement of Gipps by Sir Charles FitzRoy was more than a change of governors. It signalled a change in Colonial Office attitudes. The new man was a mild, dilatory, rubber-stamp official who confessed to having no views at all on the squatting question. This, commented Tindal, made him very popular. In March 1847 he announced that pastoralists were now to be given fourteen year leases in place of the detested annual licences, with freehold for homestead blocks. They had been given almost everything they asked for.

A century later, S. H. Roberts, described the Colonial Office's decision as fatal to the country's future.[11] 'The pioneers had become a monopolistic minority,' he wrote. 'Earl Grey and those who had departed from Gipps, had saddled Australia with an incubus that could not be shaken off, a problem that could not be solved—and the country has been paying for it ever since.'

Meantime, in the 'unsettled districts', men began to improve their runs as they had never had the confidence to do before. A buoyant new mood was now emerging. Life was something to be lived now.

'Several parties on the Clarence River,' Tindal wrote at the end of that year. 'First at Mr. Walker's on Christmas Day. Then at Mr.

Above: Tribal fight, Clarence River by C. Hodgkinson, 1845. Mitchell Library.

Below: Fishing on the Clarence by C. Hodgkinson, 1845. Mitchell Library.

[10] Tindal Family Letters, Mitchell Library, Sydney.

[11] Roberts, S. H., *The Squatting Age in Australia*, Melbourne, 1935.

Mylne's lower down. On the second day we had races and other sports, dining every evening ten in number and living in the same house.'

The Mylne brothers—a third, Thomas, had now come out from Scotland—were making their homestead the liveliest place on the Clarence. They lived with some style. Casually accepting an ancestry that went back to John of Bruce, they had enough capital from the sale of their Scottish property, Mylnefield, to begin large-scale improvements here. They had also changed the name of their Clarence run to Eatonswill. 'The Mylnes were good fellows in every sense,' Bawden recalled. 'Their home was celebrated for its hospitality. The doors were open to all. Unlimited eating and unlimited drinking were within the bounds of decorum. "Eat-and-swill" were the standing orders to their guests. Hence the name was metamorphosed into the more aristocratic Eatonswill.'

Bawden underrated their literary tastes. It was actually derived from *Pickwick Papers*, ironically recalling Dickens' rotten borough where unbridled entertainment was supposed to bring material rewards. The Mylnes, who were also good cattlemen, were unusually good hosts. James, who had resigned a subaltern's commission, came out with a rather 'wild' reputation and, so Tindal said, spent his days plaiting stockwhips and reading Waverley novels. John, the steady one, was an excellent judge of cattle and horses, while Thomas used his cavalry training for spirited cattle mustering. They had built their riverside homestead of solid cedar, with a verandah fifty feet long, a good library, well-stocked cellars and a garden of orange trees, peaches, lemons, banana palms and flowering shrubs.

Edward, whose home was described by Fred Tindal as 'the most English-looking' of them all, had now been appointed a magistrate and bought a much out-of-date set of Blackstone's *Commentaries* on English law, dated 1770.

The genial and portly John Dobie, though seldom at his station, was building a large homestead, having recently sold Ramornie to the Manning family in Sydney, buying up Gordon Brook instead. His special interest was blood horses.

1848 began as a year of promise. One event only brought the Clarence into public disrepute. This was the scandal of Kangaroo Creek.

Thomas Coutts, who had followed Craig down in 1840, appears to have been largely ignored by neighbouring graziers. On three occasions Commissioner Fry filed reports of his stockmen being killed by the local tribe. His own relations with them had been so bad that men were reluctant to work for him.

In January 1848 Fry was called out again. Tindal sent home an account of fourteen Aborigines being found dead on Kangaroo Creek, and another nine bodies washed away in a flood. They had all died of arsenic poisoning. He said that Coutts, angered by repeated thefts of flour, had given them a whole sackful, flavoured with arsenic. Traces of the poison were found in the remains of dampers they had baked and eaten.

Coutts was arrested, committed for trial in Sydney and released on bail. It so happened that he had to appear before Mr Justice Manning, part owner of Ramornie station. The judge delayed the hearing so long that Coutts was never brought to the dock at all. Reason given was that there were difficulties in finding witnesses. Two years later, ostracised locally, Coutts sold his property, taking up another at Tooloom in the ranges above Yulgilbar. He was still harassed by the local tribe. They forced him to abandon the district altogether. The epitaph to his career was written by Charles Tindal's brother, Fred. 'Coutts,' he wrote in February 1852, 'has met disaster on his new station on the Dawson River. The blacks killed some of his men and drove off his sheep.' That was the last anyone heard of him. But the Kangaroo Creek affair embittered relations along the Clarence for a number of years.

It called for some rather diplomatic handling of the people on Yulgilbar.

13
Master of Yulgilbar

Edward now had to make all his own decisions.

Yulgilbar was his alone now that his brother was up there on the hill. He could seldom have been unaware of it. On still nights, under a clear bowl of stars, in moonlight, the profile of that dominant hill was very close. Men said there was a harder set to him; he did not laugh so readily. He was now thirty-four.

'We have not agreed as well as we used to,' Tindal wrote of him at the end of 1848. 'E. Ogilvie, like many good managers, is too fond of having everything done his own way; so by mutual consent our agreement is to terminate. We shall, however, part very good friends.'

Finding himself treated like a superintendent rather than partner, the younger man had been looking around the country for some time. He had earlier hoped to buy Tabulam until an ex-army man, Captain C. H. E. Chauvel, forestalled him. Now he had managed to acquire the short-term lease of Koorelah, at the headwaters of the Clarence, and bought a thousand head of cattle with Edward's help. This was characteristic. Edward had a good money sense, enjoyed the role of a man of influence. He had inherited his father's feeling for clan involvement; and his canniness.

Physically, too, there was a good deal of his father in him. A portrait painted five years later gave him the same high-domed forehead and receding hairline, the same large Scottish nose. The painter, who was a Florentine, gave it a touch of romanticism, especially in those clear, fair flesh tones. They hardly seem appropriate to a man who had spent his life under a harsh Australian sun. He emphasised, too, the full and curling black moustaches, which created an air of gaiety, contradicted by the hard-set mouth they almost conceal. The full lower lip suggests a certain libido, but the upper one is narrow, somewhat repressive. Below the heavy Dundreary whiskers, the clean-shaven chin is outthrust and very firm. Later pictures of Edward, especially in old age, confirm the Italian artist's recognition of his steelier features, though the reflective and kindly look of the hazel eyes persisted to the end. He does not appear a robust figure, and was in fact of a rather slight build, shortish and not constitutionally strong.

Yet he had competed vigorously with Toolbillibam and others in foot races, wrestling and swimming. One is left with the awareness of strong will and a determination to succeed.

He had already done so at Yulgilbar. There was little question of that by 1850. Wool prices were rising again; cattle bringing up to £2 a head at the boiling-down works in Grafton, and Yulgilbar running thousands of sheep and cattle over three hundred square miles of country.

In less than a decade Edward had begun to change the look of this country. Tracks ran out from the head station in many directions. A series of stockmen's huts had been built nearby. Aborigines had settled once more by Yulgilbar Reach. On the far side was a bark-roofed woolshed of solid slabs. Here and there flats had been thinned of trees, allowing the native grasses to spread. Bark huts for the shepherds had gone up in all manner of once remote places. In a direct line north and south boundaries were a good forty miles apart; Tindal's 'long day's ride'. East and west it varied from fifteen to twenty miles, according to the lie of the Richmond and New England Ranges. None of it had yet been officially surveyed.

Immediately south of the homestead were the broad undulating pasturelands of the Front Run, reaching away across Fourteen Mile and Dumbudgery Creeks to the Gorge. A fantastic place, this half-mile gorge. Just below the junction of the Clarence and Mann Rivers, it compressed the strong flow of both rivers between walls of granite and blackened igneous rocks, which rose up to two hundred feet. There were deep, still waterholes, rock bars, rapids and steep falls that foamed and thundered in time of flood. The Mann, which Edward called the South River, was the powerful outlet of the Nymboida, Coombadjha Creek and many rushing streams from the high ranges. Near the junction was Heifer Station, where Edward ran his weaners and maiden cows. North and west of Coombadjha Creek (a corruption of the Kumbainggiri's tribal name) was a chain of his isolated sheep stations, mostly in small pockets of valleys, or on ridges and spurs. These had acquired names such as Land's End, Cataract, Canbarrabin, Pinnacle, Collum Collum, Tumbung, the Washpool, Nogrigar. Each flock here had its lonely shepherd and hutkeeper, to whom rations were delivered by dray every four weeks.

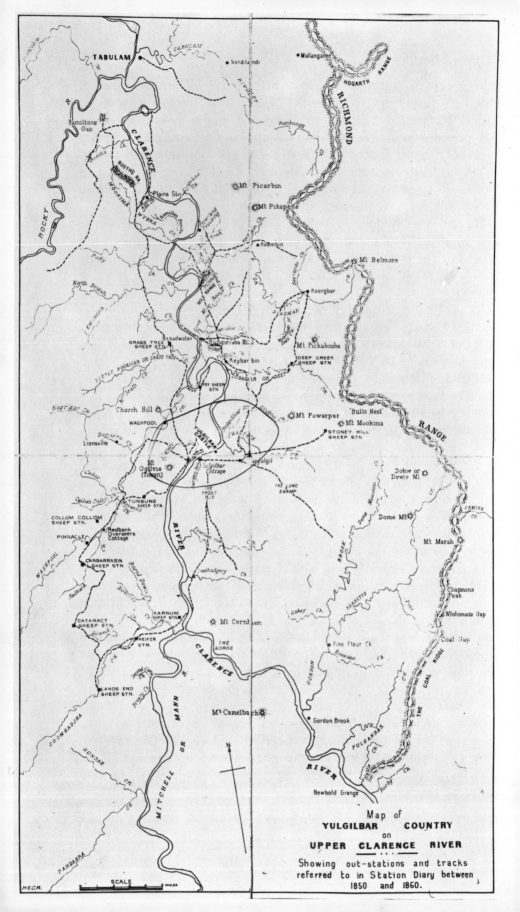

Map of
YULGILBAR COUNTRY
on
UPPER CLARENCE RIVER

Showing out-stations and tracks
referred to in Station Diary between
1850 and 1860.

From the head station, strategically placed near the centre of the run, another track ran west to Joseph's Creek, named after an early shepherd, then north across Bulgilbar, Flagstone Creek and up the long steep spur of Kungurraba Hill, from whose crest riders looked further north to the luminously blue rampart of the forested Long Mile Range. Beyond again the track wound on to Plains Station, where Edward held more cattle, and finally to Tabulam and the seemingly endless ascent to Tenterfield, Bolivia Station and New England.

Yet even this road, well travelled now by neighbouring cattlemen and bullock teams, took no account of other small sheep stations Edward had formed in hilly country east and west. Nor of the magnificent expanse of river known as the Broadwater, beneath the flank of Kungurraba Hill. It had the air of an inland lake, so broad was it, so blue and still on sunny days, though it foamed over rapids and rock bars in flood. Black swans cruised upon it. Freshwater cod, perch, bream were to be caught in abundance.

There were so many aspects to Yulgilbar. Pastoral beauty; wilderness, river flats as tranquil as England; sombre ranges; a pervading sense of the prehistoric, as in the calcified footprints of extinct monsters along the Washpool, and the Creation Day silence of the Gorge. Edward was the possessor of lands larger than an English county; a little principality over which, in unassuming fashion, he alone ruled. He rode about these lands like a feudal lord.

The squatter's life as he lived it had no resemblance to that of some verandah bosses elsewhere in later times. It was eternally demanding, consuming all his energy, committing him to a dozen different activities, problems, decisions in the course of any one day. The record of his involvement is still to be found in the station journals he kept, writing them up daily over the years.[1] Throughout the early fifties all entries were in his own rather stiff hand. Later his managers took over, leaving a detailed account of how Yulgilbar developed and prospered.

The three bulky volumes have small literary merit. That was not their intention. They were for factual reference only; a tired man's jottings after a long day on the run. Yet they have the breath of reality, echoes of hardship and hope and achievement, the realisation that, out of the day's routine, the monotonies, the unending battle against weather, human failings and isolation, something of value was being created. Day by day a pattern begins to emerge. You become

Map for Yulgilbar Station 1850–60.

[1] Yulgilbar Station Journal, Mitchell Library, Sydney.

aware of the seasonal cycle; lambing, sheepwashing, shearing, the annual cattle muster, the time for pruning vines, harvesting, the pressing and maturation of the wine. Certain names and places recur time and time again, conjuring up the feel of Yulgilbar's bygone life—the Irish, or later German and Chinese shepherds, the hard-working managers and station hands, the Aborigines little by little absorbed into a new style of living. One recognises Jimmy Cobbera, the sturdy tribesman from Merton; Pundoon, the abducted Kumbainggiri boy, growing to manhood; the proud Toolbillibam sadly transformed into King Billy with a tin name plate on his chest.

There were, nonetheless, advantages to this civilising process, for the former nomads were now being offered some security.

Edward devised an enlightened system that other squatters might well have followed, though few did. He assigned Aborigines as shepherds or hutkeepers to various flock stations, leaving a European to train them for an initial period. Hence, in subsequent labour shortages, he was always assured of men to look after his sheep. In addition, he won native loyalty and respect.

First entry in the station journal is for Sunday, 17 February 1850. It had been no day of rest for Edward.

'Reached home in the evening from Mylne's,' he wrote, 'which place I made last evening overland from the Hunter. Left Merton on the morning of Saturday the 9th, and reached Armidale on the evening of Wednesday the 13th. The weather has been very hot. For the last two days I have been almost blind with opthalmia.'

Next day he noted that the country was dry, but feed plentiful, the livestock doing well and his grapes ready for picking. He started on the vintage that afternoon. On Tuesday he found the crop so large he had to send Raby, the bullock driver, on a two-week trip to Grafton for more casks. Five days later, having borrowed others urgently from Dobie at Gordon Brook, he had eight hundred gallons of wine fermenting. On 26 February he began grinding harvested wheat into flour, filled the wine casks, set two men to fencing a sheep paddock. Of 28 February: 'Cut one of Elliot's colts in the morning. Racked off some wine as a cask was leaking. In the afternoon started for Heifer Station. Have to go to Tabulam tomorrow to sit upon a letter the Colonial Secretary has forwarded to the Bench there. Phipps en route for Koreelah to get my bullocks from Jephson.' Returning from Tabulam, where he was now local magistrate, he inspected several flocks, drafted heifers, put the herd on the road for Yulgilbar and was disturbed by the cattle's poor condition. 'Appear to have been much over-driven on their way from the Gwydir.'

Clearly the Clarence run had now been phased into the Ogilvies' widely scattered network of holdings. Brother Will bred cattle on the Gwydir, sent them across New England to Yulgilbar, which likewise had an interchange of sheep with the Commander at Merton. Breeders were also travelling to and from the Bundocks at Wyangerie and Dyraaba, Charles Tindal at Koreelah and even James Glennie, now settled at Umrigar station, under the McPherson Ranges.

Meanwhile Edward continued with his own complex operations. 5 March: 'Carted the corn crop. Racked wine again. Sent off Thomas to Tabulam to get warrants for Pundoon, Mulmul and a boy, they having broke into and plundered the store of 8 lb. tobacco while I was absent in Sydney.' More than a month passed without mention of the escapees. On 9 April: 'Made an attempt at daybreak to secure Mulmul and Pundoon. Caught Pundoon and flogged him. Mulmul escaped. Rode up to Twelve Mile station, commenced operations on the sheep.'

This flogging was hardly characteristic. Only one such action was mentioned again. Perhaps it served his purpose. Many references to Pundoon in future years revealed him as a steady worker; driving ration carts, a bullock dray, shepherding, fencing, drafting cattle. Old hands still point out the location of his chastisement. Oakey Creek is often known yet as Flogging Creek.

Even in 1850 Edward was having some success with the Yulgilbar tribe. He wrote of 'setting the blacks to pull the corn crop . . . Blacks still cutting bark.'

Month after month he was perpetually in the saddle. He rode great distances almost daily, yet still found time for a hard day's work at many remote locations. One day he is in Tabulam; the next at the South River, or visiting Eatonswill or Gordon Brook in connection with cattle, or equipment, or horses. One day he notes attending Grafton's boiling-down works. The next he has ridden another sixty miles to Yamba, where a vessel taking his wool clip to sea has run ashore. Soon another station name begins to recur.

This was Fairfield. Exactly when or how he came by this 100,000-acre mountain run is not on record. He appears to have acquired it initially on occupational lease. It was on the western boundary of Plains Station thus giving him a large extension of his original run. Edward put Robert Smith in charge, linking it with his own cattle-breeding programme.

In May he finished drafting cattle on the South River, sent them off to Grafton and made a long ride north to Tabulam, guiding Bishop Tyrrell of Newcastle back to Yulgilbar.

The Bishop's travels had obviously been timed to make Grafton for its first annual race meeting. Edward, Tindal, and Wellington Bundock were among those who entered grass-fed horses. It was a memorable occasion. His journal noted:

> On Friday, the 24th May, I was thrown from my horse on the racecourse, and broke my left arm midway between the shoulder and elbow. On Tuesday following I was able to walk about again. The bone was, I think, then united. Next day I was strong enough to walk out to the boiling works and attend to my business. By Friday last, the seventh day after the accident, I was able to leave on my way homeward. Let the first two flocks of fat wethers going down to be boiled today between Dobie's and this.

Who said he was not a robust man?

Three weeks later he was searching for more country in the ranges. 'Started out with Pillar [sheep overseer] to explore a piece of country high in the mountain at the head of Ewingar Creek.' Reaching home again next evening, he noted 'there is room for a small station up on the shelf of land I have been to look at. Last night was mild up at the height we camped, but frosty down here.' He was not a man to waste time for, a month later, he rode out with Ellen and Bundock across the river to see two flocks en route for the new station up Moam Creek.

Subsequent months revealed something of the hazards, emergencies and unexpected developments he had to meet with instant action.

> Went to Tabulam to prosecute Anderson for leaving his flock in the yards all last Sunday Week. (9 July). Went out to Foy's Station to look for some sheep seen last evening astray on his run. (13 July). Went up Moam Brook to see some country that the Blacks speak of. (14 July). My imported bull, Syntax, reported sick shortly after I returned home and died in less than half an hour while we were attempting to bleed him. (17 July). Busy all day starting Elliott, Nordblad and two blacks on way to Hall's Station to bring down cattle. One of the blacks was thrown and the horse not recovered till evening. (7 August). Pilar came in to say all the flocks have started lambing and took away a lot of men. Frost last night, which has cut up the young grass terribly. (11 September). A good deal of rain fell last night, ground now begins to look moist and grass ready to grow. Went up the run to look at lambing flocks. Heavy thunder shower fell in evening. (25 September). Hands at the Washpool making huts for own accommodation. Buried John Henry (who died this morning) by candlelight. (4 October). Set Casey to learn to shear, Hough to make presses ready for work. Put a lot of bark on woolshed roof to stop leaks in thatch. (17 October). Washed McGrath's flock, but had a nasty job of it, rain began to fall in showers. Shearing of Armstrong's flock not completed; about 400

left. (19 October). Casson's dray loaded with 10 bales wool and drew across river, but stuck at the bank. (22 October). Weather cleared. Tried to cross Armstrong's flock—shorn—over river, but too much water. (24 October). Set hand to mow oats for hay. Brady's flock shorn today. (4 November). Rams were shorn today—*the last flock!* (6 November). Cut and branded all the colts. (26 November). Awfully hot day, with west wind. Pillar so ill with inflammation of lungs I did not like to leave him. Thermometer 106 in the shade. (3 December).

Winters could be cold, especially at nights, even in this sheltered valley. There were wild westerlies, frosts, driving rains, sudden freshes down the river, sometimes floods. As the year ended the country heated up. Winds became furnace draughts, drying up grasses. Temperatures remained high all night, and sleep could be difficult. In times of sickness men had to sit it out and cure themselves. Edward left only the briefest account of the sheep overseer's illness. The following day he wrote:

'Started at sunrise for Heifer Station to select cows to come down for breeders this year. Pillar much better this morning, and, I think, out of danger. Very weak and unwell myself, the combined effects of the great heat and a slight attack of influenza, from which I have scarcely yet recovered. Heat so great last night I was obliged to leave my room and lie upon the grass flat.'

Next day, having looked over several flocks, he cut out 159 cows at Heifer Station. 'I am still so weak I was obliged to get off my horse and lie down several times today.' The day after, which he spent writing letters at the homestead, he noted, 'Took a blue pill last night, and began a course of Rhubarb and Ipecacuanha pills today. Feel much stronger.'

Ten days before Christmas he rode off, with one stockman, for Dobie's station, intending to ride through New England to Merton. 'Returned to port, disabled,' he wrote that evening back at Yulgilbar, 'Booth having been thrown about five miles along the road, his fall causing the escape of the packhorse and my spare horse. I am now resolved not to make another start till I can get Jimmy (Cobbera) to take with me.' To do this meant riding next day down the other side of the river to Heifer Station. Reaching it, he found 'Hamilton just getting delirium tremens.'

It seemed that some men's Christmas began early.

Christmas 1850 was the last the family was ever to spend together. Events were now taking them in separate directions.

Fred Tindal, who had come out to join his brother towards the end of the year, wrote of finding 'Captain and Mrs. Ogilvie alone at Merton, where they seldom saw their sons. Of this Mrs. Ogilvie often complained. But the Hunter estate can only support about 1000 sheep and some horses, and the sons look after the different stations on the Gwydir, Balonne and Clarence.'

Though Merton had by this time grown to a thriving township, with two inns, stores and St Mathias church on the hill, Mary had come to find it lonely. The Commander, in his usual solicitious way, encouraged her to spend more time with friends in Sydney. He bought a house for her in Edgecliff. Fairlight was a comfortable sandstone house with a view of the Harbour, an easy carriage drive from town.

Edward, too, had decided he could now live with a shade more comfort. The journal notes his return by horse to Yulgilbar—this five hundred mile ride was becoming commonplace—on 28 February. 'The servants and the sheep I sent per the *Meg Merrilees* have now been here about a week.' Next day he added, 'Installed my new servants, and engaged my late ones, Handock and his wife, as shepherd and hutkeeper.'

It was a significant entry. Here was the first instance of anyone on the Clarence engaging a married couple for outside station work. A new type of settler was arriving from Britain. The presence of wives on these stations promised to bring about a more settled atmosphere. The following week he mentioned sending one of his station hands across to Wyangerie, taking a nurse and cook to join his sister's establishment.

There was something almost euphoric about his entry on the Sunday. 'Divine service morning and afternoon. Pleasant day. Some clouds floating about.'

All told, a new sense of optimism begins to pervade the journal. After his earlier experiences it all seems too good to be true. Despite repeated temperatures above 100°, lack of rain and summer feed, the vintage began well, corn and millet produced a good harvest, the lambs looked healthy, the bullocks on the South River were putting on condition. The Aborigines had also become increasingly cooperative.

'Went up to Ewingar early,' he wrote on 19 March, 'as the blacks reported that old Bush is ill and unable to take out his flock. Found him laid up, and got a black gin to take out the flock.' On the 31st, he 'rode out to see the blacks who are cutting bark on the new line of road'. Three days later, when a watchman rode in from Tumbung to report a German shepherd had lost 500 weaners in the scrub, Edward recorded, 'Took Elliott with me and searched the mountain all day, but 250 still missing at night.' Next morning he 'took a lot of blacks and succeeded in finding all the lost sheep except about 20.'

A notable change from the spearing and roasting they had indulged in a few years earlier. The employment of Aboriginal women was also something new.

In May, Yulgilbar had a visit from Commissioner Fry. Edward spent two days with him, riding about the station on the annual inspection. The laconic comment in Edward's journal quietly revealed the remarkable advances made. 'Fry assessed the runs at 2,000 sheep, 2,500 cattle on Yulgilbar, and 1,500 cattle at South River.'

It was a clear indication of his changed station policy; a factor becoming general throughout the Clarence Valley. Pastoralists were now turning away from sheep to cattle. It was a trend that followed Richmond River practice, where men had discovered all too clearly that the humid coast and hinterland were just not suitable for sheep. Their flocks were being steadily boiled-down, and not replaced.

Six months later Edward made an accounting that further clarified the position. Completing his boiling-down accounts for the year, he wrote: 'Find that the sheep, 953 culled ewes, netted 4/10½ per head; the W. and E.O. cattle, 406 head, including 47 weaners, 39/8, within a fraction; and the Hall's, 104 head, 33/6d per head. W.O. sheep £77.12.9, Cattle £237.7.8. Total £315.0.5.'

Yet, during that first critical decade, it had been sheep alone that enabled him to found and stabilise his runs. More than 16,000 of them had been overlanded from Merton, and their time was not finished yet. The journal made frequent references to the new German rams he had brought north, emphasising his resolve to improve the quality of his flocks with a hardy Saxon strain.

And then, with the suddenness of a Clarence thunderstorm, the sky of his hopes seemed to split open. Everyone's future was menaced. 'By the papers and letters received yesterday,' he wrote on 1 June, 'we have the first authentic account of the gold discovery near Bathurst. I fear our prospect of labour for the next lambing and shearing is very bad.'

It was an understatement. More than the prospects of lambing and shearing were involved. The destiny of the entire country was threatened with drastic change; its economy, the social order, the kind of people migrating, jobs, concepts of freedom, the future of a nation still in process of emerging. It was not yet possible for any to understand the full implications under the clear, wind-flecked skies of Yulgilbar. How could they recognise that a revolution in men's thinking and actions was already under way, as drastic as any of the social upheavals that had lately erupted in Europe, turning popular attention towards a still formless and bemused antipodean society on the far side of the world.

The articulate Charles Tindal expressed it with more pungency.

'I suppose you have already heard of the discovery of a second California in this country,' he told his father. 'At present all the working men are headed for the mines, and are leaving this district by the shipload for Sydney. Wages are expected to rise so as to destroy all profits on sheep farming.'

More than a thousand men were at once washing creeks for gold in the Blue Mountains. Within two months there were three thousand of them on the Turon River alone. Pastoral centres like Bathurst were drained of their working population. Great numbers left Sydney, Melbourne, even placid Adelaide. In the newly separated colony of Victoria a mass exodus occurred. Police deserted their posts; clerks and counter jumpers abandoned stores; windjammers in Port Phillip Bay were left as bare as their masts. Another big strike at Mount Alexander, followed by Ballarat and Bendigo, provoked hundreds of diggers into the frantic demolition of tranquil landscapes that had hitherto known only the quiet browsing of sheep. The country was being swept almost clean of shepherds and shearers.

Threading through the journal now were several German names: Nordblad, Cram, Munt, Rosenstein. Germans had begun to emigrate to Australia late in the 1840s, due largely to a colonising scheme sponsored by a British philanthropist and banker, George Fife Angas, who saw this as a means of providing hard-working peasant settlers in South Australia. Perhaps the credit should also have gone to the King of Prussia, whose stubborn persecution of a particular Lutheran sect drove thousands of families out of his territories. Others arriving in Sydney soon proved themselves more conscientious workers than British migrants, so that station owners readily offered them jobs. They were brought out under an indenture system, with their fares paid, though they had to sign an agreement not to look for work elsewhere for two years. 'Germans are very careful with sheep,' stated a Legislative Council report on immigration. 'They are very quiet and orderly men, and excellent shepherds.' Nor did these people show the least desire to desert for the goldfields.

They had only one disadvantage. Accustomed to the tamer, closely settled landscapes of Europe, they were bewildered by the vast, often trackless Australian bush. Its hazards were dramatised by a series of journal entries in the winter of 1851.

'In the evening heard that Joseph was lost,' Edward recorded on 23 June. 'He left the Five Mile station last evening to come home, but has not since made his appearance. Sent out Phibbs with Pundoon to look for his tracks, but they returned at night unsuccessful.'

Next morning he sent Phibbs upriver with a party of Aboriginal trackers, while his superintendent Elliott searched east of the dray track the German had obviously missed. Edward who had to inspect a new flock station at the head of Paddock Creek, kept a look-out for tracks as well. One of the two stockmen riding with him found Joseph's tracks late that afternoon. They followed them until dark. The tracks led them in a great circle. When night came they were back at their starting point. As experienced bushmen they knew that, once a man started wandering in this aimless fashion, he was in serious trouble. Edward rode home in the dark. At sunrise he had a packhorse saddled up, took an Aboriginal tracker with him and enough food for forty-eight hours. They spent their entire day tracking up and down a series of creeks, through dense scrub and over a range to the head of Deep Creek, which was a long way further from home than Joseph's original starting point. Here they discovered his first night's camp. That meant they were still two days behind him.

On the 26th he wrote, 'Breakfasted at daybreak and were off on the track before sunrise. Followed it across the heads of different branches of Deep Creek, then down that creek, then across the ranges to Paddock Creek and up that creek till dark, when I left the camp to get a [further] supply of provisions and a second black to track, as two can keep the track and get on quicker than one. Got in late. There was a hard frost last night which has cut up the bananas.'

On the fourth day he wrote,

> At about midday came upon the second sleeping place [that of Tuesday night] some distance above the Dome Mountain, so that we are now two and a half days behind the chase. I begin to feel very fearful that Joseph may die of hunger before we can overtake him. We saved much time this afternoon through picking up the track where it returned on itself. The blacks say that the evening's track is a day fresher and that a camp must have been passed on the part of the track we avoided, so we are now on his yesterday's track. Ran him down by dark to pathway leading from Dobie's cattle station to the head station, so that we feel little doubt of his having made a station by this time. Hard frost again last night.
>
> Saturday, 28th. Ran the track to one of Dobie's sheep stations this morning, and there learnt that the lost man found one of the shepherds on Thursday and started on his way home yesterday. Turned our horses' heads homeward and got in about one o'clock.

In those six days they must have ridden well over a hundred miles, from daylight until the late hours, with very little sleep and only hard rations eaten hurriedly beside their weary horses. No wonder Edward wrote, of that rainy Sunday, 'Stayed at home and read the papers, which have accumulated rather.'

There was another moral to this search. Few men admitted it, but survival in this harsh and lonely country often depended on Aboriginal sympathy and skills.

Though Edward seems early to have conceived the squatter's traditional distrust of shearers—'Had a regular rumpus with the shearers today,' he wrote in October, 'the shearing is so bad I cannot let it go on longer'—he was always on the best of terms with both Germans and Aborigines. In later years those who worked on Yulgilbar described him as a hard man, very demanding, but always fair. He had strong opinions also on the right way of doing things.

According to Ellen, this applied equally to his Aborigines. He had even 'issued orders that no blacks should be admitted into the back yard without the proper amount of clothing. On one occasion whilst I was there I found a man sitting with an air of proud consciousness in his bearing, attired in a collar, hat and a pair of boots. His dignity suffered somewhat by being promptly kicked out.'[2]

He must have felt very sure of these people to have done that.

By 1852 he had reason for it. The journal records the employment of one named Warral as a shepherd for nine shillings a week. This was the first instance of any Aboriginal being given a regular wage. Others were soon engaged to build barns, huts, a dingo-proof fence to protect weaned lambs, and to cut down scrub for new pastures. Perhaps the sweetest job of all went to a youth by the name of Tommy. When a German named Happ proved himself hapless at shooting cockatoos, the blunderbuss was handed over to Tommy. His pride can only be imagined. It was a post of great importance and responsibility.

They were threshing and grinding wheat at the time. As usual white cockatoos descended in huge flocks. Losses were considerable. The new worker rated a special mention in the journal for 14 February 1852.

'Tommy watching cockatoos.'

---

[2] Bundock, Mrs E. W., *Early Recollections of E. D. S. Ogilvie of Yulgilbar*, 1894. Archives, University of New England.

14

A Good Time Coming

Within a year of the discovery of gold Yulgilbar had few Europeans workers left. The names that recur in the station journal are nearly always German, Aboriginal or Chinese.

'Sent three of the Chinese up to Keebarbin to take flocks at Grasstree,' Edward wrote in February 1852. It was the first reference to them, as if they had just arrived. Due to the general labour shortage, the Pastoralists Association had at last won the right to import Indian and Chinese coolies, though these did not arrive in any large numbers. They, too, were brought in under the indenture system, being obliged to remain with the same master for five years. Each man's fare cost his employer £15. The standard wage was £7.4.0 annually, and this had to be paid in gold or silver coin. He had also to be given free one pair of boots, trousers and a shirt each year, while the weekly ration was fixed at 10 lb rice, 2 oz tea, 13 lb beef or 14 lb mutton. Indians, according to an official report, were generally preferred to Chinese because 'they were not so subject to gusts of passion at some misunderstood trifle, and do not so often leave their sheep in the hurdles or go away in a body.'[1] Edward appeared to have little option. Indians were rarely available.

The tendency of these Chinese shepherds to be careless with sheep was soon borne out, one Ng Vooi being a particular offender. Presumably, as the regulations prescribed, he was fined for each sheep he lost, or its value deducted from his pay. Yet, in general, they appear to have worked well. The journal mentions them building yards, sowing and harvesting crops and, in the case of Chia Oor, working with Joseph the vine dresser in the homestead garden.

One wonders what language they spoke to each other.

Ellen Bundock disagreed with the popular concept of the Chinese

[1] Select Committee on Immigration, Legislative Council, 1852.

as unreliable station hands. In her experience, she wrote, they made good, trustworthy shepherds. Edward even employed them in the homestead as cooks. 'We had never seen Chinese before,' Ellen's daughter, Mary, remembered afterwards. 'We were delighted with them. The cook was very good to us, making special cakes for us, and his delight was to get my doll and plait its hair in a pigtail and make it as Chinese-looking as possible.

'One day we saw a most gorgeously dressed person riding up to the house at a slow pace. His hat, an enormous straw one as large as an umbrella, was carried by a black, who walked beside his horse. His dignity impressed us very much. We ran in to tell my uncle that the King of China was coming to see him, and were much disappointed to find he was only one of the shepherds coming in his best dress to visit his friend the cook.'[2]

Having now lost most of his trained hands, Edward had to push himself harder than ever. He was personally involved in almost every activity, perpetually in the saddle, often spending several nights away from home. He carried a tent and pack with him, sometimes sleeping on the ground. At other times he camped in some shepherd's hut. He had huts of his own as well in several places, notably at the Broadwater where cattle were mustered, at Heifer Station and on the South River. The journal refers to the chimney he had built for winter warmth at Broadwater. He set the stone around the fireplace himself, while attending a muster there. He was never inactive. There were also sudden emergencies that kept him from the homestead for prolonged periods. One of these occurred at the very time that Ellen and her children had come to stay with him in April.

Before they arrived he had written, 'The country is drying up in the most extraordinary manner. The grass is assuming a withered appearance almost all over the run, and would not burn in many parts where a week ago it had been green.' Then the rains started. He had ridden up to Collum Collum, telling his sister he would be back next morning. It was seven days before he returned. The laconic journal merely hints at the ordeal of that flood-bound week.

> *Friday 9.* Sent off Tinier George with 4 weeks rations for the mountains. Started myself in evening during a lull between showers. Overtook George this side of Turkey Brush and so delayed that night closed in before we reached Collum Collum branch creek. Found it too high to be crossed in dark. Rain fell in a perfect deluge while we were looking, or rather feeling for a crossing place, with much difficulty made a fire and encamped for the night.

[2] Bundock, Mrs E. W., *Early Recollections of E. D. S. Ogilvie of Yulgilbar*, 1894. Archives, University of New England.

Saturday 10. Rain fell in torrents all night. Creeks all bank high this morning and fire out. Having rekindled the fire and stowed all as snugly as I could, swam branch creek taking my shirt and hat with me, walked to Redbank leaving George (who cannot swim) at camp. Rain poured down all day, creek rising all afternoon.

Sunday 11. Rain ceased during night. Creek had gone down. Sun out after breakfast. Went down to camp, brought up George and all the packs, etc. Thomas looking for sheep left out at Collum Collum by Ng Vooi yesterday.

Monday 12. Heavy shower last night. Got men to work and renewed brush fence at Redbank. Put draft of rams to Ng Vooi's flock.

Tuesday 13. Swam creek and walked up to Canbarrabin to see how all had gone during flood. Rations just out. Brought Newton down with me and carried over some flour, tea and sugar for him on my head. Heavy rain again just after dark.

Wednesday 14. Swam rams over to flocks at Canbarrabin and Yarrom. In afternoon walked up to former, put 8 rams into Yoo Tswan's, 14 into Mickey's.

Thursday 15. Reached home via Tumbung, crossing creek at Mozimbil. Water reached the horses backs. River still very high. Crossed in boat and left horses at Woolshed.

The Clarence itself continued to flood for weeks. A fortnight later the road to Grafton was still impassable. The fat cattle mustered for the boiling-down works were unable to travel. Wellington Bundock, cut off in town by the floods, failed to return. Even the mailman was unable to make his fortnightly buggy trip. Nor was it possible to do much work on the station, for the red soils plains had become a vast bog that no horses could cross. By that time it had been raining almost continuously for six weeks.

Perhaps these bleak conditions accounted for two terse entries in the journal during that waterlogged June. 'Gave house servants notice I should prefer a charge of disobedience of orders against them, after which they became so extremely offensive in their language and conduct I put them out of the kitchen, and had their goods and chattels conveyed to a hut over the river.' Two days later, when the couple left, he sent his overseer down to Grafton to summons them for breach of contract.

Further conflicts developed at shearing time.

'Shearers stood out for 4/- per score,' he wrote on 18 September. 'I offered them 3/- and, as I would not advance on this, a number of them saddled up their horses and went off. However, as there are more coming, I daresay we shall have enough without these, who are the most flash of the lot.'

He made terms with the new arrivals, arranging to pay 3/6 'upon them binding themselves by agreement to do their work well.' Within two days a further dispute began. 'Went over to the woolshed in the evening, and found the shearers doing their work so badly I was obliged to make some examples by cutting down tallies.' Nonetheless, the season ended happily. 'Gave the shearers a grand dinner in the shed,' he wrote on 18 October.

He must have done them too well, for it was forty-eight hours before he allowed them to touch the last of his rams. 'They drank too much wine to be able to start yesterday.'

Perhaps no one thought to mention that it was Edward himself who had supplied that wine. Tindal had already described earlier the sound, light Sauterne-type wine that Edward sold to his station hands for three shillings a bottle. Even then he had some £300 worth in his cellars, returning him a good profit on ready sales.

Shearers apart, no one came looking for employment any more.

He decided to make a bid for more Germans. Hearing that a certain William Kirchner had recently arrived in Grafton, planning to exploit local tallow by setting up a candle and soap works, he wrote in his formal fashion, 'I am given to understand that you undertake to import shepherds from Germany under indentures to serve for two years at £16 per annum wages, with a single ration £13 to be paid to you upon arrival of each man, and that the sum will be repaid by the shepherd to his employer by two annual instalments of £6.10s. each. I wish to procure six shepherds upon these terms. If it could be effected I should prefer making the engagement for four years and paying them £20 annual wages.'

Clearly the answer was unsatisfactory. He replied a month later that 'I think it very objectionable that I should bind myself to pay the passages of men brought over from Germany, though I might never see them or be otherwise aware of their arrival than by the production of a certificate of the Master of the vessel that he had landed the men in Sydney.' He also reminded Herr Kirchner that he had noted another disturbing fact, that the shepherds, or even vine dressers, men sent abroad for often turned out to be merely untrained labourers.

He was not a man to be caught by these stratagems.

Again, towards the end of the year, further correspondence revealed the battle he was still having to survive. It was all very well for new chum immigrants like Henry Parkes, through his agitational newspaper the *Empire*, to campaign against the growing wealth of 'Shepherd Kings'. Yulgilbar, at least, was not in this class yet. Writing to a now unidentifiable Whistler, Edward apologised for his forgetfulness in renewing his squatting licence, adding that 'I may mention that I would wish to delay squaring up till I get either tallow or wool to market. The outrageous delay which has occurred with the former having brought me into very shallow water, if not aground.'[3]

At a time when many northern squatters were turning over to cattle, Edward reiterated his belief in wool. His sheep were doing well, he wrote, 'and perhaps the black shepherds are improving in their craft. If that old scoundrel Kirchner would only send me the German families he has been so long amusing me with the expectation of, and I had them settled and a little broken in to their work, I should not feel so shaky.

'In the meantime I keep a good heart, and never doubt, though the ordeal we are passing through is rather severe, there is 'a good time coming', and we shall turn right side uppermost at last. The tide of population that is now rolling in must shortly give a value to beef and mutton that will far more than compensate for all our hopes and increased expenses. As for shepherds, there must soon be an ample supply of used up gold seekers available.'

He was not far wrong. Within a year his station journal mentioned several unemployed men walking into Yulgilbar, asking for work.

At Christmas time he decided to celebrate in a most unexpected style. Instead of going south to Merton, he arranged a house party of his own. It was the first time he had ever sent out specific invitations. Charles Tindal, had he not been in Sydney, would have been much impressed. He had long deph red the fact that Clarence settlers saw so little of one another.

Edward began preparation for his all-male guests three days in advance. He had a new flat-bottomed boat hauled up from Grafton, launched it on the long reach. He set up a tent outside the homestead, and huge festive decorations, then personally chose and killed a special 'Xmas bullock' to be roasted whole. He celebrated Christmas Eve by having the first hot shower ever on Yulgilbar. It was a portable shower he had rigged up for his guests.

Christmas Day arrived with the temperature well above the century mark and smoke from distant bushfires blacking out the hills. His guests rode in from different directions to the parched Front Run. First Walker of Newbold, then the Falstaffian figure of John Dobie; then John Mylne with two neighbours from Ramornie named Chauffert and Etienne Bordier Roman. The two Frenchmen, with the mysterious Baron de Milhau, had brought the station two years earlier from the Mannings and were now in process of selling again.

---

[3] Ogilvie Family Papers, Archives, University of New England.

'We made a night of it,' the journal stated briefly.

Edward added, somewhat shakily, on Boxing Day. 'All used up. Lying about and good for nothing. Came to in the evening again. Poor Barnes was found dead in his bed this morning and buried in the evening. Weather gets worse and worse. Country looks very dry. The air is filled with smoke. The sun sets and rises as red as new copper.'

Poor Barnes, presumably a station hand, had no further mention. Nor was his death allowed to interfere with their party. The day following they 'made a day of it upriver among the swans, and succeeded in bagging three, besides one we caught alive and let go again.' On the final night they dined on swan soup and roast swan, and in the morning the visitors left for home. Edward wrote:

> All party departed and left me feeling very lonely and out of spirits. Set to work to put by all extra things, etc. Took down tent and the like. Desperately hot day. When will this awful weather cease? Currie prepared to depart, and as he takes his wife with him, I do not know what I shall do for a housemaid.

On New Year's Eve the mercury rose to 106°.

There was to be no relief from that heatwave for several weeks. At least the New Year brought some cheering news. From Sydney his father wrote to say he had solved Edward's staff problems, having engaged two immigrant families and a couple of single hands. They were due to arrive in Grafton by the next ship. Edward rode down to meet them, sending them home with Awer, his bullock driver, while he stayed on to see a new draft of bullocks through the boiling-down works.

For these arrivals fresh from England, sitting for days on a lurching, unsprung dray, the first sight of this country must have appalled them. Temperatures remained daily above the century. It was little cooler at night. Fierce westerlies blew from the mountains like a furnace draught. The landscape was blotted out by dense bushfire smoke. Each morning, Edward noted, the sun rose as a dull red ball, vanishing an hour before sunset into the foggy pall of smoke.

Nor did February bring much improvement. Cooler days were rare. Thunderstorms cannonaded around the ranges. Torrential rains fell. There were other and more human crises to be dealt with as well. Mrs Awer, for instance, was suddenly taken ill with severe pains in her side, and not a doctor this side of Grafton. 'Bled and physicked her,' Edward wrote casually in his journal. 'Left her much better and in less alarm.'

There could have been no worse weather for the annual vintage.

Somehow the grapes were picked and pressed, though much of the crop had been damaged by humidity and rain. 'Looking over the vines today,' he noted in mid-February, 'I made the agreeable discovery that the maggot, which has hitherto confined its ravages to the peaches and apples, has now found out that grapes will also suit its taste.'

Yet, in a larger context, these were minor irritants. A new bouyancy became evident in those unflagging pages. The economy was fast improving. Tallow prices had risen; so had the returns for hides and wool. The Mylnes, judging by their rate of spending and entertainment, were already doing well. Dobie, who now had a good cattleman as manager, was dividing his time between his chief love, horse-breeding, and a seat in the Legislative Council, to which he had been appointed two years earlier.

Charles Tindal, too, had at last found the station he wanted. This was Ramornie. It was a magnificent buy. He had bought it at auction in Sydney from Baron de Milhau, paying no more than the price of its cattle, with the run and two hundred head of calves thrown in free.

The Frenchman, a refugee from the Paris Commune of 1848, had evidently been no cattleman. Bred in a chateau on the Narbonne, he had let the place run down, even the gardens, so that Tindal and his brother had several hard-working years ahead of them to make it productive again. Meantime the Baron, adapting himself to a more workaday environment, rode off—presumably with the beautiful baroness Tindal regretted never having sighted—to a short-lived gold-rush near Armidale. He was next reported to be unsuccessfully rocking a cradle, not the nursery kind, on the Peel River diggings, after which he became plain Mr de Milhau, a postal inspector. Ramornie still remembers him by Frenchman's Creek, a tributary of the Clarence.

Edward now felt confident enough of his future to engage an experienced new arrival from England. This was Thomas Hawkins Smith. A kinsman of Sydney Smith, the London journalist soon to write lyrically of an Australia he had never seen for Charles Dickens' *Household Words*, Thomas Hawkins reached Yulgilbar just in time for the big event of the year.

This was the annual cattle muster.

Throughout summer, stations habitually left their herds to roam as they pleased, fattening on the swamps and the sweet grasses brought up by humidity and rain. Towards the end of February, with cooler weather returning, the boggy country drying out, firm enough for stockhorses again, the general musters began. It was a job for all hands; for any man who could ride. It meant riding, too. Hard riding. Since there were no fences, the cattle were scattered for miles; up ridges and mountain spurs, into the heads of remote valleys, down gullies whose undergrowth and scrub made them hard to find. Stockmen now had to live for weeks in the saddle, sleeping out on hard ground night after night, rising before daylight to spend long days at a canter or gallop after the young steers and fast-footed heifers. It was a contest of wits and will. The stubborn beasts resisted confinement after their months of freedom. They had to be out-ridden, flushed out of hiding, blocked and shouldered and turned till they were brought at last, reluctantly and bellowing, into a sizeable mob down on the open flats.

Mustering on the open range has always been among the most strenuous occupations of pastoral man.

A mob of a thousand beasts or more rings upon the sun-heated plain. The dust rises. The trumpeting, restless herd can be heard a mile or more away, stirring up brown dust under the great bowl of cobalt sky. A dozen horsemen ride around the cattle, watchful, checking each attempt at a break. Then the cutting out begins. The fat bullocks and the steers are drafted to a second mob for droving down to Grafton. The cleanskins have to be branded; the young bulls cut. It needs a skilled man with a rawhide rope to single each beast out, lassoo him by the foreleg or horns, throw him bodily to the dust. It is a time of great excitement; of rushes and sudden alarms; of shouting, confusion, cursing; and an occasional spill from a horse.

It was well into April before the various Yulgilbar herds had been fully mustered, and the breeders settled on pastures for the winter.

During this time Edward had also to make the round of his sheep stations, set other men planting crops and solve multifarious problems with inarticulate workers for whom English was not their natural tongue. It was a rare day indeed when he could write in his journal, 'Walked with Smith up the Pinnacle and saw Billy's sheep. Remained a good while on the mountain top enjoying the splendid view. Clouded morning, but afterwards lovely day again.'

Perhaps this sense of well-being was related to his growing financial security. Some inkling of this is revealed by a journal entry in April, when he summarised the profits from his turn-off of cattle to Sharp's boiling works. A consignment of 471 head of cattle had realised him from 35/5d to 44/8d each, according to various gradings. This returned him £977.14.10, without including the sale of hides.

Nonetheless, this did not preclude him from writing an angry letter to Kirchner, complaining at the high costs charged for bringing out more German shepherds. The fares he had already agreed to pay; and, anyway, these were by agreement deducted from wages at the end of the second year. What had angered him was the amount of rations his agent wanted him to pay for en route.

'At Grafton and even here 50 miles inland,' he wrote, 'the charge for a full ration for a week does not at the present moment exceed 6/2d, while you have charged 1/6d per day, or 10/6d per week, in Sydney, where of course the cost is less. I cannot but think you might have arranged for their remaining on board while they were transferred to another vessel.'[4]

He repudiated his agreement, declining to take most of the men hitherto agreed upon. Kirchner's reply is not on record. Four months later, however, Edward wrote again, sending a cheque for £50.10.0, which ignored all charges for 'a number of hands I have released'. Kirchner was clearly not yet in a position to argue with these upriver squatters.

The swing towards prosperity on the Clarence was expressed in Charles Tindal's enthusiastic letters home. Early in 1853 he told his father that tallow had risen to £33 a ton, and that their expectations were even higher. In another letter he declared that 'I seriously hope that after boiling-down in June we shall have seen the last of such a waste of good meat. We have a small boiling-down plant at Ramornie, which I intend to alter into a salting or a preserving meat establishment. Cattle stations, and indeed all property, must rise tremendously before long. According to our last returns we boiled down last season sufficient for 100,000 mouths at the rate of 10 lbs of meat per man per week. The cattle in this colony have not been allowed to increase in the last four years.'

Though nothing more was heard of his ambitious plan—at least for some years—Tindal was among those shrewd enough to anticipate the coming boom. Within twelve months tallow prices were to increase to £58, doubling the price of cattle on the hoof.

Main cause of this was rumours from Europe of approaching war. Tallow had larger uses than making soap or candles. It was also an essential material for greasing guns. When the Russian Tsar threatened to invade Turkey's provinces in Asia Minor, the French government, traditionally nervous of Tsarist ambitions, declared itself ready to protect the Turks, while the Emperor Napoleon III none too secretly attempted to involve Britain in its plans for mobilisation. In September 1853 the Turks declared war. Britain and France soon joined them. Tallow soared.

---

[4] Ogilvie Family Papers, Archives, University of New England.

Fred Tindal, having earlier written that only the continuing labour shortage prevented him and his brother from making a trip home, then sent his father some remarkable news in March 1854.

'Everybody is to get rich and go home in a steamer,' he wrote. 'Do you see the Sydney papers? The *Empire* is at present attacking the squatting system. The "Shepherd Kings" have however their champions in the press. Many large fortunes have been made in the last year or two by squatters, and from the number which have left for England, I should fancy you must be overrun with Australian "nabobs".' He listed several Clarence men who were also planning to go; Dr Dobie, John and James Mylne, and Frederick Walker. Finally, he added, 'The Ogilvies, with Edward, are the last I have heard as intending to return home.'

This was news indeed.

What Tindal failed to mention was that the great W. C. Wentworth was also preparing to leave for London. His was a political mission; to shepherd a new constitution for New South Wales through the British parliament.

His plan for a fifty member assembly, to be elected by popular vote, had already been endorsed. Despite his now reactionary stance, Wentworth was realist enough to recognise the mass pressure for a more representative style of government, though he hoped to dampen it with an upper house that had to approve its legislation. He wanted this to consist of wealthy 'men of merit', elected for life. His idea was to model it on the House of Lords. The opposition at once provoked mass ridicule for such a scheme. Radicals like Henry Parkes and Daniel Dehieny wanted to know if Queen Victoria was going to create a new race of Australian peers; a 'bunyip aristocracy'. Were they now to be governed by Lord Wombat, Earl Kookaburra and the Duke of Wagga Wagga?

Nor did the patrician orator with his flowing white mane of hair endear himself to the populace by his attacks on democrats. Such men, he declared, were ignorant 'levellers, communists and socialists'. In the subsequent uproar the self-styled elder statesman was more than ready to pack for his voyage to a more respectful Westminster.

Edward did not appear to have given anyone but the Tindals much inkling of his ambitions to travel. Throughout 1853, indeed for the early months of the year following, his journal continued its matter-of-fact chronicle of day-to-day station events.

During July another significant visitor arrived. This was a government surveyor, W. W. Darke, who had laid out the town plan for Grafton. Edward spent four days riding through his country with Darke, 'measuring and marking out my plot of ground for purchase at the head station.' Within six months he was to be given a 325-acre freehold on this homestead block. Next he claimed a similar freehold block at the Plains Station, with a further 160 acres on Fairfield. The holdings were registered jointly in his father's and his own name. The Ogilvies had finally secured long term ownership of these Clarence lands.

Two months later, returning from a visit to Wyangerie, Edward broke his journey at the Lismore station on the Richmond River. His laconic journal entry hardly did justice to that much discussed event.

'Fry's wedding came off last Monday at Lismore,' he wrote.

Nothing was said about his being chief witness at the ceremony; nor of the astonishing youthfulness of the bride. The swaggering, worldly commissioner, with his twirling moustaches and scent of Macassar oil, had succeeded in winning the station owner's daughter aged fifteen. The story goes that one of the guests, arriving after all the rest had assembled in the homestead, found a slender girl in a child's dress alone on the verandah. She was crying.

'What are you sitting out here for, child?' he asked.

She answered through tears, 'I'm going to be married in there.'

On Yulgilbar the year of 1853 came to an end with the usual excesses of heat, thunderstorms, deluging rain. The shearing passed off without incident. Edward bottled the last of his wine, saw his paddocks ploughed afresh for wheat and corn, put his newly acquired sire Prince among the brood mares and rode off to spend Christmas with the Bundocks. From this period the station journal lost the sharp, personal touches Edward brought to its daily entries. It was written up in a new hand; by Thomas Hawkins Smith.

It began to look as if Edward were really preparing for the overseas travel that Fred Tindal had forecast.

'This voyage to Europe,' he confessed later, 'had for years been the dearest object of my wishes, and the constant theme of my daydreams.'[5] If this were indeed so, he had kept it very close to himself.

The real motive had nothing to do with any celebration of sudden wealth. Nor was Edward by any means wealthy yet. The explanation was first voiced through another of Charles Tindal's letters, telling his father that Edward and his parents were to sail for Europe in July. 'They propose wintering in Italy,' he wrote somewhat inaccurately,

---

[5] Ogilvie, E. D. S., *Diary of Travels in Three Quarters of the Globe*, London, 1856.

'so you will probably see them in about a twelvemonth. You will not find much alteration in Captain Ogilvie.

'But Mary Ogilvie is almost blind.'

This was the first hint anyone had been given of her condition. No one outside her family had been aware of it. They knew of her blinding headaches, and that was all. According to Ellen, the servants at Merton had long been puzzled by her habit, when inspecting the house linen, of holding each piece very close to her eyes. They had put it down to eccentricity. Now she was advised to see a first class eye specialist, which meant travelling to Europe.

William wanted her to go by the first available mail steamer. Yet, in Ellen's words, he was 'not yet solvent', and could hardly afford to remain so long away. To raise sufficient cash he decided to mortgage Merton.

It was a sad reflection on all those years of struggle that, at the age of seventy, this resolute old boy still had to go to the brokers. Yet, soon afterwards, young Fred Tindal sent his father a tasteless and uncharitable anecdote about him. 'I did not expect a very high popularity from the Ogilvie party. Charles Walker had rather a narrow escape from William Ogilvie. He had accepted his invitation to Merton, and accordingly called at the Club, but found Ogilvie incapable of the journey or anything else, so he came home direct.'

Few men had more justification than the old Commander to a little quiet tippling; especially in his own club.

The time for Edward's departure from Yulgilbar arrived at last.

Thomas Hawkins Smith, who had not troubled to keep up the journal during his employer's five-month absence at Merton, left a detailed record of the last month of preparations. Much of the time was spent riding around Yulgilbar, which Smith was now to manage. They visited every flock station, mustered the last of the cattle, watched the ploughing and seeding of wheat paddocks, broke in horses, had a bridge built for sheep across a deep creek, saw the last wool bales hauled off to Grafton by dray and plotted the course of several wire fences, a significant innovation to offset the continuing shortage of shepherds and stockmen.

On 30 June Smith noted: 'Mr. Ogilvie packing wine to take with him to England.' This was for more than the pleasures of the table. Edward had plans to show his wine overseas against those of Germany and France.

Finally, on 8 July, everything was ready.

'After some difficulty, necessarily attending on so many horses, Mr.

Ogilvie started today for England, Elliott and Churchill helping part
of the way to Gordon Brook, making a large party, being no less than
19 horses. Beautiful weather.'

Edward described his leaving in more lyrical fashion. At no other
time in his life did he express himself so feelingly. He was rarely a man
to commit his private thoughts to paper. Yet, affected by the beauty
of that scene under 'the clear, blue, transparent Australian sky,' he
recalled it nostalgically in a book he published later on his overseas
travels.[6] Behind the somewhat stilted and sentimental phrases, was a
profound love for Yulgilbar.

He rode at the head of a party making for the Front Run. Climbing
the hill that looked back at his homestead, he reined in and let the
others go ahead. He sat there, at the very place where 'beneath cedars
planted with my own hand, but now stately and spreading trees, a
broad slab marks the lonely grave of a brother.

'Beneath me, at the foot of the slope, surrounded by garden and
vineyard, its modest roof of thatch shaded by willow and beautiful
white cedar, was the cottage in which I had passed the last fourteen
years—probably the happiest of my life. Among the buildings of the
farm yard, still lingering upon the spot where I had parted from them,
stood the servants assembled to farewell me; while, on the intervening
slope, in scattered groups, were numbers of the dark children of the
forest, some reclining in the shade of the great trees, others in silence
watching, others wailing and in lamentation.'

Then he put spurs to his horse and caught up with the others. They
made quite a cavalcade. Robert Smith, of Fairfield, and an Aboriginal
stockman Denny were to ride right through with him to the Hunter,
taking charge of eleven of the best station horses he intended to have
'turned into cash in Sydney'. They also had two well-loaded pack-
horses. Riding with them as far as the Yulgilbar boundary went Thomas
Hawkins Smith, J. R. Elliott, the sheep superintendent, and an overseer, Churchill.

As soon as two of that escort turned back, the horses began to cause
trouble, as if also reluctant to leave their home pastures. 'They were
very fresh and difficult to manage,' Edward wrote. 'Being too many
in each hand, they got foul of the trees, struggled and pulled different
ways to the great peril of their necks. Breaking their strong halters of
bullock hide, some got free, gallopped off, and were with difficulty
overtaken and recovered.'

Late in the evening they reached Gordon Brook, where Dobie's
manager had their horses paddocked, offered them 'a cheerful fireside'

[6] Ogilvie, E. D. S., *Diary of Travels in Three Quarters of the Globe*, London, 1856.

and beds for the night. Next morning those spirited horses gave more trouble, delaying them on the next fifteen-mile stage to Newbold Grange, then on to Ramornie. There was more serious trouble than horses here, for Edward and Walker argued bitterly over a boundary dispute that was not to be settled for another ten years.

Soon after daylight the Tindal brothers saw them off on the lonely route to the New England Ranges. 'For the next two weeks,' Edward recalled, 'I had only a tent for home.'

Since the cutting of a new road down from the ranges, Edward had given up the longer, circuitous route through Tabulam, Sandy Hill and Tenterfield. It was not much of a road, merely a steep, rutted track winding up spurs and ridges. Drays were able to negotiate it only in good weather. It passed through Kangaroo Creek, over Coutt's Crossing and the headlong Nymboida River, climbing steeply up a series of mountain escarpments to Guy Fawkes and the Ebor Falls. The route, in fact, kept very close to Craig's Line, and, probably, to the original track down which the Ogilvies had come to the Clarence all those years before.

It was very much a sentimental journey he was making.

The first twenty miles, before they struck that track, was across country. Since the manager was still with them, and an Aboriginal rider lent by Tindal, they were able to quieten those horses by the time they made camp. Next day, reaching the first of the ranges, the three horsemen were on their own. Edward led one packhorse, which carried his tent and personal gear. The 'merry and good-natured' Denny led the second, weighted down with flour, tea, cooking pots and his own form of sleeping bag made of possum skins. They made dinner camp in true bush style beside the Nymboida; billy tea, boiled slices of beef and johnny cakes, which Edward called leather jackets, freshly kneaded on bark and baked in the ashes.

Next day they had a twenty-mile waterless stretch before them, mostly stiff climbing. They spent that night beside Cloud's Creek and the morning was frosty. The cheerful Denny was overcome with homesickness, and had to be jollied back into the saddle. It took them another three days to reach the Guy Fawkes River. Each morning the frozen ground cracked under their horses' hooves.

As Edward lay in his sky-blue tent that night, listening to the thunder of Ebor Falls, he must surely have thought back to that tense encounter so long ago. Here, in this lonely but beautiful place, four horsemen in red shirts and cabbage tree hats had confronted the sullen Craig. All around them had been sheep and cattle, the drays chartered by Dobie and the Mylnes, and watchful overlanders squatting on the grass. Had it been asking so much, after all, to join that party. Yet Craig had refused. 'Very well, we'll find our own way—and be there before you.'

They had found their way; found Yulgilbar. It had been a triumph to remember. And now few people even remembered Craig. He was merely a paid hand on Ramornie.

The following morning the party rode into a bitter westerly, pushing their horses, cantering them whenever possible, for the shelter of the Snowy Mountains near Armidale. Snow fell at one stage, much to the alarm of Denny, who had never before seen rain so cold that it froze. The 'ruthless' westerly winds continued for days. One morning they awoke to find their saddle packs frozen over. 'The horses, when they attempted to drink, only bobbed their astonished noses against the solid ice, in some places nearly an inch thick.' Next day there were icicles hanging from the horse's noses; a hoar frost whitened their backs; and ice crackled under their hooves as they rode for Moonbi Pass and the warmer country below. Winter in New England was no time to travel; and this was a more bitter winter than most.

They were down to salt meat only when they crossed the Peel River, camping near the A. A. Company's head station at Goonoo Goonoo.

On the day before they reached the Liverpool Range, they were able to pull off their greatcoats, woollen comforters and gloves, riding in shirtsleeves again under the warming sun.

After a pleasant camp on Warrah, Edward delayed the morning start by gathering 'some of the finely-scented Myall wood that grows on these plains. I wished to carry a few specimens to England.'

After making camp at the foot of the range, Robert Smith left them to visit some nearby friends, returning with 'a famous supply of roast beef, a hot loaf and a bottle of home-made wine, which he produced with some triumph.'

Despite the wine, Edward's first impressions of the valley were depressing ones. He had not ridden this way for some years. 'Formerly,' he wrote, 'the traveller returning from the solitudes and scattered stations of the great squatting districts of the interior, felt his heart gladden in passing down the fine valley of the Dartbrook. Every four or five miles neat homesteads surrounded by fruitful orchards and spacious flower gardens gave evidence of prosperity and content, while luxuriant vineyards, well tilled fields and numerous cornstacks attested to the fertility of the soil. All this has badly changed during the last three years.'

He was shocked by the atmosphere of neglect and decay; houses were roofless, crumbling amid weed-choked gardens. Fences were broken; sheep grazing on what had formerly been harvested paddocks.

It was the other face of a land grown affluent from gold. Half the valley's people, certainly nearly all its labouring men, had abandoned it for the diggings. 'A few farmers, encouraged by the recent high prices for corn yet struggle on against exorbitant wages and a short supply of hands, but even their lands look ill-cultivated, and their houses unkempt, neglected.'

The next night was spent outside the village of Scone. Here Edward had a remarkable encounter. In the figure of a stooping, lonely shepherd was the symbol of the devastating changes European ambitions had brought upon the land. He described how he first saw him, alone, squatting under a tree, barely concerned with the sheep feeding in the paddock of a ruined farm. The old man caught sight of Edward, rose up and walked towards him.

'With his keen eyes intently fixed on me, with a gesture of surprise and delight, he pronounced my name. I at once recognised him as an Aboriginal named Coolan, son of a chief of the once powerful tribe that dwelt in this neighbourhood; and who had often been the companion and attendant of myself and brothers during our hunting and fishing excursions.'

They talked for a while, reminded one another of the old times around Merton, arranged to meet after Edward's companions had made camp.

An hour or so later Coolan joined them round the fire. He brought with him a roasted possum as a gift for Denny. Then he sat in front of the flames, lit his pipe and began 'his melancholy tale'.

He told how the once numerous tribes of the Camilarrai [Kamilaroi], who in his boyhood roamed the plains and camped in the valleys of this wide district, hunted the kangaroo, sat at the council fires, made war or peace, and were the proud, free masters of the land; how the warlike Marowancal, the Tooloompikilal, the Gundical and the fine intelligent tribe of Paninpikilal, to which he himself belonged, had all sunk, dropped off, died and gradually disappeared, the miserable surviving remnants, some half dozen broken men, all gaining a livelihood like himself by tending sheep. It was fate, he said, and he expected soon to follow those who had gone before. Yet he admitted that a taste for ardent spirits, and the drunken habits into which his people fell, had doubtless much influenced their rapid melting away. An inscrutable deity would seem to ordain that the savage man must yield his place upon the earth to civilised man. Not one of the tribes enumerated had ever come under hostile collision with the white intruders, but had from the first occupation of their country remained on terms of perfect amity with the stranger. Yet all had been as surely and wholly swept away, as though to destroy and exterminate had been the aim of the newcomers, instead of the human desire to preserve and support their dark-skinned brethren ever evinced by the settlers in their locality.

Despite those touches of piety, his somewhat naive belief in his fellow settlers and what constituted civilisation, Edward's attitude was both humane and rare. Not that it was of much practical help to the old shepherd. Yet what could he have done? He was about to leave the country; Merton was mortgaged and cutting down on staff; to offer money would have been fruitless, considering the availability of rum.

They rode on next day for Merton. Edward found no one left in the village he knew. The gold rushes had swept the district clean. Even his parents had left, having already packed up and travelled down to Sydney.

Surprisingly Will was home. His brother had ridden in from the Liverpool Plains expressly to meet him. It was like old times again, the two of them yarning together. A fire going in the cottage; good Merton wine. They talked of future plans, of all that remained to be done in the back country, of their mother's return with her sight restored.

The two brothers rode down to Maitland with the others, boarded the steam packet for Sydney and left Smith and Denny to take the horses on by road. Some days later those finely-bred Yulgilbar horses brought good prices at auction, the best of them selling for £75. Will remained in town to see the family off on R.M.S. *Madras*. Before she sailed, he told Edward, 'Take care of yourself so I can see you back again.'

It was the last time the two brothers ever saw each other.

15

The Grand Tour

They sailed for England down that same broad and sunlit waterway they had entered in very different circumstances all those years ago. Thirty years exactly.

Since R.M.S. *Madras* was anchored in mid-stream, they boarded a lighter at the new, semi-circular quay. It took them past the high wooden hulls of barquentines and clippers, whose tall masts, spars and rigging were cross-hatched against a pale, clear winter's sky. The crowded foreshores of Sydney Cove proclaimed a busier, more prosperous city than the slatternly convict settlement of their arrival. Clearing Dawes Point, they looked back at close-set streets and solid buildings reaching away for miles, the row upon row of labourers' cottages climbing the slopes of Woolloomooloo, the mansions of the successful on the heights around Elizabeth Bay. Some of these were their friends. They could even make out the four-square sandstone facade of Fairlight in the distance, leased now until Mary's return.

They had a place in this city now. They belonged. Thirty years ago they had sailed into this splendid harbour owning nothing, possessed only of uncertain hopes, letters of introduction, a few hundred pounds. Now they were leaving behind them property, several hundred square miles of land, an established reputation. They had not done too badly, after all, in those thirty years.

They sailed on 20 August 1854.

Sailed was the right term. Though the P & O listed *Madras* as a steamer, she cruised out at sea under canvas as well. The sea air, Edward noted, gave new zest to all of them, even if he was as usual among the first to go down with *mal de mer*. His indomitable mother, he added, soon proved herself among the best sailors aboard. Apart from the Commander, of course. He would doubtless have walked the decks as soon as the liner cleared Sydney Heads. The old couple settled down comfortably in the first-class saloon with Deas Thompson, now going to join W. C. Wentworth for the House of Commons debate on the new constitution. Edward found other congenial company in his three-berth cabin. Sharing it were a Moreton Bay squatter and Major Briggs, an Indian Army man, 'both gentlemen and agreeable fellows.'[1]

He was already slipping into the clubman's jargon of the first class smoke room.

The diary he kept on the voyage, and subsequently throughout Europe, gave many insights into his developing sophistication. After recasting it in narrative form, he was to have it published at his own expense in London.[2]

Prefacing it with the modest hope that it might be of interest to his friends, he took modesty further by omitting his name from the cover and title page. Its authorship was attributed merely to 'An Australian Settler'. If this *Diary of Travels in Three Quarters of the Globe* was no great literary achievement, it did preserve the only record of his journeys and experiences. The narrative form he gave it was much in line with other books of the time, written by prosperous English milords making the traditional Grand Tour of Europe. Here now was one of Tindal's 'Australian nabobs' to show that successful colonials could travel in equal style. Nonetheless, his account has considerable value. It reveals an entirely different Edward.

The euphoric moods of ocean voyaging enveloped him early. The hard-living, dedicated bushman is swiftly replaced by a more indulgent character resolved to enjoy the world. It was as if this hitherto dour, rigidly disciplined man of forty were suddenly enjoying a delayed youth; a youth he never had either the leisure or ready cash to liberate. After his experiences in Europe he would never be the same again.

There were even discoveries to be made before leaving his own continent. None of the Ogilvies had hitherto seen Melbourne. They were in two minds about this brash, hustling, newly affluent city with its Americanised ways and fixation on gold. It became something of a shock to realise that the semi-feudal, exclusive society they had adopted three decades ago was outmoded, as it would be soon in Sydney as well. They felt more at home in the dignity and quiet of provincial Adelaide. Once the usual turbulence of the Bight was behind them, the last landfall amid the solitudes of King George's Sound, they had only the

[1] Ogilvie, E. D. S., *Diary of Travels in Three Quarters of the Globe*, London, 1856.
[2] *ibid.*

blue and immeasurable expanses of the Indian Ocean to fill out idle, sunlit days on deck.

Ceylon, too, was something of a dream sequence. They adopted the role of tourists, drove up the elephant road to Kandy, took their leisure under the coconut palms, admired the natives whom Edward, remembering his Aborigines, thought 'very sleek, well-fed and well conditioned'. At Aden, where the uproar of coaling by raucous Africans made sleep impossible, Edward spent his one oppressively hot day ashore riding out to the British garrison's fort. In his shrewd cattleman's fashion he hired a spirited pure-bred Arab grey. He and his fellow squatters also talked Arabian horsemen into impromptu races which, in true Australian style, they matched with their money.

The voyage ended at Suez.

As the Canal was still only in de Lesseps' mind, passengers had to travel overland to Cairo, then Alexandria, boarding another ship for Mediterranean ports. The old Commander, delighted with their passage through the desert, wrote Ellen a long letter describing the fast two-wheel carriages that, with two mules and two horses in the traces, took them at a full gallop right through to the capital. There they were overwhelmed by the uproar of crowded streets, Egyptian hucksters and the bazaars. They moved into Shepherd's Hotel, delighted in the pageantry of the Pasha's palace guards, visited mosques, saw Dervish and belly dances, haggled for carpets and rugs, went cruising on the Nile and, leaving Mary in town, made an expedition by donkey to the Pyramids, reinforced by a hamper of exotic foods, beer and wine. Mary consoled herself by riding around Cairo on a donkey of her own. Merton and Yulgilbar had never been like this.

Edward, however, astounded Britishers and fellaheen alike by his outrageous colonial behaviour. When their guides demanded more money to ferry their party of sahibs across a deep canal, he did just what he would have done if Washpool Creek had baulked him in flood.

'Losing patience,' he wrote, 'I quickly stripped, and packing my clothes on my head, swam across.'

Whatever his loss of caste, there was no further arguing over money.

During this four-week sojourn in Egypt, Edward took himself off on a trip up the Nile, visited a slave market and was duly appalled by what he heard of the jealousy, intrigues and cruelties practised in nearby harems. Back in Cairo he was shocked by reports of the disastrous Allied campaign in the Crimean War. News arrived of troop transports destroyed in the Black Sea by Russian guns, and of the so-called victories at Balaclava and Inkerman resulting in the death of several thousand British troops. Despite the efforts of that saintly virago Florence Nightingale, treatment of the sick and wounded had become a world-wide scandal. Major Briggs was going to the Crimea, so Edward decided to go along with him. Why he should have evinced this sudden interest in warfare was not explained, unless he felt some personal involvement through the supply of tallow. He went with his parents to Alexandria, from where they intended to sail to Malta, then booked a berth on an Italian steamer for Constantinople.

The ship was filled to the gunwales with pilgrims returning from Mecca. But only Moslems of the male variety, to his disappointment, were allowed on deck. All he was able to see, through the bars of what resembled an outsize chicken coop, were 'a pair of bright eyes peeping, or a glimpse of a female form reclining amid pillows and cushions.' At Smyrna they were further weighted down with Turkish soldiers, 'such a dirty set of ragamuffins was never seen'. They steamed past the site of ancient Troy, saw snow upon legendary Mount Ida and entered the Dardanelles, where British and French warships were soon familiar sights. Again there were disturbing glimpses of female flesh. 'Some Greek beauties with dark eyes and graceful figures came aboard, only to be whisked out of sight.'

Soon he was enchanted by the broad, mirror-calm Sea of Marmora, then the fantasy of the Golden Horn, growing upon the horizon in a mirage of soaring minarets and cupolas.

News from the front was less enchanting. In Constantinople no one talked of anything but the blunders, inefficiency and stupidity of British army leaders. 'I went to bed that night with a sadly altered feeling about the war, and with much less confidence in the ability of my country to do everything better then the world besides.' He read scarifying despatches published by the London *Times*, talked to disillusioned army officers in his hotel, visited both French and British military hospitals. The French impressed him greatly, so did their Sisters of Charity, but he found his own compatriots horrifyingly short of medical supplies, unable to cope with their overflowing wards, and totally lacking in the famous sense of British efficiency and order. What further disgusted him was the sight of at least twelve hundred sick and wounded, without blankets or warm clothes, lying in the snows behind the hospital.

Somehow he won permission from the commanding general at headquarters to visit Balaclava. Leaving on a troop-ship just after Christmas, he confessed himself glad to leave 'the filthy muddiness of this city', where the only evidence of Christian ethics had been drunken British sailors carousing 'to the great scandal of the sober Turks'. The Turkish ladies he found more intriguing, even if he decided it was their yashmaks that gave them their allure. By veiling their coarser features, he wrote, only their splendid dark eyes were exposed.

Edward was developing a fixation for these intriguing eastern ladies.

At Balaclava Bay he watched Allied preparations for a crucial battle with the Russian army, which at that moment occupied the fortified heights above Inkerman Valley, a few miles away. An army officer even took him on horseback through the British lines to the battlefield. Not even official war correspondents were given such opportunities. Edward casually rode through a sea of mud and desolation, past the rotting corpses of men and baggage mules, looked through field glasses at the enemy's defences, and even entered front-line trenches, where snipers sent musket balls perilously close to his head. He returned from it all unscathed, but no more keen about war.

The report he wrote was a scarifying indictment of British military disarray. He described its demoralised army 'perishing of cold, wet and hunger, within sight of the most abundant supplies', because no one had troubled to complete a road between battlefield and harbour. Shiploads of warm clothes, blankets and medical supplies failed to reach overcrowded field hospitals, while troops remained bootless, though a whole shipload was cruising around the Black Sea with no authority to land them.

Had Edward been writing despatches for a newspaper, he might have won himself a reputation. As it was, the calamities had passed into history by the time his book appeared. His experience had value only in revealing other aspects of the British establishment he had once admired.

He returned to the Golden Horn on a ship so filled with wounded he was sickened by the 'dreadful odours'. Malta, where he rejoined his parents, appeared an unreal, almost paradisal world. He was 'seduced' by the Mediterranean sunshine, gained honorary membership of the naval and military club, went to picnics and dances, a ball at the governor's palace and had only one jarring encounter in his two month sojourn. This was on meeting a certain General Sir George Browne at a friend's house. The general's complacency about the Crimean War shocked Edward, especially when he dismissed *The Times* corres- pondent's critical despatches as 'impertinent exaggerations of one who would meddle in matters he cannot understand'.

Malta's ingrown society eventually decided Edward to travel further. He complained of it as 'a priest-ridden community', that 'English rule has deprived the carnival of all its ancient license, excitements and extravagances.' Yet he managed to enjoy carnival time all the same. He wrote of the gay tradition in which women pelted menfolk with sugar plums, and vice versa. 'I myself engaged in one or two such sharp contests that I was obliged to treat myself to a new hat.' Having taken lessons in the Italian language, he sailed for what he hoped would prove livelier encounters in Sicily.

His instinct was right.

He was lucky enough to meet 'a French gentleman travelling for pleasure', passed a gay night with him aboard a French warship returning from the Crimea, and wrote, 'A somewhat too lengthened investigation of the merits of various Sicilian wines has resulted in a headache that renders me not undisposed to remain quiet today.'

Italy captivated him from the beginning.

The vitality of its people, its beauty, the sunlight, bright colours, the spontaneity of life entered so deeply into him that he was never able to forget the country, and returned to it again and again. Nor did he make any attempt to conceal his enjoyment in the *Diary*. In the Sicilian village of Villafrate he and his gay companion paid two blind musicians to play for them half the night, the Frenchman ending by dancing a tarantella with the female one. They explored Greek and Roman ruins, drank regional wines, took in every theatre, hillside cafe and restaurant they found, admired the singing in village masses and visited noted monasteries, including one in Palermo where Edward conceived doubts as to 'the vows of continence by the holy friars.'

They went by steamer to the Bay of Naples, found in Capri 'all I had ever dreamt of Italy s blue waters, sunny skies and enchanting scenery.' There he decided that 'Capri is celebrated for the excellence of its wine, and beauty of its women. The former was tasted at the Hotel de Londres, and I think it deserves its fame.'

Of the latter he was more discreet.

Some days later he asked, 'Who can sojourn in Naples, and not feel regret when the moment arrives of taking leave of this most gay, dissolute and noisy, but most pleasant of cities?' They spent days wandering through the ruins of Pompeii and Herculaneum, even longer in Neapolitan museums and galleries, rode up the slopes of Vesuvius and watched the fiery drama of an eruption. Next, having parted from the Frenchman, he chartered a *vetturino*, riding through the countryside with the luxury of a true English milord, passing mile after mile of vineyards on the road to Capua, stopping one night in the little town of Sant' Agata where he astounded a travelling French burgher by ordering a steak for early breakfast.

'*Monsieur*,' exclaimed this incredulous French provincial, '*est-ce-que vous avez commande un bifteck pour cinq heures du matin?*'

Edward assured him that it was so.

'*Mon dieu!*' he cried. He kept crying it around the hotel lounge. '*Mon dieu!*' *Les types Australiens* were clearly even more incomprehensible than the English themselves.

Passing through Villa Cicerone next day, Edward 'happened to observe' that the village had girls of remarkable beauty, and then immersed himself for nearly a week in Rome. The Grand Tour continued to unfold in terms of the Pantheon, St Peter's, the Colosseum, the Villa Borghese and some sumptuous dining at Frascati. In Tuscany, entranced by the relics of a vanished civilisation, the antipodean sheepman suddenly re-emerged.

'I observed several flocks of sheep,' he wrote, 'some of them newly shorn, which I almost instinctively went to examine. From the shepherds I learnt that the best shearers clip from fifty to sixty sheep per diem, and that their remuneration is not more than two pauls, or about tenpence with three meals daily.' What memories this must have conjured up of past woolshed disputes back home. 'The shearing is not very skilfully or neatly performed,' he conceded, 'though it is such as we should not be dissatisfied with in Australia.'

Travelling by diligence to Siena, en route for Florence, he took a poor view of fate for shutting him inside a coach for thirty hours with 'three very plain women and a lap dog'. Florence, of course, made up for it.

Florence. It influenced him and drew him back.

When his parents reached Southampton they found themselves at once among friends. Whatever happened in the outer world, English life seemed to go on just as it had always done.

Mary's great-nephew Edward Baynton met them on the wharf. His father, Commander Baynton, had remained on active service till he was sixty-five, having been drowned in Balaclava Bay only a month before Edward went there. They stayed with Mary's sister's family in Hampshire, no doubt visiting the grave of William's mother at nearby Alverstoke. The old lady had been dead only six years, living to ninety-two. Later they took the steamer across to Jersey, where Mary's two sisters were now living. 'Nothing can exceed the kindness of your aunts Jessie and Ellen,' the Commander wrote to his daughter at Wyangerie, describing how they had nursed him through a bout of influenza.

He added, with a nostalgic touch: 'Everyone seems to delight in flowers. It gives us great pleasure to see our old friends the horse chestnuts, lilacs, laburnums, hawthorn, which are coming out with so much beauty now.'

The pair decided to stay in the Channel Isles until Edward ended his Grand Tour.

'We do not know exactly where he is,' his father wrote, 'though we have no doubt there are letters from him astray somewhere. We should have been uneasy, but that Charles Marryat informed us he had a letter requesting a credit on Florence and Paris, and stated that he enjoyed his trip through Sicily very much and liked Italy so well that he should not hurry through it.'

It was an understatement. Edward was behaving irresponsibly for the first time in his life. Why worry, when he could always send to their London agents—Joseph Marryat and Sons—for more money. He was nowhere near Paris yet. He was still involved in his love match with Florence.

He was now living in some style at the New York Hotel. The name suggests one of those modern and comfortable places catering for affluent foreigners doing Europe. If that were so, he had no mind to appear in the role of an inferior colonial. He engaged a valet.

Antonio was also described as a guide and instructor in the language. He appears to have been a man of some taste, for he guided his master to all the places a lover of music and the other arts should visit. For three weeks, Edward wrote, he gave himself up to the galleries and museums of the Uffizi and Palazzo Pitti, the Bella Arte, private collections, and the enchanting Boboli Gardens overlooking the reflective Arno.

'Florence is by far the most delightful place I have yet visited; the situation, the climate, the people, are all charming, while the galleries, museums and palaces, the theatres, the studios of living artists, and the ateliers of the workers in marble and alabaster offer inexhaustible sources of amusement and pleasure.'

It was at this stage that he had his own portrait painted. He chose an accomplished artist. Pietro Milani's painting was a perceptive one. One can only presume it was a good likeness, for no other picture existed of Edward at that stage of life. It was also more than a likeness. The Florentine set special emphasis on the strong bone structure, the determined mouth, the sterner qualities of a man toughened by his bush environment. But a hint of gaiety emerged, too. Only a hint. The painter had romantic sympathies. Perhaps he divined the unusually light-hearted mood that his subject had adopted in the heady atmosphere of Florence; a mood that was by no means typical, and perhaps would never return. He gave a cavalier twist to those sweeping, well-brushed black moustaches, an exceptional brightness to the observant eyes. Here was a man at ease with life, merry in at least temporary fashion. A hint of laughter underlines the austerity.

Yet there was melancholy in those eyes as well. He had the appearance of a lonely man.

If this was indeed the artist's intention, he understood his subject well. That lonely sense was to drive Edward hard for the next year or two, allowing him little inner peace.

In the end he had to force himself to leave his 'seductive city'. He had also to dispense with Antonio. He wanted to take the man with him to see more of Italy, but there was talk of family commitments, especially a sick child. Finally the Florentine produced a compadre of his, from Venice, who agreed to act as guide instead. They travelled on to Lucca, Monte Catino, Pisa, though Edward could not resist turning back on his tracks for the grand fiesta of San Giovanni in June. On this compulsive return Florence began to seem his own city.

Even when he left for London, he made a roundabout route of it. He stayed in Genoa, Milan, Venice, Verona, Turin, crossing the French border by way of a carriage journey across the Alps and the Mont Cenis pass to Chambery, then driving into Switzerland for Geneva and Chamounix. It was July before he had even reached Paris, which curiously disappointed him. He was now the dedicated Italianate.

Like Rome, he found Paris too heavy and formalised for his taste, except for the international Exposition that had just opened. Here he recast himself in another role. He was a world-travelling Australian who had arrived. It was reassuring to find his country so dramatically represented; golden nuggets from now world-famous fields, finely-grained native timbers, wines that were 'taking high rank among their French and German rivals.'

Resolved at last to join his parents in the Channel Islands, he took a coach direct through Normandy to St Malo, boarding a ferry for Jersey. His Grand Tour—or at least its first instalment—had taken him just eight months.

In England they all stayed once more with the Bayntons. Next came a reunion with the ageing Captain Tindal near Birmingham. Perhaps the Commander brought up that old contentious issue of the 'firebrand letters'; perhaps by common agreement they ignored such bygone matters. What would have delighted Edward was to find Charles Tindal staying there. He had arrived some months earlier from Australia, rejoicing in the booming prices of wool and tallow, and in the rapid advances made at Ramornie, which he had left for the time being in his brother's hands. Fred wrote regularly, giving them all news of the Clarence. It must have gladdened the old captain to see his son back after so many years, though he would have been grieving still over the death of his third son, Arthur. The young man had only sailed for Australia towards the end of 1854, planning to join his brothers at Ramornie.

Arriving in Sydney, Arthur had taken the new Clarence-built steamer *Isabella* for Grafton, where Charles was waiting to meet him. He waited for days. No one saw that steamer again. A little wreckage was later washed up near Newcastle. No bodies were ever found.

There were other friends to meet in London or elsewhere; newer Australian friends. Charles Tindal had been right in predicting that half the Clarence would soon be found in England. Among them were John and Thomas Mylne, dividing their time between London's night life and grouse shooting on the Scottish moors, Fred Walker from Newbold, and Dr John Dobie. The portly ex-surgeon had renounced his Australian identity now. He had sold out Gordon Brook to Fred Bundock, of Dyraaba, in partnership with Henry Barnes and R. G. Massie, and had left the country for good. It was a surprising reversal for a man, who eight years before, had been attacked by a supporter of Governor Gipps for monopolising too much land. He had then possessed 128,000 acres on the Clarence and Liverpool Plains. Now he owned nothing but a parcel of shares in London's Agra Bank, which was soon to go broke and give him a fatal heart attack.

Early in September old Captain Tindal had more disastrous news from Australia. This time it concerned Fred.

In the last letter from his son, written in April, Fred had told him of a big flood on the Clarence, which had marooned him between the main river and the Orara. Two months later, Fred's jackaroo cousin, Charles Porter, sent another letter home. In the most gentle manner possible it told the old man of his son's death. 'The last seen of him,' he wrote, 'he breakfasted at Eatonswill on the morning of Friday, June 22, after which in an attempt to ford the river at Smith's Flat, he was unfortunately drowned.'

Fred was by no means the first victim of this moody, unpredictable river. There were to be many more.

The next fatality was recorded by Thomas Hawkins Smith in the Yulgilbar station journal. On 7 July 1855, he wrote: 'Crane came in during the evening and reported that Gobel was drowned trying to cross the river at the junction.'

Several days were spent trying to locate the German shepherd's body. Not until the 16th were they successful, when the manager wrote in his laconic style: 'Took Smith, Crane and six blacks and were fortunate in finding the corpse very quickly, which we buried in the river bed. He had evidently but floated this morning. Saw Wyach and his flock. All well.'

Whether all was well or not, Edward received only sporadic reports of progress at Yulgilbar. Business letters passed between the two. But it seems most unlikely that he heard much of the station's more secret history, such as the entries his manager made during 1855.

> *Friday, 9 November:* Smith came in the evening and reported the death of German Swart in the mountains. Very hot windy day.
> *Saturday, 10 November:* Went out with Smith early this morning, and on to the place where Swart was found dead. Pillar and blacks just finished burying him as I reached there, and discovered he had hung himself with a piece of greenhide. Very hot day. Wind blowing very strong from the west.

At this moment Edward was in Paris. He was one of a party of Australians, attending among other lively diversions a cattle show. The Mylnes had crossed the channel with them, with their two sisters holidaying from Scotland; probably Charles Tindal, too.

Presumably Mary Ogilvie was by this time having treatment for her eyes in London. If she was, there were no reports of any improvement. Not until the following year did the Commander find anyone really competent to cure her complaint, which was probably a cataract that few medical men then knew how to treat. They were referred to a celebrated oculist in Germany. It was quite an expedition to reach him, for he practised in the out-of-the-way provincial town of Grafrath, near Dusseldorf. They crossed the Channel once more about the end of June.

It was not clear exactly when the Commander took delivery of that unhappy letter from Wyangerie. Ellen had posted it in April 1856. Perhaps it reached him before they left London. Perhaps it was forwarded to them somewhere en route. She wrote telling them of Will's death at Merton. He had died quite suddenly on 10 April from spasms of the chest; which could only have meant angina pectoris. Neither William nor Edward had the courage to tell his mother. She was just not in good enough health to be told.

The situation was fully described in one of Edward's rare letters. Posting it in Grafrath, he apologised to Ellen for not having written earlier, confessing that 'my book will no longer serve as an excuse.' His *Diary of Travels*, which he had finished in January, was then on the point of being published by Saunders & Otley, of Conduit Street, London. He wrote:

I take advantage of the leisure hours and repose of mind under which one suffers in this insufferably dull little place to write you a more lengthy epistle. We made a very leisurely journey from London, stopping at Calais, Little Brussels (whence I made an excursion to the field of Waterloo), Liege and Aix La Chapelle. The famous oculist who as you know we came to seek at once pronounced my mother's eye to be in a fit condition to be operated upon, which put us all in spirits, in spite of the very wet, cold and dismal weather and the indifferent accommodations of this out of the way corner. After we had been here 10 days the operation was performed, but most unfortunately not with perfect success as my mother unhappily made an involuntary start whilst the instrument was in the eye, causing a little damage which brought on an inflammation, the result of which has been to again obscure the sight. Though immediately after the operation she saw quite clearly through the afflicted eye, the inflammation has now passed away and the doctor appears confident of ultimate success, treating the matter as only a question of time and speaking of the restoration of the sight as a thing not to be doubted. But, as you may suppose, we have had a fearfully anxious time of it, and are yet far from comfortable or easy. I have of course resolved not to leave my father and mother to proceed on my own journey. We hope for the best, and the tales we hear of the doctor's skill and unfailing success are so general that we feel every confidence that all will ultimately come right.[3]

There was very much more. The saddest note came at the end of his letter, where Edward sent his 'love to Bundock and to all the children'. Then he added:

We are now all in all to each other Ellen. You my only sister, I your only brother. How many of the happy dreams of youth have been crushed and withered. I will write again soon and hope to have good news to tell you of my mother as far as her eyes are concerned. Though how or when we can break the terrible news to her I cannot tell.

Edward's letter to Ellen carried other sentiments of great significance. The mature man who, in Italy, had so impulsively yielded to the upsurge of youth, who had been swept away by the intoxications of Europe, the sexuality of mysterious women such as he had never before encountered, the easy delights of the Parisian boulevards, had also been given the time to think more profoundly about the future of the land, however remote it now seemed, that had made him what he was.

It would not be possible to understand his character without reading that letter to his sister in Wyangerie half the world away. The crucial passages were prompted by his suspicion that Wellington Bundock, like Dobie and others, was tempted to renounce Australia.

[3] Ogilvie Family Papers, Archives, University of New England.

'You make frequent allusions to a resolve under certain probable circumstances,' he wrote, 'to sell off and clear out of the Colony. To this I must unhesitatingly answer *don't.*'

His argument warrants its quotation complete. It was something of a manifesto. It summed up his attitudes to Australia, his beliefs, the philosophy by which he was to stand for the rest of his years.

> With all its evils and discomforts, it is after all a life with a purpose. Particularly for those who are blessed with descendants. What can be a more worthy and interesting pursuit and purpose in which to spend one's life than founding an estate and achieving a position that those you are to have to inherit your name. I assure you that I would not, for any consideration, *not* have my Australian home and estate to return to. Did I not feel that my present vagabond wandering life is an exceptional and not a regular thing, that it is a thing with a definite limit, and not a permanent mode of life, I should not enjoy it, but I should indeed feel without a sufficient object, and discontented.
>
> Indeed I observe that most of those among our friends who sold out and left Australia are those who are most discontented. Dobie, I think I told you, is even thinking of going out to *buy* again, and Hamilton who, before he left Sydney said he would not on any account order mutton for dinner the day he arrived in England, has now so far altered his note (tone?) that, when I met him a few days ago in Paris during the cattle show, he was talking of having enjoyed the day among the sheep pens—with *his fingers among the wool again.* Therefore I say, try and devise any remedy for the evils of squatter life rather than give up. The want of servants is with you the grand evil. But as Bundock increases his flocks and herds, this evil can surely be conquered, as it is chiefly a matter of cost.

In September the Ogilvies returned to England for a notable event. This was the marriage of Charles Tindal to a Miss Anne Travers of Buckinghamshire. The newly-weds planned to return to Australia. Charles was already planning a new homestead at Ramornie.

It began to look as if this phase of overseas jaunting was over. The Mylnes were talking of going home, taking their two unmarried sisters. On William Ogilvie's recommendation, Captain Tindal decided to send out his youngest son, Frank, to join Charles on the Clarence.

The Ogilvies alone showed no urgency to return. Writing out to Charles in December, the captain told him that William and Mary were about to leave for Jersey until spring brought warmer weather. 'Edward,' he added, 'returned from his travels on the continent about a fortnight ago, and will remain in London. He is already installed at the Conservative Club, where he has fallen in with Mr. Wentworth, and renewed acquaintance with him.'

An Ogilvie in the Conservative Club. This was indeed a change from Captian William Ogilvie's radical views.

Captain Tindal went on to describe Mary's 'great spirits from the successful treatment of her eyes by the celebrated German oculist', though she had been advised to 'abstain from all excitement for some time'. Nor had she yet been told of her son's death at Merton, 'which places Captain O. in a very awkward position, as it will be quite impossible to prevent her learning the event by some means or other.'

John and Thomas Mylne finally left England on the last day of May, 1857. With them went young Frank Tindal and their two sisters. James Mylne had written from Eatonswill saying that its handsome homestead was being renovated to welcome the returning voyagers. He was also getting ready to meet the Scottish servants sent out ahead of the party. Mylnefield had at last been sold, and the proceeds allotted to ambitious station improvements. With them on board were three costly Hereford bulls and other cattle.

Their ship was the *Dunbar*.

She came within range of Sydney's South Head lighthouse on the night of 20 August. Only its beam was not visible. Heavy rain and mist blotted out the entire coastline. Because a strong sou'-easterly was blowing, the captain made a cautious approach under double-reefed tops'ls. Towards midnight he sighted what he believed to be the gap between those high sandstone cliffs of North and South Heads. He was a quarter-mile too far south and *Dunbar* drove into solid rock. Massive waves broke over her. Surf boiled around her hull. Most of the fifty-five passengers were in their cabins or already in bed. The ship broke up within minutes. There was only one survivor; a member of the crew. The place has ever since known as the Gap.

The mass funeral on Monday 23 August was watched by twenty thousand people. There were no hearses, not even a coffin. The shattered remains of 114 passengers and crew were taken through Sydney's streets in six closed carriages. Mounted police and the Royal Artillery band proceeded them to Camperdown cemetery, where the remains were placed in a common grave.

From Ramornie Charles Tindal wrote a tragic letter to his father.

'We must now bow down and submit ourselves to Providence—poor Frank has followed Arthur and Fred. May God bless you, dear father, and preserve us for another meeting in this world.'

The continent was extracting a harsh price for its settlement. Three out of Captain Tindal's four sons had been separately drowned. Four Mylnes had perished in the one calamity. The Ogilvies had also lost two of their three sons in lonely bush deaths, while Mary's brother, William White, had died in unknown circumstances in the far interior.

16

Norman Blood

Edward's life in Europe was by no means all pleasure.

He corresponded regularly with T. H. Smith at Yulgilbar, kept as much control over station activities as he could at this distance, supervised the sales of tallow and wool through the family's London agent, Joseph Marryat & Sons, and had frequent consultations with his father on their joint management problems. Captain Tindal's letters to his son made it clear the Ogilvies were prospering. 'The new shipment of tallow just arriving will have a good market,' he wrote. 'Capt. O. just sold fifteen casks at 55/6d per ton, and prices have risen since.' A month later he wrote again: 'The Ogilvies are still in Jersey, but not E.D.S., who bought sheep on the continent and shipped them by the *Wellington* from Liverpool two weeks ago.'

Edward appears to have crossed the Channel several times on business, as well as travelling England to inspect or buy livestock for Yulgilbar. One letter to Smith spoke of attending shows at York, Horncastle and Penrith, buying several stud bulls in Northumberland and shipping out a Clydesdale stallion. On another visit to Germany he engaged several more German shepherds and a groom for Yulgilbar's bloodstock. If he also took in an opera or two, art galleries and sight-seeing, this was reasonable enough.

One letter that has survived reveals the problems of management under long distance control, as well as the frustrations of his harassed manager. He complained in September 1857 of 'the very depressing account of the state of things at Yulgilbar' given him in Smith's letter of four months earlier.[1]

> The trouble, care and anxiety you have had. The loss of sheep really seems likely to become something serious, so serious as to severely lessen

[1] Ogilvie Family Papers, Archives, University of New England.

the number of bales of wool of the oncoming clip. I do hope that when you wrote matters at their worst, and that your next letter will bring better tidings. The only agreeable item of intelligence in your letter of May was your mention of the high prices of tallow and hides. I wish you had entered more fully into money matters, and given some idea of the state of accounts.

It would have been interesting to overhear Smith's comments, reading that querulous letter under the oil lamps at Yulgilbar.

The manager was further scolded for sending a cheque for £300, 'without saying what for, when I have already enough money on this side of the globe, but will need a great deal in Australia on my return to buy land. The condition of the exchanges reduces the sum you sent by two and a half per cent (£12), and it will only have to be transmitted back again.'

Again he urged him to ship over as much wool as he could to the London market, which 'continues at a famous price'. His last shipment of twenty-two bales, he added, sold for 2/6d a lb.

Edward was also angry at Smith's temerity in buying a large mob of passing cattle without approval. He said he had only heard of the deal by accident, through the herd's former owner, Malcolm McDougall. 'I feel sure it must be a bargain,' he wrote acidly, 'and greatly recommended to you by the quality of the cattle, or you would not have done so after what I said in a previous letter of my desire for *cash* on my return.' He ordered the man to sell, not buy cattle in future. It was money he needed now, not more stock.

Yet, according to Thomas Bawden, Smith had made a tremendous bargain for his master.[2] To talk of waiting eight months for written consent was unreal. McDougall had been travelling 1,005 head of cattle down the Clarence and, while crossing Yulgilbar, had been trapped by the great flood of 1857. The mob was marooned between Washpool Creek and the main river. T. H. Smith offered to buy them for £1,500, plus a thousand wethers. Cattle were then worth £4 a head. That Yulgilbar had acquired these so cheaply was due purely to the accident of flood.

E.D.S. clearly had other reasons for his apparent parsimony. He gave only a partial explanation.

'I have invested so much money,' he wrote. 'I will only repeat that for the year 1858 I shall want as much cash as I can get to work with buildings etc. You will therefore perceive that whatever the reasons

[2] Bawden, Thomas, *Three Lectures on the Early History of the Clarence.*

and inducements to do otherwise, it would be better to give cattle than money.'

The nature of that building was not explained; not at least for another year. When he did explain, it would have been the manager's turn to be amazed, for those grandiose plans had no relation to the development of his property.

T. H. Smith may even have begun to wonder if high living in Europe was turning his employer's head. It is doubtful if he were much mollified by the final passages of that long letter:

> I have just completed a tour of the northern countries, the Highlands and all the principal lakes and mountains. The scenery after so long a sojourn in this level country delighted me and I enjoyed the trip altogether extremely. I think of taking in Ireland next month. We still think of getting away during the coming winter and returning as we came by the Red Sea, but as I have yet another herd of livestock still to select, you will perceive it is impossible at present to fix the time very precisely.

When that light-hearted letter reached the Clarence, Smith was desperately coping with all manner of emergencies. There were truculent shearers to handle, blacks suspected of killing cattle, pastures withered by summer's heat. 'Hottest day I ever felt in the bush,' reads one entry in the station journal before Christmas. 'Thermo said to be 114⁰.' Above all, there were weeks of unremitting rain.

T. H. Smith was to remember this flood year for the rest of his life. Of his experiences Edward's son, W. F. Ogilvie, wrote many years later.

'The Clarence was in perpetual flood for six consecutive months, and moss grew on the sheeps' backs. The country was so sodden that rations had to be conveyed to the out-stations by blackfellows who carried them on their heads, the country being one vast bog. In one instance, a blackfellow camped for several days opposite Coombadjha out station on the Washpool, a roaring torrent, with rations for the shepherd. He felled tree after tree, and only on the fourth day found one long enough to bridge the torrent.'

Nature treated men rather more gently in Ireland.

Edward enjoyed Ireland. This was perhaps the main reason for Captain Tindal's news towards the end of that year that 'the Ogilvies have ideas of spending the next winter in Europe. Their eventual departure depends on Edward meeting a suitable person to occupy the head of the table at Yulgilbar. I have a notion that an event of this nature would influence their movements.'

Portrait of E.D.S., aged forty-one, by Pietro Milani. This was painted in Florence in
1855. By courtesy of Mrs Griselda Carson, photography by Kevin Testerm.

Pietro Milani's portrait of Theodosia Ogilvie, painted in Florence in 1859. Mitchell Library, Sydney.

The old gentlemen obviously knew more. He was not at present saying; even to his own son.

Nothing is known of what took Edward to Ireland, nor where he went there. But he was invited to one formal evening party, probably in Dublin, that was to transform his entire career. The party has passed into family legend. Many years later Edward told one of his daughters that, as soon as Theodosia de Burgh came into the drawing room, he said to himself 'that girl is going to be my wife'.

It was not to be as simple as that.

Those who knew her said Theodosia Isabella was exceptionally beautiful. It was a rare kind of beauty, delicate as the Irish landscapes he so admired, fragile almost. That she had beauty should have surprised no one. It was in her heritage. Her great-grandmother, Elizabeth Lady Mountjoy, had been one of the three models chosen by Sir Joshua Reynolds for his painting of *The Three Graces Decorating the Altar of Hymen*, subsequently bought by London's National Gallery. The other two graces were her sisters, the Honourable Mrs Barbara Beresford and the Marchioness of Townshend.

It seems unlikely that Theodosia mentioned those antecedents, at least not for a long while. Her father, after all, took even more pride in his male ancestry. There had been de Burghs in the British Isles as long as there was an England. Longer, in fact. His earliest known ancestor had come over from Normandy with William the Conqueror. In A.D. 1185 another William de Burgh, brother of that famous Hubert de Burgh who had taken sanctuary in the abbey at Merton, was granted immense lands in Ireland, fiercely opposed no doubt by the Celts. He had then married a daughter of Mor O'Brien, King of Thomond. Later a William Oge de Burgh had fought beside Henry III in France, being put to death at Athankip while a hostage of the Duke of Connaught. There had been William or Sir William de Burghs for the next seven centuries, culminating in Theodosia's father, a doctor of divinity from Trinity College, and now rector of Sandimount, County Dublin.

It was heady background for a blunt, middle-aged Australian brought up to salt beef and johnny cakes in the bush.

He began to see a good deal of the de Burghs. He delayed his return to England. He called frequently, and found the Reverend de Burgh a charming, enlightened, scholarly man. It is unlikely that he often saw Theodosia alone. It was very much a family establishment. The old rector's two wives had bequeathed to him eighteen children. Theodosia, one of the youngest, appears to have been teaching at this time, an essential activity since her father had only his clergyman's stipend.

As far as suitors were concerned, the old man would no doubt have been reserved and proud. Besides, his daughter was only nineteen; less than half Edward's age.

Despite her graceful air, her poise and apparent assurance that went with her special kind of breeding, she was still little more than a girl. She was shy and immature. A portrait painted of her a year later in Italy reflects all these complex traits. It is a lyrical painting. The unknown artist chose his materials well. He painted her in pastels. The rich colours of her dress, the ruffled lace at her neck, the gloss of that dark hair framing an oval face emphasised the delicacy of her features. The complexion is pale, almost transparent, giving her an unworldly look, a haunting innocence. Taken singly those features are not beautiful. The nose is a fraction too long and narrow, the blue eyes set too wide, the chin not strongly moulded, and the mouth curiously uneven, with down-turned, petulant creases at the corners; a child's mouth still. Yet it is a haunting and lovely face, with a touch of sadness; insecure. Somehow the painter has given this charming and generous girl-woman a parsonage look. The puzzled eyes follow you around a room.

After some weeks Edward went back to England.

England was never to be quite the same. He drove himself harder, became involved in all manner of projects. There were wool sales, the tallow market, cattle shows. He developed a sudden interest in cavalry saddles. Hearing of a contractor left with ten thousand saddles ordered for the Crimean War, now ended, he tried to enlist Captain Tindal in jointly buying nine thousand for Australian stations. He proposed alterations for outback conditions, adding knee puffs and saddle plates, saying they would be a good buy for 36/6d each. Eventually a quantity were shipped out to Ramornie, Yulgilbar and Merton.

But there was still no decision about going back himself. Captain Tindal was now complaining of this indecisiveness. He had plans to send his daughter Mary, as well as cattle, to Ramornie under Edward's care. And now these damned Ogilvies were even of a mind to settle in England. The New Year passed. Then, in May 1858, he reported that Edward had gone to Hamburg. He was selecting another group of Germans for Yulgilbar. But these were no ordinary shepherds. They were brickmakers and stonemasons.

Some extravagant new project was clearly taking shape in Edward's mind.

In June he went back to Ireland again.

A month earlier T. H. Smith had written asking E.D.S. to come home as soon as he could. Major changes were occurring on the Clarence. Hundreds of men were arriving from the south, swelling Grafton's population, invading the back country. Gold had been discovered in the region. Prospectors were even camping and digging on Yulgilbar itself. So long as they possessed Miner's Rights no one could stop them.

The existence of gold in those hills was not exactly news. There had been a rush to the Rocky River diggings, near Fairfield, back in 1856. T. H. Smith had, in fact, written of two hundred men landing from one ship alone. It was naturally of concern to Edward, for the alluvial mining was only twelve miles from his Fairfield run, where his new manager George Smith—his father Robert having just died—now had more work than he could cope with. He was also the licensee of the hotel at Fairfield, Edward having bought it before he went abroad. Though that rush was short-lived, every man there had won himself anything from £100 to £1,000 in a few months, and many of them remained. Now there was even a township named Drake, whose butchers were buying beef from local stations, among them Fairfield and Yulgilbar. It was a pointer to better times. Instead of driving cattle to distant boiling-down works, station men could sell locally at double the price, up to £5 a head. In mid-1858 there was a renewed rush to Drake, while one group of prospectors washed a little gold from the Washpool on Yulgilbar.

More disturbing was a despatch from Charles Tindal.

> Our Legislative Council keeps us in alarm. An assessment bill of £7.10. on every 250 head of cattle has been passed, and a notice served that no leases will be renewed for lands within the settled districts. This includes about one-third of Ramornie. The reason for this is that land may be thrown open for sale, and as long as the Government confine themselves to selling land no great harm will be done; but they talk of giving the buyers of a few acres an unlimited right of commonage over all the unsold adjoining land. I have now bought 160 acres at £1 an acre under my pre-emption right. This includes the house, men's huts and the cultivation paddocks, and as Ramornie possesses very little land fit for the plough, and is rather difficult of access, I consider myself tolerably safe.

E.D.S. could have congratulated himself on being far-sighted enough to buy those freehold blocks on Yulgilbar, the Plains Station and Fairfield back in 1854. During his absence abroad he had also applied successfully for another 187 acres on Yulgilbar across the river, and 169 acres of Heifer Station. His holdings were reasonably protected. But the implicit threat remained. Throughout New South Wales and Victoria there was now a popular demand for land. On every goldfield the easy alluvial deposits were petering out. It was the day of deeper reef mining, which called for machinery and capital. The independent miner was being pushed out by companies. For the first time there were unemployed men in the cities; others carried their swags into the bush. A few arrived even on Yulgilbar, where they were given work felling and stumping trees.

As unemployment grew men began demanding the right to farm, to own a few acres of their own. A clamour for closer settlement was beginning, with its emotional slogan of 'Unlock the lands'. This could only mean the squatters' lands. It really was time for Edward to be thinking of home.

In July, 1858 Captain Tindal had some real news at last for the Clarence.

'The Ogilvies,' he wrote, 'have finally determined to go out either in October or November at the latest. They propose shipping their heavy luggage by a Sydney trader next month. Edward is at present staying in Ireland, where he appears to have been very hospitably entertained; and I tell his mother that she may expect him to bring back a wife with him.'

The old fellow was always brilliantly informed.

Edward's courtship was a rapid one. Probably he had proposed to Theodosia on his earlier visit; or by letter, soon afterwards. It seems likely that she—or her father for her—had delayed an answer. She was, after all, still a minor. There was a considerable difference in their ages. Edward had had his forty-fourth birthday while actually staying at Sandimount. She had celebrated her twentieth only three months before. Which was not to say, as that Florentine painter had shown, that he could not be as youthful and gay as many younger men. There were other considerations, too. Theodosia was not strong. She suffered badly from asthma; she was said to have 'a weak chest'. In that case, Edward may have answered, she needed a better climate than damp old Ireland. Sunny Australia was the ideal place for anyone so deprived. Again there were questions of distance. De Burgh's daughter had never been out of Ireland before. Now this impetuous, persuasive colonial was wanting to take her to the far end of the globe. What did anyone know about Australia, anyway? How would they ever see her again? To a cloistered and patrician, if impoverished, ascetic like the Reverend de Burgh it would have appeared a barbarous land of gold-diggers, speculators and the most vulgar nouveaux riches. Not that the Ogilvies were quite in that class.

Yet the man obviously had prospects. More than that; he had

arrived. He was the owner of lands larger than an Irish county. In addition, he was devoted to the child; passionately so. He would do anything for her, give her anything. No doubt he had already promised all manner of comforts and possessions she could never gain in a lifetime here. At this stage Edward probably told her of the new home he intended to build for her.

Those Germans from Hamburg were not going out to the Clarence merely to build stone barns or cowshed walls.

He would have described for them the great new mansion he had in mind. Perhaps he showed them sketches and plans as well. He had certainly been working on designs since his earlier tours of Europe; particularly in Florence. The site for the big house he had already chosen. It had been chosen many years ago; perhaps during his first occupation of Yulgilbar. The place was to be built close to the spot where he and his brother had camped nearly twenty years before, close to that ironbark tree under which they had rigged their tent. It was a superb position. From the broad terrace they would be able to look down on the sunlit and tranquil waters of Yulgilbar Reach. He would have gardens laid out at the foot of the entrance steps. He would have ornamental trees planted there, with sloping lawns by the river, and a circular carriage drive for the arrival of guests. He was thinking in terms of at least thirty bedrooms, and a staircase of local cedar, a spacious drawing room with french windows opening on to the terrace, servant's quarters for a large staff, an inner courtyard with Florentine archways, a marble fountain and flagstones like those that elegant craftsmen had fashioned in mediaeval Italy.

Nowhere in Australia had anyone built anything of quite this scale and design. It would be a home to make any de Burgh happy.

Whatever he told her, Theodosia accepted him.

Ireland is a land of fables and magical stories. Unlike this vision of Yulgilbar, few of them were expected to become real.

Edward would surely have made the distant Clarence Valley appear exciting. All those pasture lands to ride over, with her own horses; and a vast countryside as beautiful as Ireland in its fashion; smoky-blue mountains, clear rivers and creeks, waterfalls, picnics along their own private reaches, boatings and visits to Sydney in the season. She was a country girl; she loved horses. She rode well. Yulgilbar offered the promise of life larger than an Irish parsonage.

Hence he was able to produce the engagement ring he had hopefully brought with him from London. It was a magnificent ring. The single sapphire—a match for her Irish blue eyes—covered her finger from the knuckle to the first joint.

The excited letter Edward sent to his mother in London is no longer in existence. Her reply has been preserved. She wrote it from the house they were renting in Welbeck Street. The date was 4 August 1858.[3]

> My dear Edward,
> Not mentally merely but most heartily do I embrace you and congratulate you on having found The One who will cheer and brighten all your life to come and from the very depths of my heart do I rejoice in your present joy and future happiness. I am quite prepared to love the sweet amiable girl you describe who is to be so much to us all. Set your mind at rest on that matter and never mind my face which is become too hard to be an index of my mind. The outpouring of your heart, my dear son, shows how full it was, now there is room within it for all the happiness there is in store for you.
> Your ever affectionate mother
> Mary Ogilvie.

They were married on 2 September at Donnybrook church, outside Dublin. A postscript to the occasion went from Captain Tindal to Ramornie a fortnight later.

'Edward Ogilvie and his bride are expected this evening from Ireland. He has taken lodgings near his parents in Welbeck Street; but Mrs. O. tells me he does not intend to introduce her to them before tomorrow—no doubt wishing to create the most favourable impression.'

The following month he, and many other friends, went down to Gravesend to farewell the Commander and Mary on the first stage of their voyage home. They travelled on s.s. *Teviot* as far as Malta, where they would wait for the Edward Ogilvies, who had gone direct across the Channel for a honeymoon on the Continent.

'I think it is probable that the senior couple will settle down in the neighbourhood of Sydney,' wrote Tindal after seeing them for the last time. 'Let us hear what is thought of the Bride on the Clarence. We consider her pretty, with easy and elegant manners, very natural and unaffected. I expect she will be feted, and hope she will have her health; indeed in *that* particular it is probable that the climate of the colony will prove a benefit to her.'

Edward inevitably travelled through Europe by way of Florence. It was a city he felt compelled to show her. By now he knew it intimately. He would have taken her around his favourite galleries, palazzi,

The twenty-year-old Theodosia de Burgh at the time of her marriage to E. D. S. Ogilvie in Dublin, 1858. Courtesy Miss K. Bland.

[3] Ogilvie Family Papers, Archives, University of New England.

mediaeval churches and open squares. He would have shown her the special facets of architecture that had so attracted him, and which in more modest form he was soon to reproduce in the mansion he built for her.

It was the most enchanting period in his life. To possess her in the Florence he loved, to pass long idle days in these piazzas and terrace restaurants, to sense the admiration of passers-by for this exquisite, fair-skinned young woman with her innocent wonder was enjoyment of a kind he had never yet known. Who could have imagined so much happiness after those many years of fly-blown sheep, hard rations, the sweat and discomfort of dust-blown cattle camps, the brutishness of those illiterate, rum-soaked men of his upbringing on the Hunter.

Here he commissioned that unknown artist to paint her portrait. He sat near her at each session in the studio, clearly as absorbed in her beauty as the Florentine. It is unfortunate the man never signed that painting. Edward was to treasure it all his life. It crystallised for him the one moment in time when he was supremely happy. This lovely, still immature girl; the intoxication of life in this handsome, old world city; the feeling that for the moment nothing else in existence mattered; the painter would not have been insensitive to the climate of their emotions.

And yet . . . one wonders why he so emphasised her sadness, that lost, child-like quality that implied that she was still very much alone. There is nothing in this portrait of the high spirits, the talkative gaiety that others said came naturally to her in Australia.

In Florence there were other more practical matters to arrange as well. Orders and commissions.

It delighted him to walk with her into the studios and courtyards of Florentine craftsmen, looking at their work, discussing designs, asking for specifications. He commissioned a marble fountain for the courtyard to be built at Yulgilbar, two carved stone lions for the terrace steps, a chandelier for the big dining room. They spent days choosing and rejecting. And goodness knows how long it would be before they saw the finished products, crated and shipped across the oceans, clumsily unloaded on the wharf at Grafton, and finally hauled over that dusty, pot-holed road up the Clarence.

The hazards ahead meant nothing to Theodosia. She would be seeing that mythical country, too, for the first time.

On board *Teviot*, two days before berthing at Malta, the Commander wrote a long letter to Ellen Bundock at Wyangerie.

We are (at length, you will say) embarked on our return to the colony. It has been much rougher than we had any right to expect at this season. Your mother is now sitting on deck chatting with Lady Young and some other agreeable ladies. You know, I presume, that Lady Young is the daughter of our old friend Charles Marryat. She has made a short visit to England and is now on her way back to her husband in Van Diemen's Land. Your mother has not done as well as I had hoped, and appears to feel the annoyances and inconveniences much more than on the homeward voyage. Our plan is to remain a month at Malta, where Edward and his wife will join us and then go on together by the November packet, so that you may expect us in January.

Before we left London Theodosia had a severe chest attack, but was recovering fast when we came away and expected to follow in about ten days, making easy journeys to Marseille.

It had not been a promising beginning. Theodosia was far less strong than even her family had realised before she left Dublin. Edward would have to be very tender and considerate of her, especially when they returned to the rugged environment he took so much for granted on the Clarence. Something of this was implicit in what the reflective old Commander wrote. Health was a subject very much in the foreground of his thoughts; especially as his condition, according to Edward, had several months earlier been 'very alarming'. Towards the end of his letter he said, feeling the nostalgia of leaving England for the last time:

The kindness and attention we have continued to receive from very dear friends, and the reluctance we could not but feel at parting with them all required a good deal of resolution to overcome, and has I fear shaken your mother not a little. I am, I suppose, of a hardier nature, for although I feel the parting acutely, I am now in very robust health— happily we are spared a good deal of it, as a large portion of our friends were absent from London when we came away.[4]

Robust health or not, he became seriously ill two days before the ship reached Sydney. They berthed in Woolloomooloo. He had a high temperature and was too weak to travel further. Edward found a bed for him in a guest house nearby. This was St Kilda, in Woolloomooloo Street. The doctor they called said there was little he could do. What he needed, above all, was rest; and time. They all stayed at St Kilda with him. Three weeks went by. His health showed no improvement. Most of the time he was in a semicoma.

The old Commander died here on 10 March 1859.

He had celebrated his seventy-seventh birthday only a month before.

[4] Ogilvie Family Papers, Archives, University of New England.

17

The Master Builder

The ten Germans from Hamburg reached Yulgilbar by bullock dray at the end of October. T. H. Smith was pretty laconic about them in the journal, as if he regarded them as a damn nuisance. It was, after all, his busiest time of year.

Shearing had started. Flock after flock had to be washed, brought into the woolshed across the river. Heavy rains had set every creek running a banker. The Clarence itself was rising fast. Several times the shearers refused to handle wet sheep, and the usual disputes occurred. To disrupt things further the bishop and Reverend Arthur Selwyn rode in from Grafton, obliging him to give all hands a day off for divine service. And now he had these Germans to waste his time. They were bewildered by the country, lost themselves in the bush, spoke only a few words of broken English and had no idea how or where to find the right materials for building.

He had to find suitable trees for the sawyers, Paetke and Bauer; the right quality of clay for the brickmakers; Aborigines to cut and dry great quantities of grass for them, and valuable workers like Jimmy Cobbera to cart it to the site where they were puddling their clay. Next he had to lecture those axemen how to split shingles, how to select the right trees and, in God's name, to look after the tools they kept losing in the scrub. When those sawyers wanted special timber for rafters and posts, he went out again, locating a magnificent stand of red cedar on Long Swamp. They dug the pit for their crosscut saw at a place still known as Sawyer's Creek. Two months later he was angered to find that the splitters had cut hardly any shingles, and had 'a great rowing' with the brickmakers for making none at all.

It was all desperately frustrating. Especially as he was totally in the dark about building plans. All he had been told so far were the types and quantities of materials required.

He was in no doubt that the big house would be a long time building; probably years. He would just have to live with the present turmoil until the master returned to take over. For T. H. Smith running a station meant handling sheep and cattle, not coping with a mob of truculent foreigners in a backblocks construction camp. Yet he was one of the best managers Yulgilbar had, even if his successor claimed that he had neglected to muster and brand a considerable number of the half-wild cattle running in the more inaccessible foothills of the New England ranges. For almost five years he had been in sole control, greatly increasing turnover and productivity. He was deeply interested in this country. He had also a shrewd understanding of the new directions it was taking. The Clarence was becoming far more open to the world outside.

Gold escorts were beginning to come through from the ranges at Drake. Another strike was reported at Tooloom farther out. Teamsters had begun carting supplies to the fields from Grafton, camping on the run. Cattle buyers from the south were coming up, one of whom had recently arrived with a commission to buy up to four thousand head, if these could be found on the Clarence. The old system of boiling-down was on the way out. In fact, Kirchner's tallow enterprise at Grafton was to go bankrupt within a year, its works converted to a sawmill. Big travelling mobs were starting to pass down the river, for expanding populations in Sydney, Melbourne and elsewhere had boosted the demand for live beef on the hoof. Already the main local outlet for cattle was two meat-salting works on the outskirts of Grafton, offering some hope for a future export trade.

Smith felt that E.D.S. had been too long abroad. He was still trying to run Yulgilbar as it had been in the early fifties. He was out of date.

Hearing that his ship had at last reached Sydney in February, Smith sent a man down to meet the next coastal steamer in Grafton. E.D.S. and his bride were not on board. Instead more German builders came ashore. With them were also two English stonemasons. Smith had to set about building more accommodation for them all. Two more steamers arrived without the Ogilvies. Finally a letter came, giving 'the melancholy news of Captain Ogilvie's death'.

Edward added that he was now compelled to remain a while in Sydney. There was a great deal to be done. It took him two months to wind up his father's affairs, have his will proved, re-register Merton and other holdings in his and Mary's names, and settle the long delayed probate on Will's estate, for his brother had died intestate.

The Commander's estate was finally valued at £75,000.

It came as a surprise to all of them. After all those difficult years, the mortgage on Merton, their absence abroad, he had died a prosperous man. The irony of it was that most of this wealth had been earned in the years they were out of the country. They were able to pay off the mortgage at once and, since there was now no one to run Merton, to lease it for five years. The lessee was the new owner of Edinglassie, Edward White—no relation to Mary—who took up his option to purchase at the end of that five-year term.

It was the end of an era on the Hunter. After thirty-three years there was no longer to be an Ogilvie on Twickenham Plains. When the sale went through, Mary persuaded White to agree not to demolish Merton Cottage. The bill of sale stipulated that it should be preserved for ever.

At least she would never want for money again. In the terms of her husband's will, she acquired his half-share in the Clarence River properties. She had also that comfortable sandstone house, Fairlight, in Edgecliff. Since she was now too 'embonpoint' to walk much, Edward helped her to buy a carriage, and engaged a housekeeper and coachman. She soon became a familiar sight in Edgecliff Road, taking afternoon drives and visiting her friends.

There had been one unusual clause in the Commander's will. It was typical of the old man. He had instructed his executors to have his funeral 'conducted in the simplest and least expensive manner, and wholly free from the absurd and grotesque mannerisms practised by undertakers.'

They did as he wished. They buried him quietly in Camperdown cemetery on the outskirts of Sydney.

Among the second party of Germans to reach Yulgilbar was an elderly, self assertive character named Betelmann. Since he was to take charge of building operations, Smith left him to cope with his troublesome compatriots, returning to station work. The English stonemasons, the Wilmot brothers, being experienced craftsmen, were no problem. All they wanted was high quality sandstone for the outer walls, which were to be built of solid blocks three feet thick. He found them two large deposits—one six miles out on the Tabulam road, the other a mile upriver on Joseph's Creek—and left them to quarry and dress it. It was actually freestone, light in colour, with a coarse, open grain and soft to cut, though it hardened rapidly when exposed to the air.

Two of these Germans had brought wives with them, which meant more huts to build. To employ married workers had always been Edward's policy. He thought it made for a settled work force. It did not work out that way at all. Within two weeks the camp was in uproar.

Fierce, inexplicable arguments developed between Betelmann and the wife of a carpenter, Frau Melzer, obliging Smith to find the foreman fresh quarters elsewhere. A few weeks later he was confronted by another angry lady. 'She says she was beaten by Betelmann,' he wrote in the journal, 'which I am inclined to believe is false, but which has created a regular row amongst them all.' Thereupon Frau Eggert complained of being too sick and bruised to leave her bed. Her husband, without telling anyone, took off for distant Grafton to find a doctor, and had to be saved from perishing in the bush.

Relief came at last with another letter from Edward. He was finally coming home. Smith harnessed up the buggy and drove down to meet him. While in Grafton he took out a summons against Betelmann for assault, the writ being served by a mounted trooper the following week.

It was a bleak period for the Ogilvies to arrive. Theodosia's first sight of the Clarence was through deluging rain. It continued for two days. Grafton's streets were bleak and empty. Even when they did leave, the long buggy ride over sodden roads so exhausted Theodosia that Edward decided to take her no further than Gordon Brook.

Perhaps he had forgotten how rough and crude this country was. Now, concerned about her health, he began to realise how little his own home had to offer her. It was a very masculine establishment. The Cottage, he still called it. Nothing had been added since he and Fred shared it years ago. It was comfortable enough for active, outdoor men, despite its bare floors, the walls hung with bridles, stockwhips and guns, the billiard table for the amusement of idle males. For so feminine a woman as Theodosia there was nothing. He arranged with the Bundocks for her to stay indefinitely; at least until he could make it a more attractive home.

Meantime he lived as a part-time bachelor.

He rode across to Yulgilbar every few days, returned to his wife for the rest of the week. He drove himself hard, drove his manager hard as well. He had the cattle mustered, rode out with Smith to inspect them, questioned him about the poor condition of the newly arrived stud bulls, toured the scattered sheep flocks—now wholly shepherded by Germans and gins—and badgered the brickmakers and sawyers for quicker results. Dissatisfied with the rate of progress, he ordered an immediate start on building.

He took the now ailing Betelmann down to the site, marked out the exact dimensions of the house, had the undergrowth cleared and sent more men to begin the excavations.

This was soon the busiest place on Yulgilbar.

Men were set to breaking and gathering up stones by the river.

Others hauled them up the slope on sleds, drawn by horses or bullocks. Others again built rafts to ferry more stone from the crossing. It was solid and chunky serpentine suitable for the foundations. A bullock driver was brought from Grafton to haul in grey gum logs and cedar posts from Bulginbar Creek. The dependable Jimmy Cobbera carted bricks from the kiln, scantlings and freestone blocks. They worked with such energy that the first scaffolding was going in by mid-August.

Theodosia was still at Gordon Brook. The journal referred to her as being very ill. The nature of her sickness was left unstated. She was now also three months pregnant.

Now that the new house was well under way, Edward decided to do something about the Cottage. He had the rooms replastered and painted. A German tradesman named Junker added a stone fireplace and chimney to warm what was to become Theodosia's sitting room. Even Betelmann, no longer hobbling about on a stick, was put to whitewashing the ceilings, which must have somewhat deflated his self-importance.

The new mistress of the Cottage came over at last towards the end of winter. This first mention of her in the journal, which had been silent for three months, was in October. Now written in a new hand, it referred to a drive she made with Edward out to the Washpool. Since this beautiful spot was only a few miles out, it seems likely to have been her first sight of Yulgilbar country.

The effect she had on the station blacks was startling. They had never seen a woman like her before. The only European females they had known before were middle-aged servants, the wives of station hands or those quarrelsome Prussian fraus. Now this slender and graceful Irish girl came among them, with her smooth white flesh, her groomed and glossy hair, the soft lilt of her voice. It was afterwards said that, whenever Edward was out bush—he would not have tolerated it had he been home—the Aboriginal women and their piccaninnies would come and sit around the cottage, just waiting for her to appear on the verandah. They sat on the ground and stared at her, admiringly. Such beauty was quite alien to their experience.

That three month gap in the journal had been caused by the resignation of T. H. Smith.

Perhaps the arrangement was a friendly one; perhaps not. There had been grounds enough for disagreement during Edward's long absence abroad. There was also the friction caused by Betelmann and his obstinate workers. At all events, ill-feeling between the two men was evident soon afterwards.

Smith, whose sister was married to Fred Bundock, curiously enough moved to Gordon Brook just as the Ogilvies moved out. He had bought Massie's share in the partnership with Barnes and Bundock and took over the management. Within a few years he became sole owner.

From early November until March 1860 the journal was silent again. The cause this time appears to have been Wilson the bookkeeper, whom the new manager wrote off in March as 'getting more idle and thoughtless every day'. E.D.S. was certainly too occupied to trouble about it any longer. Any free time he had went to looking after Theodosia.

The child was born on 18 January.

Whatever her health, Theodosia seems to have had no trouble in childbirth. However, Edward would not allow her to breast-feed the baby. He considered the practice unladylike, and brought a strong young Aboriginal girl up from the riverside camp as a wet nurse. Though his motives were distinctly puritan, he must have shocked fellow settlers fearful of intimacy between the races, especially in so sensitive a region as mother's milk.

On his next visit to Yulgilbar, the Reverend Selwyn baptised the child Mary Isabel.

There was a growing feeling along the Clarence, especially in Grafton, that Edward's personality had altered since he went overseas. He was said to have become aloof, overbearing, even arrogant. 'Mr. Ogilvie returned a changed man,' wrote R. C. Law two generations later.[1] 'Five years in the stuffy society of mid-Victorian England and his marriage altered him entirely.'

Possibly so.

Yet Victorian society was not all swallow tails, crinolines and antimacassars. Nor was there any evidence of the Ogilvies being entertained, even accepted by the higher echelons of British society. Most of their time had been spent with old friends or relatives, or with visiting Australians like the Tindals and Mylnes. As for Edward, he was more frequently on the Continent than in London. His values had changed, nothing was more certain. The elegance of European life had come as a revelation, its arts and architecture, the highly civilised life of Florence. No sensitive man could have returned to the crude, materialistic, often mindless atmosphere of the backblocks and remained unaware of the contrasts.

The main influence on any change in attitudes, one suspects, was the de Burghs; that ancestral environment, the easy assumption of aristo-

[1] Law, R. C., 'A Clarence Pioneer', *Clarence River Historical Society Journal*, Grafton.

cartic values, even without wealth. Perhaps the old dean, despite his courtesy and charm, had been a little condescending. Who were these colonials, anyway? Perhaps Edward himself had been overawed, determined to match their unconscious pretensions. If this were so, his ambitions to transform Yulgilbar into a grand manorial estate were understandable. In designing his great mansion he was challenging the de Burghs, creating at the same time a monument for his love and admiration for the beautiful Theodosia.

He would also have been out of sympathy with the new social currents he found on his return. He had left Australia before Eureka. Now there was mass clamour for equal rights, a levelling of standards and prestige, a larrikin set of opinion against the once mighty squatter. These attitudes were now being voiced regularly in the new democratically elected parliaments of Melbourne and Sydney. Having dined in the Conservative Club with W. C. Wentworth, who equated democracy with the revolutionaries of the Paris Commune, he found himself back in a land where Jack insisted on being his master's equal. At least in the cities and towns. His fellow pastoralists were equally determined to remain the nation's elite.

The new mood was particularly evident in Grafton. Men no longer raised their hats to the squatter, stood aside as they entered a store or reserved for them the best hotel accommodation. A different class of men now ran the town. Its first municipal council had been elected in 1859. Influenced by radical gold diggers and small selectors downriver, it had an anti-squatter caste. The mayor, J. E. Chapman, was a bootmaker. Its aldermen comprised Thomas Bawden, now an auctioneer, two publicans, two storekeepers and three small farmers. Not a pastoralist among them.

Townsfolk were persuaded to regard Edward as 'the ultimate in squatter conservatism, [who] expressed his contempt for the changing society by the building of a castle at Yulgilbar.'[2] That he never termed it a castle, forebade others to do so in fact, made little difference. He was also said to have shown contempt for the town by importing workers from overseas, used only building materials he found on the station, and bought little from local merchants and storekeepers. Yet it must have been clear that Grafton could not have provided the experienced stonemasons and skilled tradesmen he needed to match the aesthetics of his design. No matter. He was a snob; a silvertail.

What further compounded this ill-feeling were his plans for a new port on the Clarence.

[2] Davies, A. E., *History of the Clarence River and Grafton*, M.A. thesis, University of Sydney, 1953.

This portrait of Edward Ogilvie by Tom Roberts was painted at Yulgilbar in 1894.
Reproduced by permission of Mrs Norah J. Roberts and the Mitchell Library.

A century later—Yulgilbar Castle today.

Yet is was not Edward who first chose it. The riverside hamlet of Lawrence—originally known as the Devil's Elbow—was a product of the Timbarra gold rush. Impatient diggers for the Rocky River field had jumped ashore there, refusing to stay aboard for another twenty miles to Grafton. Besides there were shoals and sandbanks beyond this point; and a twisting, hazardous channel that pilots called the Elbow. Even before this, Richmond River settlers had adopted the embryo port for their bullock drays and produce. It became the logical river link with both the Richmond and New England, whatever Grafton's merchants had to say about it.

E.D.S. quickly saw its possibilities.

He could bring his Fairfield and Plains Station cattle out this way. He could also cut a road through the Richmond Ranges direct from Yulgilbar. He began buying up land on the outskirts. He leased a large area beyond for cattle resting paddocks. He planned his own wharf, a cattle ramp for direct loading on to coastal steamers, a wool store. Soon he owned more land than anyone else in town.

T. H. Smith need not have worried about Edward being out of date. He was now in front of them all, looking a long way ahead. If boiling-down were finished, he would now ship away his cattle live, taking advantage of high beef prices in Sydney and Melbourne.

His master-stroke, or so he then thought, was to invite Thomas Bawden to manage his Lawrence affairs. Bawden, having come overland with Craig at the age of nine, knew everyone in the region, had worked on several stations and was an experienced auctioneer. He was also an alderman on the Grafton Council. This was really a case of Edward putting his hand in the lion's cage, and expecting no one to bite.

The two men went into partnership together.

E.D.S. was equally astute in his choice of a replacement for T. H. Smith. To judge by his journal entries, Mr Watt was an efficient, if critical and sometimes irascible, young man. He had been brought to Yulgilbar in 1860, after the sale of Will Ogilvie's Liverpool Plains stations, which he had managed, and given an unusually good salary of £400. His first entry on 6 March 1860—also mentioning Edward's departure on a five-week trip to Sydney—was crisply written, informative and far more detailed than his rather slapdash predecessors. Day after day he summarised events so fully that the book remains a vivid picture of just how large stations like Yulgilbar were run. Nothing seems to have escaped that sharp, sardonic eye.

Hagen breaking up limestone; Melzer off duty, bad leg; Eggert hoeing the vineyard; Cooper making yokes and filling up casks in the cellar;

Bauer working for Mrs. Ogilvie and making a baking table; Pemberton
with cart to Broadwater with fencers; blacks have today cut 119 sheets
of bark. Counted the ram flock, found all correct.

This independent character seems not to have cared whether or not
his employer read his sometimes caustic comments. After one especially
frustrating week when downpours turned the station into a vast swamp,
stopped work on the building, destroyed thousands of newly-made
bricks and caused a landslide to bury the lime kiln, he wrote: 'It is
indeed time that someone was here to take an interest in the station.'

Perhaps Edward read this entry on his return. At all events, he took
a more active role in sheep and cattle work in subsequent weeks.

Theodosia appeared at this time to have settled happily into
Yulgilbar life. The manager wrote of Bauer and Melzer making
furniture for her, Hunt doing maintenance work on the carriage
Edward had bought for her in Sydney, and another German paving
a pathway to the child's nursery. She began also to go out riding on
her own. Even the station hands thought her a good horsewoman,
despite the handicap of riding side-saddle. She now had her own
riding hack, and cantered light-heartedly over the Front Run and river
paddocks.

She might have been happy. The manager was not.

'Gardener troublesome today,' he wrote in April, 'assuming an
impertinent tone with Mrs. Ogilvie, also myself. Severely reprimanded
him. I have also had to reprimand Eggert, Hanlon and Hunt for laziness,
and the storekeeper for neglect of duty. I certainly never had a more
lazy, useless lot of men to deal with. They almost drive me wild by
their horrid laziness.'

In the latter half of the year she had to give up riding. One imagines
that, even had she wanted to go out still, Edward would have firmly
discouraged her, or confined her to the carriage. She was expecting
their second child. Florinda Ellen was born in the Cottage on 12
January the following year. If Edward were disappointed in her giving
him another girl, he would have kept it to himself. Mary was far less
considerate. Unaware of biological truths, she accused her daughter-in-
law of being unable to produce the son that Edward wanted as the
eventual heir to Yulgilbar.

If resentment in Grafton was any guide, his new venture at Lawrence
was becoming a success. Already the recently formed Clarence and
Richmond River Steam Navigation Company had made it a regular
port of call. Skippers welcomed the chance to lighten their cargo

before steaming through the Elbow and skirting those variable shallows, even if Grafton's merchants detested the whole scheme.

The energetic Bawden was changing the character of this little township. Its population had not yet passed the fifty mark, yet trade had doubled. Though there was already a jetty at the downriver end of the straggling one-street hamlet, Edward insisted on building another of his own. This hardly increased his local popularity. But he was not the man to be beholden to others, to share enterprises; or their profits. Things had to be done his way, under his control, or not at all. As a result, the township reproduced a replica of itself. There were now two Lawrences, a mile apart. And a post office half-way along the river-front.

Shipping found it had to make two calls into this divided port. The bottom end handled mail and cargo for the Richmond or New England carrying trade. Bawden & Co. looked after Edward's enterprises at the top end, where he had built a wharf near the mouth of Sportsman's Creek. (The name derived from that pioneering visit of s.s. *King William*, which had put its passengers ashore here in 1839 for a day's sport with fowling pieces.) He had a store here, too, for his shipments of Yulgilbar wool; a race for loading cattle on the hoof, and sundry other business activities managed by Bawden.

On the high red bluff immediately above this wharf he had begun the building of a hotel. It was a fine spot. From the hundred-foot crest, overnight guests and casual drinkers would be able to look out at the splendid flow of the Clarence, exactly two miles wide at this bend.

No matter if a competing hotel was already building at the bottom end. This little empire of his must have its own hostelry as well.

While the brief Timbarra boom lasted men continued to arrive in impressive numbers. There was, after all, plenty of trade to keep two rival retail stores in business at either end of town. There was even a new 'American Conveyance' to take passengers along the rough and rutted road through Traveller's Rest, Wyan, Camira to the diggings and New England; even if, on the steeper mountain pinches, they had to leave their swags on board and walk. The diggings also kept thirty-five bullock teams busy on this route, as well as a gold escort of mounted police. When, after 1860, hundreds of diggers began leaving in disgust, Lawrence trade continued to prosper from the exodus.

The disgust of these diggers was due not so much to a decline in gold, but to the new class of fossickers coming in. They were Chinese coolies, yet these 'untouchables' of an incipient White Australia did not pass through Lawrence. They were freighted up to Grafton at so much a score, and the xenophobic Europeans retreated out of neurotic fears of cholera, opium-smoking or plain demeaning equality.

Edward, in his usual timeless fashion, spent much time riding the back country, determined to make a direct road link with Yulgilbar. The journal mentioned three prolonged trips he made away from the station. He made his own surveys and tree marks, took parties of men out to clear tracks, had them crudely graded and surfaced, and even charmed money out of the Government in Sydney for culverts, a causeway and the paving of swampy sections. This private route for his cattle and drays eventually followed Camira Creek to its source, crossed the Richmond Range to Dome Mountain, then kept to a series of ridges through the top end of Gordon Brook to the Long Swamp and home paddocks on Yulgilbar. Though long disused, it is still known to old hands as Ogilvie's Road.

Henceforth, whenever he wanted to travel to Sydney, he rode or drove to Lawrence, boarding a steamer there. Grafton rarely saw him, except during the races in what became known with mixed feelings as Squatter's Week.

Matching these advances at Lawrence was the accelerated progress of his German builders. Even the loss of that cantankerous Betelmann had no ill effects. Whether his foreman was sacked or resigned Edward never bothered to mention. It was probably the former, since Betelmann took out a summons against him in Grafton, claiming unpaid wages of £13.7.6. Nothing more was heard of him; he did not even go to court.

On 2 May the journal carried a triumphant entry: 'Foundation stone of new building laid.'

On the same day a second brick kiln was burnt in. The first was dismantled and carted to the building site, which suggested that work was beginning on the basement structure. The Wilmot brothers now began building the wine cellars and other store rooms, while others fabricated a huge underground storage tank for the domestic water supply. This was a remarkable innovation of Edward's; probably unique in Australia.

Other working parties scoured the back country for more limestone deposits, set up fresh brick kilns in favourable areas, and in August the first scaffolding poles were cut and brought to the site for inner walls. The station ledger recorded the impressive amount of work done by those two stonemasons before the end of that year. They were credited with having supplied 2,231 perches of rubble work which, at eight shillings a perch, earned them £892.8.0. Further excavation work and stone cutting brought the total to more than £1,000.[3]

[3] Yulgilbar Station Ledger, 1860–67, Clarence River Historical Society, Grafton.

Before they were finished this emerging mansion was to absorb 3,500 tons of serpentine rubble, a thousand tons of freestone and 110,000 hand-made bricks. This great quantity of bricks set many problems. To find the sand and clay was not difficult. The major shortage was a substitute for lime. Edward solved this by borrowing the technique Charles Tindal had used three years earlier while building his homestead at Ramornie. Tindal had been obliged to send bullock drays right down to the sea coast at Yamba, on the Clarence mouth, where so many generations of Aborigines had left great piles of mussel and oyster shells. Burning this shell made a kind of lime.

It was a long slow journey. The teamsters had to take their drays fifty-six miles to Grafton, then another ten miles through dense scrub and wheel-choking sand to the Yamba headland. It took those bullock teams at least two weeks to travel each way. All told, those drays made more than a hundred of these journeys.

Towards the end of the year, the Wilmot brothers were shifted to fresh projects. William Wilmot began building the stone stables, while John worked with Junker on the mansion's surface walls.

With the work so far advanced, it was now possible to gain an overall impression of this monumental building. It was being built in the form of a hollow square. The excavations covered an area of ninety-one feet by eighty-five. The front terrace, still to be paved, spanned the complete width of the house, with full-length french windows looking out at Yulgilbar Reach. Eventually there would be a row of eight doric columns supporting a massive canopy, and a broad flight of sandstone steps leading down to lawns and formal garden. The upper storey, still in Edward's sketch plans, would carry the large front windows of seven bedrooms, with twin towers of unequal height at either side. The western tower, on the river side, was to be fifty feet above the ground. Each of these towers, and the roof coping between them, would be crenellated like a mediaeval castle.

The master plan called for the building of forty rooms, including extensive servants' quarters, a large kitchen and cool rooms on the ground floor, and a series of family and guest bedrooms on the upper level.

The unique feature of this remarkable building was to be an inner courtyard forty foot square, with pillared archways giving the effect of cloisters, and above this a square of wrought-iron balconies overlooking the paved flooring.The centrepiece would be a marble fountain Edward had commissioned before leaving Florence. The first floor passageways would be reached by a great staircase of local red cedar. The craftsman capable of creating this had still to be found.

At the back of the house Edward was already planning to build a coach house and stables. Further back, high above the river, was to be a large laundry, also of freestone and serpentine to match the main building. A carriage drive passing the eastern side of the house to a grand circular sweep fronting the entrance steps had still to be laid out. There was plenty of time for that. But he was already discussing the double entrance gates and sandstone pillars with the stonemasons. He had also planted two monkey puzzle trees that would eventually add to the manorial splendour of this entrance.

In later years his curious concept of towers and battlements prompted men to talk of a Moorish design. That roofless inner courtyard, with its blend of sunlight, cool green plants and splashing fountain, was also said to have had a Moroccan influence. Ellen Bundock herself compounded this theory. She wrote of her father's 'dream home, a type in use in Morocco and southern Spain where the Moors had lived as conquerors for some five hundred years.'

She propounded, in fact, exactly that dream castle idea which Edward was to spend the rest of his life contradicting. It made him extremely angry when people used the term castle at all. Others came to call it Yulgilbar Towers. He detested this, too. For him this was to remain simply the Big House.

It seems strange that Ellen never discussed the design's origins with her father. Or, if she did, that she passed them off with that one superficial phrase.

There is strong evidence to suggest that the inspiration did not come from Spain at all. Certainly not from Morocco, which Edward never visited. The key is surely to be found in his beloved Italy.

One of his grand-daughters has recently described its origins in more convincing fashion. 'I used to think,' wrote Miss Kathleen Bland, 'that Yulgilbar was a sort of Scottish castle adapted to the hot climate. But, on further study, I am now convinced that the buildings which really influenced him were mediaeval Italian. The place he loved best was Florence.'[4]

These battlements were not some symbolic defence of an embattled squatter's privilege, but a tribute to the fine craftsmanship of bygone Florentines.

Miss Bland pointed to the crenellated roofs and tower of the Palazzo Vecchio which Edward, on several return visits, had so much admired. There are similar roof lines in other parts of the city. The cool inner courtyard he planned may well have stemmed from the church of

[4] Letter to author, 3 April, 1971.

Santisima Annunziata, or the Lucia Giordano room in the Medici
Palace, for both have similarly rounded archways and slender columns,
complete with marble fountains. Even the high-arched doorways he
designed to link drawing room and library may have been derived
from the Pitti Palace or Stibbert Museum. The theory is intriguing.
It is highly probable that Edward desired to surround himself for life
with remembrances of *la bella Firenze*.

He had, in fact, already commissioned a Florentine artist to copy
an early 16th century painting by Raphael Sanzio, said to have been
influenced by Michelangelo. This was the *Portrait of Cardinal Dovizi*,
which he had greatly admired in the Palatine Gallery. The copy was
destined to hang above the drawing room mantelpiece in his new house.

Edward's vision was a heroic one. His attempt to recreate the
magnificence of Florentine architecture on the banks of the Clarence
overlooked certain factors. Neither his Germans nor those English
masons were Renaissance craftsmen. The materials they had to work
with were not, with the exception of some imported paving stones, the
marbles or travertines of Italy. They had to make do with whatever
could be found on Yulgilbar, and work with crude techniques and tools.
Nor, for that matter, was Edward anything but the most amateur of
architects. The copying of any masterpiece requires a high degree of
training and aesthetic disciplines.

The monument he was in process of creating was, in effect, a folly.
It was a grand gesture, nonetheless. A folly to be cherished amid the
raw, simplistic landscapes of the antipodean backblocks.

18

Free Selection Jack

Grafton's new weekly newspaper, *The Clarence & Richmond River Examiner* carried a bold advertisement in August 1861. It was not to win many friends among Grafton folk. Written with the flamboyance of an auctioneer, it read in part:

COMMERCIAL HOTEL
LAWRENCE

Thomas Bawden begs to inform his friends and the public generally that he has opened the above hotel. Wines, spirits and beers are of the best quality. Tabling will be first class. Accommodation unequalled in these districts and unsurpassed out of Sydney. He feels most confident that one visit will satisfy the most fastidious. Persons travelling up country can be supplied with horses for their changes.

Ellen Bundock paid it one visit soon afterwards. Perhaps she was too fastidious. She was not very complimentary about that unequalled accommodation and first-class tabling. All the same, Bawden must have stocked Yulgilbar wines.

The flourish of this grand opening was somewhat eclipsed by the competing Lawrence Hotel, which had opened a month earlier. But what must have puzzled local guests more was the absence of the owner. In later years Edward, accompanied by Theodosia, would make manorial appearances here, driving by carriage around the gravelled drive to the front steps, pausing to look at the splendid river below.

Yet on this occasion he remained at Yulgilbar. This was not surprising. Within a week a public announcement was made that the partnership between Ogilvie and Bawden had been dissolved.

Edward's choice of a partner and agent had not been so wise after all. Though Bawden had a reputation for honest and hard work, he had overspent himself. His creditors had caught up with him. When one William Wilson sued him for failing to meet a promissory note for £100, plus a bill of exchange for nearly as much, he was on the way to bankruptcy. Since the summons was issued against Bawden and Co., agents for E. D. S. Ogilvie, it began to look as if Edward might have to settle.

The case was to drag on for a full year. Edward engaged expensive counsel in Sir William Manning, travelled to Sydney for Supreme Court hearings, but no forensic brilliance could offset his agreement with Bawden when dissolving their partnership. Both had agreed that Bawden should take over the company's assets, and that he should meet all debts. Since he was now in no position to pay, Edward had to do so. This surprisingly unbusinesslike arrangement cost him several hundred pounds, as well as heavy legal expenses for both sides. What disillusioned him more was that Bawden's evidence was given in favour of Wilson. The result was a feud that lasted many years. Edward was not a man to enjoy being on the losing side.

Though Bawden wound up his affairs and returned to Grafton, the two neither met nor spoke again. In later years there were odd hints that their falling out might have had more personal overtones. It was said there were remarkable likenesses shown in photographs of Edward and Bawden's son. Others dismissed this as small town gossip.

At all events, E.D.S. conceived what was almost a passion for litigation. His lawyers were kept active on numerous large and small disputes. He lost almost as often as he won. This seemed hardly to concern him. It was as if he derived some rare pleasure from taking his opponents before the courts, dragging out his disputes in public, persisting in rear guard actions when he could not hope to win.

Nor was he any longer on speaking terms with T. H. Smith. When Smith refused any longer to allow him to take his cattle from the South River across a Gordon Brook river paddock, E.D.S. was forced to make a difficult crossing of the Clarence and take them up the other side. This continued for years.

Further legal matters—probably connected with the unfinished Bawden affair—caused him to be absent from Yulgilbar that Christmas. He was still in Sydney when Theodosia arrived by horse in Grafton alone. The event was remarkable enough for W. A. B. Greaves, Oliver Fry's successor, to note in his diary, 'Mrs. Ogilvie rode in from Yulgilbar today, en route for Sydney to her husband, detained there by illness.'

This was no easy ride for a young woman still unfamiliar with the bush. She was also expecting her third child, in little more than a month. It began to look as if she were not nearly so frail as was commonly supposed.

William Frederick was born in Sydney on 2 February 1862. At last Edward had his heir.

He had all the more reason now to develop and protect his lands. And they were in need of protection during 1862. His fourteen year leases had just expired. All over the country landowners were under threat of resumptions. New attitudes were being expressed in parliament. The chief inspiration for these was Free Selection Jack.

John Robertson had already been premier once, resigning in favour of Charles Cowper, William Ogilvie's old adversary of those bygone Church Lands days. Robertson had stepped down simply to concentrate wholly on a new land act he was determined to have passed. This was to open up crown lands for agriculture. Edward knew the rough-spoken ex-secretary of lands only too well. In their youth, when the Robertsons raised sheep at Jerry's Plains, they had been family friends. That was before the man's increasingly radical views made him break with W. C. Wentworth over support for the squatters. Since then he had campaigned for manhood suffrage, vote by ballot, national education, state aid for religion and the free selection of public lands. Dangerous socialistic talk.

In 1861 Robertson had won a majority vote for his Free Selection Act. The law now allowed any man to select any block he liked on crown lands, even before anyone surveyed it. He could pick out from forty to 320 acres, and set himself up as a farmer. All he had to do was pay a deposit of five shillings an acre, promise to live on his block for three years and put in improvements valued at £1 for each acre.

Already landless men of this type were appearing on the Clarence and Richmond. Many were unemployed. Others were disappointed goldminers. None had any capital whatever. All they wanted were a few acres of land, enough to grow crops, run cows and scratch a living for their families. Groups of these 'cockatoo' farmers had even now settled on the river banks between Lawrence and Grafton, laboriously clearing scrub and head-high grasses. More were beginning to look in the direction of the Upper Clarence, where they saw only huge cattle and sheep runs monopolising what they regarded as good agricultural land. Moreover, they were being encouraged by that dour, crusading Presbyterian, the Reverend John Dunmore Lang, who wanted to see a new peasantry settled on the rivers and small farms by the hundred, replacing the squatter.

It was for this reason that Charles Tindal—now in England again—had organised a petition of Clarence landowners to Queen Victoria. Edward had been among those who signed. The petition appealed for the separation of the northern rivers from New South Wales, enabling them to join the newly formed State of Queensland. At once the Clarence member of parliament, one Hoskins, publicly attacked 'the reactionary squatters who want to ally themselves with Queensland, because of its plantation attitudes and cheap foreign labour.'

Her Majesty was gracious enough to ignore the colonial altercation.

E.D.S. at once took other protective action. He anticipated the passing of John Robertson's act by an approach to Crown Lands Commissioner Greaves. Though no attempt had been made to resume any of his land, he wrote to say that those subject to rent and assessment had already been 'materially reduced', while the charges on them had not. He continued:

> Of my leasehold lands I have purchased upon my Yulgilbar run about 5,000 acres, and this will according to the spirit of the forthcoming Land Law entitle me to the free use of 15,000 acres of the adjacent lands, making a total of 20,000 acres for which I am entitled to claim remission of rent for the coming year.
>
> Besides this there is a further quantity of about 22,000 acres withdrawn from my lease by the formation of the reserves, of which I received notice through your letter of the 12th of June last. Upon these grounds I think I am fairly entitled to a remission of at least one third of the amount of revenue and assessment heretofore charges.[1]

With five thousand acres of freehold, and the entitlement to graze the rest on renewed leases, Edward had his flanks well protected.

The proclamation of the Free Selection Act created widespread popular enthusiasm. It also deepened the divisions within expanding towns like Grafton, where anti-squatter prejudices were on the increase. Throughout the bush every shearer, bagman and out-of-work miner began to sing the ballad of the Free Selector. They sang of 'the victory John Robertson has won, now the Land Bill has passed and the good time has come.'

> No more with our swags through the bush need we roam,
> For to ask of another there to give us a home;
> Now the land is unfettered, and we may reside
> In a home of our own by some clear waterside.

Only too often, however, this turned out not to be the selector's true home at all.

'Honest Jack' was one of those utopians who believed their fellows needed only common justice to live freely and generously together. This most democratic act of his was supposed to remedy past inequalities, give every man a reasonable livelihood and create a nation of contented

[1] Ogilvie Family Papers, Archives, University of New England.

yeomen farmers. Instead all manner of new terms entered the Australian language. Men began to speak of peacocking, or picking the eyes out of land otherwise of little value; of dummying, or occupying supposedly free land to protect the squatter; of pre-empting, which meant secretly buying a block before it was legally thrown open for sale. As G. W. Rusden put it, 'the scramble for land at a fraction of the value for which it could be sold by auction was rapacious. Frauds and demoralisation, cupidity of selectors, sometimes sharpened by gratified revenge; cupidity of squatters, resorting to unusual if not illegal acts. Any scoundrel anxious to live beyond the purview of the authorities could select before survey the most convenient and secluded nook for his own or his comrade's villainies.'[2]

There was nothing as wild as this on the Upper Clarence. It remained as peaceable as ever. Yet men like Edward were accused of being rigidly opposed to agriculture. This was not precisely true. He was only opposed to anyone wanting to practise it on his own lands.

'One of Mr. Ogilvie's main activities,' wrote R. C. Law long afterwards,

> was the defence of his station from free selectors. He exercised his rights of pre-emption in securing the home run and the South River and Plains station, and by means of volunteer land orders purchased by him, he not only peacocked nearly all the permanent waterholes on the back country, but put together a large area of freehold at the Top Plain.
>
> He contrived that most of the roads left between or reserved in his freeholds led either into rocky declivities or deep water or both, and so blocked nearly all the fords, and almost all practical access to the back lands available for selection. Even the river ford to Lionsville could only be reached by crossing his freehold. The result of these and other means of repression was that practically the only selections on Yulgilbar during his life were made by his own employees, or by persons who were quickly disheartened, and in either case the holdings were very soon absorbed into the station.[3]

Nonetheless, selectors did establish themselves on Yulgilbar. At one time there were six of them, occupying twelve hundred acres. They built bark huts along the river, as far as Tabulam. Only one was a *bona fide* settler. The rest had agreed to camp on their blocks, surrendering them again at the end of the prescribed three years, at a reasonable profit, to Yulgilbar. These dummies were paid thirty shillings a week while they stayed on their land.[4]

[2] Rusden, G. W., *A History of Australia*, London, 1888.

[3] Law, R. C., unpublished journals, Grafton.

[4] Local informant to author.

The exception was one dogged selector named McColl, who took up land well away from the river. According to a former station hand, his sheep were impounded each time one of them wandered outside his boundary. 'It was like a dingo getting in among a mob of sheep,' the former mail driver William Hamilton said. 'The old fellow had no chance at all.' After being forced off his block, he selected a second one. This time it was right on the river. The Yulgilbar manager had him fenced in, denying him access to any road. From then on the determined old man kept a flat-bottomed boat, and came and went by the river.

It was seven years before these issues broke surface. Finally three selectors on the Washpool, debarred from crossing Yulgilbar to their land, sent a petition down to the Lands Minister in Sydney. They asked for the right to use that same ford approached through Edward's freehold.

The district surveyor, Grafton's *Examiner* reported, 'having gone to Yulgilbar for the purpose of laying out this road, Mr. Ogilvie has been put upon his mettle, and has got up a petition against its proclamation, stating that he is willing to grant it on "suffrage" [sic]. Of course, this is to say Mr. Ogilvie's toadies may pass through, but none others. To this petition, we learn, are attached the names of some of the sham free selectors of Mr. Ogilvie's nomination, some of whom, it is stated, are to be remunerated in some way or other. The question is now whether Mr. Ogilvie, as one man, is to reclaim the road, or whether the general interest of the public should be considered.'

The Examiner added that those 'toadies' were not only 'in that gentleman's employment, but lived at Tabulam thirty miles from the Washpool, having no interest in that particular road.

'Conduct like Ogilvie's,' it concluded, 'has set people of the colony against squatters as a class.'

Edward had been abroad during the devastating flood of 1857. He was back in time to watch the next great torrent surge through Yulgilbar in 1861, its brown and debris-topped waters washing down whole tree trunks, struggling bullocks and dead sheep, smothering rock bars and falls, churning to an awesome height through the narrowing cliffs of the Gorge, sweeping away the splintered remnants of stockyards, fences, huts half-way down to Grafton. 1863 brought an even larger flood.

On Plains Station a stockman was drowned. At Tabulam, where the river rose to nearly seventy feet, five people lost their lives. One of them, a policeman with a wife and six children to support, was marooned on a rooftop, being last seen on his knees, as if praying, as his entire cottage was swept away. At Yates Flat, the crossing for Plains Station, the vehicle punt was washed right down to the Clarence Heads, while several teamsters camping there never saw their drays again. Remnants of packing cases were later found near Grafton, other articles off Lawrence, while bagged flour and a box of boots finished up on the beach at Yamba.

Men estimated the current's velocity at ten miles an hour, for one of those drays, still loaded, was seen passing Lawrence, two hundred river miles away, within twenty-four hours.[5]

The Clarence, in its more violent moods, was no river to treat lightly.

Even old hands were shocked by its destructive power. They had known nothing like it in earlier years. Yet anyone who had ridden the soaring, uninhabitable escarpments, the granite-walled ravines and deep sunless canyons of its tributaries knew something of its elemental force. They could read it in the massive boulders choking channels miles from their mother rock, the heaped stones and shale high above normal levels, the detritus of past inundations in the upper branches of stout trees.

But now there appeared to be some cyclic change in the seasons. Rainfall since 1857 had been without precedent. For weeks at a time each year the stations had been waterlogged, their stock work disrupted and harvest ruined.

Yulgilbar's sheep had suffered badly. Years earlier T. H. Smith had told Edward this country was just too hard for sheep. He had seen those losses in the period of his employer's absence overseas. In the mid-fifties the place had supported thirty thousand. Now they were down to half that number. They were badly affected with footrot, bottle, catarrh, while the spiky-burred spear grass worked into their fleeces and skin, eventually killing them.

At last Edward decided to sell. He was lucky to find a buyer almost at once. W. H. Buchanan, a New England sheepman, bought practically all of them, travelling them three hundred miles up the ranges to Tenterfield, past wintry Ben Lomond and out to Coonamble, claiming not to have lost a single animal. Though Edward retained one or two flocks—he was still selling a few bales in England three years later— Yulgilbar was wholly given over to cattle.

It was the end of an epoch.

He had battled through to prosperity on the backs of sheep, opened up the back country with them, shaped the contours of his vast, partially freehold estate. Now there were to be no more jumbuks milling through races, gates and drafting yards. No inarticulate shep-

[5] Law, R. C., unpublished journals, Grafton.

herds shambling behind them in their cabbage tree hats, no gins squatting beside portable sheepfolds, no metallic sound of distant sheep bells drifting down wooded valleys or the green shoulders of hills. This, after all, had been his life for almost thirty years; since boyhood.

There were larger inducements for the changeover to cattle. They ran free, needed fewer men to work them, had to be mustered only once or twice a year and were reasonably well adapted to the climate. Again the market for beef was beginning to look promising.

From now on Edward was to concentrate on building up his herds, and improving the breed. He began to buy well-bred stock from the A.A. Company at Tamworth, and soon had shorthorns that were among the best cattle in the north. 'In the checkered shade and sunlight of forest oak and native apple trees he rode about with his stockmen,' wrote N. C. Hewitt of Edward. 'His men admired him for his knowledge and skill.'[6]

Because he was so absorbed in completing the big house he rarely went to Sydney, even though he now arranged for Theodosia to stay south. It was unreasonable to expect her to cope with three young children in so remote a place as Yulgilbar, especially as she was now expecting a fourth. Her health was not good enough for this rugged living. He leased a comfortable house for them on Darling Point, slipping away from the Clarence for brief visits every now and then.

It was a good arrangement in many ways, for Buckhurst was near his mother's home. Mary was sentimentally devoted to her grandchildren, taking them off her daughter-in-law's hands a great deal. This may not have made Theodosia very happy, for she appears never to have been at ease with her somewhat overpowering mother-in-law. Her letters to Edward at Yulgilbar hinted at her nervousness. It was sometimes said, too, that she found him rather brusque and dominating. That shortness of breath people spoke of was itself revealing. She was said to preface every conversation with a sharp intake of breath, beginning each time with an 'Oh . . . Edward,' and an almost apologetic air.

Nonetheless, she was profoundly attached to him, writing of how much she missed him whenever he was away from Sydney.

In June 1863 she wrote from Buckhurst saying how glad she was to hear he had had a good sea trip home. She had now engaged a Miss Manning to look after the children, and had spent the previous day with Mrs Ogilvie. Curiously she never called her anything else, even with Edward. 'We went for a drive as far as Government House, then

[6] Hewitt, N. C., *The Daily Examiner*, Grafton, 24 October 1932.

in the evening let the cook, housemaid and coachman go into town together to see the illuminations,' while they watched a fireworks display over the Harbour from her mother-in-law's bedroom window. Presumably this was part of the Queen's birthday celebrations. Theodosia added that the English mail had just arrived and, because of heavy rain, she had sent the coachman out to post the letters on to Yulgilbar. It was plain that she was not living in any great discomfort.

Mary, who seldom went out at all these days, had now added a large, tower-like room to Fairlight, which occupied most of the upper floor. She had become too stout to use the stairs frequently, and made each journey out-of-doors a major expedition.

Towards the end of June Theodosia wrote to Edward again.

> Your two nice long loving letters came to me this morning and made me so happy. I am enchanted to be missed and also enchanted at your description of dear Yulgilbar. I do indeed wish I was there. All the happiest days of my life have been spent there and they shine out in such strong relief that the many days of anxiety about you, darling, are forgotten. You should not say all you do about being nasty some-times; it was part of your illness and you made up for it so lovingly then that I never minded it in the least. Besides have I not often erred in the same way myself without your excuses. You must forgive and forget much, at any rate we love each other dearly and that is all happiness to me.[7]

She wrote of her delight at hearing how pleased he was with the progress of the big house. 'There is nothing I would like better than to walk through it and come up at once if we could manage it. I do so hope, darling, that this will find you on your way to me. I know it will be very tempting to stay a little longer at Yulgilbar, but I want you back so much.'

There was naturally much talk about the children. 'Baby has repeated the performance of walking alone, but he is very shy about it. Mary is very sociable, both she and Flora are very good. Mary asks very often when the big ship will bring Papa home.' But there was again wariness about her mother-in-law. She was terrified of offending the old lady by having Ellen Bundock's daughter to stay with her at Buckhurst, instead of going to her grandmother. 'Oh, Edward dear, I am beginning to long for you to come home again.'

This letter also gave some insight into the success of Edward's cattle-breeding. A newspaper report had just written of a record bullock turned off by Yulgilbar, weighing a sensational 1,200 pounds.

[7] Letter in possession of Mr and Mrs John Ogilvie.

This massive bullock was to be much discussed by cattlemen in later years. Common belief was that the beast had been a full-grown bull castrated by mistake.

Early in July she wrote again, expressing her 'great pleasure that you have at last fixed a time to come home. I only hope that nothing will prevent your coming to your dear wife.'

This time there was more talk about the servants than her children. She was concerned at the prospect of having to find another housemaid, though 'you will be glad to hear that the coachman is reconciled to his wife, and that she lives in Sydney with the three boys. Wilks had applied to be released, just as she was getting perfection in her business and, though I like to have a person so respectable and that the children know, yet I am afraid of having to teach again.'

It was her only reference on record to the shadow of her impoverished life in Ireland. One need hardly wonder that she had slipped so contentedly into the new mode of life Edward had been able to give her.

'Here people are very gay,' she wrote, 'and the opera goes on every night. We are going to go very often when you come back.'

Once more she hinted at the tension between her and Mary. She wrote of refusing an invitation to Government House, having hoped it would not arrive before his return. 'This is the second time since you left. They were both for evening parties, and I think if I could have had the courage to face Mrs. Ogilvie I should have gone, but she would have been annoyed.' There was a suggestion of panic as she mentioned the old lady again, for at once she wished she were up north again at Yulgilbar. 'I wrote to Ellen,' she continued, 'telling her I should be very glad to have her for a week or so when she was staying with grandmama, but that the latter would be annoyed if she came to me and not to her.'

Her husband returned to Sydney soon afterwards, remaining in town for the rest of the year. One can assume he took his wife to the opera a number of times, since singing was one of the rare Ogilvie passions. The children were exposed to music from an early age. It was to be among the family's chief delights in later years at Yulgilbar.

Edward was soon to have other good reasons for spending a good deal of his time in Sydney. He had been offered a seat in the Legislative Council. Since this carried no salary or expenses, apart from generous attendance allowances, it was the type of role only a well-to-do man could afford. He told his friends he regarded it as a 'public duty'. The official confirmation of his appointment reached Buckhurst on 23 November.

The Honourable E. D. S. Ogilvie, M.L.C. took his seat in the upper house next day. In this dignified clubman's atmosphere he found himself with old friends. Among its senior members was the Honourable E. Deas Thompson, recently created a Commander of the Order of the Bath. Two other new members were admitted the same day; Edward's former Queen's Counsel, Sir William Manning, and the Honourable John Blaxland.

Edward attended almost every day during the pre-Christmas session, spoke during the debate on a bill for the prevention of scab in sheep, was appointed to a select committee vetting the City Bank Bill and cast his vote in a number of unimportant divisions. It was not an exciting session. The Council, however, was not designed for excitement, but largely to review, veto or defuse the more dynamic legislation initiated in the lower house. It was all rather like passing his days at the Australian Club, but with legislative authority.

The day on which he did not appear was when Theodosia had her fourth child at Darling Point. Theodosia Isabella was born on 11 December.

It was during this period that Edward took to driving with an Aboriginal boy in livery on his carriage step. He had brought the lad down from Yulgilbar, drawing a fair amount of attention in Sydney's workaday streets.

A good deal more attention came with his attempt to take the liveried boy into the Australian Club. It seemed there was a by-law to prevent such untoward adventures.

A bush blackfellow in the Australian Club!

Yulgilbar claimed Edward once more throughout most of 1864. He spent hardly any time in Sydney, and was even absent from Legislative Council debates, except for one day, until the end of the year. That single attendance had been to vote in support of a Loyal Address to Her Majesty Queen Victoria on the Birth of a Prince. 'We are thankful,' declared these august colonials, 'that we have the privilege, as members of that great Empire on which the sun never sets, to share in the rejoicing.'

Edward was likewise concerned that the sun should never set on his Yulgilbar estate.

He negotiated a revision of the boundaries between Plains Station and the neighbouring Cheviot Hills. This station comprised country resumed from Fairfield, whose lease he had transferred to his former employees, the Smith family, rather than see it pass into the hands of strangers. The realignment of boundaries ensured that he would have an unbroken stretch of country adjoining Yulgilbar.

Now he came under attack from a new quarter; and from a fellow landowner. His southern boundary with Newbold was being disputed. The argument had, in fact, been going on in desultory fashion for many years. Now it came to a head.

The Hanging Rock Valley had always been a kind of buffer zone between Charles Walker's Newbold and what Edward called his Cattle Station on the South River. This was at the far end of his first-class cattle country, below the Gorge. The narrow valley, which ran to the head of Hanging Rock Creek, had been claimed by both men.

That disputes of this kind should occur was not surprising. None of these Clarence runs had ever been properly surveyed. No boundary fences existed. Men had always run their stock according to the lie of the land, establishing its limits by a mountain range, creek or line of scrub. Besides, they had all had more country than they used. This was not the case any more. Edward was prepared to defend every square mile of his land, even if it meant litigation.

In one of numerous letters written on the Hanging Rock affair, he made it clear that he had regarded this valley as his since he first took up Yulgilbar in 1841.

'I occupied the H.R. Creek with cattle two years before Walker advanced a claim to it,' he wrote to the current crown lands commissioner, Richard Bligh. 'I have occupied it continuously for 24 years. On all occasions when the right to the ground has been disputed, Walker has been the attacking party and I in defence. Your accusing me of endeavouring by my pertinacity to "worry my adversary out of a portion of his run" is about as just as it would be (comparing great things with small) to accuse the Circassians of endeavouring to worry Russia out of a portion of her territory.'[8]

This was only the final cry of exasperation. The conflict had been smouldering away since July 1854, when he left for Europe. Stopping overnight at Ramornie, he had had a tense meeting with Walker on their borders. T. H. Smith, being his manager, supported him. Charles Tindal did not. Writing to his father, Tindal said, 'There was a slight coolness between myself and Edward on parting. I had been arbitrator between him and Charles Walker on a question of boundaries, and gave it in favour of the latter.'

Since Tindal was a close friend, his opinion seemed likely to have been a valid and reasoned one. Nonetheless, Edward continued to defend his position on returning. It was still unresolved in the 1860s. Edward, at least, claimed it was unresolved. The Commissioner for

[8] Ogilvie Family Papers, Archives, University of New England.

Lands in Sydney had staged an inquiry, appointing two arbitrators, one nominated by each side. They gave a joint decision in favour of Walker.

'The arbitrators were misled by the production on the side of my opponent of a false map,' E.D.S. later wrote to the Minister for Lands. Perhaps he was not surprised by the Minister's lack of sympathy, for he happened to be John Robertson. Refusing to accept the award, he took the whole question to court, applying to have it set aside. R. C. Law later reported that 'Ogilvie made charges of corruption on the part of Walker and his own arbitrator, Fisher, and charged both with breaking their promise to inspect the land and depriving him of the chance of calling further evidence. The court did not believe Ogilvie and declined to disturb the award.'[9]

To complicate matters, Walker then sold Newbold to W. A. B. Greaves. The new owner, who retired as crown lands commissioner in 1863, was in a position of strength, having been familiar with the official files. Stubbornly persisting, Edward kept the fight going for two more years. He visited the Lands Department offices in Sydney where, being an M.L.C., he was able to have easy access to the records. What he discovered there prompted him to write angrily to Richard Bligh, who had taken over the crown lands office from Greaves in Grafton. He expressed his 'very great surprise and mortification' at finding an adverse report from Bligh himself to the Lands Minister in May 1865.[10] He added:

> Surprise that one who has all along maintained the most friendly relations with me should at the same time have thought proper behind my back to put forth the most slanderous statements imputing to me conduct in the highest degree dishonourable and even dishonest. Mortified that one whom I have long regarded as a friend should have evinced so much readiness to believe me capable of such conduct as that of which I find myself accused. The passages in your letter to which I particularly refer are the following.
> "That Mr. Ogilvie by letter formally withdrew all claim to Hanging Rock Creek and acquiesced in the first award"
> "That no misrepresentation (even if there were any) of the position of Hanging Rock or Camelback could affect the clear intention of both sets of Arbitrators to give to Walker the valley of the Hanging Rock creek or Mr. Ogilvies' formal recognition of the first award and distinct resignation of all claim, and that the second reference to arbitration was only obtained by Mr. Ogilvie's refusal to ratify his own written promise".

[9] Law, R. C., unpublished journals, Grafton.

[10] Ogilvie Family Papers, Archives, University of New England.

"Trusting that your sense of justice will not permit the pertinacity of Mr. Ogilvie to worry a less influential adversary out of a portion of his run assigned to him by two sets of arbitrators confirmed to him by the Supreme Court and guaranteed to him under the hand of Mr. Ogilvie himself."

The whole of the statements and inference embodied in the foregoing extracts are neither materially or wholly the truth, but I wish for the present chiefly to call your attention to those portions which I have underlined as containing three statements and assumptions which are at the same time the most defamatory and the most easily capable of refutation.

"The course of events will determine whether it will become necessary for me to produce proofs of the falsehood of these slanderous statements or accusations at another time and in another place." I shall now only state for your information that I never did acquiesce in the first award but on the contrary protested against it from the first in the most emphatic terms and further that the documents dated Ramornie 4 of July 1854 and bearing my signature was prepared and placed before me by the Arbitrators by whom I was required to sign it as a condition precedent to their going into the case Mr. Walker being at the same time and in like manner required to sign a similar document.

You have I repeat within your reach evidence of the utter groundlessness of the slanderous statements which you have thought proper to place on record to my injury and prejudice and in now calling upon you (as I feel it my duty to do in the most unconditional terms) to retract those slanders I afford you an opportunity to retrieve an error and to recede from a wrong which a just man should be glad to avail himself of.

Further letters came and went. The tone grew more bitter. Bligh accused him of trying to provoke a personal quarrel. Edward replied that the quarrel was not of his making. 'I have explained in what way you have wronged me and have pointed out how and where they can find the proofs of your error. Meet me I again suggest at Moriarty's office and I am certain that the truth will become manifest to you in half-an-hour by the examination of half-a-dozen documents which I can point out to you.'

Whether they met or not, he lost the battle. Hanging Rock Valley was erased from his run.

Simultaneously he was fighting on another front. Grafton merchants had found another hopeful way of isolating Lawrence. Perhaps Edward should have blamed the turbulent Clarence. When that 1863 flood destroyed the Yates Flat punt, teamsters found it almost impossible to travel the Lawrence–Tabùlam road. The Government was persuaded not to replace it. Instead the Mayor, Alfred Lardner, surveyed a new and more direct route to New England, travelling straight up the mountains south of the Clarence to Glen Innes. This meant that all downriver traffic would have to pass through Grafton.

Edward campaigned against the new road, and was attacked by both the Grafton and New England press for doing so. But Lawrence's trade was now too well established. Besides it was now living largely from the river. Schooners, shallow-draught droghers with stern wheels, all manner of water craft had stimulated local trade, while ocean-going vessels landed cargo and carried away produce from the hinterland.

The Commercial Hotel, under new management, was also prospering. It was even offering a special service for travellers on horseback. Newspaper readers in Grafton were now promised 'no charge for paddocking horses, having secured grassed, well-watered paddocks from the Honorouble E.D.S. Ogilvie, M.L.C.'

Also advertised, for the entertainment of customers, was a musical box in the bar. This was a genteel Victorian counterpart of the modern juke box.

Civilisation was coming to Lawrence.

19

Castle Waters

When Edward rejoined his wife in Sydney late in 1863 the big house was structurally complete.

Junker and John Wilmot, according to the station ledger, had been paid off in August. They had at last finished the stonework, after three hard-working years. As well as building the outside walls, they had also constructed the ninety-foot wide front terrace, a wall to support it and broad entrance steps. The large flagstones were laid in a 'court diamond' pattern, and used up 6,000 feet of stone. This alone cost E.D.S. £508.14.9 in contract wages.

All this flagging had involved slow, laborious work. To begin with the stone had to be carted ten miles by bullock dray from the bed of a watercourse on the Tabulam road. The place is still known as Flagstone Creek.

These stonemasons had become very much an integral part of Yulgilbar, for they were not to complete the last job until 1867. This was the building of stone piers for the impressive entrance gates three hundred yards north of the house. All told, they were employed on house and grounds for seven years.

The final stages were clearly approaching when, in June 1864, a painter and glazier named Andrews arrived. When he was paid off ten months later the many rooms had been painted and fifty windows, some of them full length, fitted with glass. Yet another painter followed him, remaining until November the following year.

Presumably George Eccles was no ordinary housepainter, though nothing more has been learnt of him. It seems almost certain that he was engaged for more elaborate work. This was to paint the cornices and frescoes beneath the high ceilings in the dining room, drawing room and library.

Another remarkable craftsman was brought to Yulgilbar in October that year. This was a Scottish carpenter named John David Farquhar. The brief four months he spent there produced the most remarkable results. He cut and set in position the cedar panelling for living rooms and corridors, did other essential woodwork and, finally, created the stairway that was to remain a showpiece of the mansion for the next half-century.

This, too, was of beautiful polished cedar. It rose from the main hallway in one broad flight of steps that turned at ninety degrees to reach the upper floor. One of Edward's grandchildren, Mrs F. J. Sabine, later described it as having the grace and delicacy of a bird's wing.

Legend has it that Edward had him build a secret room on the upper floor, perhaps in one of the towers. If so, it remained so secret no one ever located it. There were, however, several rooms on a third level, which could only be reached by the two steep and narrow wooden staircases in the towers, after which those who used them had to walk across the flat, leaded roof surrounded by battlements.

Meantime a shipment from Italy had arrived, via Sydney, at Lawrence. It included some heavy crated objects, difficult to transport and very costly. Among these were two lifesize stone lions, replicas of those carved by Canova for a Florentine tomb. These were to be set on pediments each side of the entrance steps. There was also the beautiful, two-tiered fountain of Carrera marble Edward had commissioned before leaving Florence. At least this was reasonably simple to transport, when lashed on to a dray; always supposing it did not capsize on the boggy or pot-holed tracks. A third large crate was a much more touchy proposition.

This contained a cut crystal chandelier, also from Florence. It defies the imagination how those teamsters took it without damage along those seventy miles of rough back tracks and over the ranges to Yulgilbar.

By the time all these treasures were installed some of the forty rooms were already occupied; though probably only the servants' quarters— and a bedroom for Edward when he came up. Evidence was to be found in the station ledger, which accounted for the laundering of household linen from July. A Mrs Henry Muller was then paid for the washing of fifty dozen and eleven pieces at the reasonable rate of two shillings a dozen. The account was debited to 'Yulgilbar Towers'.

Surely Edward did not see this account, or he would never have paid it. The name was taboo. No fancy names like Yulgilbar Towers for him. It had to be modestly the Big House, or plain Yulgilbar.

From the beginning Edward had resolved to give his mansion an elegant setting. Scenically, the surroundings were magnificent; the great rounded flanks of Mount Ogilvie, the splendid river, the gentler hills and pastures on the eastern bank with their park-like trees and picturesque clumps of grass trees. But he wanted landscaped gardens as well. He enclosed four acres around the house for this purpose, fencing it to keep the cattle out. It was more than good fortune that enabled him to employ a man who was probably among the best gardeners in Australia.

Gustav Stenmark had migrated from Norway around 1850, finding work at once in Sydney's Botanical Gardens. When Edward's father advertised for a head gardener at Merton, Stenmark applied for the post. The Commander could hardly have refused him. His credentials were astonishing. He had been employed as an undergardener for the King of Norway, working in the palace gardens at Christiana. To prove this, he produced an elaborate, embossed reference in Norwegian— with a translation confirmed by the British consul—as a gardener of 'ability and indefatigable industry'. Whilst at Merton he had married the Scottish immigrant girl whom Mary had engaged as her lady's maid, so both already felt a close involvement with the Ogilvies. Edward brought them to Yulgilbar, giving Gustav a strongly built Irish undergardener to do the heavy work.

By the time of the housewarming in 1866, both grounds and gardens were in beautiful condition. There was none of the raw, half-planted atmosphere common to new houses.

From the unfinished double entrance gates a gravelled avenue approached the house at an angle, describing a full circle about an island of lawn and shrubs. Two paths, enclosing a much larger expanse of lawns, followed sloping ground flanked by trees. The centrepiece for this garden took the form of a circle enclosing a five-pointed star. This was later said to have been based on a Moorish design, on what authority no one knows. Of more significance was the orange tree growing at its centre. This had been brought out as a cutting from Napoleon's grave on St Helena. Several vine cuttings in a second small vineyard beside the river also came from this grave.

Stenmark planted many imported and native trees around the house, nurturing the monkey puzzle trees at the gates and, in the lower garden, a magnolia whose blooms were later to float in the basin of the courtyard fountain. He introduced ferns, palms and creepers into that courtyard, too, making it a marvellously cool refuge from the heat of summer months. Also he took great care with the ironbark tree beneath which Edward and Fred had camped on the night of their arrival. Now aged and gnarled, with some of its upper limbs dying, it is still carefully preserved some hundred yards from the rear of the house.

Strange how rapidly men's accounting of the past vanishes. There is no record of just when the mansion was fully occupied, nor its opening celebrated. Nor were there any but vague estimates by out-siders as to the exact cost of building. N. C. Hewitt calculated it at about £40,000, a high figure for the time considering the cheap labour costs and availability of local materials.

In August 1865 Edward, writing from Sydney to the Reverend Selwyn[1], mentioned the 'nuisance' of having to leave Buckhurst for another rented house in Rose Bay, since Yulgilbar was shortly to be ready for them. There was another good reason for this discomfort, for there had been two more additions to the family. Twin girls, Maude and Jessie, had been born in December, 1864. Edward naturally remained in Sydney throughout December and attended the Legislative Council meetings until it adjourned a few days before Christmas. He was certainly on the Clarence early in January, for the *Examiner* reported a verdict in the Grafton court against him, when Dr Simon Belafonte was awarded £20 for an all-night ride he had earlier made to attend Theodosia and a sick child at Yulgilbar. Edward had objected to his charge of £25, paying him only £15. The jury there-upon decided that a fair charge would be to split the difference. Reflecting current Grafton antipathies, the *Examiner* gave the report some prominence.

Yet the same weekly did not trouble to report the Yulgilbar house warming at all, even though it must have been the Clarence River's event of the year.

Though it became a family tradition that 'many distinguished guests' came to celebrate, no one remembers who attended the party. Charles Tindal and his wife would certainly have been there, for they had just returned to Ramornie after four years in England. So would Mary Ogilvie, the Wellington and Fred Bundocks, T. H. Smith, the Reverend Arthur Selwyn and probably the bishop. Curiously, Graham Mylne—last surviving brother at Eatonswill—made no mention of the event in his otherwise copious diary. He had nothing to say beyond reports of his own strenuous cattle mustering and imprecations against excessively humid weather. Others who would obviously not have been invited were W. A. B. Greaves of Newbold, the antagonistic Richard Bligh and Thomas Bawden.

A contemporary photograph of Yulgilbar with Mt Ogilvie in the background.

[1] Selwyn Papers, Mitchell Library, Sydney.

The fact was the *The Examiner* had never much concerned itself with Yulgilbar, except for the movements of gold prospectors and Edward's troubles with free selectors. Mostly it would have been unaware even of Edward's comings and goings. He rarely visited Grafton, took no part in its annual races—Thomas Bawden, in addition to being mayor, was also president of the race club—and the two men were careful not to meet. For the rest, whenever he went to Sydney or returned, he used Lawrence not Grafton as his port.

What really made that day memorable for the district was the entertainment E.D.S. arranged for his station workers. He organised a sports day down on the flat, between the river and Colley's Hill. In later years this would be occupied by a tennis court, a croquet lawn and bowling green. Now everyone on Yulgilbar, regardless of colour or class, gathered down there to watch foot races, wrestling and other contests at which the blacks especially excelled.

According to mail-driver Jack Hamilton, whose father was present that day, the magnificently-built young Tommy Ryan won most of the events.

Poor Tommy Ryan. He found himself in no end of trouble soon after. The mounted police thought him a desperate character. Having already escaped from Copmanhurst gaol by overpowering the warder, he was arrested again on the Upper Clarence, handcuffed and escorted downriver by two troopers, riding his own horse. The story of his escape was told by Duncan Macfarlane:[2]

> Proceeding along a narrow cutting by the river in single file, Tommy in the centre, his escort, in view of a steep mountain range on one side and the river on the other, gave the rear member the opportunity of joining the leader for conversation. Eventually they cast a glance back at their prisoner, who was not to be seen, though his mount was pacing steadily along. Tommy had sufficient resource to disengage his arms from the wristbands, plunge into the river and make for the opposite bank.

His thefts and assaults had made him too much a wanted man to remain free for long. Macfarlane told of his subsequent arrest and how he was sentenced to a term behind the supposedly impregnable walls of Grafton's gaol. They were not so for Tommy. He eluded the sentry, climbed the wall, walked unrecognised through the streets and dived into the river, which was three-quarters of a mile wide and running strong. He was caught again eventually and, after serving one more

[2] Macfarlane, D., 'Aboriginal Races', *The Daily Examiner*, Grafton.

sentence, decided the whitefellow law was too strong for him. He kept out of trouble from then on. 'Poor old Tommy,' remarked a former Yulgilbar cattleman, 'there wasn't much wrong with him. He was just too strong to handle.'

Prominent among the spectators on that famous sports day was old Toolbillibam, frail and white-haired now. Jimmy Cobbera would have been there, too—an elderly man now—and the hard-working Pundoon.

Perhaps the old chief reminded Edward of those wrestling matches of more than a quarter-century ago. There had been no polite applause or laughter in those days. Perhaps the stout and greying Charles Tindal spoke of them, too. Both his former adversaries would have realised that this was no longer the proud, dignified figure they had first encountered on this same open ground beside the Clarence. Now he wore the shabby breeches of station handouts instead of ceremonial belt and kangaroo skins. On his bony chest was the customary inscribed crescent made of tin, hanging from a cheap metal chain around his neck. Edward, in his well-meaning fashion, had given it to him as a badge of note. It was a humiliation nonetheless.

The wording on it read: Billy, King of the Yulgilbar Blacks.

There was even a coat of arms crudely engraved on it. This depicted an emu and kangaroo rampant, holding between them a helieman; a tribal shield. Later one of Edward's descendants was to cliam that 'it was from this coat-of-arms, sketched by my grandfather for King Billy, that the crest for the South Wales was taken.'[3] *New?*

Maybe.

Even at this stage, it seemed, E.D.S. was becoming fascinated with the heraldic symbols of the feudal manor.

Visitors arriving for that house party may well have felt themselves in Europe rather than on the Clarence. They rode or drove down that long, tree-shadowed driveway to the front of the house, pulled up at the broad entrance steps, guarded by its two Canova lions. Aboriginal grooms held their horses as they dismounted, leading their riding hacks, carriages or buggies around to stables and coachhouse at the back. To walk up those stone stairs, whether in crinoline or hot and formal suit of serge, engendered something of the solemnity of visiting Government House. There was even a Union Jack flying on the west tower's flagstaff.

[3] Sabine, Mrs F. J., *The Daily Examiner*, Grafton, 1964.

Edward and Theodosia would have been on the flagged terrace to greet them, standing beneath the canvas sun awning supported by those eight Doric columns. Through the tall doorway of hand-carved cedar was a vista of long hallway with black and white marble tiles, the soaring, bird's wing stairway and the cloistered cool of the inner court with its marble fountain playing.

The french doors of the drawing room were likewise open. This long, airy room with its high ceiling, frescoes and glittering, eleven-foot chandelier had been furnished with impeccable Victorian taste. It was, in the usual manner, overcrowded. There was no room for another picture on the clean, whitewashed walls. A huge gilt mirror above the marble fireplace reflected the assembled company. At one end was a rosewood concert grand. There was an embossed buhl cabinet filled with plate and chinaware, the family's cedar furniture brought up from Merton, occasional tables, a Venetian vase inlaid with gold, beautiful wrought table lamps, candelabra, chintz chairs and sofas and the splendidly carved oak settee that Edward had bought form Sir Charles FitzRoy when he left Government House for England.

The long dining room, on the eastern side of the house, had become something of a family portrait gallery. Here were Hay's paintings of William and Mary, looking suitably regal side by side, the unknown Florentine painter's lyrical pastel study of Theodosia and Pietro Milani's swaggering portrait of Edward at forty. Amid the almost ceiling-high bookshelves of the library, the high and narrow archways Edward had so admired in Florence created a mood of withdrawal and repose.

Despite those ceiling heights and some cross-ventilation, the house was uncomfortably hot at this humid time of year. That internal courtyard fashioned another climate altogether. Again direct sunlight was screened off by canvas stretched above the upper balconies. A dozen archways, white pillars and an eight-foot wide arcade blended with the tree ferns, potted palms and creepers that Gustav Stenmark had nurtured with such skill. Several rooms, including a large billiard room, opened on to this cool and peaceful little square. The sculptured marble fountain from Florence gently spilled water from one basin to another. It had a reflective sound. Perhaps someone had already floated frangipani blooms or the first few magnolias in that lower basin. There was an almost convent-like repose in this elegant courtyard,

The drawing room (above) and the dining room (below) at Yulgilbar. Photographs by Kathleen Ogilvie were taken in 1894. Tom Robert's portrait of E.D.S. hangs over the mantelpiece. Courtesy Miss K. Bland.

especially when the ladies of the house began to use it as a retreat in summer time.

All that was so far missing was the travertine paving stone which did not arrive from Italy until April.

At night there would have been music.

Theodosia loved the piano. Probably even Edward, freed by wine and good company from his inhibitions, sang. He had a good voice. The Schubert, Mendelssohn, Italian arias they played would not have been unfamiliar to at least a few of their guests.

I would like to think that, when the last visitors retired to those many upstairs bedrooms, Edward walked out to the front terrace alone. It had been a night of triumph. His night. He had at last achieved almost everything he set out to do. His mastery of Yulgilbar was now complete. It belonged to him and his heirs for ever.

The night would still have been hot. It always was in January. Unless there were thunderclouds over the western mountains, or summer lightning silently forking the distant sky, the air would have been clear for all that humidity. From beneath those columns he would have looked down at the dull sheen of Yulgilbar Reach; Castle Waters, as a later generation would come to call it. It was very still. Perhaps a blacks' fire or two glowing under the hill; or starlight glinting on black water. Swans fluted intermittently; a sad and haunting cry. And all this great spread of country, ringed about by the dimly visible hills and ranges, curiously one-dimensional under the vast pale cupola of sky, was land that he had brought out of a wilderness, made productive.

Even its solitudes, the overwhelming silence of it all, must have filled him with a kind of triumphant awe. This was his country; and he himself had made it so with his own hands and will.

Charles Tindal had come home with expansive ideas.

His vague plans of twelve years ago, to preserve meat instead of boiling it down, had come to fruition at last. In England, with his father's help, he had succeeded in forming a company to market whatever he produced abroad. The Australian Meat Company had a subscribed capital of £100,000, planning to set up a well-equipped meatworks on the river bank at Ramornie. It was to have its own wharf, warehouse and a head office in London. 'My father,' wrote his son, Charles F. Tindal, later, 'corresponded with Baron Liebig, re meat extract, who told him of a chemist in England who could give him all details, and Ramornie was making it only a few months after the Liebig Company started in America.'[4]

[4] Tindal Family Letters, Mitchell Library, Sydney.

The building of this works began late in 1866. It was an ambitious project. Cattle were to be bought from surrounding stations, as well as coming from Ramornie, slaughter yards would be built and a packing plant supplied with tins and pine cases from the works itself. In addition to preserved beef, Tindal intended to export tongues and other meats for which there had hitherto been no sale. One potential market he had in mind was contract supplies for the British army and navy; contracts which did come about within a few years.

The new steam-driven plant would clearly be of great advantage of Yulgilbar.

First disappointment, from Edward's point of view, was that the company was prepared to pay no more than 12s. a hundredweight, dressed. They had also to be prime cattle. Hence he continued to ship his, wherever possible, to southern markets through Lawrence. Yet this was not easy any more. Depression had struck at cattle-breeders once again. 'Most of them,' wrote L. T. Daley, 'were improverished after buying up large sections of their runs to protect themselves from the selectors. At the same time the price of cattle and sheep dropped to levels as low as those in the depression of the forties.'[5]

Edward himself admitted that he was now running Yulgilbar at a loss. 'We have not yet realised the advantages expected as a result of the high prices and scarcity of meat in England,' Edward wrote to Joseph Marryat & Sons in London. 'Cattle-holders are not willing to accept the old prices, but have not yet found a market at new. The good time comes very slowly.'[6]

To worsen matters pleuro-pneumonia was spreading northward from Victoria where herds had been badly infected. Yulgilbar suffered very seriously. A considerable amount of his herd died or had to be destroyed. This was another hazard of the climate. Cattle tick thrived in the humid scrublands. It was the devil's own job to eradicate them from either grazing or travelling herds until inoculation became a practical proposition.

Yulgilbar appears not to have suffered too badly, but the drop in prices forced E.D.S. to shelve for the time being his developmental plans. Just how difficult it had become to dispose of prime cattle was evident towards the end of 1866. Once more he had to threaten litigation. His opening gambit was a letter to P. N. Trebeck, a Sydney commission agent:

[5] Daley, L. T., *Men And A River*, Melbourne, 1967.
[6] Ogilvie Family Papers, Archives, University of New England.

I sent you a telegram last Wednesday re sale of cattle to F. White and I now address you on the same subject.

Mr. Weaver arrived here on the morning of the 2nd. At that time we had more than half the cattle gathered for him, a beautiful lot of steers and I think superior to any lot yet sold. Mr. Weaver saw them on Monday and again on Tuesday, when to our very great surprise he said he did not like them, and as he had no reason to doubt that they were a fair sample of the herd, he should decline the purchase altogether.

I at once told Mr. W that I could not agree to the sale being repudiated in this way. He pleaded instructions from Mr. White, but I pointed out that such instructions could not override a written contract. It must seriously damage the reputation of my herd to turn out again as rejected the whole of a draft of cattle collected for delivery. I pointed out that a clause was provided in the contract for settling disputes, and asked Mr. W to show me such cattle as he objected to, but he replied that he objected to all and to the quality of the herd generally adding that Mr. White had pointed out to him before he started certain bullocks running in a paddock and had desired him to bring nothing that was not equal to those and as he did not think my cattle equal to those sample beasts he could not take them. Ultimately I agreed to give him time to communicate with his principal by telegram and we signed a memorandum on the back of the contract extending the time for delivery to the last week in September. Mr. Weaver then left for Grafton and I have not since seen or heard from him.[7]

Two weeks later he wrote again, tempering anger with a tinge of caution. It was a matter of almost desperate importance to retain the sale.

I now propose (unless the mail due here on Sunday evening next alters the position) to collect the remainder of the 600 head of cattle before the termination of the month, and, should there be then no person here to take delivery, to call in some uninterested party to bear witness that the cattle are ready for delivery and then turn them out and commence proceedings against Mr. White for breach of contract. Should the end of the month arrive before I hear from you on this point I will keep the cattle in hand till I get your telegram. I hope however that Mr. White will come down himself and take the cattle or desire his agent to do so and not drive matters to extremity. I feel certain that he could be well satisfied with the cattle as they are really good and that all this trouble is caused by some crochet of Mr. Weavers. He acknowledges that the cows of the herd are good and large yet thinks fit to consider the brothers and braying of these same cows small.

Nonetheless, when a reverse situation developed soon afterwards, E.D.S. was swift to take advantage of events to cancel a contract much as White had done.

[7] Ogilvie Family Papers, Archives, University of New England.

He had arranged to buy a mob of a thousand bullocks from Francis Girard, then ending his life on a Richmond River property. He sent Bill Hamilton, overseer of his Broadwater run, across to take delivery. Before he could do so, the river came down in flood. The cattle were marooned. When the flood subsided not a beast was left alive. Edward, being familiar with the fine writing of that contract, refused to pay. Technically he was right. The cattle had not been handed over to his representative. Girard went broke in consequence.

Beyond the law of contracts, this hard country had another law. A man's own survival came first.

Yet nothing angered Edward more than any implications that he was a difficult or unjust man to deal with. It was a subject that particularly disturbed him at the end of this year. There had long been friction between him and the former Yulgilbar manager, Watt, who had been subsequently transferred to run the Plains Station, and had now resigned from this.

'On the occasion of our late painful conversation at the Plains Station,' he wrote to him in November, 'when I acceded to your resignation, you cast aspersions upon my conduct of so serious a character that, having allowed myself full time for cool reflexion, I have come to the conclusion that I ought not to allow such aspersions to pass unnoticed. You asserted that before coming to me you knew I was 'considered a bad master' and 'warned' that if you had 'anything to do with me I should throw you over.' Such accusations coming from you I feel to be not only peculiarly unmerited and unjust, but contrary to the truth.'[8]

Edward reminded him of how he had taken him over from his late brother's properties, increased his salary, persuaded his mother to give him a gratuity of £150 and 'upon your representing that this amount fell short of your expectations, a further gratuity of £250.' At that time, he added, he had complete confidence in the young man's ability, treated him as a friend, and had only recently come to realise he had 'overestimated his capacity' in management. He recalled a free exchange of opinions on this matter in 1863, after which Watt had asked for leave of absence for health reasons. Though Edward continued to pay him a half-salary, even paying part of his expenses on a visit to New Zealand, where he acted 'in my interests,' he confessed that he had always hoped that Watt would find something that better suited him and not return. Sure enough in 1865 the resignation came, written from the Plains Station.

At this point his curious love-hate attitude to Watt intervened.

[8] Ogilvie Family Papers, Archives, University of New England.

Theodosia obviously liked him, for several letters to her husband made friendly inquiries about him, which suggests that Edward partially at least shared her view.

Now, having gained the resignation he wanted, Edward made a volte-face.

'I could perceive from the language of your letter that you had been prompted by feelings of pique arising out of a misconception of my meaning in a matter of which I had spoken to you on the previous evening. I therefore thought it right to explain and remove this misconception, and having done so, to leave it to you to choose whether to adhere to or withdraw your resignation. You chose to withdraw it and, although I should have preferred that your decision had been the other way, I had the satisfaction of feeling and knowing that I had acted disinterestedly and in fidelity to the call of friendship.'

There was very much more. The points at issue became increasingly complicated. After Watt had 'readily acquiesced' to a reduction of salary because Yulgilbar was no longer paying, further disputes arose over expenses, his right to use station horses, the sale of another horse that Edward had only reluctantly parted with out of friendship. The end was inevitable. They parted.

Yet Edward, whatever his eagerness to go to law, was never unfair with his workers. His son-in-law, C. W. Bundock, described him as a 'strict disciplinarian. He was always just and his employees had a strong affection for him. He, on his part, was always keenly interested in the welfare of his old hands.'[9] A hard man, but a fair one, was the way Stenmark's daughter described him, after working as a housemaid. 'If he found he had been wrong, he would apologise to anyone on the staff he rebuked unfairly.'

In some ways he was beginning to mellow. He was now very much the family man. And a prolific one at that. The seventh Ogilvie child, Mabel Harriet, was born in the big house on 16 May 1866.

[9] Bundock, C. W., *The Sydney Morning Herald*, 25 January 1923.

20

Queen and Consort

The pastoral industry was now entering its first long period of stable development and prosperity. There were only to be two other comparable periods right through to the mid-20th century. The first lasted an uninterrupted twenty-five years.

It became almost impossible for the owners of large estates not to grow wealthy, given reasonable intelligence and managerial skills. The markets for beef, mutton, wool, hides, bloodstock horses were all rising, even the hitherto unsaleable by-products of slaughtered animals. Only in the far outback and tropic north was there any kind of frontier situation left. It was the age of the overlander, the million-acre man, the Costellos, Bluey Buchanans, Duracks and MacDonalds who drove great herds over thousands f miles of outback plains, desert and arid red ranges to form vast holdings that were like European principalities. For the men of the 'inside country' there were no such dramatic scenarios left. They had become settled people, prosperous, living in comfortable homesteads, within moderately easy reach of civilisation despite their rough bush tracks, primitive transport and a reliance on the horse and buggy.

The turrets and ornamental gardens of Yulgilbar were by no means typical. But many pastoral families were now living on a similar scale, notably in the Riverina, Victoria's Western Districts and New England.

Even the climate seemed to be changing, becoming less severe. There were no extremes of drought and torrential rains, such as had driven sheep out of the Clarence and Richmond valleys. Summers remained fiercely hot; winter frosts sometimes blackened pastures; rivers and creeks still rose in destructive flood. Nothing would ever check the Clarence's turbulence. In 1867, for example, a great flood surged through Tabulam and Plains Station, where one of Edward's contract fencers simply vanished. His bridle was later found in an oak tree above Mookima Wymbra Creek,. his coat away on the Rocky River and, some weeks later, his body on the Washpool Plain ten miles away. Floodwaters swept through the streets of Grafton, where its inhabitants had a desperate struggle to save homes and possessions, while the Ramornie meatworks had machinery washed away and thousands of pounds worth of damage done.

These rare excesses were accepted as part of the natural order. Life stabilised itself again. On Yulgilbar it returned to its pleasant and upholstered manner.

Theodosia gave glimpses of this in a letter she wrote to her brother Maurice de Burgh, in Ireland. Though undated, it had references to the children that placed it at some time in mid-1867. Obviously writing for the first time in many years, she reminded him that she had now been married 'eight or nine years', a curiously vague attitude to what she assured him was a successful marriage. 'Very happy years they have been for me', she wrote, then added:[1]

> My little children now number seven. The youngest is just over a year old, and my twins, Maude and Jessie, are in their third year. They are dear little creatures and very fond of each other. Maude is the prettiest child I have. She reminds me of Emma when a child. Jessie is quite different in every way from Maude. Mary, the eldest, is a bright merry girl and rather a troublesome child. Flora is a strangely old-fashioned child, like her father in face. Willie in his sixth year is a very sensible little fellow. He is the best looking after Maude, but is a little like her, and my namesake is a sharp clever little creature who is very interesting, but at present takes a great deal of watching to keep her from mischief. She is papa's pet and was remarkably like me from the time of her birth, so he called her Theodosia. Now you know the names of them all. It is a long string, is it not?.
>
> We have a very fine house and the situation is most beautiful. Edward is now very well indeed and he likes the country life and the business that takes him constantly on horseback and out of doors. Much better than living in Sydney. He takes me out riding and driving very often and we sometimes row up the river in a boat with the older children and have a picnic, which charms them greatly. We have quite enough visitors to be pleasant, indeed sometimes all my spare rooms are full, so we are not wanting in society. The only serious drawback to our happiness is the want of a church and clergymen. We have an occasional visit, and for the rest we read divine service every Sunday morning for the benefit of those in the house and on the station. And we have family prayers every morning. There are few children about as the servants who come to reside here as stockmen, gardeners or farming men etc. are usually unmarried or without family.

[1] Undated letter in possession of Mr and Mrs John Ogilvie.

Her accent on religion was only to be expected from a clergyman's daughter. Daily prayers in the dining room before breakfast became a tradition; the family on one side, servants the other. No doubt she was responsible for the large number of religious books on Edward's ceiling-high library shelves. Alongside Thackeray, Moliere, the standard English poets, were Stackhouse's *History of the Bible*, de Burgh's *Life of Christ*, and volume after volume of *Sermons* by such forgotten clerics as Oxenden, Horsley, Pitman, Bushfield, Baxter, John Venn, Disney and the celebrated Bowdler. There was also a personally autographed volume by Bishop John Wilberforce, who had been largely responsible for the abolition of slavery.

After Edward died, Robert Leycester Dawson wondered 'whether Mr. Ogilvie used to spend his Sunday afternoons reading all those volumes of sermons. It would need a long life'.[2]

He seems more likely to have spent his leisure hours with the biographies of Napoleon and Nelson, his many works on natural history and travel, the popular *Waverley Novels*, *Wines of the World* and *Debrett's Peerage*, 1866 edition. There was also an imposing series of large, calf-bound, gilt-embossed volumes much in vogue among successful Victorian gentlemen. Though they had a wide range of classic titles, the actual volumes were box-like dummies without printed pages inside.

The library, however, was to have a lively influence on the Ogilvie children, most of whose formative years were passed at Yulgilbar. They were all well read, with a taste for poetry and music, despite a lack of formal education made inevitable by the station's remoteness.

All in all, it was a good life they had.

'The isolation of early days was only relative,' wrote C. W. Bundock. 'We were always busy. There were always friends and relatives staying at the homestead, sometimes for weeks. We had riding, fishing, shooting whenever we wanted it. We had plenty of good reading. If you wanted to go anywhere you got on your horse and went, road or no road. It was all one to us. There were no fences except close to the stations. People who were friends would come three hundred miles every year to stay a few weeks about Christmas, and then there was plenty of amusement for all. We took life much more leisurely than now and got more out of it. My mother often said to me that the happiest days were the old rough ones when our wants were few and simple.'[3]

Elsewhere he wrote—and this applied equally to Yulgilbar—'every-

[2] Dawson, R. L., letters 1823–43, Richmond River Historical Society, Lismore.

[3] Bundock, C. W., *The Sydney Morning Herald*, 24 January 1923.

one had a vineyard and made his own wine. It was jolly good wine, too.' Edward, soon to win an overseas award for one of his dry whites, was also making a palatable red wine and distilling brandy as well. His main vineyard was on a well-drained slope near the entrance gates, with a smaller one below the house by the river.

But there were often shortages as well as plenty.

Bundock wrote of how their provisions were brought out in bulk by bullock dray, once or at the most twice a year, of how these were frequently bogged down for weeks, or delayed by flooded creeks and rains. 'The return of the heavily loaded dray was quite an event in our lives. When there was no flour we had to live on maize crushed and boiled. Sugar came up in casks, shipped out from the West Indies. It was dark brown, treacly stuff, which would stick to anything you threw it at. The hard lumps were said by the facetious to be the remnants of niggers boiled in the pans.'

Even at this time the new farmers along the Clarence and Richmond were discussing the feasibility of growing their own sugar cane. A few had even begun to plant, though most were awaiting Edward's promised inquiries on the best type to grow. The climate was right for it; water was no problem; there was land in abundance. Edward volunteered to take samples of the sugar they harvested down to Sydney for advice. He also went into the economics of building a crushing mill himself at Lawrence. Nothing came of it all. Perhaps he was alarmed by the outlay of capital needed; or the organisation required. At all events, people at Lawrence became critical of his inaction. They were even more critical when rumours spread that he planned to revive a defunct boiling-down works instead, with its notorious fumes and stink.

The truth was that Edward had begun to slow down. He had enough enterprises to handle already, without trying to launch an unproven sugar industry. Some said that he owned too much of the town as it was, and was in fact holding it back. Harold Woods even suggested that his primary interest in Lawrence was 'an indirect protest against the encroachment of the agriculturalists on the domain of the squatters.'

Yet in 1867 he relinquished one of his town blocks. He made a gift of it to the Church of England. Theodosia drove over some time later to lay the foundation stone of what was soon to be Lawrence's first church, a weatherboard structure overlooking the contemplative waters of Sportsman's Creek.

In July that year she gave Edward their eighth child, Edward David.

The astonishing fact was that, despite her recurring illnesses, despite seven pregnancies—including twins—in little more than eight years,

Theodosia Ogilvie at thirty, photographed by Freeman of Sydney.   Courtesy Mr and Mrs John Ogilvie.

she still appeared as young and fresh as ever. Paintings may stretch the truth a little—photographs cannot. During a visit to Sydney in 1868 she was photographed by Freeman, who ran the fashionable studio of the day. He made a beautiful study of her. Naturally she looked more grown-up and mature in expression than that earlier pastel portrait in Florence. She was, after all, ten years older. There was a touch more sophistication in her hair style, choice of jewellery and costume. Yet her face was as relaxed and tranquil as ever, still almost childlike. Freeman made her the kind of woman who would never grow old. It was hard to believe she was then the mother of eight children; or that she was twenty-eight.

With the birth of Edward David there were now two potential heirs to the E.D.S. properties. In the manner of the times, female children barely counted, however well they were to be provided for. For the man of property it was the male line alone that mattered.

Travelling, as they did each year to Sydney, was now quite a problem. Coastal steamers were hardly designed for family comfort, especially with so many young children. Even a buggy and horse journey down to Lawrence made quite an expedition. If it was anything like Bundock's experiences, there would have been all kinds of unexpected hazards. 'On all trips,' he wrote, 'everything was carried in a swag in front of your packhorse. It was not uncommon to see ladies' most intimate garments being shied all over the scenery by a fractious packhorse. I must be one of the few people left who knows how to pack a crinoline with three-eighths of an inch tape into a packbag.'

Bundock may have been amused by such incidents. Edward, probably, was not.

He made it a habit now to spend at least two months a year in the city, feeling that Theodosia needed a break from the loneliness of Yulgilbar. Sometimes they spent Christmas in town, giving the children the rare chance of going to parties at the homes of their friends. Since he had also reasons of politics for spending much time in Sydney, he rented a large house in Forbes Street, using it as a family *pied à terre*. Barham, with its ballroom and many bedrooms, made a splendid home for entertaining. It was also an easy drive to Parliament House and his other club, the Australian in Macquarie Street.

If the often esoteric debates in the upper house gave him little opportunity to influence political life, he became known as a good and conscientious committee man, with sound values on the conservative side. Men spoke with less enthusiasm of his speeches, which were said to be so dull that even his friends left the visitors' gallery.

Yet, with the beautiful Theodosia beside him, he made a considerable impact at receptions and parties. She had a way of unconsciously taking over a room when she entered it, apparently unaware of the stir her looks inevitably caused. Among their friends they became known as the Queen and her Consort.

On such occasions the Honourable E. D. S. Ogilvie, M.L.C. had to take second place. Proud of the admiration she evoked, he was happy to give her precedence.

At home on Yulgilbar their situation was subtly reversed. Theodosia would always have been father-oriented, for the Reverend de Burgh had been an elderly man from her birth. Having since transferred her affections to another man much older than herself, she would have accepted Edward's decisiveness without question or regret. Besides it was his proper role to direct their family affairs. This now large household was becoming more demanding of his time and energies. Even with no guests staying, his children made perpetual calls on him. He read to them, entertained them, taught and disciplined them, and took charge of morning prayers. It was an austere household much of the time. At meal times at least four children would have sat with their parents at the long dining table, waited on by servants. The younger ones remained mostly in their nursery quarters upstairs, where they saw more of the nursemaids than their mother. Each baby was also breast-fed by a wet nurse engaged for the pre-weaning months. With her periodical lung trouble Theodosia became less inclined to climb the staircase to their rooms. Much of her days were, in fact, spent reclining on a sofa in the drawing room.

Perhaps she was already becoming disenchanted with the Big House, as she was certainly to do in later years. As a showplace it was fine. For domestic comfort certain drawbacks were already apparent; especially in winter months. The huge chandelier and candelabra were rarely lit except for guests. Mainly they used kerosene lamps and candlesticks. Those long corridors could be very gloomy after dark, a little scary for young children. In winter the thick stone walls made both living and bedrooms depressingly cold. Not even big logs blazing in marble fireplaces could fully warm the large, high-ceilinged drawing room or library. There was also repeated trouble with the flat roof, which leaked badly after heavy rains. Another time a thunderstorm shattered one of the french windows and flooded the entire drawing room. It was not all home comforts.

Only on special occasions did the mansion become lively and ablaze with light.

In 1869 Edward and Theodosia, already expecting her ninth child, drove into Lawrence to meet the new governor on his first tour of the north. Earl Belmore and his lady landed with great ceremony at the Ogilvie wharf, where gay bunting, streamers and loyal slogans gave the river bank an air of carnival. A salute of guns was fired, a formal address of welcome read and townsfolk cheered the vice-regal cavalcade as it took off to the backblocks and Yulgilbar.

The Queen's representative was said to have been entertained there in very lavish fashion. The Florentine chandelier with its thirty-nine candles glittered above the formally dressed guests in the long drawing room. The butler, footman, parlour maids and grooms had been carefully rehearsed in their duties, and the children sent upstairs long before the dinner hour arrived, with its silver dishes and tureens, crystal glassware and the starched rustle of parlourmaids' uniforms.

The same year brought another eminent visitor. On this occasion the table talk at dinner was probably more guarded. Their guest was John Robertson, now premier of New South Wales for the second time, as well as being the elected member for the Clarence district since 1866. Since he had won the popular vote of townsfolk and small selectors, there would not have been much accord between the pair, even if they met from time to time in Sydney's Parliament House. It would be fascinating to know what took place between these two men of radically opposed views, despite their common origin as Hunter squatters, and how Free Selection Jack reacted to the grandeur of Yulgilbar.

His principal motive in coming upriver had been to visit the grave of his boyhood friend Peter Cunningham Pagan, near Tabulam, though he would inevitably have called at other stations *en route*.

Given his populist attitudes, he was probably more impressed by the achievements at Ramornie than Yulgilbar. Charles Tindal's meatworks were now treating eighty head of cattle a day and had a secure export trade. This was also a model community supporting a large number of settled families.

Nothing quite like it existed anywhere else in Australia.

> There was no rent at Ramornie works. The Tindals considered that the villagers should have their cottages free. Each family could run a horse and cow on the property, the weekly agistment being sixpence for a horse and ninepence for a cow. The works, with its village and paddocks, covered 45 acres. If a breadwinner died, then his dependants were looked after. The village had several streets, a church, a school (at one time attended by 100 children), a store and reading room. Each cottage had its garden, well kept and full of flowers. Erstwhile residents speak of the carefree atmosphere. All night long the men on shift would be singing and whistling. Oranges were sold at fourpence a dozen. First grade peaches and passionfruit grew wild along the banks of Cattle Station Creek. There were amusements and to spare—dances, concerts, visits from the travelling circus, races every pay day and a breaking-up ball at the end of the season.[4]

Yulgilbar was also employing a large number of men and women by this stage. However, apart from station work, these were mostly domestics catering for the family's private existence. By 1870 Edward had 115 employees on his books. Perhaps there were also further additions to the nursery staff, for another daughter, Emmeline Martha arrived in June that year.

[4] *The Daily Examiner*, Grafton, undated extract.

The solitude of Yulgilbar was severely shaken when more of those damned fossickers found gold on the run in 1871.

E.D.S. had always known those free selectors would be a fatal influence. Though a little gold had earlier been found on Nogrigar Creek, when a few small nuggets were raffled in Grafton for £10 each, no more had been heard of it. The prospectors had taken their picks and pans elsewhere. Now parties of work-shy men had sneaked up the western side of the river, scouring the hills and scrubs around Nogrigar, and located alluvial deposits and rich outcrops that started a full-scale rush. The first of these strikes, in the mountains west of the head station, they named Solferino. This was discovered by an Italian migrant named Paolo Marcolino.

Edward, from his continental reading, would have known this to be named after an Italian town where Emperor Napoleon III had defeated the invading Austrians. Now there seemed little likelihood of his defeating the invaders of the new Solferino. And so it turned out. Less than a year later more gold was found at Lionsville, half-way between the Italian's strike and the head station at Yulgilbar. Within a few months four thousand people were living and working there. At Solferino the Garibaldi mine became so productive that some £140,000 worth of gold was won in two or three years. The first inn to be built there did such fantastic trade that a newcomer offered to buy it for £30,000. The offer was refused. As it transpired, the rejection was a foolish one, for the field only lasted a few more years.

Since mining rights took legal precedence over grazing, there was nothing E.D.S. could do to halt the increasing traffic over his run. Nor did Yulgilbar benefit in any way financially. He owned the pastures solely, and none of the wealth below the ground accrued to him. Within the first year a public road had been surveyed across the centre of his run, intersecting the Tabulam road at a place called Baryulgil, fording the river between the manager's cottage and Mount Ogilvie. Fortunately it was half a mile from the Big House, and thus did not destroy its manorial calm.

Edward's efforts to keep his lands free from outside interference had other motives, too. The finding of gold had a disruptive effect on his station workers. A number of them left, not unnaturally preferring to take the chance of a lucky strike rather than work for wages, then only one pound a week. The Aborigines were also demoralised. In his patriarchal fashion, Edward had tried to protect his people from the debasing white men's values. Anyone found giving them liquor was at once dismissed. Nor would he tolerate their surreptitious visits to the women in their camps.

Once prospectors and working miners were free to come in, he was powerless.

'With a few exceptions among the older ones,' wrote Mabel's daughter, Jessie, years later, 'their capacity for work and their morals became completely undermined, and their camps became little hells when the white men with their bottles of liquor visited them. The tumult would last for many days. I can remember as a child hearing the screams and shouts and raucous laughter from the camps about half a mile away when these representatives of the Christian white race visited the heathen natives.'[5] In her time the all too prevalent factors were alcoholism, venereal disease and half-caste children. As one old hand expressed it, 'the camps became brothels.'

One night Edward was brought down to the settlement by the sounds of wailing and lamentation. All the tribe was gathered there. They were mourning the death of his oldest and most faithful employee. This was Jimmy Cobbera.

The old fellow had been his last link with that great trek through the mountains of thirty and more years ago. The keen young lad from Merton, a full-blooded Kamilaroi, had stayed with him all those years, shepherding his sheep, driving bullock drays, timber-cutting, fencing, building stone fences and drafting yards. A strong affection had grown between these two men of different races.

'On the day old Jimmy died,' Herbert Rogan, a former head stockman told me, 'the station people rolled him up in a blanket and dug a grave for him. But the old people didn't want that. They dug him up again, piled up a load of bushes and laid him on them. Then they set fire to him, making sure he did not go to the beyond with a devil inside him. His remains are still buried up there on Laundry Hill, looking down on the Castle.'

In later years other station Aborigines were to be buried on this hillside. Among these was the part-European horse breaker, Billy Faraway, whom Rogan described as 'the smartest man that ever crossed a horse,' and 'King Bobby', Toolbillibam's successor to the embossed tin plate.

Yulgilbar Reach remained, as it had always been, a tribal burial place.

The Big House, wrote one of Edward's grand-daughters after she married and left home, was always to be remembered by 'the languorous scent of magnolias and gardenias, and an old-fashioned, but very

[5] Street, Jessie, *Truth or Repose*, Sydney, 1966.

fragrant rose.' There were flowering trees and shrubs all around the house; fresh cut flowers in the living rooms; flowers floating in the fountain. It was a pleasant atmosphere in which to grow up.

At Christmas a large river oak was brought into the courtyard, decorated with Chinese lanterns and candles. It was Theodosia's job to distribute presents off it to her own family, the staff and their children. Each year, too, the Ogilvie children performed a play in the drawing room for Edward's birthday, and the buhl cabinet was always stocked with games; ludo, backgammon, draughts and spillikins. The children seemed always to be acquiring new pets. Edward brought them in live parrots and cockatoos. There was a tame emu that lived in the garden. 'My grandfather,' wrote Kathleen Ellen's daughter, Kathleen Bland, 'never allowed kangaroo hunting on the station, considering it a cruel sport. My mother remembered him coming up to the nursery when she was a small child, taking a baby kangaroo out of his pocket and putting it on the floor, telling them to take care of it as its mother had been killed. It became a great pet and was called Flop.' Yulgilbar Reach was also declared a sanctuary for waterfowl and platypus.

When the children reached an age for schooling, Edward decided they would have to be given some form of education at home. He built a schoolhouse near the entrance gates, and hired a resident teacher. When Graham Mylne heard of it, he asked if he could send his sons and daughters across from Eatonswill, which meant boarding them there during terms. 'Since our family had six children and the Ogilvies eight,' wrote the eldest Mylne son, also Graham, 'this really made a regular school. We had a cranky and dotty old schoolmaster, with a crankier wife, and we hated the place.'

They may have hated it, but it united two families in a way that distances had never made possible before. The result was several lifelong friendships and, in two cases, marriage between the clans. When the young Mylnes went home for holidays, the Ogilvie children adapted the schoolroom as a special retreat of their own. They made it a place where they could amuse themselves, play, read books and indulge in the fantasies of childhood away from parental disciplines.

Soon, with father's indulgence, they were given another retreat, too. This was a picturesque little temple he had designed on a clifftop overlooking Yulgilbar Reach, a replica in sandstone of ancient temples to Diana that Edward had seen during his Italian journeys. There had been one in Sicily, for instance, standing on a high cliff above the Mediterranean. It was a scene he had described in his *Diary of Travels*. The structure he had built here was octagonal, open except for pillars at the sides, with stone seats from which they could look out at the mountain ranges and silent river.

Mother and daughters formed the habit of driving up here in a pony cart on sunny days. They sketched and painted the superb scenery around them. Before long Edward's concept of a temple, for that matter all thought of extinct goddesses, was disregarded. They came to call it simply the sketch house.

In her early teens, Jessie—elder of the twins—was to paint a charming watercolour sketch here, still treasured by the family. The scene she painted will never look quite the same. At the foot of the slope were open pastures; a few head of cattle grazing; English trees with rust-coloured autumn foliage in the background; and the Big House invested with all the splendour of a Scottish castle; or, more aptly perhaps, like Government House in Sydney, even to the Union Jack flying on a high mast above the western tower.

It was a romantic childhood picture of all that a home in the country meant to her.

Her mother, too, was happy enough when out of doors. Despite so large a family, there were no great hardships. She had plenty of servants, nursemaids, a housekeeper to look after her domestic needs. She went riding when she felt well enough, had a groom to look after her horse. This was a fine thoroughbred bay named Nestor, a valuable gift from Edward. The horse was so spirited, she claimed, that no one else could ride him. 'On one occasion,' wrote Kathleen Bland, 'a man came to stay who said it was impossible that Mrs. Ogilvie could ride any horse he could not control. He insisted on mounting Nestor, with the result that he was immediately bucked off, to the great amusement of the family.'

The ability to ride was, after all, a matter of family pride; even among the youngsters. It was inherited as much from Grandmother Mary as Theodosia.

Though Mary, on her now rare visits, had long given up riding, she liked to drive around the property in a dog cart, drawn by a quiet old pony. One afternoon, after she had been away for several hours, a guest in the house said he was worried at her failure to return. He asked Theodosia, 'Aren't you afraid the pony may have gallopped away with her?'

Her daughter-in-law replied, 'Well, I can't think of anyone else who would dare to.'

Grandmother was well known at this time for her imperious moods. Despite her bluff affection for them, her grandchildren were a little scared of her. Like Queen Victoria, she knew how to stand and stare.

One day an unnamed grand-daughter, rebuked for some misdemeanour at the foot of the staircase, cried out defiantly, 'I hate you. I hope you'll soon be dead.'

Mary pointed imperiously upstairs. 'Go to your room, Child. You'll stay there till *I* tell you to come down.'

There was a great deal of life in the old lady yet.

Her favourite was the elder boy, William. She had still not forgiven Theodosia for having all those daughters. Many years before her death, she wrote him a tender letter, leaving instructions with her bank that it was not to be opened until he married. Written on the black-edged notepaper she had continued to use since the Commander's death, the letter was dated 23 July 1866. Accompanying it was a carefully sealed box. She wrote:

> My darling Willie,
>   When you open the box with your name on the lid and the articles of silver plate within it belonging to you, you will also find this letter and it will recall to you memories, if you have not entirely forgotten her, the loving grandmother who has packed the box with her own hands and who had bequeathed it to you as a small memorial of your beloved and honoured grandfather whose name you bear. You will be a married man then and I trust find as much happiness in the marriage state as full as my own, but for many many years. God bless you,
>   your loving grandmother,
>   Mary Ogilvie.
>
>   Goodbye once more and try not to forget me. The hand that writes this will be cold when your eye deciphers it. Once more may God keep you.[6]

The box contained the silver spoons and forks her husband had used in the officers' mess on H.M.S. *St George*.

Mary's attachment for the boy began early in his life. Whenever the family went to Sydney, she singled him out for special attentions, even having him to stay alone at Fairlight. She liked to send him out driving around Edgecliff and down to the harbour in her carriage. The solemn-faced little boy sat always on the box seat beside coachman and groom.

In the past there had never been an opportunity to indulge her own sons in this way.

One suspects that she had also a good deal to do with his education. Perhaps it was she who convinced Edward that the boy should have something more than an Australian schooling. At all events, at the

[6] Ogilvie Family Papers, Archives, University of New England.

age of twelve he was sent to Ireland, where Theodosia's family arranged for him to board at a private school in Dublin. From the Morven School's book of rules, it was clearly an academy for young gentlemen. The headmaster's printed instructions counselled all boys 'to take part in the services, joining in the responses . . . to behave during mealtimes as they would at their parents' table . . . to pray in their bedrooms *before undressing* . . . not to talk to the servants . . . to discountenance all coarse and improper language . . . and in their whole conduct to remember what is their duty as the children of gentlemen and members of a Christian Family.'[7]

William was thus adequately prepared to go on to St Columbus College, where he was eventually to become captain of the football team.

A forceful new character made his appearance on Yulgilbar in the mid-1870s. He had arrived first with a team of horses, engaging in contract work for stations. Deciding that he liked the look of the place, he asked E.D.S. for a permanent job and stayed. Sydney William Penrose was another Englishman, energetic, well-spoken, with a good deal of personal charm. Edward put him in charge of cattle grazing west of the river, found him a house in Lionsville and confidently left him to run this large tract of country whenever he left for Sydney.

The eastern portion remained in the hands of a second superintendent, Brown, who occupied the Cottage. But not for long.

Penrose was a persuasive man. On what ground he did so was never made clear, but somehow he convinced his employer that Brown was not the best man to manage the station. In the end it was Brown who resigned. Penrose moved into the Cottage and was given control of the whole run. Henceforth it was Mr Penrose who gave the orders, made most of the managerial decisions and recommended modes of action to Edward. The Ogilvies took to spending more and more of their time in Sydney.

It was in Barham, for instance, that their tenth child was born in May 1874. Theodosia was thirty-five when she had Kathleen Ellen which, under normal circumstances, was no excessive age for motherhood. But she was beginning to tire of so much travelling between her two homes. Nesta Griffith, making one such sea voyage, described the rough conditions obtaining in a communal cabin shared by twelve women; the cramped deck space; the pitching and rolling in high seas; and the perennial hazard of crossing a shallow bar at the Clarence mouth, which could only be done on a high tide in a flurry

[7] Ogilvie Family Papers, Archives, University of New England.

E. D. S. Ogilvie was sixty years of age when this photograph was taken in Sydney in 1874.

of surf. Even then it took the best part of a day to sail up the broad, but winding river, past mangrove swamps, scrub, small farms cleared for maize and patches of bright green sugarcane near Lawrence, where a few hopeful farmers were growing their first crops for a privately-owned mill. Beyond this again was a fifty-mile drive by four-in-hand over the ranges to Yulgilbar.

Though Theodosia was now given a three-year respite from child-bearing, yet another was born in April 1877. It was a remarkable tribute to her health; the comfort of her surroundings; and the midwifery of the times that she had hitherto had so little trouble. All her ten children had lived, grown healthy and strong; which was more than could be said of most other bush-bred families. Every settlement in the backblocks had its residue of child graves.

The birth of her third boy was a very difficult one. She had a long and agonising labour, during which one of her hips was broken. She was never able to walk again. Hubert de Burgh, sickly from the beginning, lived only seventeen days.

A second grave was dug beside Frederick's up on the stony hill. Engraved on the headstone later brought up by bullock dray was the text:

> Born in health and beauty
> On 18th April and snatched
> away on 15th May, 1877
> "O God Inscrutable Are Thy Ways
> Nevertheless
> Thy Will Be Done"

It was the death of this child that prompted the Ogilvie legend of the curse on the third son.

Edward attributed this legend to the Scottish clan from which, with little more evidence than a similarity in name, he claimed descent. 'Somewhere in the 13th century,' wrote Mrs Josephine Sabine, 'the third son was said to have committed an act of sacrilege. The priest denounced him and told him that no third son of his branch of the family would live to have a child. They might marry and live to a great age, but would never leave a descendant.'[8]

Superstition thrives on vague tales of this nature. Given the high infant mortality of past ages, especially in impoverished Scotland, the frequent wars and murderous nature of clan feuds, childless men cannot have been uncommon in most large families. Even without unspecified sacrilege and magician-priests, the third male child was commonly in a fairly poor condition, physically or financially, to marry and reproduce. Nonetheless, the facts can be made to fit. The two-weeks-old Hubert was inevitably childless. Edward's brother Fred died without marrying; Commander William's younger brother, was still a bachelor when drowned at sea, though who could be sure he left nothing behind in some seaport or other. Details of earlier generations remain unknown.

In Theodosia's case the cause seems to have been not so much a third son but physical exhaustion after such prolonged child-bearing.

[8] Stevens, F., and Sabine, J. F., *The Pathfinders*, manuscript, Mitchell Library, Sydney.

21

Australian Octave

Theodosia never properly recovered from that last traumatic childbirth. For the rest of her life she was to be a cripple.

The following year, while under medical treatment in Sydney, she had a letter from the elder of the twins, Jessie, expressive of the loneliness of those children up at Yulgilbar. Father was also away from home. Jessie, now thirteen, wrote in affectionate, impulsive terms, though there were hints of the little mother who felt responsible for her three younger sisters.

> My very dear Mama,
>
> I was so sorry to hear you were not so well, I hope you are quite well now. Maude and I got such a nice letter from William, he said he expected you would all be at home when the letter reached me, how I wish you were, Mama dear, we all want you so much. I am sure you will not be able to come home for a very long time. We gave the children the doll's house on Mabel's birthday. It was a rainy day so we had a waggon and brought it down, and then I went into the house to set the children up in the still-room. When it was carried up we put it on the balcony and arranged it all, it looked so very pretty, and then we got a sheet and held it up in front while two of us went to get the children. Then we dropped the sheet and let them see it, they were so surprised.[1]

After more gossippy information about her sisters, Jessie added a postscript: 'The camellias are so beautiful now, especially the white ones, we sent some to Mrs. Penrose last Saturday.' The Penroses, though still at this period out at Lionsville, were now on closer terms with the Ogilvies than any other manager had been. The children, with their parents away so often, accepted them almost as part of the family.

[1] Ogilvie Family Papers, Archives, University of New England.

Despite the many servants, they had also learnt to look after themselves and make their own amusements.

This did not in the least mean they could do what they pleased. Edward had rigid views on how young ladies should be brought up. Their hours were regulated; their studies, even their outdoor life. He taught them early how to handle a horse, and encouraged them to ride, though he would not let them go out cattle-mustering and always sent a stockman or groom along with them. Nor were they allowed to enter the stables or saddle their own horses. They had to wait, in the proper gentlewoman's habit, on the entrance steps until a groom brought their horses around to the front.

There had always to be a right way of doing things. Edward insisted on that. He was a tough-fibred old bushman who, even in his middle-sixties, thought nothing of riding up to Tabulam for a court session and returning the same evening. He drove others equally hard. He had firm opinions on family behaviour, where his daughters went and who should be allowed to call on them. Young, unattached males were given special scrutiny. The girls were all given bedrooms in a wing of their own, on the eastern side of the house, which could be reached only by a flight of stone stairs at the back of the tower. Since this was out of bounds to males it became known as Paradise Lane.

Father's sense of decorum extended also to guests staying in the house. There was a definite social code to be observed. Dress was all important. It became the custom to assemble in the drawing room or library for drinks before dinner, after which they were expected to change into more formal clothes.

Stories of dining at Yulgilbar became somewhat apocryphal. It was often said, especially among Grafton folk who had never sat at table there, that Edward insisted on every male guest wearing a dinner jacket, which was patently absurd since travelling bushmen did not have such wear. One can hardly imagine stock inspectors, surveyors or cattlemen struggling into starched shirts and black ties. It was also rumoured that Edward kept spare dress suits for visitors, having them laid out by butler or valet on each guest's bed. No attempt was made to explain how the lean, corpulent, short and tall all managed to adapt themselves to the same suit of clothes without looking like galahs at table.

Robert Leycester Dawson thought the tale exaggerated, 'a way of raising a laugh in town at Mr. Ogilvie's expense.' But he added, 'there is little doubt that it had some foundation in fact, and that on special occasions dress suits were worn at the Castle. For example, on notable holidays, like the Queen's birthday, or when visitors from England were staying at Yulgilbar. I am quite sure that my father on his many visits never wore dress clothes nor have I heard him mention others doing so.'[2] On many other stations, he wrote—notably Wyangerie, Kyogle and Ramornie—women were expected to wear evening, or semi-evening dresses for dinner, while men wore formal lounge suits.

Yet there were ceremonial occasions on Yulgilbar when guests were brought into dinner by a Highland piper and fifer playing suitable Gaelic airs. The idea was no doubt borrowed from the late Major Archibald Clune Innes, one-time superintendent of convicts, who also entertained his guests with bagpipes in his terraced mansion outside Port Macquarie. Unlike E.D.S., however, his indulgences soon sent him bankrupt.

Dawson's father, who stayed often at Yulgilbar as crown lands commissioner, had other comments to make on the reception of visitors. 'I have heard him say,' his son wrote, 'that, although the stables were magnificent, and the mangers all that could be designed, there was frequently nothing at all in them, and he had to turn his horses, with empty bellies, into bare and close-cropped paddocks. In short, the Lord of the Manor was close-fisted and mean in little matters.'[3] The wife of one Yulgilbar manager once said that 'it was common knowledge that visitors' horses were never fed.'

This did not at all mean that visitors themselves were not well entertained. Edward, being an abstemious man, rarely ate or drank much himself. In fact, one grazier's wife remarked on the rather spartan fare. 'A manservant would appear at your elbow with a great silver dish,' she said. 'When he took the silver cover off, you would find only a single mutton chop.' Yet he enjoyed displaying his own wines and brandies, and had good reason for doing so. His whites won a certificate of merit and two first-class awards at the 1879 Intercolonial Exhibition in Sydney. Four years later he was awarded a silver medal at an international show in Calcutta.

Just as the old Commander had encouraged his sons in the art of making wine, so did Edward with his elder boy. Detailed notes, in William's hand, were later found among the family papers, apparently copied down at his father's dictation. These were written soon after his return from Ireland. If the methods are now somewhat old-fashioned, they followed sound principles of wine-making. These were his formulae:

[2] Dawson, R. C., *The Daily Examiner*, Grafton, 23 January 1939.
[3] *ibid*.

1. White Wine

Grapes to be picked about 2nd week in February. Gathered early in morning while still cool. Any green bunches to be rejected; unevenly ripe bunches to be picked over. Spread about 4 inches over bottom of treading tub.

When all berries crushed, door is lifted, and all is sent through. Tread till underneath tub is full, then press. Fill press, put on cover and screw down. Pressed mass to be turned over with fork, and fresh grapes added till all is pressed.

Leave in press all night.

Put rag round fomenting bins, put them in bung holes of newly filled casks; fill with water, and put a tin upside down over them. When no sound to be heard, at end of probably 4 or 5 days, rack into sulphurated casks, and, at once, put on slide and put in cellar; each cask as soon as it is racked.

Put dregs in vinegar cask.

2. Red Wine

Grapes gathered about week later than white grapes; early in morn. All green grapes to be rejected. Trodden (like white grapes) in tub. Not pressed. Take stalks only from them by sieve or rack. Put in large cask without a head, and cover it with a bag.

Watch every day; it will form a 'head' and rise 9 inches. When the head begins to subside, and feels cold, then draw off into sulphur casks. Draw it off through a bag or straw cap nailed over the bung hole. Put in cellar at once.

Press the head and put in vinegar cask.

3. New wine; White and red

When in cellar, paste 4 brown papers over bung hole. Every cask and jar must be quite full. Visit it daily. In first 2 or 3 weeks it, especially the red wine, will probably have to be racked several times. Place your ear daily to bung hole, and if any sound is to be heard, rack into sulphured cask. Fermentation must be stopped before the 'must', or grape juice parts with its sweetness. Casks should not be filled up until fermentation has quite ceased. Racking is no longer necessary in a fortnight, or 3 weeks.

Red wine *may* be filled up with white.

Bottling time was a lively period, attracting the family and friends down to the cellars. Spigots were driven into the casks and the wine drawn off amid much gaiety and sampling of the new vintage. Even the lubras were brought into these activities, washing old bottles for the new wine. They gathered around the outside stairs of the cellars, where they were issued with shot which they dropped into the bottles, then dipped them into a tub of sudsy water and cheerfully rinsed all day.

With both parents so much in Sydney, life on Yulgilbar was now tending to be reflected through the children's eyes. Their letters, diaries and records reflected the growing up of a new generation, while Edward had long ceased to be an innovator. For him, life flowed along smoothly enough. He had an assured turn-off of cattle, established business affairs at Lawrence and his comfortably padded seat in the council chamber. His children, meanwhile, were establishing life patterns of their own.

There were only the eight girls now. Young Edward David had been sent off to England to train for the Royal Navy on H.M.S. *Britannia*, Dartmouth College, while William's name had been entered for Balliol College Oxford. He was due to go overseas within two years. The station school had been abandoned. Both the dotty old school-master and the Mylnes were gone. Instead a governess, Miss Tregear, had been engaged, mainly to teach the younger girls. Lessons still took place in the schoolhouse, now also known as the Lodge. But it was used just as often as a kind of clubhouse for the family's leisure hours.

Before Theodosia retreated to Sydney, she had made it more than that. Depressed by the chill rooms and draughty corridors in the Big House, she decided to move in there. In recent times it has been suggested that she was then suffering from melancholia, brought on by the loneliness of the station, the lack of near neighbours and the almost annual pregnancies that kept her largely confined to her boudoir next to the drawing room. The Victorian ethos decreed that visibly pregnant ladies verged on the indecent in public. Whatever Edward thought of her attitudes, he humoured her by furnishing a bedroom as she wanted it and adding a few extra comforts. Her daughters were even less happy about the arrangement.

'It will be nice to have you home again,' wrote the seventeen-year-old Theodosia Isabella to her father in February 1881, hoping he would find time to write to her. 'I have only had two letters from you in all my life, and we always prize your letters, because we know you have very little time.' But her first concern was for her mother.

> We all hope that when Mama sees the house first from the top of the hill, she will change her mind and not stop at the horrid little school-house. We have a cane chair all ready in the hall for her to get into directly she comes, and be carried up to her own room. It will be such a pity if she does stay at the schoolhouse. Mama will be able to stay there when the winter comes, for it is so cold up there at night that, when we were living there, we used to have four doubled blankets and as many waterproof shawls as we could get over us, and then we were hardly warm enough.
> Jessie used sometimes to wake up with cramp in her feet from the cold, so I am sure that would not do for Mama as there are not enough fireplaces in any of the bedrooms.[4]

[4] Ogilvie Family Papers, Archives, University of New England.

Another letter from Maude at the same time expressed her excitement at seeing her mother soon. 'Won't it be nice when we are all at home together again,' she wrote, 'and how pretty everything will look, especially Mama's room.'

The sixteen-year-old younger twin told her father how well they were all progressing with their studies at home, due largely to Miss Tregear. 'I think that if we continue steadily on as we are now, we will in some way make up for all our lost time. Miss Tregear is more sensible with Emmeline and Kathleen. She began, I think, to find out that giving way to them in everything wouldn't do, and has been stricter lately. For two hours on Wednesday afternoon we go out and sketch with Miss Tregear, it is very pleasant in some ways, but I don't think I will ever be able to make a respectable sketch.'[5]

They must have been delightful afternoons. All these young girls, scarves and dresses blowing in the wind, gathered about the Temple of Diana. They brought a touch of arcadian Greece to the wooded hills and mountains, with the splendid Clarence River flowing broadly by below.

It was a long time since Mary had visited Yulgilbar, and her grandchildren. Now she would never come to the Clarence again. It was not a long illness. She died peacefully at Fairlight on 23 August 1881, soon after her ninetieth birthday.

Hers had been a long and rewarding life. At times it had been little short of a heroic one. It went back to the storms and discomforts of a female convict ship, the tensions of raising a young family on the once remote Hunter River, the magnificent defiance of an angry, spear-rattling tribal horde, the periods of poverty and depression. Who could have begrudged her those final years of luxury in Edgecliff with her carriage and groom, the pleasure of her grandchildren around her, the dowager image she introduced to the drawing rooms of Darling Point and Rose Bay.

A long procession of draped carriages, with black-plumed horses, drove through Sydney's eastern suburbs on the way to the cemetary at Camperdown. She was buried beside the old Commander in the family tomb.

Edward remained in town for the reading of the will.

The old lady seemed to have forgotten nobody. She left Fairlight and its valuable furniture to her one surviving son, as well as her half-interest in the Clarence properties and Bawden's still unredeemed mortgage. Her daughter, Mary Ellen, was given £8,200, plus the

[5] Ogilvie Family Papers, Archives, University of New England.

principal and interest on W. C. Bundock's mortgage of Wyangerie; Bundock and her grandson William Frederick were each left £2,000, while every other grandchild was given £1,000. There was also an endowment to Prince Alfred Hospital at Camperdown, providing for three large wards to be built for 'naval officers and gentlemen of the country without friends.' She asked for an inscribed marble tablet to be set at the entrance in memory of Commander William Ogilvie and their two sons, William Kitchenham and Frederick Henry.

Despite the brusqueness of her later years, Mary Ogilvie remained, as she had always been, a very humane woman.

What did young girls dream of on those sunny afternoons at Yulgilbar? Some of the answers at least can be found in a thick, black-bound notebook Mabel kept from March, 1883. She carried it about with her, making notes, setting down her thoughts beside the river, above the waterfall on Joseph's Creek, or lying on the grassy slopes of Mount Currey. On the same hilltop she copied out an unidentified poem on 'Creation's Wondrous Choir', and gummed to the page a fragile bunch of lyrebird feathers.[6] There were other poems on grief and pain, on religious inspiration, on marriage, mysticism, the 'eternal nature of music'. She copied out long summaries of Ruskin's essays, Newton's *Dream of Gerontius*, an account of Bach playing before the Prince Elector at Dresden, a prose poem by Turgeniev, and Tennyson's verses on Sir Galahad. Perhaps Sir Galahads were scarce on the Clarence.

Strangely, the only news on record of Theodosia's health was in a letter from Edward David at Dartmouth. 'I am delighted to hear that my mother is getting so strong and well,' he wrote to his father in Sydney. 'But I think it is a pity she can't stay at Yulgilbar for the holidays.'[7]

The eighteen-year-old naval cadet was now growing into a man of the world. He wrote of the social contacts he had made through his friends, the country houses he stayed at, the ladies of title who entertained him and asked his father 'to look up some of the fellows arriving on the *Nelson*, especially Lambton, who is the brother of the Earl of Durham and was very kind to me when I first came here.' The letter ended with a curiously adolescent concession to his father's strong feelings about tobacco. 'I think, Father, I may safely tell you that I have not been tempted into smoking. I am sorry to say there

[6] *ibid.*

[7] *ibid.*

are boys on board this ship who go out on Sunday afternoons on purpose to smoke, but still if they are caught are severely punished.'

When Theodosia was considered fit enough to return north, her family persuaded her not to live in the schoolhouse. She was unable to walk now. In the daytime they carried her around in a chair. At night servants took her up to her bedroom on a litter. When she went out of doors, the children wheeled her in a bath chair. Occasionally she rode in the pony-cart Mary had used. Yet the spirited Irish girl could still break through the rugged-up cast of an invalid.

The girls saw that she was never alone. They fussed over her, wheeled her bath chair around the terrance and the grounds, sang for her at nights in the drawing room, played the grand piano and harmonium. Music became the unifying force in their lives.

'All the family had good voices, the brothers as well,' wrote Stevens and Sabine.[8] 'One could have made a name on the concert platform as a ballad singer. But Mr. Ogilvie would never have consented to that. These eight sisters, and their brothers, were devoted to Gilbert and Sullivan operas. Being so large a family, they used to give quite a good rendering of them in the great flower-filled drawing-room.'

There were frequent performances of these light operas. The girls made all the costumes, sometimes with the help of the housekeeper and maids, while jackeroos, if they had any sort of voice, were asked to fill the male roles. They staged performances for visitors, though the most regular audiences were the staff, both house servants and station hands. It was something unique for the owners of the manor to entertain their employees.

These employees were also well able to entertain themselves. At least when the family was not at home. One parlour maid who worked there later told how some of the maids dressed up in those Gilbert and Sullivan costumes, while jackeroos and stockmen chased them around the house.

Mabel began a second diary in 1884. There were many references to playing the piano or harmonium for mother, evenings of singing, picnics up on Mount Currey, lessons in French and dancing and shopping visits by buggy to town. More significant were her references to certain classes she took herself in the schoolhouse.

These were given for the children of the station Aborigines. On no other property had anyone attempted this. It was an unique experiment, and a rewarding one.

[8] Stevens, F., and Sabine, J. F., *The Pathfinders*, manuscript, Mitchell Library, Sydney.

It soon became a commonplace for visitors to comment on how well-spoken were Yulgilbar's native stockmen. It was Mabel who gave them their command of English. Along the Clarence men said they could always pick 'Ogilvie's blacks' by their cultivated voices.

According to Mabel's diary, the whole family had moved south by mid-1884. For the first time in her life she was given some formal education, spending two terms at a private girls' school. They were all invited to parties and dances, went swimming at Redleaf's harbourside pool, listened to Mother's account of the most recent opera Edward had taken her to, and saw him off by carriage to 'important' debates in the Legislative Council. There was also an unnamed Madamoiselle who came to Barham to teach them French. Soon afterwards she mentioned also that Father had begun inquiries about sea passages for them all to England. The far country called Overseas was beginning to draw him again.

Thirty years earlier it had been his mother's failing eyesight that took him abroad. Now it was Theodosia. Convinced that she needed specialist attention, he decided to give the family some experience of Europe as well.

Perhaps there were other motives, too. Australia now had little to offer him. He had land and prestige. Money was no longer a problem. Yet he was out of key with the new social moods. Even in Lawrence his popularity had declined. Those who lived there were protesting against his 'slaughter house and yards, from which the stench is indescribable.' *The Examiner* published a letter complaining of the dangerous state of his landing wharf, where people disembarking off ships were imperilled by half-wild cattle being driven into his yards. A campaign developed to have the place closed down.

He was also heckled at a public meeting in Tenterfield, where one faction supported his proposals for a railway line down to Lawrence, while another equally vocal one wanted New England to be linked through Glen Innes and Grafton. One 'ill-mannered person,' in Edward's words, had even had the effrontery to shout at him to 'speak up'. To which he replied with dignity, 'I am speaking loud enough for those who are disposed to listen.'[9]

The trouble was that not enough people were disposed to listen. The railway finally went to Grafton, cutting out Lawrence.

A touch of paranoia seemed to overtake him at this time. He quarrelled with neighbours, fell out with old friends and even the Legislative Council no longer gave him any pleasure. He disagreed

[9] *The Examiner*, Grafton, 1880.

with those he had previously supported. 'The Honourable E. D. S. Ogilvie was a courageous and upright man,' wrote R. C. Law.[10] 'He was very sensitive as to his honour as a gentleman, and any real or fancied imputation would rouse him to strong resentment. The loss of friends was often due to this.'

Passages were booked on a P & O steamer due to leave before the end of the year. He made a farewell visit to the Clarence, taking three of his children with him. Meanwhile he sent Theodosia and the other daughters to stay with friends at Moss Vale, believing the dry air of the southern tablelands would be good for her. Mabel recorded their movements. 'After staying in Grafton, off to Gordon Brook. Jessie and William riding, Papa and I driving. Glad to get to bed in schoolhouse.'

By this time Penrose had moved into the Big House, having been installed as full manager. She described a ten-day tour they made of Yulgilbar and Plains Station—the old Heifer run had been resumed several years before—and the bush pleasures of dinner camps beside creeks, nights under the stars, sleeping at out-stations, shooting and cooking wild duck, talking to stockmen and her father's favoured selectors. There was much hard riding, too; up ridges and mountain slopes, along sunlit valleys, until they reached the headwaters of the Clarence and Mitchell Rivers. From one mountain spur they could look right down that great valley that Edward had claimed and mastered forty-five years before.

He was now a man of seventy. 'A small, spare man with mutton chop whiskers,' was how R. L. Dawson described him at this time. Yet he could still sit a horse with ease; still ride with the best of the younger stockmen.

On their return to Sydney they travelled by a new route. This emphasised the way the country was changing. They rode up to Tenterfield, stayed overnight in the new Royal Hotel, went by spring cart to Glen Innes, which had just been connected with Sydney by railway, and made a cold journey in the guard's van of a freight train to Armidale. There they were able to board a passenger train for Newcastle, enabling them to attend two Sunday church services before taking another on to Sydney.

It was an easier journey than that packhorse trip of 1840. Edward had taken no small role in pioneering the new Australia. Yet he no longer felt part of it.

[10] Law, R. C., *Clarence River Historical Society Journal*.

To see Florence again. What more could a man desire?

Since the Suez Canal was now open, the mail steamer took them direct to Naples. They travelled overland to his 'seductive city'. He would not have found it much changed in all those years. For Theodosia it may have been a little saddening. All those years ago. The free and exhilarating life they had shared. The plans they had made together. Their prospects of an easy, free-riding life in far-off Australia, as wide as Yulgilbar's pastures, unshadowed as the sunlit antipodean skies. Now she could only see it from the seat of a bath chair. On the other hand, she had her children with her. To watch their youthful exuberance in this lovely old city would have been a sure reward.

They stayed only a few weeks. Though Theodosia's health seemed much improved, he was anxious to take her to a London specialist. They made a few friends, chiefly through the British legation, went to operas, galleries and receptions. A remarkable friendsnip grew between Edward and Robert Browning, though it was hard to conceive what subjects an Australian cattleman and the ageing poet could have had in common. There was, of course, one. Their passion for Florence.

Impatient for medical advice, Edward cut their visit short, travelling on to Paris towards the end of May. Here a letter was waiting for them from William, saying he had passed his first exams at Oxford. 'I feel quite grand at having a son who is an Oxford man,' his mother wrote back impulsively. Edward, congratulating him in more sober fashion, told the boy that 'your mother, who is very well, has been out for some hours each day.'

Perhaps he meant only to reassure his son, for both knew how ill she had been for years. In London specialist opinion was utterly discouraging. Though her family never spoke of it, it seems clear that her 'weak chest' was an euphemism for consumption. Edward was advised to rent a house for her in Torquay, reputed to be England's mildest resort.

He sent the two youngest girls to boarding school in north London, taking the others down to Devon. He engaged a private nurse, had a doctor make regular visits and made her last year as comfortable as possible. His single-minded concern for her found expression in one incident his daughters long remembered. This occurred when young Graham Mylne, now a British army officer, arranged for some friends to take them to a ball. It was a big occasion. They ordered new evening gowns from London, talked of nothing but this rare night away from home. While they were dressing, a girl friend arrived to admire their ball gowns, running straight upstairs without first calling on Theodosia below. Edward staged a furious scene. 'When you come to my house,' he said, 'you will kindly pay your respects to Mrs. Ogilvie first.' He refused to allow his daughters to go to the ball.

Perhaps his motives were understandable. He wanted the invalid Theodosia to feel herself still the centre of her family. But his harshness so angered Mylne, he devised a protest. He knew the old man had a phobia about smoking. Next day he found a pretext to borrow his carriage, driving his friends around town while they chain-smoked cigars, strewing ash and butts all over Edward's favourite travelling rug.

Despite the sunshine, the long English winter was too much for Theodosia. She died on 23 March 1886. She was only forty-seven.

Edward now began his second lonely odyssey.

Even with a family around him, he became rudderless and alone. Without Theodosia he had no more direction to his life. He took his daughters back to London, rented a large furnished house in Queen's Gate Place. He had no plans for the future. It seemed pointless to return to Australia, which was doing well enough without him. His seat in the Legislative Council had been declared vacant; his business affairs were being well enough managed; and Penrose wrote reassuringly of progress at Yulgilbar. Besides four of his children were now being educated in England. William, enjoying himself at Oxford, had been chosen to row for his college; Edward Junior had yet to pass out of Dartmouth; while Emmeline and Kathleen were both doing well at Brondesbury School. It was the kind of place that combined good education with social prestige, an advanced school run on much the same principles that Dr Arnold had introduced for boys at Rugby.

Meanwhile he kept the other six girls close to home. The eldest of them, Mary, was now twenty-six; the youngest, Mabel, twenty. It was a strange household; one old man in his seventies and all those restive young women. They were soon familiar figures around Queen's Gate. When father wanted to go walking, they all went out together. The girls followed him in Indian file. What made them more conspicuous was the style of dress he made them wear. Just as his widowed mother had gone on using black-edged notepaper for thirty years after her husband's death, so did Edward insist on tokens of mourning. He wore a black crepe armband, while the girls had to drape black veils over their faces when they went out. They hated it. Their only compensation had been, before leaving Torquay, to learn that the undertaker's name was also Ogilvie. He declared that their conspicuous mourning dress was the best advertising he had known. They hated it more when their younger brother brought his gay-living naval friends to the house, where they were expected to make only the most subdued talk with these hobbled young spinsters in black dresses and veils.

It was Edward David who brought it to an end.

'Don't you know, Father,' he said, 'that everybody's talking about you. They want to know who is this suspicious foreign gent parading the streets with a gang of kept women in harem veils.'

They were ordered off next day.

Six months after Theodosia died, Edward returned to Florence. This time he took only Kathleen, leaving her sisters to stay with friends. His main objective was to have another portrait painted of Theodosia. A posthumous one. They stayed with new friends he had made there, the Reverend Robert Loftus Tottenham and his wife. Tottenham was chaplain to the British legation, and seemed to know everyone in Florence. However, it was Browning who had recommended the painter Edward commissioned for Theodosia's posthumous portrait. Gordigiani was a well-known artist who had already done a portrait of the English poet. This painting now hangs in London's National Portrait Gallery.

Edward spent long hours in Gordigiani's studio, discussing Theodosia's nature and appearance. He gave him a copy of the photograph Freeman had taken of her in Sydney at the age of twenty-seven. He even brought from London her favourite blue satin dress.[11] These sessions provided a melancholy echo to those of that other studio on their honeymoon.

The artist's room had then been charged with life, their mutual love, the exuberance of her personality. Now there were only two men alone, a discarded dress, memories. It was one of the strangest commissions an artist was ever given. If only he had at least sketched Edward in those grieving hours. It was a study that Rembrandt would surely have done.

Yet perhaps it gave him the release he so desperately needed. In sitting beside the artist, guiding his brush strokes almost, pouring out to him all he remembered of this beautiful woman, as if attempting to breathe life into her again—he was finding release from the misery within.

He returned to London after this catharsis. He took a more active role in social life again. He arranged for Mary and Florinda to be presented at Buckingham Palace, and was himself received by Queen Victoria. A West End photographer made a study of him in court dress, before he drove to the palace. Posed against an artificial background of Roman splendour, he made a curiously archaic figure with

[11] Bland, Kathleen, letter to author, May 1971.

his velveteen, cutaway coat and knee breeches, buckled court shoes, gilt-handled sword, cocked hat and white gloves in hand.

He had become an old man now. The features had been fined down; the complexion was paler than any bushman's had the right to be; the long, white moustaches and mutton chops had grown straggly and thin. This was an altogether different Edward from Pietro Milani's black-haired, adventurous cavalier.

Towards the end of 1887 he made another brief visit to Florence. This time Mabel was with him. Because everyone had spoken so highly of her natural contralto voice, he arranged for her to have singing lessons. The professor he chose was so impressed he escorted her home, then asked to see her father. He said he would like to train her because she had the makings of an opera singer. Edward's reaction astonished him. How dared he suggest it? His daughter. Appearing on the stage.

There were no more singing lessons.

Back in England he became troubled by the way his sons were growing away from him. He rarely saw them any more, except for an overnight visit when they came to London. Both had much more exciting friends of their own. William's occasional letters mentioned having breakfast in college with the Prince of Siam, staying with the youthful Lord Morpeth at Naworth Castle, Cumberland, and all manner of house parties, dances and receptions. His father, though undoubtedly impressed by these social connections, was also concerned at his changing attitudes. Once the boy graduated, he would have to go back to the remoteness of a cattle station, learning the more serious business of handling stock and management. His gay life in London, the flighty girls and idle banjo playing, had to be ended. It was time this frivolous young man was packed off home. The girls, too, were beginning to find their father rather much of the Victorian stereotype. Within the next two years, as one of the family later expressed it, four of them were to escape into matrimony.

That curious friendship between Edward and Robert Browning flowered at this time. The two old men spent a great deal of time in each other's homes, for the poet lived in De Vere Gardens nearby.

Browning was also charmed by the girls, who made a great fuss of him, talked of poetry and sang for him. He was so enchanted with their voices that he called them his Australian Octave. Mabel especially would have enjoyed these meetings, for she had always had a girlish passion for his poems. Before leaving Yulgilbar she had copied some of his verses into her notebook, and in London wrote out another sad

E. D. S. Ogilvie in court dress for his presentation to Queen Victoria in 1888.

love poem, *Ferishtah's Fancies*. He gave her a signed photograph of himself, which she kept for the rest of her life.

What especially pleased Browning was that they made no attempt to treat him as a celebrity. They had a genuine love for his poetry; and for his genial nature. Browning said he found them a welcome change from the 'sitting worship' of certain other light-headed young women, whose effusions he found irritating.

Kathleen was given an autographed copy of his *Pied Piper of Hamelin*.

The last letter they had from him was dated 8 May 1888. This was written to his 'beloved octave' after they had sent him flowers for his birthday the day before. It was a single note, written with great tenderness.[12]

> My dear Eight; what a peculiar as well as a pleasant privilege it is, to love each one of you as if there were eight of you to love, and the whole eight as if they were one and indivisible. Your beautiful flowers will gladden my room for a season, and your dear words will stay in the heart they have assuredly gone to. Remember me always as most affectionately and gratefully yours
> Robert Browning.

The whole family was then united in London, the last time they would ever be so. William, having graduated from Oxford, sailed for Australia, where Penrose had been instructed to make him familiar with all aspects of station work. Obviously he would not be able to take over from his father without a long refresher course. Edward Junior, meantime, had been posted to overseas service on H.M.S. *Imperieuse*. Then the eldest girl, Mary, became engaged to the youngest son of Charles Tindal, who had now retired to live in Sussex. In June she married John Travers Tindal at Worthing, then sailed with him for the Clarence, where his father had given him his own station, Karrabil, a sub-division of Ramornie. Five months later the twenty-two-year-old Mabel married a distant relative, Charles Lillingston, then on home leave from the Bengal forestry department. A much older man, by at least twenty years, he had a great deal to offer her. As a senior official in the Indian civil service, he lived and travelled in some style as well as keeping a comfortable home in Suffolk.

With no regrets for lost opportunities in opera, Mabel happily left London and the restrictions of paternal living.

Six weeks after her marriage, Edward had a letter from William to say that he, too, had been married. This was also a stylish wedding,

[12] Letter in possession of Miss K. Bland, England.

Above: Browning's Australian Octave, 1879. From left to right (standing) Mabel, Mary, Emmeline, (sitting) Theodosia, Jessie, Maude, Flora with Kathleen on the floor. Courtesy Miss K. Bland.

Below: Browning's letter to Kathleen. Courtesy Miss K. Bland.

Dear Miss Kathleen,

I was in hopes to have seen you when, according to your kind desire, I called to see you before you go to School. Will you accept this little book for my sake; which contains a poem of mine, and illustrations which may make it more amusing?

You must remember me as always, yours affectionately

Robert Browning

for it took place in the fashionable St Mark's, Darling Point. The bride was an old school friend, Ethel Maude, Graham Mylne's daughter from Eatonswill. The clans were continuing to inter-marry.

With four of the remaining girls—Emmeline and Kathleen were still at school—Edward took off for Italy at the end of the year. London society had no more to offer him.

He rented a splendid villa, where he could entertain in proper fashion. The Villa Margherita, now an orthopaedic hospital, was one of the most handsome Renaissance houses in the city.

'When my mother came over to join the family,' wrote her namesake, Kathleen Bland, 'they were all very happy here. They enjoyed the beauty of Florence, the art galleries and wonderful balls, many of which were given by the Florentine families who were then still living in their old palaces.'[13]

It was the golden age of Florence as well as expatriate Australian squatters.

[13] Letter to author, May 1971.

22

Duke of Yulgilbar

'I am one of those who hold that people of every country should have a knowledge of the geography and history of the country in which they live.'

This was how Thomas Bawden began a remarkable series of public speeches in June 1886 at the Grafton School of Arts, which Richard Bligh had founded thirty years before. It was his inaugural address as president. As with two further addresses he gave two years later, it drew a large audience. Clarence people were becoming conscious of their achievements, taking pride in what an earlier generation had done to make their own prosperity possible.

Bawden was just the man to recount the story. He was once more a successful businessman, had represented the region in parliament for eleven years and had grown up with the river folk from the beginning.

Now he reminded his audience of many long forgotten events, of the hardships and adventures of an earlier generation, of just how much toil, ambition and risk had gone to the making of a now comfortably-living community. Threaded through his narrative were all the main events and personalities that had transformed this region within living memory from unexplored jungle to productive pasture lands and farms. He recalled the runaway convicts, the cedar-cutting camps, *King William's* voyage of exploration, Craig and the overlanders, the Orara and other massacres, the achievements of men like Charles Tindal, Dr Dobie, the Mylnes and Ogilvies. He had much to say on the spirited career of the old Commander, on the long and exhausting trek his two sons made through the ranges and their pioneering successes on the Clarence.

Of more recent events he was less than complimentary. That old feud with Edward continued to rankle. The Grafton *Argus* reported him as saying that:

Yulgilbar was a station noted for the number of colonial experienced
hands usually to be found on it. Of the earliest of these may be mentioned, Mr. C. G. Tindal, the present owner of Ramornie. Then came
the Elliotts, Mr. W. H. Thomas, Mr. Thos Hawkins Smith, who spent
the first years of his colonial life at Yulgilbar. Many of these owe much
of their subsequent success in life to the industrial training and thrifty
habits set them by Mr. Ogilvie . . .

In the early days the Ogilvies struggled very hard and displayed a
large amount of enterprise and untiring industry, so much so that is
scarcely to be wondered at if they came to look upon Yulgilbar as
theirs by right of conquest from barbarism, and therefore had acquired
a right to a patent of nobility, under the style and title of 'Dukes of
Yulgilbar.'

Bawden had an acid tongue. The title was his own invention. It
gained currency nonetheless. He knew his audience. Edward's aloofness
from Grafton had long rankled.

Yet that last sweeping statement ignored many creative factors in
his adversary's life. Bawden passed over those courageous years when
first forming Yulgilbar, his humane approach to the Aborigines, the
splendid confrontation with Toolbillibam, the generous paternalism
he adopted towards his station workers and the very considerable feat
of making Yulgilbar into one of the finest cattle runs on the river.

What especially angered E.D.S., when told of it in Florence, was
Bawden's final estimate of his success.

Mr. E. D. Ogilvie has been a prominent figure on the Clarence for the
past 48 years. Possibly, if he had identified himself more fully with the
people, and sympathised more with their progress, his circle of personal
friends would have been greater than it is, and he would have been
more popular with the masses than he appears to be. Possibly he cares
nothing for these things. But I cannot help remarking that, with the
influence Mr. Ogilvie could have exercised, a man with broad
sympathies and progressive views would have rendered the district
important service.

Bawden's strictures were difficult to refute. Edward had never
sponsored any public cause, nor given money to charity. His one
altruistic gesture had been to propose the local bishop's health at a
Grafton luncheon, followed by a donation to the cathedral funds.

Now, in his long absence abroad, he was confirming Grafton's
unfortunate view of him as a silvertail. Questions of ancestry had
always fascinated him. In Europe this became an obsession. Perhaps
his friends, the Loftus Tottenhams, were the involuntary cause of it.
The urbane old chaplain liked it to be known at the legation that his

father had been Lord Robert Ponsonby Tottenham, Bishop of Clogher, and his grandfather the first Marquess of Ely. A certain cachet was to be derived by entertaining and being entertained by the Tottenhams, for it gave Edward access to the homes of the well-to-do English colony, as well as the Florentine elite. For his daughters, after the solitudes of Yulgilbar, life had suddenly become rewarding, at times ecstatic. Father mellowed in this atmosphere, he gave them more freedom, allowed them to go out to parties and balls. He felt secure in doing so, for the chaplain's daughter acted as their chaperone. Alicia Georgiana Frances Tottenham, a mature, intelligent woman in her early forties, conceived a great affection for these girls. They, in turn, became attached to her. They drew from her some of that maternal warmth the sick Theodosia had rarely been able to give.

But Edward, hypersensitive in these matters, had no mind to accept the Tottenhams' friendship in any spirit of patronage. They had to be on equal social terms.

He appears to have made his first approach to the London College of Heralds late in 1886, soon after his first return visit to Florence. He was staying at Great Malvern when a reply reached him from H. Farnham Bourke, who wrote:

> I don't want to raise your hopes for nothing—but I have been looking into the Ogilvie affairs, and believe if you come from the man *I believe to be your ancestor*—you are certainly entitled to one, if not three Peerages. I can only say it looks very like it—and I am so much interested in it that I have told off two of my clerks to conduct all the evidence we can get here. If we have to get to the Scottish records, it will be an expensive search. I hope to get the Admiralty evidence next week (unable to find any R.N. background beyond father, till the discovery of a civil merchant grandfather.)[1]

He listed as possible, if yet unproven, ancestors Baron Banff, Lord Deckford, the Earl of Findlater and an unnamed baronet. A further letter sent to the Hotel de Russie, Florence, said he had an agent at work in Edinburgh, but it would be necessary to pre-pay certain sums, because the man had been taken off other work.

Next year came a letter from Somerset House to his new address in South Kensington, arranging an appointment during which they could discuss the feasibility of further searches for 'proof of your claim to the Peerages you alude to.'

Another year went by before Mr Bourke reported any success. This was merely to confirm the identity of his grandfather James, the

[1] Ogilvie Family Papers, Archives, University of New England.

Holburn Hill merchant. 'He was son of another James, who is described as a "gentleman", and I have further particulars of him, and many interesting facets connected with your family history to form a foundation for building up your pedigree.'

There followed, some months later, 'a further request' for £50 to meet expenses. E.D.S. appears not to have been over-eager to spend money on his pedigree, for no receipt was sent for another three years. By this time there were two further unpaid accounts. The first, for ten guineas, was for the Somerset Herald's search through records, wills and registry offices involving the Commissariats of Aberdeen, Banff, Brechin, Moray, St Andrews, Edinburgh and Dumfries. All these failed to prove any link with the ancient Scottish families he had nominated.[2] An additional twelve guineas was needed for the 'registration of pedigree from the grandfather in the records of the Heralds' Colleges.' This much of his pedigree he knew already.

The quest dragged on for another two years, when two more letters reached Edward at the Villa Santa Margherita. One granted approval for the unconventional spelling of his new family motto *Tout Jour*. 'As for the crest, I have no evidence of user beyond the lion on old Mrs. Ogilvie's candlesticks, but your letter and the impression of your seal (similar, as you claim, to that used by your father) enable me to have the question again considered, and I hope soon to let you know that the point will be conceded.' The second letter read, 'I am glad to be able to tell you that the old crest (with the addition of certain necessary "differences" for a cadet family) and the motto will be allowed. Please send me, by the end of the current month, your cheque for the balance of the official fees on the Patent of Arms, namely the sum of £67.15.0'[3]

His still unsuccessful search was running into money. He had already paid £65.3.3 three years earlier for a draft of the pedigree. This was the equivalent of a sizeable draft of cattle from Yulgilbar.

The ultimate irony was that his own son, William, with no effort on his part, had acquired for his children an authentic lineage that Edward could not attain for himself. Through their mother, they could now trace their ancestry back through twenty generations of Mylnes, through John of Gaunt and the Duchy of Lancaster, to the royal line of Stuarts.

Yet Edward was convinced there was only one missing link between his own great-grandfather—James Ogilvie, Gentleman—and the

[2] Ogilvie Family Papers, Archives, University of New England.
[3] *ibid.*

Findlater Ogilvies. According to Burke's *Extinct Peerage*, this family was descended from the first Earldom of Seafield, created in 1638 and lapsing in 1811, after which descent had continued through the female line, when the family's name became Grant Ogilvy. There were rumours that the last heir to the title had vanished abroad, probably in the Netherlands, while James Ogilvie, Gentleman, was also supposed to have come from there as a young man. Edward became convinced that the one proof separating him from the earldom was a missing 18th century marriage certificate. Even for rich Australian squatters, it seemed, it was easier to pass through the eye of a needle than enter the peerage.

The baffling fact was that both the Findlaters and his own forebears had used the same family crest. At least, by 1892, he was given permission to patent his own coat-of-arms. This was published, with biographical notes in the sixth London edition of *Armorial Families*. Along with his antecedents and issue, his approved status as a gentleman was announced in this fashion.

> *Armorial bearings:* Argent, guttee-de-poix, a lion passant gardant gules, holding in the dexter paw a trident in bend sinister or, in chief a chaplet of roses also gules, and in base a portcullis sable. *Mantling:* gules and argent. *Crest:* on a wreath of the colours, a lion rampant gules, charged on the shoulders with an anchor gold, gorged with a chaplet of roses argent, holding in the dexter fore-paw a plumb-rule erect proper, and resting the dexter hind-paw on a saltire or. *Motto:* Tout Jour.

By this time, however, he had another claim to the company of peers. In December 1889, during a Christmas visit to London, he married Lord Tottenham's grand-daughter.

It is not clear whether or not he and Alicia Georgiana Frances Tottenham first announced their engagement in Florence, or whether it was an impulsive decision. At all events, her father had just retired as chaplain to the legation, taking his wife and daughter back to England. It was a quiet wedding, as befitted a widower of seventy-five. His bride was thirty years his junior.

When his son William was asked what he thought of that lost title, he said: 'How in the world could a man grow better sheep by calling himself Lord Seafield?'

The fact that he said sheep, not cattle, revealed an unexpected divergence in Edward's dream for an heir to Yulgilbar.

After William returned to Australia in mid-1888, he went straight to the Clarence. Having been so many years abroad, he knew little of the country, nor of cattle-breeding and management. His father wanted him to learn from the beginning. Penrose took him at his word. The manager sent the young man up to Plains Station where he became little more than an out-station superintendent. He was placed in the position of any other jackeroo.

Even after his marriage to Ethel Mylne, he found himself excluded from the mainstream of station life. He wrote to his father complaining that Penrose was keeping him out of the way, that he was learning nothing. What passed between father and son was never disclosed. But Penrose continued to live comfortably in the Big House, remaining in firm control. On the occasions when the couple came down to stay a night or two, it was made plain to them they were visitors.

William chafed under this offhand treatment. Yet there was little he could do. His father trusted Penrose absolutely, accepting whatever advice or reports he gave. It seems likely that none of these reports would have particularly favoured an angry young man who, in the manager's view, was a mere untrained college graduate.

For William it was an impossible situation. There was certainly no way of resolving it by correspondence. A single exchange of letters between Yulgilbar and Florence took four months; and there were limits to what could be said by mail. That such letters became terser, more candid, can be taken for granted. They appear to have done nothing to undermine Edward's trust in his manager. Besides it was all rather remote. No raised voices reached him in the Villa Santa Margherita's drawing room, or its tranquil, sunlit gardens. Amid the sober pleasures of the expatriate British colony, William would have appeared a mere trouble-maker. Besides, the boy was young. He could afford to wait a year or two.

Those who worked the station were by no means so uncritical. Penrose was becoming known as a 'verandah manager'. He had never been much of a horseman. Now, growing stout, he began to find the saddle rather troublesome for long riding into the back country. His one attempt to demonstrate his bushcraft had almost ended in disaster.

This had happened two or three years earlier, after taking a draft of Yulgilbar horses down to the bloodstock sales at Tamworth. Riding with a single Aboriginal stockman and a packhorse, he had followed the now well-used road through Tenterfield and New England. On the return journey he made a rash decision. Perhaps he was trying to emulate his employer's overlanding feat through those almost impenetrable ranges south and west of the Clarence. This meant trying to rediscover the old, disused Craig's Line, which had long ago reverted to wilderness and heavy scrub. To complicate matters they carried the proceeds of the sale, in gold sovereigns, packed in two saddlebags.

'After crossing the Dividing Range,' wrote a Grafton *Examiner* correspondent,[4] 'Penrose and the black encountered some of the most broken and thickly timbered country imaginable, and this soon became too difficult for the horses to negotiate. They abandoned both horses and saddles, and continued on foot, carrying the saddle bags of sovereigns slung around their shoulders with straps. Every so often the black would climb a tree to find a landmark. Eventually they won through, weary and almost done, their shoulders sore from the weight of the sovereigns, which caused the straps to cut deeply into their flesh. Search parties were sent back for the horses, but these were never found.'

His stockmen were not impressed with their manager's performance.

There were other reasons for their mistrust. These must also have been known to William. Penrose had been given permission to maintain a small breeding herd of his own. Its numbers showed a remarkable increase in the years of Edward's absence. Whenever cleanskins were mustered in remoter reaches of the run, a good number seemed to acquire Penrose's own brand. More selectors had also come to take up small blocks on Yulgilbar, especially along the river frontage. As usual these were dummies. But rumours became current that the agreement they made for the later surrender of their blocks was not with the station, but Penrose personally.

Again there was Penrose's unfortunate appearance in the Grafton courts. A young girl, whose parents had worked for a while on Yulgilbar, brought a paternity suit against him. He defended the case, persuading the jury of his innocence. Perhaps, had he not taken further action, Grafton opinion would have given him the benefit of the doubt. But Penrose then sued the girl for defamation of character, and had her sent to gaol.

In 1890, despairing of a *modus vivendi* with Penrose, William decided on stronger action. He made his father an offer to buy Yulgilbar. It was a fairly desperate bid, for he had little capital. It would also have meant buying out the rest of the family.

Among his posthumous papers were found two pages of pencilled notes, headed 'Yulgilbar expenses, 1888–90.' These consisted of rough calculations, estimating the current value of the station, his share in it and how long it would take him to pay off the purchase

---

[4] Undated newspaper cutting from *The Examiner*, Grafton.

price. He estimated its total value, based on the ruling price of £1 an acre, as £100,000. If his father could be persuaded to make the station over to his children, excluding the two married daughters, he calculated that he could pay off the other five-sixths in a period of time. It was a desperate, long-term estimate, even with the help of his wife's sizeable income from the Mylne properties. He found that it would take him up to thirty years.

Furthermore, his calculations had a despairing marginal note, relating to the estimate of stock numbers: 'What chance of finding a cattle count?'

Penrose was still running the station close to his chest.

Nothing more was heard of these ambitions. Clearly Edward had no intention of relinquishing his ownership. Nor did William receive much encouragement from his wife to wait his time. She had grown to dislike Yulgilbar. She shared Theodosia's reactions to its cold winter moods. She found the silence along Yulgilbar Reach oppressive. The sombre mountains around it gave her a touch of claustrophobia.

It was Ethel who finally persuaded William to renounce his inheritance.

In 1891 he wrote to his father saying he wanted to buy a station of his own. He had found a sheep run in New England that appealed to him. Whatever coolness now existed between the two, Edward agreed to advance him £2,000. He remembered that loan to his death. His will stipulated that it be deducted from interest due to his son on the Yulgilbar estate.

By the end of the year William was the owner of Ilparran. It was excellent sheep country, nearly four thousand feet up in the ranges, west of Glen Innes. He worked hard to develop it into a profitable run.

Now Edward had to face a new dilemna. He had to find another heir to Yulgilbar.

If conditions in Australia had remained normal, it is unlikely that Edward would ever have left Italy. He had now been comfortably abroad for nine years. He had become an accepted part of the Florentine establishment. But the laws of economics began to exert pressures of their own.

The first alarm was sounded by his sister Ellen. Writing from Wyangerie, she warned him that, unless he came home soon, he might well lose Yulgilbar altogether.

Perhaps she exaggerated. But what she told him produced an immediate change of plans. The Bundocks' warning succeeded where his son's had failed. He learnt why Yulgilbar's revenues were falling off, even though just as many cattle were being sold. He learnt of those dummy selectors. It had become impossible to obscure the facts any longer. Several of them—each with 320 acres on conditional purchase, and another 960 of leasehold—had run themselves into debt and had to surrender their blocks.

Confirmation was later to be found, after Edward's death, in his own register of properties. This listed nineteen selectors who had held a total of 8,000 acres under conditional purchase; all of them in choice positions along the river or on grazing flats. Among these was one strategically-placed block named Baryulgil, later to become a township for the station. (The name was simply Yulgilbar re-formed.) The entire list had then been cancelled, entered under a new heading, and Edward's ownership restored.[5]

During his absence, Penrose had another run of luck. On a steep spur running down to the river, only a quarter-mile from the Cottage, he discovered payable gold. It was close to the surface, requiring only open-cut methods with a few paid workers. Penrose Reef became a steady producer for a number of years, even though some dubious characters worked on it from time to time. One of these was Deeman, a murderer wanted by the police in several States.

What this small-scale mine did prove, however, was that gold now paid better than cattle or land. By the time Edward was ready to leave Florence, a new economic crisis had struck·Australia. It was the end of a boom period that had lasted twenty-five years.

'Something irrecoverable passed from Australian community life in the last lean years of the old century,' wrote Brian Fitzpatrick.[6] 'What took place was like the ending of a childhood; the curtain's fall on wide-eyed expectation, the entrance instead of uncertainty, doubt and mistrust. The second Australian land boom—fifty years after the first in 1840—had collapsed, with calamitous effect upon a host of speculative financial houses, widespread unemployment and deterioration of wage standards.'

As Fitzpatrick pointed out, Australians were not equipped to deal with the economic mayhem their simplistic, money-hungry attitudes had caused. They seemed to believe that land existed only to make quick money; endless money. It was as if all gamblers were pre-ordained to go on winning. They gambled on the stock exchange, turning it into a casino; gambled on land values; on cattle and wool and sheep.

[5] Register of Properties, Clarence River Historical Society, Grafton.

[6] Fitzpatrick, B., *The Australian People*, Melbourne, 1945.

Gold digging at the Penrose Mine, Yulgilbar. Photograph by Kathleen Ogilvie was taken in 1894. Courtesy Miss K. Bland.

And when, as was inevitable, the overloaded markets crashed, they had not the least idea why.

Even in the Renaissance calm of Florence, Edward must have been kept informed. Besides the English papers made much of the new industrial anarchy in Australia. Massive strikes by shearers and maritime workers were fought with extreme bitterness, reproducing the class warfare more common to Europe. The City of London cut back its investments; export prices for meat and wool dropped continually; more than twenty land banks in Sydney and Melbourne crashed. Edward, with Alicia and his youngest daughter, was actually ocean-bound for Sydney when the prestigious Commercial Bank, temporarily, closed its doors. This was late in 1893.

The nineteen-year-old Kathleen was now the only daughter to remain with him. All the others, except Flora, were now married, while she too had elected to stay in England. Theodosia was now Mrs Lewis Boyle; the twins, Maude and Jessie, had married close friends in Loftus Townsend and Tancred Armstrong, of the Colonial Secretary's office; Emmeline had become Mrs Archibald Campbell. Meanwhile Mabel had gone to India with her husband, while Edward David was on active service aboard H.M.S. *Imperieuse*.

There could hardly have been any worse time to arrive in Sydney. A full-scale depression had begun. What Edward learnt of his own affairs prompted him to hurry home. They travelled by steamer to the Clarence, were met by the Penroses at Lawrence, and moved into the Big House to end his nine-year absence.

Yulgilbar, at least, was still solvent. No one, even Penrose, could have called it prosperous. Apart from ruinous cattle prices, a succession of dry seasons had much reduced turn-off and carrying capacity. There had been no real drought since 1888, but rainfall had continued to be scarce, and his herds desperately needed building up.

Edward resumed his control of stock-raising as though he had never been away.

He was indestructible. Though now approaching eighty, he could still swing a leg over the saddle, and rode around the station as he had always done. His stockmen admired him for his vigour and down-right approach. 'If you wanted a job off him,' one old hand said, 'you had to bowl right up to him, and look him straight in the eye. He looked you straight in the eye, too. If he thought you were all right, you'd get the job.'

He was blunt in his dealings always. He had his own stringent rules. You broke them at your peril. He was known, for instance, to have great compassion for horses. Alec Rogan spoke of one flash stockman he caught trying to make his horse buck by digging in spurs. He was sacked on the spot. Another, sent up to the Cottage to pick up some branding irons, was confronted by Edward at the paddock gate.

'How come your horse is sweating like that?'

The man said he had been ordered to hurry.

'Don't take it out on the horse. You'd better see Mr. Penrose and get your money.'

It is difficult to imagine Alicia—Alice as she was now known—adapting easily to the rough texture of cattle station life, though she would have found the Big House comfortable enough. She was always the practised hostess; charming, groomed, intelligent. They entertained a great deal. Noted visitors from the city or overseas came to stay. There was even a world-travelling guest of title now and then; the kind that Edward would have read up in his latest edition of Debrett before greeting him at the lion-flanked entrance steps. For his wife the problem was more in reconciling her drawing-room talk with the earthy, less class-conscious accents of the locals. The station Aborigines bothered her a little. She did not find it easy making common ground. They had responded in quite different fashion to the exquisite young Theodosia. But that was an earlier generation; and a long time ago.

There was one curious confrontation during her first week on Yulgilbar. Each time she went to the side entrance she found a stout, grey-haired lubra squatting outside the door. Nothing was said. The woman merely stared. Alice found that scrutiny unnerving. At last,

Alicia Ogilvie in the courtyard at Yulgilbar, taken by her stepdaughter Kathleen. Courtesy Miss K. Bland.

with some impatience, she asked: 'Do you want something? If not, please go away.'

The lubra looked at her impassively. 'I see you'm little bit flash, missus. I bin Missus Ogilvie longa time afore you.'

Even Edward, if she told him, would have found this hard to explain. How did one describe a feudal relationship with tribal employees, the Aborigines sense of belonging, the role of a wet nurse in family affairs.

In December 1894 Yulgilbar had a visit from one of the most distinguished men ever to stay at the Big House. Tom Roberts arrived by horse from New England, alone. He looked very much the bushman, wearing white moleskins, high riding boots and a trim, v-shaped beard. He carried his swag across the saddle bow, and camping gear, brushes, oil paints and rolled canvas in the saddlebags. He was now at the peak of his early success, having already shown one of his masterpicees, *The Golden Fleece*. Originally called *Shearing At Newstead*, this had been painted in Duncan Anderson's woolshed at Newstead Station, near Inverell.

He had just finished another large canvas, *Bailed Up*. Duncan Anderson had helped him reconstruct an authentic encounter between a Cobb and Co. coach near Glen Innes, lending him some station workers and horses as models. Riding on to Tenterfield, Roberts

Tom Roberts at Yulgilbar in 1894 with painting gear. Photograph by Kathleen Ogilvie. Courtesy Miss K. Bland.

camped for a while on the old Rocky River goldfield, where he painted *On The Timbarra*, before coming down the Clarence through Tabulam.

He stayed several days at Yulgilbar. The opportunity was too good to miss. He was commissioned to paint Edward's portrait.

He was given the study, next to Edward's library, for a studio. His subject sat for him there for several days. Both family and house staff were nervous about the situation, for Roberts liked to smoke a pipe while he painted. Edward detested smoking. No one was ever allowed to do so in the house.

Outside the closed door everyone waited for the explosion. They heard match after match struck. The half-heard flow of talk went on. No protest came. Edward, it seemed, had at last met a character as strong as himself.

When the portrait was finished, Roberts carried it into the courtyard to dry. It was still there, propped against one of the archway columns when Billy, Edward's Aboriginal groom, walked through from the kitchen. Sighting the picture, he stopped guiltily, said 'Good morning, Boss', then gave it a closer look, giggled and ran back to the kitchen.

Edward's daughter Jessie was later to describe it as 'a speaking likeness.' It was more too. Setting him against a rich burgundy background, Roberts caught the essence of the man in his last vigorous years. It is a strong, confident, almost domineering face. The face of a man who knows exactly what he wants from life. Half-turned away from the artist, hands clasped behind his back, very erect, Edward looks the viewer straight in the face, despite the cast in the right eye, suggesting the onset of age. It is a shrewd, hard gaze; assessing and aware, though the expression has been slightly softened by the half-smile beneath those flowing white, well-brushed whiskers. Here is the Victorian father figure in excelsis. This is a masterful character. And a masterly portrait.

When Tom Roberts passed through again the following year, he may have realised that he had painted Edward just in time. The old man was showing his age now. Another humid summer seemed to have withered him, though he had escaped the hottest months by renting a house for his family down in Bowral. His mind was beginning to slow. He was growing a little eccentric. Rarely going on horseback any more, he drove about in the basket gig that Theodosia had used, drawn by the same old white pony, which was now almost blind.

His main preoccupation now was the future of Yulgilbar. He referred to it, significantly, as the succession. He had to make up his mind who was to be his heir.

Nor was he altogether happy about its present management. One imagines that, on his return, there had been some straight talking between Penrose and his employer. Whatever was said, they continued to work together. There was no alternative, as he made clear when the Lillingstons, now with two small children and their ayah, arrived during a year's sick leave from India in April 1895.

'About a month after our arrival,' Captain Lillingston wrote, 'Mr. Ogilvie offered me the managership, with a sub-manager under me. This I refused, informing him that I felt entirely incompetent to take up such a position, that such work would not have been at all to my taste.'[7] Besides, he added, he was expecting soon to be made head of the Bengal forestry department. 'It would be folly on my part to throw up my appointment and pension, due after five-and-a-half years' more service, in order to take a more or less subordinate position as manager of a cattle station in Australia.'

It was not hard to understand his point. This stout, sun-reddened, extroverted man, with a taste for well-cut safari jackets and cavalry-style riding boots, had grown accustomed to the life of a sahib. When the Lillingstons travelled through India, they had their own marquee, a team of elephants and turbanned bearers to wait on them. No wonder he said that 'life on Yulgilbar could never be exciting.'

[7] Confidential letter circulated to members of family, Ogilvie Family Papers, Archives, University of New England.

Edward did not mention the subject again for another four months. Then, while out riding with Lillingston, 'he went straight to the point, and asked me if I would like to be a squatter. I told him that, if I had a place like Yulgilbar, I would like it, but otherwise it would be a different matter.

' "Well, Charles,' he said, 'I am an old man; I may not live for another year; I have given deep thought to what best should become of Yulgilbar when I am dead and gone. I had hoped my eldest son would have succeeded me, but he had the chance and refused." '

Beneath that seemingly casual statement was clearly a deep hurt. For thirty years he had treasured the belief that William would become his heir. He had given half his life to the building of a great estate, and now his chosen heir had rejected it. The second boy had revealed himself equally indifferent. Edward David had never shown the least desire to identify himself with the station or its management.

Lillingston then said that Edward discussed the claims of his children one by one, coming at last to Mabel, whom he called his favourite daughter. His final decision was to leave Yulgilbar to her.

At this point he made a proposal that, in his son-in-law's words, were to cause 'very serious misunderstandings' among others of the family. Some of them claimed later that he had offered the Lillingstons an income of £1,000 a year to live on the property. Lillingston, in a confidential letter drafted by his solicitors, vigorously denied it. All Edward had said, he insisted, was that the Big House would need a great deal of money for its upkeep. He wanted it maintained in proper style, whatever the cost.

Out of all Edward's heart-searching one crucial factor emerged. It was Yulgilbar, above all, he loved. At all costs it had to be preserved. Even those who owned or managed it took second place. There were to be no absentee owners.

He told Lillingston that, if his wife accepted the inheritance, he could never be more than her agent, or representative. Other members of the family would be paid annuities out of the estate, 'but he would expect us to make Yulgilbar our home; and that he would look to me to interest myself in the work of the estate and to throw my whole heart into it; and not to look on it purely as a speculation, from which I was to get as much money as I could and to care little or nothing about the interests of the property and those working on it.'[8]

Here Edward came to the core of his problems. It explained why he had retained Penrose, despite those adverse reports. Penrose had

[8] *ibid.*

a wealth of inside information that no one else, without his confidence, could obtain.

'He wished me to act at the agent of my wife in all matters,' Lillingston wrote in that confidential letter, 'and to study Colonial political questions &c. Mr. Ogilvie wished me also to promise that I would personally visit every portion of freehold land and carefully inspect the boundaries thereof, in order that I might know what land was freehold and what was not. The only person now cognisant of the boundaries of the different freehold lots being Mr. Penrose, and in the event of anything happening to him, were I not thoroughly acquainted with the boundaries of the freehold land myself, very considerable complications might ensue, and the estate become involved in litigation and mulcted in heavy expenditure.

'I faithfully promised that I would do all he wished.'

Significantly, when Lillingston suggested that Edward discuss the whole question with Penrose, his father-in-law would have none of it.

He insisted that the only others to be taken into his confidence were relatives at present staying in the house: his wife, Mabel, William and his wife, and Kathleen.

And so, for the time being, it rested. The Lillingstons left for England to complete their year's leave.

At Christmas, as usual, the Ogilvies went south again. Edward rented the same large house in Bowral. Yet even these normally cool southern tablelands were hot this summer. The whole country was enduring the most intense heatwave in living memory.

Edward spent much of his time indoors. He had urgent reasons for doing so. He was trying to complete the last draft of his will. It was a complicated document; one that was to cause much dissension and misinterpretation in coming years. The complexity of its wording and sentiments must have taken weeks to set in satisfactory order. According to arguments in court thirty years later, and learned opinions by King's Counsel, its meanings were never made wholly clear. During the final stages he brought his solicitor up from Sydney. He must have stayed over Christmas, for the document was signed and witnessed on Boxing Day.

There was little holiday spirit in the house that year.

When it was done at last, Edward may have felt like a man shriven. He spent the next month in relaxed fashion with his family, even went riding outside the town. It was no mean feat for a man in his eighty-second year to sit a horse still, even if he put it to no more than a jog-trot.

He had, after all, lived in the saddle for sixty years. And this was the way he died.

Late in January, returning home from an afternoon ride, he passed under the railway bridge at the outskirts of town. At that moment a train approached the bridge, its wheels thundering directly overhead. The horse bolted. The old man failed to control it, and was thrown.

He died from his injuries within a few days.

The date of his death was 25 January 1896. His long and vigorous life had spanned the best part of the century. And it had been the best part. The 19th century was the golden age of the squatter. From then on the splendid world of the pastoralist would never be quite the same, never quite as expansive as it had been from the time the first adventurous squatters drove their flocks and herds to the frontiers of settlement, first on the Upper Hunter, and then to the inhospitable Clarence Valley.

Yulgilbar, too—despite his chosen heirs—was never to be run with quite the same single-minded passion as Edward David Stewart Ogilvie brought to his lands and possessions.

His family and a few friends attended the funeral service at Bowral, following which his body was taken to Sydney, then placed aboard s.s. *Kallikina* for Grafton. There it was laid in state in the cathedral, making the final journey by dray along the Coaldale road through the ranges to Yulgilbar.

This was now the principal road to the station. There had not even been a track when Edward and his brother first cantered across those splendid pastures to form Yulgilbar. Now, fifty-six years later, his remains were carried over the very same route he had pioneered.

His body was placed in the high-ceilinged library at Yulgilbar for another day. Then station hands carried him up that steep and stony hill, putting him to rest beside his brother.

It was a day of sorrow for Ogilvie's Blacks. They gathered on the flat, watched the pall-bearers carry his coffin to the crest of the hill, sending him off with much the same hushed and respectful awe they had shown on his first departure for Europe.

'Beneath me, at the foot of the slope,' he had written on that far-off occasion, 'still lingering upon the spot where I had parted from them, stood the servants assembled to farewell me; while, on the intervening slope, were numbers of the dark children of the forest, some reclining in the shade of the great trees, others in silence watching, others wailing and in lamentation.'

Whatever changes had come to the world outside, an air of tribal unity and ceremonial remained on Yulgilbar.

23

Heirs and Successors

Edward's choice of a family motto had great significance. *Tout Jour*, apart from being old French, had a very specific meaning. This was quite different from *Toujours*, to be translated as *Always*. The phrase he chose meant *Forever*.

For him Yulgilbar had been a passionate involvement. His belief in destiny. Even after death, it must not be allowed to pass from his chosen heirs and successors. It was his road to immortality, a challenge sent into the great void of time. Those to whom he passed it must always be Ogilvies.

Whether or not it was his fault that he failed is of no importance any more. He could have secured the succession, had he not alienated his elder son; or kept the younger one closer to him. Since this was not to be, his logical choice was Mabel, even though she no longer carried his name. His complex will was largely designed to reshape the situation. But there are limits even to the decrees of law. It had been easy enough for him to instruct his solicitors to ensure that any successors adopted the name of Ogilvie. Human nature tends to follow different courses, impervious to legal formula.

The first eight of those thirty-six clauses were simple enough. These dealt mainly with the disposal of his possessions and effects, and certain minor legacies. Alice was given an immediate legacy of £500; Penrose another £300. His former heir, William Frederick, was left his best gold watch and chain, with a few trinklets as well.

To Alice he bequeathed all the personal treasures he had accumulated over half a century. She acquired his furniture, jewellery, plate, glassware, china, books, manuscripts, pictures, prints, musical instruments, wines and liquors; his horses, carriages, harness and saddlery; and all the additional prints, paintings, furniture and household goods still stored in Florence. She was also to have the use and enjoyment of what he termed the 'principal Mansion House' until her death. Anything she did not want was to pass to Mabel.

The complications began with clause nine.

The Yulgilbar Estate, which was put in the hands of three executors and trustees—his son-in-law Tancred Armstrong, Sydney William Penrose and John Tindal—was to be held by them in trust for Mabel for the duration of her life. On her death it was to pass, still in trust, to her eldest son, and then to his heirs; or, if the first son failed to reach twenty-one, to the next brother, if any, and then down through the same line of descent. If the Lillingstons had no eligible son, then the estate was to pass to William Frederick's eldest son, and on through the same order of precedence.

The ultimate aim was to ensure that Yulgilbar remained always within the Ogilvie family, and was never sold or even mortgaged. Even if it were to be held by a Lillingston, the son must immediately change his name to Ogilvie on gaining the inheritance.

So much for the actual ownership. Edward's other nine children— including the disinherited William—were also to benefit from the estate. The will directed that a valuation be made on his death, and that a sum equivalent to two-thirds of the total value be paid to them over a period of years in annuities. This meant that most of Yulgilbar's revenue had to pass into a trust fund, so that Mabel was unlikely to accumulate much wealth, however well the station supported her. This was to have critical implications for the future, especially when her own son made unreal demands on her.

That this complex will caused hard feelings among some family members was only to be expected. As soon as it was read, Charles Lillingston was accused of having unfairly influenced a senile father-in-law, promoting his own interests over Mabel's sisters and brothers. Indignantly denying this, Lillingston had his English solicitors draft a lengthy and printed document, which was sent in confidence to all close relatives. This described his relationship with Edward from their first meeting, the old man's offer to make him manager, his own support for other family members and a declaration that he intended to act only as his wife's agent and business manager, without taking personal control.[1]

Meantime he had resigned from the Indian civil service. After a brief visit to England, where he sold his Suffolk home, he brought his family out to Yulgilbar, arriving early in 1897.

It was to remain in their possession until Mabel's death nearly

---

[1] Confidential letter, Ogilvie Family Papers, Archives, University of New England.

thirty years later. The widowed Alice returned to Florence, where she died in 1921.

Yulgilbar, without its founder, was never to be quite the same again.

Hard times continued to the turn of the century. When the economic depression lifted, several years of drought followed. The 1899–1901 drought devastated the whole of eastern and central Australia, and is referred to by old hands to this day as 'the grandfather of all droughts.'

Eventually the good seasons returned. Yulgilbar prospered again. But E. D. S. Ogilvie's memory did not easily fade. After more than half a century, he had invested it with his own special character. Exactly what this meant in terms of personal achievement was vividly reflected by one of his daughters.

The letter Jessie wrote after his death was the most touching tribute anyone had paid to him.[2]

She wrote it after returning from England with her husband, Tancred Armstrong, who had been notified of his appointment as a trustee. They reached Sydney on s.s. *Austral* in March 1896 with her sister Theodosia (Zoe) and her husband, Lewis (Lou) Boyle. Some days later, the sisters went by train to Tenterfield with their step-mother, whom they called Steppie, and thence by road to Fairfield and Yulgilbar. The long, intimate letter to her other sisters overseas was begun at the White Rock Hotel, Fairfield. Although she was an Australian returning home, everything had become so strange to her that she wrote like a visitor to her own land. She described how they had spent two days with the Macarthur–Onslows at Camden Park, which 'reminded me of an Italian villa or an Indian bungalow.' Then came the long train journey 'through the wild country, but some of it quite beautiful.' In Glen Innes they were met by her brother, William, and his wife. 'Dear old Will,' she wrote, 'was a good deal altered and didn't look at all Colonial, only he is rather different from other people. He seems very happy and pleased with his home out here. Ethel says he was dreadfully cut up about not being with Papa when he died, but you see the doctors never thought it necessary to send, it was so sudden at the last.'

Next day they went on to Tenterfield, where they were met by Penrose and John Tindal. 'They gave one the feeling of being taken care of at once.' Yet the town looked as strange and quaintly colonial as Glen Innes had done, with 'that curious dry hard look that Australian country towns have.' They drove off for Fairfield that

[2] Letter in possession of the late Sir Kenneth Street.

afternoon in two buggies, enchanted by the wild and beautiful country-side. The next morning they drove on again to Tabulam, and down the familiar track to Yulgilbar. The second part of her letter carried a new date; 18 March. It reads:

My darling sisters, I am in the library. We have been here three days, and it is so very strange. The day I wrote last we started off in the afternoon and had a really lovely drive as far as Tabulam, and there we stopped at the funniest little inn you ever saw, there was an out-station feel about it that was really very fascinating. We had twenty five miles of driving across country, but although it was very extraordinary it was not at all frightening, the horses were so wonderfully good and obedient, and the country was really lovely. I think we are seeing it now at its best, such wonderful green grass everywhere, and some of the trees are pretty, and such lovely wildflowers. There has been lots of rain, and there was a delicious green freshness everywhere.

It was so strange arriving at Broadwater—the dear little place—it is very pretty, but was so small. The hut had been done up for us with flowers, and Mrs. William Hamilton and all the children looked so nice and *so* pretty, they are a wonderfully good-looking family. From there the cousins, Alice and Mr. Penrose went by boat, and I rode in with Jack.

It looked very grand and lovely, the dear old place, only it all looked so much nearer, and the clearing over the river made such a difference, and took away much of the wild look; all the way from the little hill to the door things seemed so much smaller and balder somehow. The same way with the court and all, and the garden seemed nearer. It was such a strange feel, as if I had grown twice as large myself—and there was a strangeness about everything, as if I had had all my life between and this was coming back in a dream of the past. I have no *intense* feeling about anything—even the missing dear papa, I only miss him as I miss mother here, in a faraway, vague way. It seems rather dreadful of me, but things are very strange with Alice here and the cousins.

But now and then one feels a pang to think that he is not here any more to arrange things—dear Papa—but it is almost as if the past was quite, *quite* gone and one was living in a dream, among old memories in intensely new surroundings. Mrs. Penrose was here to greet us, she is such a dear and so helpful to us.

The servants have all been so nice—what good servants they are, so anxious to do all they can for us, and there is the same old charm about the rooms and some of them are really very well furnished—the bed-rooms, I mean, and the library and dining room are really delightful though a little bare. I love the drawing room, too, in a way, though one sees it is not furnished right for a hot climate, but the whole house has a curious feel about it, and one is content to leave things as they are. The sad thing is the lower garden and the ceilings. The lower garden is a wilderness simply, and the vineyard. I shall not go into the garden more than I can help, at least beyond the trellis, but the park and the country round and the river, and the views about are quite lovely. In the balcony and the front verandah and some of the bedrooms that we do not use, large pieces of the ceilings have fallen down. It was the awful storm that we heard about in the summer that did it.

We do not feel in the least lonely at night and the court is so very pretty with lots of ferns in pots looking so fresh and green.

This morning I went up to the cemetary to see it. It was such a lovely morning, so fresh and clear, and with a very cool breeze and such wonderful freshness in the air, and the walk there was so delicious, all through the grass, and the birds were singing all round. I thought of you all there and laid some white flowers on the grave.

I was so glad to think that dear Papa was resting in a place he loved so well—just near the cottage that he brought mother to at first. What a wonderful thing it was, his opening up this country and making this place—there is much sadness in it too, for the dear old place is so far away, and has brought so much trouble to him since—I wonder how things will all end about it. They have buried dear papa in the vault and all the cemetary has been tidied up and there have been some flowers planted—there are lovely trees all round and it is very pretty. We must put up a cross, dears, dont you think? Alice and I thought so, and we will consider about the words to put on it afterwards. I think a marble cross, quite plain, would be nice, when we can see to it. Steppie and I are going to find some verses, and tell you about it next mail.

It was so strange this morning to think of all my darling sisters, all so far away and I alone by Papa's grave, thinking of his life all finished where he had spent all the happiest part of it. I like to think of him at rest there. It seems so right and fitting, and life would have been full of worries to him now, for land is a great trouble out here it seems to me, and it seemed hard at his age that he should still be fighting here. I am very glad to feel that he is at rest after all his work. I realised the peace of it all there this morning, though of course one does miss him here so much for our own sakes. One never realised till now how one leaned on him.

My dear love to all from your very loving sister,
    Jessie.

Jessie's cross was placed on the hilltop soon afterwards. It was not marble, but granite. It stood six foot high on a broad plinth; quite plain as she desired it. The words they chose came from the Book of Proverbs and Ecclesiastes: 'The path of the just is a shining light which shineth more and more unto the perfect day . . . Whatever thy hand findeth to do, do it with all thy might.'

On the landscapes below life flowed on as peaceably as before.

The cattle were mustered and drafted; bullock teams hauled their drays in from Grafton; visitors came and went by carriage or sulky; Aborigines fished and drowsed by the river. Though a new master occupied the castle—as Charles Lillingston liked to call it—management remained the same. At least for a while.

Lillingston had assured his wife's family that he 'desired nothing more than that he [Penrose] should have an absolutely free hand, and he will never receive anything but unqualified support from me.'[3]

Two years later the manager made a very different decision of his own.

No one ever explained his motive. Least of all Penrose. One day he went into Grafton and never came back. He took nothing with him; neither clothes nor possessions. He left his wife and son behind. The Clarence never saw him again. From time to time there were rumours of him living in Sydney. Then, in February 1900, came news that he had died.

His body was brought up to Grafton by train. They laid him, as Edward had been, in the cathedral. Over his grave they set the largest headstone in the cemetary. Penrose, after all, had left his family well provided for. His estate was valued at £20,000.

Yet, even then, curious rumours persisted. Some said he was not dead at all. They hinted that—like Lasseter in another context—he had merely departed for a better life in this world, taking ship for the United States. As for his coffin, it was said to have contained 'a dead Chinaman from Sydney,' the extra weight being made up with lead.

The Clarence has never been without its legends.

In Grafton Captain Lillingston reversed his late father-in-law's image by making it his headquarters. Unconcerned with Lawrence, where the Ogilvie assets were progressively sold, he became a popular figure in town, a good mixer, especially at race meetings and clubs. He was also in demand as a court interpreter. The growing Indian community on the Clarence and Richmond, brought in originally as cane cutters on sugar farms, were typically litigious, and Lillingston was the only local to speak Hindustani. A few townsfolk thought him a bit flash, on account of his dashing manner when driving a four-in-hand.

Whenever he drove to Grafton, men said, he stayed overnight at the Half-Way Inn, a once notorious shanty on the Coaldale road, then entered town at a full gallop next morning with fresh horses, claiming that he had driven right through from Yulgilbar.

Under Penrose's successors, the station began to prosper again. The great drought was followed by a run of good seasons. New markets in beef developed, especially in the frozen meat trade to Britain. The

[3] Ogilvie Family Papers, Archives, University of New England.

first World War accentuated both prices and demand. Even though Lillingston was unable to prevent the resumptions Edward had feared, Yulgilbar did not greatly suffer, due to improved breeding methods. Its 98,000 acres were reduced to 40,000 by the end of the new century's first decade. Yet, by introducing a Devon strain into its Shorthorn herd, they were able to turn off cattle at four years old instead of eight. The only restraining factor was the conservative control of the trustees, which gave managers little scope for initiative or taking quick advantage of markets.

And so matters remained until 1925. This was the year Mabel died, during an epidemic of Asian flu. She, too, was buried amid Aboriginal lamentations beneath the afternoon shadows of her father's granite cross.

The grand days of Yulgilbar had come to an end.

Never again would there be a family living permanently in that expansive turreted mansion. No more formal parties in the long drawing room. No grooms to hold the visitor's horse at the entrance between those Canova lions. No more evenings of music around that mellow rosewood grand. For half a century it had seemed as if the sounds of singing were part of Yulgilbar; in all the years Theodosia had lived there; and afterwards, when Mabel played and sang, the girl who might have made a career in European opera.

'She really had a most beautiful voice,' wrote her elder daughter, Jessie. 'One of my greatest pleasures in the evening was to sit on the verandah, outside the drawing room window, and look over the broad expanse of lawn and river at the starry sky above, sometimes with the moon shining, and listen to mother singing. I have heard many celebrated singers, but they never had the perfect setting mother had.'[4]

With her death the survival of Yulgilbar was threatened again. The cause was another family feud.

The Ogilvie clan, it seemed, was fated to fall out with one another; fathers and sons especially. First Edward had broken away from the old Commander, forming Yulgilbar. Next William was estranged from his father. Finally Charles Lillingston's son quarrelled with both father and mother over his inheritance.

Edward George Grey Lillingston was a most unlikely heir. He had shown not the least interest in Yulgilbar since the age of eight, when his parents sent him to school in England. Later he went to Sandhurst, joined the British Army, saw action in France during World War One and settled down in post-war London. Then, wanting to marry a girl of some social pretensions, he described himself as a rich Australian

[4] Street, Jessie, *Truth or Repose*, Sydney, 1966.

cattleman. His future in-laws checked his credentials. Though his aunt, Jessie Armstrong, assured them he was expected to inherit Yulgilbar, he had to admit to having no present income at all.

By 1921 he was pressing his mother for a marriage settlement; preferably in the form of a regular income. She told him she was in no position to do so. Yulgilbar's profits were still going to pay off those annuities. Besides she felt an obligation to put some money aside for her two daughters. Edward persisted.

Despite his father's opposition, he persuaded her to sign a legal agreement. This gave him a half-share in station proceeds during his mother's lifetime; the proviso being that, after he inherited Yulgilbar, he continued to pay the other half to his sisters. This was totally opposed to the spirit of his grandfather's will. His new demand presupposed absolute ownership of the property. To secure this, Mabel had to buy out other possible claimants, which meant William Frederick's two sons. They were reluctantly persuaded to accept a cash settlement. Though Edward was given the money he wanted, he so antagonised his own family that no one ever spoke or wrote to him again; except through solicitors.

Financially, too, he gained nothing by his ruthless attitude. On his mother's untimely death, only four years later, he found himself sole owner of Yulgilbar, but with only half its revenue. Still in England, he tried to have that agreement set aside. When this failed he threatened to sell Yulgilbar unless his sisters, Jessie and Eve, relinquished their interest.

'My sister and I were most distressed,' wrote Jessie. 'Grandfather had explored and opened up the country and built the Castle. Mother had been born there, and my sister and I spent much of our childhood and some of the happiest years of our lives at Yulgilbar. The magic of the place was in our blood. We did not want to sell it and take the risk of it being neglected and becoming a ruin.'[5]

They urged him, if he must sell, to preserve at least the heart of the property. They asked for the retention of the Castle and a thousand acres of parkland surrounding it. Finally they proposed buying it themselves, then offering it to the Government as a national memorial.

The absentee brother declared, largely out of spite, that this was impossible. Yulgilbar would have to be sold in its entirety. Otherwise, he claimed, it would not be saleable at all. He was supported by the trustees, especially Tancred Armstrong, the last of the original appointments still alive. The sisters challenged them in the Equity Court. Once

[5] Street, Jessie, *Truth Or Repose*, Sydney, 1966.

more those involved provisions of the will were argued, made the subject of learned opinions by King's Counsel. The court found in Edward's favour.

In 1926 Yulgilbar was sold. It was bought by a syndicate for £90,000.

As Jessie feared, the old home was soon on its way to a ruin. The new owners were principally interested in the run for its cattle. A new manager moved into the Cottage. The castle was left empty.

The Lillingstons' old gardener, George Colgate, was kept on as caretaker. He looked after it as best he could, did a few repairs, tried to keep vandals out. When he died, the Big House also began to die. During World War Two, when building materials were unobtainable and manpower scarce, roofing iron was removed for essential station buildings. Vandals stripped lead sealing from the turrets, selling it to coastal fishermen for sinkers. Damp began to affect the walls. Heavy rains caused the ceilings to collapse. The post-war years recapitulated the story of Nelson's decaying manor house in Merton nearly a century and a half before. Vandals broke in, smashed windows, ripped away cedar doors, architraves, panelling, even that magnificent staircase. This was wrecked by intruders piece by piece, balustrade after balustrade, for firewood. By the 1950s the great mansion was little more than a shell, littered with fallen masonry, broken floorboards and rotting timbers.

It was the end of a century–old dream.

Yet it was the dreamer himself who destroyed it. He had dreamed of founding a dynasty. His sons, and the sons of his sons, were to live there forever, perpetuating his name. Instead he alienated his original heir, set his descendants at odds with one another, and involved them in costly litigation through a capricious, eccentric will. Other men became masters of the magnificent cattlelands he pioneered; Edward Lillingston's name was swiftly forgotten; even his own children disowned him; while the continuing line of Ogilvies had to turn to successful grazing elsewhere instead of building on their grandfather's tradition.

Since that time Yulgilbar's direction and ownership has once more changed. Its pastoral lands have been further reduced in size. Yet, despite Edward Lillingston's argument, the station remains as productive as ever.

The Castle, too, has been restored.

Its facade is no longer the way Edward Ogilvie designed it. The twin towers have gone. There is no upper storey. Its huge kitchen

Yulgilbar Castle after the First World War. Photograph by courtesy of the late Sir Kenneth Street.

quarters have been shorn away. The stables have vanished as have the schoolhouse and the cottage by the ornamental gateway. To have restored all this would have cost anything up to half-a-million dollars. The towers had become dangerous, and had to be demolished. Most upstairs rooms were beyond restoration. Nonetheless, a great deal of money was spent on redesigning, replacing whole sections of the outer walls, strengthening the terrace pillars and transforming the interior into an elegant modern home.

The barren, weed-choked gardens have also been replanted, and visitors can stand once more on the broad terrace, looking down at the tranquil spread of Castle Waters as they did in Edward Ogilvie's time.

The Clarence flows by as steadily and vigorous as ever. The river will outlive us all.

Bibliography

Official Records

Historical Records of Australia, series 1, Vols. II–XXVI
Despatches from Governors, 1821–49
Colonial Secretary's Correspondence, 1826–32, N.S.W. State Archives, Mitchell Library
Register of Convict Ships, 1825
Votes & Proceedings, N.S.W. Legislative Council, 1835–47
Journal of the Legislative Council, 1863–85
Clergy & School Lands Corporation, correspondence and reports, 1825–33, State Archives, Mitchell Library
Magistrates Letter Book (Merton), 1832–42, State Archives
Merton Bench Book, 1832–34, State Archives
Muswellbrook Bench Book, 1834–43, State Archives

Published Works

Abbott, J. M. H., *The Newcastle Packets*, Sydney, 1934
Bateson, C., *Convict Ships*, Glasgow, 1959
Burke's Colonial Gentry, London, 1895
Clark, C.M.H., *Select Documents of Australian History*, Sydney, 1950
Cunningham, P., *Two Years In New South Wales*, London, 1927 revised edition, with preface by David S. MacMillan, Sydney, 1966
Curr, E. M., *Reminiscences of a Squatter in Victoria*, Melbourne, 1883
Daley, E. J., *Men and a River*, Melbourne, 1967
Dangar, H., *Index & Directory to Map of the Hunter River*, Sydney, 1828
Fitzpatrick, Brian, *The Australian People*, Melbourne, 1945
The British Empire in Australia, Melbourne, 1949
Griffith, Nesta, *Some Northern Homesteads of N.S.W.*, Sydney, 1949
Harris, Alexander, *Convicts and Settlers*, London, 1837

Madgwick, R. B., *Immigration Into Eastern Australia, 1788–1851*, Sydney, 1959

Mudie, J., *The Felonry of New South Wales*, London, 1837

O'Byrne, W. R., *Naval Biographical Dictionary*, London, 1849

Ogilvie, E. D. S., *Diary of Travels*, 2 vols., London, 1856

Roberts, S. H., *History of Australian Land Settlement*, Sydney, 1924
    The Squatting Age in Australia, Melbourne, 1935

Rowley, C. D., *The Destruction of Aboriginal Society*, Canberra, 1969

Russell, Jack, *Nelson & The Hamiltons*, London, 1967

Russell, H. Stuart, *The Genesis of Queensland*, Sydney, 1911

Rusden, G. W., *A History of Australia*, London, 1888

Ryan, J. S., *The Land of Ulitarra, Early Records of the Aborigines of the Mid-North Coast, N.S.W.*, Armidale, 1970

Street, Jessie, *Truth or Repose*, Sydney, 1966

Therry, R., *Reminiscences of Thirty Years in New South Wales & Victoria*, London, 1863 (suppressed edition)

Walker, R. B., *In Old New England*, Sydney, 1966

Warner, Oliver, *A Portrait of Lord Nelson*, London, 1958

Wood, A. W., *Dawn in the Valley*, Sydney, 1971

Unpublished Documents

Bundock, Mrs E. W., *A Memoir of E. D. S. Ogilvie of Yulgilbar*, Mitchell Library
    Early Recollections of E. D. S. Ogilvie, University of New England
    Notes on Early Recollections at Richmond River, Mitchell Library
    Notes on Richmond River Blacks, Mitchell Library

Bawden, Thomas, *Three Lectures on the Early History of the Clarence*, University of New England

Davies, A. E., *History of the Clarence River and Grafton*, M.A. thesis, Sydney University, 1953

Dawson, R. L., letters to N. C. Hewitt, Clarence River Historical Society, Grafton

Eyre, John, *Journal*, 1836, Mitchell Library

Gardner, William, *North & Western Parts of New South Wales*, Mitchell Library

Hobler Manuscript, Mitchell Library

Harrison, B. W., *The Myall Creek Massacre and its significance in the early squatting period*, B.A. (Hons.) thesis, University of New England.

Ogilvie Family Papers, University of New England

Register of Properties of E. D. S. Ogilvie, Clarence River Historical Society, Grafton

Stevens, John F., *The Runaway (Richard Craig)*, roneoed, Mitchell Library

with Sabine, J. F., *The Pathfinders*, roneoed, Mitchell Library
Yulgilbar Sheep Book, Mitchell Library
Yulgilbar Station Journal, Mitchell Library

Newspapers and Periodicals

The Sydney Gazette, 1825–35
The Sydney Herald, 1831–40
The Sydney Morning Herald, 1840 to date
The Monitor, 1830–40
The Clarence & Richmond River Examiner, 1859 to date
The Maitland Mercury, 1840 to date
The Muswellbrook Chronicle, 1860 to date
Historical Studies, 1940–55
Mankind, 1890–95
Royal Australian Historical Society Journal
Clarence River Historical Society Journal
Richmond River Historical Society Journal
The Daily Examiner, Grafton

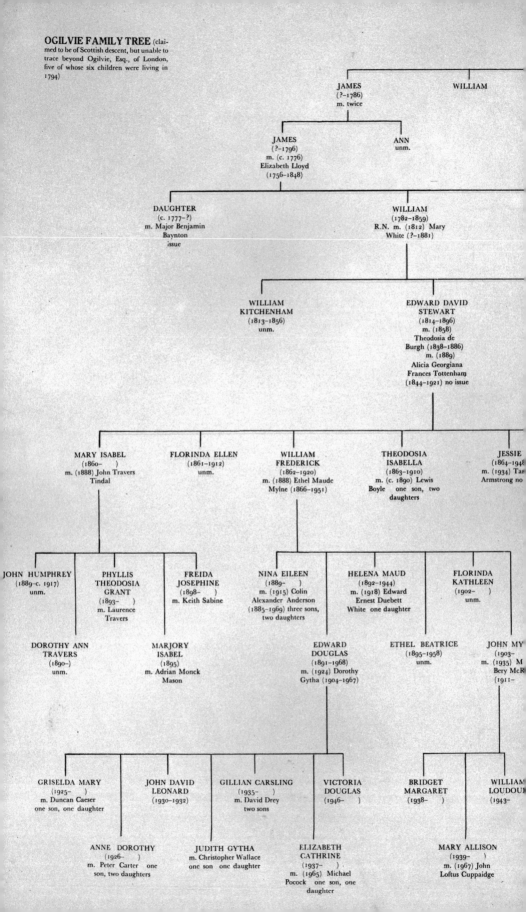

OGILVIE FAMILY TREE (claimed to be of Scottish descent, but unable to trace beyond Ogilvie, Esq., of London, five of whose six children were living in 1794)

JAMES
(?–1786)
m. twice

WILLIAM

JAMES
(?–1796)
m. (c. 1776)
Elizabeth Lloyd
(1756–1848)

ANN
unm.

DAUGHTER
(c. 1777–?)
m. Major Benjamin
Baynton
issue

WILLIAM
(1782–1859)
R.N. m. (1812) Mary
White (?–1881)

WILLIAM
KITCHENHAM
(1813–1856)
unm.

EDWARD DAVID
STEWART
(1814–1896)
m. (1858)
Theodosia de
Burgh (1838–1886)
m. (1889)
Alicia Georgiana
Frances Tottenham
(1844–1921) no issue

MARY ISABEL
(1860–)
m. (1888) John Travers
Tindal

FLORINDA ELLEN
(1861–1912)
unm.

WILLIAM
FREDERICK
(1862–1920)
m. (1888) Ethel Maude
Mylne (1866–1951)

THEODOSIA
ISABELLA
(1863–1910)
m. (c. 1890) Lewis
Boyle   one son, two
daughters

JESSIE
(1864–1948
m. (1934) Tar
Armstrong no

JOHN HUMPHREY
(1889–c. 1917)
unm.

PHYLLIS
THEODOSIA
GRANT
(1893–)
m. Laurence
Travers

FREIDA
JOSEPHINE
(1898–)
m. Keith Sabine

NINA EILEEN
(1889–)
m. (1915) Colin
Alexander Anderson
(1885–1969) three sons,
two daughters

HELENA MAUD
(1892–1944)
m. (1918) Edward
Ernest Duebett
White   one daughter

FLORINDA
KATHLEEN
(1902–)
unm.

DOROTHY ANN
TRAVERS
(1890–)
unm.

MARJORY
ISABEL
(1895)
m. Adrian Monck
Mason

EDWARD
DOUGLAS
(1891–1968)
m. (1924) Dorothy
Gytha (1904–1967)

ETHEL BEATRICE
(1895–1958)
unm.

JOHN MY
(1903–
m. (1935) M
Bery McR
(1911–

GRISELDA MARY
(1925–)
m. Duncan Caeser
one son, one daughter

JOHN DAVID
LEONARD
(1930–1932)

GILLIAN CARSLING
(1935–)
m. David Drey
two sons

VICTORIA
DOUGLAS
(1946–)

BRIDGET
MARGARET
(1938–)

WILLIAM
LOUDOU
(1943–

ANNE DOROTHY
(1926–)
m. Peter Carter   one
son, two daughters

JUDITH GYTHA
m. Christopher Wallace
one son   one daughter

ELIZABETH
CATHRINE
(1937–)
m. (1965) Michael
Pocock   one son, one
daughter

MARY ALLISON
(1939–)
m. (1967) John
Loftus Cuppaidge